Cases in Communication Law

Cases in Communication Law

Third Edition

EDITED BY PAUL SIEGEL

ROWMAN & LITTLEFIELD PUBLISHERS, INC.
Lanham • Boulder • New York • Toronto • Plymouth, UK

Published by Rowman & Littlefield Publishers, Inc.
A wholly owned subsidiary of The Rowman & Littlefield Publishing Group, Inc.
4501 Forbes Boulevard, Suite 200, Lanham, Maryland 20706
http://www.rowmanlittlefield.com

Estover Road, Plymouth PL6 7PY, United Kingdom

Copyright © 2012 by Paul Siegel

All rights reserved. No part of this book may be reproduced in any form or by any electronic or mechanical means, including information storage and retrieval systems, without written permission from the publisher, except by a reviewer who may quote passages in a review.

British Library Cataloguing in Publication Information Available

Library of Congress Cataloging-in-Publication Data

Cases in communication law / edited by Paul Siegel.—3rd ed.
   p. cm.
  Includes bibliographical references.
  ISBN 978-1-4422-9040-2 (pbk. : alk. paper)—ISBN 978-1-4422-9041-9 (electronic)
  1. Mass media—Law and legislation—United States—Cases. 2. Press law—United States—Cases. 3. Freedom of speech—United States—Cases. I. Siegel, Paul, 1954–
KF2750.C375 2011
343.7309′9—dc22
                                                                2011018087

∞ ™ The paper used in this publication meets the minimum requirements of American National Standard for Information Sciences—Permanence of Paper for Printed Library Materials, ANSI/NISO Z39.48-1992.

Printed in the United States of America

Contents

List of Cases	ix
Preface	xi
1 Introduction	1
The U.S. Judiciary	2
Understanding Legal Citations	3
A Word about the Editing of This Volume	4
2 First Amendment Principles	7
Brandenburg v. Ohio	8
Hess v. Indiana	9
Wooley v. Maynard	11
Johanns v. Livestock Marketing Association	15
U.S. v. O'Brien	19
Morse v. Frederick	25
U.S. v. The Progressive	29
U.S. v. Stevens	35
3 Libel: Common Law Elements	45
Greenbelt Cooperative Publishing Association v. Bresler	46
Nichols v. Moore	49
Amrak Productions v. Morton	52
Stanton v. Metro Corporation	55
Kaelin v. Globe Communications Corporation	60
Diaz v. NBC Universal, Inc.	66
4 Libel: Constitutional Considerations	71
New York Times v. Sullivan	72
Gertz v. Welch	78

	Philadelphia Newspapers, Inc. v. Hepps	83
	Peterson v. Grisham	86
	Brock v. Viacom International, Inc.	90
5	**Invasion of Privacy**	**95**
	Time, Inc. v. Hill	96
	Solano v. Playgirl, Inc.	100
	Neff v. Time, Inc.	104
	Holman v. Central Arkansas Broadcasting Company	107
	Boring v. Google, Inc.	109
	Zacchini v. Scripps-Howard Broadcasting Company	112
	Owasso Independent School District v. Falvo	115
6	**Copyright and Trademark**	**121**
	Eldred v. Ashcroft	121
	Campbell v. Acuff-Rose Music	129
	Bourne Company v. Twentieth Century Fox Film Corporation	135
	ProtectMarriage.com v. Courage Campaign	143
	Tillman v. New Line Cinema Corporation	145
	The Sheldon Abend Revocable Trust v. Spielberg	148
7	**Access to Government Information**	**157**
	Saxbe v. Washington Post	158
	Baltimore Sun v. Ehrlich	160
	National Archives and Records Administration v. Favish	166
	Acker v. Texas Water Commission	173
	Doe v. Reed	175
8	**Covering the Judiciary**	**183**
	Sheppard v. Maxwell	184
	Nebraska Press Association v. Stuart	188
	Press-Enterprise v. Superior Court (I)	193
	Presley v. Georgia	196
	Press-Enterprise v. Superior Court (II)	201
9	**Protecting News Sources**	**205**
	Branzburg v. Hayes	206
	In re Grand Jury Subpoena, Judith Miller	210
	Zurcher v. Stanford Daily	215
	Cohen v. Cowles Media Company	219
	Chevron Corporation v. Berlinger	223

CONTENTS   vii

10 Regulation of Advertising   233
    Virginia State Board of Pharmacy v. Virginia Citizens Consumer Council   233
    Central Hudson Gas & Electric v. Public Service Commission of New York   237
    Rubin v. Coors Brewing Company   242
    Citizens United v. Federal Election Commission   247

11 Sexually Oriented Speech   261
    Miller v. California   262
    Stanley v. Georgia   265
    Osborne v. Ohio   268
    Ashcroft v. Free Speech Coalition   272
    U.S. v. Williams   281

12 Broadcast and Cable TV Regulation   293
    FCC v. Pacifica Foundation   294
    Fox Television Stations, Inc. v. FCC   299
    Turner Broadcasting System v. FCC   311
    Motion Picture Association of America v. FCC   320

13 The Internet   327
    Reno v. ACLU   327
    MGM Studios v. Grokster   335
    Fair Housing Council of San Fernando Valley v. Roommates.com   345
    Bradburn v. North Central Regional Library District   352

About the Author   361

List of Cases

Note: Cases marked with a square bullet indicate availability of supplementary materials on the author's website, www.paulsiegelcommlaw.com. Detailed instructions for finding specific images and/or video clips are given in the text. Electronic versions of this book have hyperlinks leading directly to the pages on the website.

Acker v. Texas Water Commission	173
■ Amrak Productions v. Morton	52
■ Ashcroft v. Free Speech Coalition	272
Baltimore Sun v. Ehrlich	160
Boring v. Google, Inc.	109
■ Bourne Company v. Twentieth Century Fox Film Corporation	135
Bradburn v. North Central Regional Library District	352
Brandenburg v. Ohio	8
■ Branzburg v. Hayes	206
■ Brock v. Viacom International, Inc.	90
Campbell v. Acuff-Rose Music	129
Central Hudson Gas & Electric v. Public Service Commission of New York	237
■ Chevron Corporation v. Berlinger	223
■ Citizens United v. Federal Election Commission	247
Cohen v. Cowles Media Company	219
■ Diaz v. NBC Universal, Inc.	66
Doe v. Reed	175
Eldred v. Ashcroft	121
Fair Housing Council of San Fernando Valley v. Roommates.com	345
FCC v. Pacifica Foundation	294
■ Fox Television Stations, Inc. v. FCC	299
Gertz v. Welch	78
In re Grand Jury Subpoena, Judith Miller	210
Greenbelt Cooperative Publishing Association v. Bresler	46
Hess v. Indiana	9
Holman v. Central Arkansas Broadcasting Company	107

■ Johanns v. Livestock Marketing Association	15
■ Kaelin v. Globe Communications Corporation	60
MGM Studios v. Grokster	335
Miller v. California	262
Morse v. Frederick	25
Motion Picture Association of America v. FCC	320
National Archives and Records Administration v. Favish	166
Nebraska Press Association v. Stuart	188
Neff v. Time, Inc.	104
New York Times v. Sullivan	72
■ Nichols v. Moore	49
Osborne v. Ohio	268
Owasso Independent School District v. Falvo	115
Peterson v. Grisham	86
Philadelphia Newspapers, Inc. v. Hepps	83
Presley v. Georgia	196
Press-Enterprise v. Superior Court (I)	193
Press-Enterprise v. Superior Court (II)	201
■ ProtectMarriage.com v. Courage Campaign	143
Reno v. ACLU	327
Rubin v. Coors Brewing Company	242
Saxbe v. Washington Post	158
■ The Sheldon Abend Revocable Trust v. Spielberg	148
Sheppard v. Maxwell	184
■ Solano v. Playgirl, Inc.	100
Stanley v. Georgia	265
■ Stanton v. Metro Corporation	55
■ Tillman v. New Line Cinema Corporation	145
■ Time, Inc. v. Hill	96
Turner Broadcasting System v. FCC	311
U.S. v. O'Brien	19
U. S. v. The Progressive	29
U.S. v. Stevens	35
U.S. v. Williams	281
Virginia State Board of Pharmacy v. Virginia Citizens Consumer Council	233
Wooley v. Maynard	11
■ Zacchini v. Scripps-Howard Broadcasting Company	112
Zurcher v. Stanford Daily	215

Preface

Cases in Communication Law is designed to be used as a supplemental text in courses focusing on media law and freedom of speech in the United States. As was true of the second edition, the chapter sequence mirrors that found in my *Communication Law in America*, Third Edition, also published by Rowman & Littlefield.

The majority of the cases presented here (forty out of sixty-four) were decided by the United States Supreme Court and are binding precedents on all jurisdictions nationwide. But such controlling legal precedent does not exist for every important principle in media law. Therefore also examined here are provocative lower court cases, whether from federal or state courts.

Eighteen of the cases here stem from highly visual artifacts, and thus where appropriate I direct readers to the related page on my website (www.paulsiegelcommlaw.com). Ten of those eighteen cases involve TV programs (from *Family Guy* to Showtime's *Bullshit!* as well as the epithet-boasting awards show appearances by Bono, Cher, and Nicole Richie, and the infamous Janet Jackson "wardrobe malfunction") or films (including *American Gangster*, *Bowling for Columbine*, *Crude*, *Disturbia*, *Hillary: The Movie*, and *John Q*), and the relevant clips can be seen on the same website. Most of the remaining visuals are still photos from magazines, newspapers and books, and readers will be directed to these artifacts, too. An icon appears in the margin alerting the reader to check the website, and specific navigation directions are given in footnotes. The electronic versions of this book have hyperlinks at each icon, which will take the reader directly to the material on the website.

1

Introduction

There are many sources of communication law in the United States. Chief among the United States Constitution's relevant provisions are the Free Press and Free Speech clauses of the First Amendment, which tell the Congress that it shall "make no law" abridging either one. Individual state constitutions also have provisions that mirror the First Amendment, although sometimes these have been interpreted so as to give a state's residents more rights than Americans in general enjoy (such as a right to leaflet on the grounds of privately owned shopping malls).

The legislative branch of government, whether a city council, a state legislature, or Congress itself, also has an important role to play in the creation of communication law. This mechanism is the one that produces everything from federal copyright law and state libel and obscenity laws to local ordinances governing how many newspaper racks may be placed on public streets. Some areas of communication law involve more than one level of legislation. Advertising is regulated both at the federal and state level. The cable television industry is regulated by a complicated mosaic of federal legislation and contracts entered into between cable franchisees and local governments.

The executive branch also creates communication law, in several ways. The president (with the consent of the Senate) appoints federal judges, as well as the top officials at such agencies as the Federal Communications Commission (FCC), the Federal Election Commission (FEC), and the Federal Trade Commission (FTC). By the simple act of signing an executive order, presidents can greatly affect the flow of information, such as by creating new rules governing how aggressively and timely officials will declassify once-secret documents.

This book, however, focuses exclusively on published decisions from the judicial branch, mostly the United States Supreme Court, but also lower federal and state courts. That focus can be justified in two ways. First, judges are often called upon to rule on the constitutionality of the other governmental branches' actions. In *Citizens United v. Federal Election Commission*, for example (see chapter 10), the Supreme Court struck down portions of the Bipartisan Campaign Reform Act, while in *Johanns v. Livestock Marketing Association* (chapter 2), the Court upheld key provisions of the Beef Promotion and Research Act. The Fourth Circuit Court of Appeals, in *Baltimore Sun v. Ehrlich* (see chapter 7), told the governor of Maryland that the First Amendment does not require him to return disfavored reporters' phone calls, as long as he treats them fairly when it comes to invitations to press conferences otherwise open to all. By reading court opinions, then, we see the machinations of the other branches of government as well.

The second reason for focusing on court decisions is that they are the most revealing and rhetorical among legal documents. Judges have to make arguments just as much as do the opposing counsel who appear before them. Lower court judges have to word their decisions clearly and defensibly, so as not to be overturned on appeal. Appellate courts, consisting as they do of anywhere from three to almost two dozen judges, especially must produce rhetorically compelling opinions to attract enough votes to form a majority. To a large extent, this is why court decisions are generally more comprehensible to non-lawyers than are statutes themselves.

The U.S. Judiciary

We should first realize that there is not one judicial system in the United States, but rather a federal system, a system for each of the states, and one for the District of Columbia. That is fifty-two systems in all, without even counting the courts governing such places as Puerto Rico or the Virgin Islands.

The structure of the judiciary itself need not be a source of complete bewilderment, however. Indeed, the hierarchy of courts in the states is almost without exception modeled after the federal system. There are three layers. At the bottom are the trial courts. In the federal system they are called federal district courts. The names of the trial courts vary greatly from state to state, but are most frequently (and somewhat counterintuitively) called superior courts.

Litigants who are unhappy with the trial court result have the option of bringing an appeal to the next layer of the judiciary. In the federal system, and in that of most states, these are called, intuitively enough, appellate courts. In the federal system these appellate courts govern a specific region of the country, called a federal circuit. There are thirteen such circuits. Eleven of them are given numbers. The Appellate Court for the Eighth Circuit, for example, governs the states of Arkansas, Iowa, Minnesota, Missouri, Nebraska, North Dakota, and South Dakota.

There is also an appellate court for the District of Columbia. That particular court has jurisdiction over most appeals from decisions of the FCC and other federal agencies. The thirteenth federal appellate court is the one for the Federal Circuit, a special court created by Congress in 1982 to handle such specialized appeals as patent and trademark cases.

Litigants who are not satisfied with an appellate ruling can sometimes take their grievance one step higher. The pinnacle of the judiciary in both the federal and state systems is also an appellate court, but it goes by a special name. The highest federal court is, of course, the United States Supreme Court. The highest court in almost every state is also referred to as a supreme court, although there are some exceptions. New York's highest court, for example, is its Court of Appeals.

Although we often hear aggrieved parties vow that they will take their cases "all the way to the Supreme Court if necessary," in fact this is romantic fancy because the justices of the Supreme Court have tremendous latitude about which of the thousands of appeals filed there annually will be heard. In recent years, the justices have issued only about seventy-five or so decisions—seventy-three in the 2009–2010 term. Many state supreme courts have similar discretion to determine which cases they will hear. As such, often litigants are realistically limited to having their grievances heard in two, rather than three, rungs of the judicial system. In the federal system, two rungs often becomes three even without Supreme Court intervention, in that litigants unhappy with a three-judge panel of a Circuit Court of Appeals can sometimes persuade all of the judges in that circuit—this can be as many as two dozen or so—to rehear the case. This is called a rehearing *en banc.*

Of the sixty-four cases represented in this volume, forty are United States Supreme Court decisions, fifteen are federal appellate decisions, and seven were decided at the federal district court level. The book also includes two state supreme court cases. Nineteen of the cases presented here are new to this edition. Cases that needed to be discarded from the previous edition in order to make room are still easily available on my website, www.paulsiegel commlaw.com.

Understanding Legal Citations

Each of the court cases excerpted in this book has not only a name but also a citation. The citation tells you a fair amount of information about the legal dispute, not the least of which is where you can find the full text of the opinion, should you decide to read further.

Although there are several published (and online) sources for the full text of Supreme Court decisions, the citation format provided in this book except for very recent cases refers to the Court's own official volumes, called *United States Reports* (abbreviated *U.S.*). The very first case appearing in these pages is *Brandenburg v. Ohio*, the citation for which is 395 U.S. 444 (1969). This tells us that the full text of the Court's opinion can be found in volume 395 of the *United States Reports*, beginning on page 444. The case was decided in 1969.

Federal district court opinions, when they are published at all, appear most conveniently in a series from West Publishing Company, based in Saint Paul, Minnesota, called *Federal Supplement* (or F. Supp., with more recent cases in the second series of the *Federal Supplement*, abbreviated F. Supp. 2d).

Federal appellate decisions are found in another West publication called the *Federal Reporter* (abbreviated simply as *F.*) This publication went into its second series (F.2d) in 1924, and began its third series (F.3d) in 1994. Some federal appellate decisions appear instead in a publication called *Federal Appendix* (Fed. Appx.).

Each state's judiciary publishes its own case reports. Thus we may see references, for example, to the *Wisconsin Reporter* or the *New York Supplement*. Academic libraries at most colleges without law schools do not bother to subscribe to each and every state's reporters. Rather, they tend to subscribe to yet another West series of publications. West's regional reporters conveniently break down the states into seven separate areas—the Atlantic (*A.*), the Pacific (*P.*), the Northeastern (*N.E.*), the Northwestern (*N.W.*), the Southern (*So.*), the Southeastern (*S.E.*), and the Southwestern (*S.W.*). Some of the regional reporters are in their second editions, some in their third.

You have probably figured out already that the generic format of legal citations is volume number, name of publication, first page number where the court case can be found, and date (preceded, if needed, by a shorthand label for the actual court). There are some further complications you may encounter. For example, sometimes when cases are not destined to be officially published, or if they are too new to find their way into a real volume, we provide instead a citation given by the LEXIS database. Indeed, it is fair to say that researchers read court cases and other legal documents online far more frequently than they do in an official printed reporter. Thus the volume numbers and page numbers from traditional citations, while still the preferred usage, are becoming somewhat fictional—"if I went to the shelves, this is where I would have found it."

A Word about the Editing of This Volume

The editing of this volume could aptly be described as *purposefully heavy-handed*, and necessarily so. Most of the court cases found in this volume, if read in their entirety, would take up five to ten times as many pages as the excerpts offered here. Yet the publisher's intention and my own were to expose you to a fair sampling of court cases within each chapter's areas of case law.

How were the cases cut down to size? Several strategies were used. It was helpful to delete the footnotes from the original cases. In those few instances where the information found in the footnotes was essential to understanding the case, that information was moved up to the main text instead.

Whole lines of arguments deemed distracting from the main point of a court case were also deleted. Some of these were rather generic. Courts often have to consider whether one or more parties to a lawsuit are eligible to sue or can be excused from a lawsuit, or indeed whether they came to the right court to state their claims. These arguments of standing, immunity, and jurisdiction have been surgically removed from the cases here.

Sometimes issues that are related to communication law are nonetheless distractions from a case's main point. In *New York Times v. Sullivan*, for example—the landmark libel case excerpted in chapter 4—one of the plaintiff's arguments was based on the Supreme Court's not-yet-evolved doctrines applicable to commercial speech. That argument was excised. Similarly, it is hoped that the detailed excerpts offered in chapter 9 from *Branzburg v. Hayes*—involving a *Louisville Courier Journal* reporter's subpoena to appear in front of a grand jury—will suffice to teach the case's main lessons, even though the Court's discussion of the facts surrounding two companion cases involving other media outlets has been deleted.

Beyond these strategies, a heavy hand was taken to any jurists' long-winded prose or unnecessary redundancy. Internal quotations to earlier cases were generally omitted. These interventions sometimes resulted in sentence fragments that had to be combined, and to portions of text that had to be moved up several paragraphs. To aid readability, the use of ellipses and other editors' tools to alert readers of deletions has been generally eschewed.

Users of this volume, especially if they have occasion to compare one or more of the case excerpts offered here with the original, full-text versions, will be in the best position to assess whether the purposely heavy-handed editing succeeded.

2

First Amendment Principles

In this chapter we examine decisions in which the courts have outlined the First Amendment's scope and meaning, starting with *Brandenburg v. Ohio*, a 1969 decision stemming from a prosecution for "criminal syndicalism" against a Ku Klux Klan speaker. The *Brandenburg* test, still good law, says that political speech is protected by the First Amendment unless it is likely to produce "imminent lawless action." The second case, *Hess v. Indiana*, is an example of the test's application, and suggests that the Court takes seriously the earlier decision's "imminence" requirement.

Another issue fundamental to the First Amendment's scope is the posited right not to speak. *Wooley v. Maynard*, one of the Supreme Court's many statements on this issue, has often been cited as an elegant paean to silence. Following up on *Wooley*, we offer *Johanns v. Livestock Marketing Association*, in which the Court tells us that the right not to speak is inapplicable when the speaker is the government, even if select individuals are compelled to provide the funds for that speech.

U.S. v. O'Brien asks us to consider in what circumstances communicative conduct that does not involve the vocal cords is to be counted as "speech." The emerging "*O'Brien* test" tells courts how to evaluate government regulations that are aimed at the *non*communicative component of an agent's conduct, but that have an effect on that agent's message.

Our next case also involves symbolic conduct, but in *Morse v. Frederick* the Court discounts the agent's communicative intent, perhaps in part because he himself admitted he was not quite sure what, if anything, he intended to convey with his "Bong Hits for Jesus" banner, and perhaps also because he was a minor and the punishment involved was thus public school disciplinary actions, rather than a fine or a threat of jail time.

Next we examine the matter of prior restraints on the press by reading *U.S. v. The Progressive*, in which a U.S. district judge issued an injunction against publication of an article the government argued could lead to nuclear annihilation.

Finally we examine *U.S. v. Stevens*, in which the Court declines to remove depictions of "animal cruelty" from the protection of the First Amendment.

▪ *Brandenburg v. Ohio*
395 U.S. 444 (1969)
Per Curiam opinion:

The appellant, a leader of a Ku Klux Klan group, was convicted under the Ohio Criminal Syndicalism statute for "advocat[ing] . . . the duty, necessity, or propriety of crime, sabotage, violence, or unlawful methods of terrorism as a means of accomplishing industrial or political reform" and for "voluntarily assembl[ing] with any society, group, or assemblage of persons formed to teach or advocate the doctrines of criminal syndicalism."

The record shows that [the appellant] telephoned an announcer-reporter on the staff of a Cincinnati television station and invited him to come to a Ku Klux Klan "rally" to be held at a farm in Hamilton County. With the cooperation of the organizers, the reporter and a cameraman attended the meeting and filmed the events. Portions of the films were later broadcast on the local station and on a national network.

One film showed 12 hooded figures, some of whom carried firearms. They were gathered around a large wooden cross, which they burned. No one was present other than the participants and the newsmen who made the film. Most of the words uttered during the scene were incomprehensible when the film was projected, but scattered phrases could be understood that were derogatory of Negroes and, in one instance, of Jews [such as "Bury the niggers," "This is what we are going to do to the niggers," and "Send the Jews back to Israel."]. Though some of the figures in the films carried weapons, the speaker did not.

The Ohio Criminal Syndicalism Statute was enacted in 1919. From 1917 to 1920, identical or quite similar laws were adopted by 20 States and two territories. In 1927, this Court sustained the constitutionality of California's Criminal Syndicalism Act, the text of which is quite similar to that of the laws of Ohio. *Whitney v. California*, 274 U.S. 357 (1927). The Court upheld the statute on the ground that, without more, "advocating" violent means to effect political and economic change involves such danger to the security of the State that the State may outlaw it. But *Whitney* has been thoroughly discredited by later decisions. See *Dennis v. United States*, 341 U.S. 494, at 507 (1951). These later decisions have fashioned the principle that the constitutional guarantees of free speech and free press do not permit a State to forbid or proscribe advocacy of the use of force or of law violation except where such advocacy is directed to inciting or producing imminent lawless action and is likely to incite or produce such action.

Ohio's Criminal Syndicalism Act cannot be sustained. The Act punishes persons who "advocate or teach the duty, necessity, or propriety" of violence "as a means of accomplishing industrial or political reform"; or who publish or circulate or display any book or paper containing such advocacy; or who "justify" the commission of violent acts "with intent to exemplify, spread or advocate the propriety of the doctrines of criminal syndicalism"; or who "voluntarily assemble" with a group formed "to teach or advocate the doctrines of criminal syndicalism." Neither the indictment nor the trial judge's instructions to the jury in any way refined the statute's bald definition of the crime in terms of mere advocacy not distinguished from incitement to imminent lawless action.

Accordingly, we are here confronted with a statute which, by its own words and as applied, purports to punish mere advocacy and to forbid, on pain of criminal punishment, assembly with others merely to advocate the described type of action. Such a statute falls within the condemnation of the First and Fourteenth Amendments.

Reversed.

POINTS FOR DISCUSSION

1. Should incitement of violent illegal action (such as "bury the niggers") be treated differently under the *Brandenburg* test from advocacy of nonviolent action (e.g., tax evasion) or even advocacy of "victimless" crimes (e.g., having an extramarital affair)?
2. The *Brandenburg* test requires courts to consider whether a speaker's utterance is "likely to produce" lawless action. Does this mean that an ineffectual leader incapable of delivering a rousing speech enjoys more First Amendment freedoms than does a dramatic and talented rhetor?

▪ *Hess v. Indiana*
414 U.S. 105 (1973)
Per Curiam opinion:

Gregory Hess appeals from his conviction in the Indiana courts for violating the State's disorderly conduct statute. Appellant contends that his conviction should be reversed because the statute is unconstitutionally vague, because the statute is overbroad in that it forbids activity that is protected under the First and Fourteenth Amendments, and because the statute, as applied here, abridged his constitutionally protected freedom of speech. These contentions were rejected in the City Court, where Hess was convicted, and in the Superior Court, which reviewed his conviction. The Supreme Court of Indiana, with one dissent, considered and rejected each of Hess' constitutional contentions, and accordingly affirmed his conviction.

The events leading to Hess' conviction began with an antiwar demonstration on the campus of Indiana University. In the course of the demonstration, approximately 100 to 150 of the demonstrators moved onto a public street and blocked the passage of vehicles. When the demonstrators did not respond to verbal directions from the sheriff to clear the street, the sheriff and his deputies began walking up the street, and the demonstrators in their path moved to the curbs on either side, joining a large number of spectators who had gathered. Hess was standing off the street as the sheriff passed him. The sheriff heard Hess utter the word "fuck" in what he later described as a loud voice and immediately arrested him on the disorderly conduct charge. It was later stipulated that what appellant had said was "We'll take the fucking street later," or "We'll take the fucking street again." Two witnesses who were in the immediate vicinity testified, apparently without contradiction, that they heard Hess' words and witnessed his arrest. They indicated that Hess did not appear to be exhorting the crowd to go back into the street, that he was facing the crowd and not the street when he uttered the statement, that his statement did not appear to be addressed to any particular person or group, and that his tone, although loud, was no louder than that of the other people in the area.

The Indiana Supreme Court placed primary reliance on the trial court's finding that Hess' statement "was intended to incite further lawless action on the part of the crowd in the vicinity of appellant and was likely to produce such action." At best, however, the statement could be taken as counsel for present moderation; at worst, it amounted to nothing more than advocacy of illegal action at some indefinite future time. This is not sufficient to permit the State to punish Hess' speech. Under our decisions, "the constitutional guarantees of free speech and free press do not permit a State to forbid or proscribe advocacy of the use of force or of law violation except where such advocacy is directed to inciting or producing imminent lawless action and is likely to incite or produce such action." *Brandenburg v. Ohio*, 395 U.S. 444, 447 (1969). Since the uncontroverted evidence showed that Hess' statement was not directed to any person or group of persons, it cannot be said that he was advocating, in the normal sense, any action. And since there was no evidence, or rational inference from the import of the language, that his words were intended to produce, and likely to produce, imminent disorder, those words could not be punished by the State on the ground that they had "a 'tendency to lead to violence.'"

Accordingly, the judgment of the Supreme Court of Indiana is reversed.

POINTS FOR DISCUSSION

1. Clearly the *Hess* decision emphasizes *Brandenburg v. Ohio*'s "imminence" requirement. But why should "imminence" make a difference? Is a speaker who directs audience members to loot the downtown *now* any less culpable than one who advises them to take a brief lunch break first? Is the real issue the presumed opportunity for intervention to stop the violence from taking place?
2. If you were trying to predict in advance whether Hess's utterance was likely to lead to unlawful action, what would your guess have been? After all, he was surrounded by over a hundred followers (unlike the mere dozen or so "hooded figures" who listened to Brandenburg's racist speech) who had already broken the law (by blocking traffic, for example). Are courts likely to use their own "20-20 hindsight" when applying Brandenburg's "likely to produce . . ." requirement (i.e., speeches that *did* result in illegality were therefore "likely to produce" illegality)?

▪ *Wooley v. Maynard*
430 U.S. 705 (1977)
Chief Justice Burger:

The issue on appeal is whether the State of New Hampshire may constitutionally enforce criminal sanctions against persons who cover the motto "Live Free or Die" on passenger vehicle license plates because that motto is repugnant to their moral and religious beliefs.

Since 1969 New Hampshire has required that noncommercial vehicles bear license plates embossed with the state motto, "Live Free or Die." Another New Hampshire statute makes it a misdemeanor "knowingly [to obscure] the figures or letters on any number plate." The term "letters" in this section has been interpreted by the State's highest court to include the state motto. Appellees George Maynard and his wife Maxine are followers of the Jehovah's Witnesses faith. The Maynards consider the New Hampshire State motto to be repugnant to their moral, religious, and political beliefs, and therefore assert it objectionable to disseminate this message by displaying it on their automobiles. Pursuant to these beliefs, the Maynards began early in 1974 to cover up the motto on their license plates. In May or June 1974 Mr. Maynard actually snipped the words "or Die" off the license plates, and then covered the resulting hole, as well as the words "Live Free," with tape. This was done, according to Mr. Maynard, because neighborhood children kept removing the tape. The Maynards have since been issued new license plates, and have disavowed any intention of physically mutilating them.

On November 27, 1974, Mr. Maynard was issued a citation. On December 6, 1974, he appeared in Lebanon, N.H. District Court to answer the charge. After waiving his right to counsel, he entered a plea of not guilty and proceeded to explain his religious objections to the motto. The state trial judge expressed sympathy for Mr. Maynard's situation, but considered himself bound to hold Maynard guilty. [For this and subsequent violations, Maynard was fined $75 and served 15 days in jail.]

On March 4, 1975, appellees brought the present action, [seeking] injunctive and declaratory relief. Following a hearing on the merits, the District Court entered an order enjoining the State "from arresting and prosecuting [the Maynards] at any time in the future for covering over that portion of their license plates that contains the motto "Live Free or Die."

The District Court held that by covering up the state motto "Live Free or Die" on his automobile license plate, Mr. Maynard was engaging in symbolic speech and that "New Hampshire's interest in the enforcement of its defacement statute is not sufficient to justify the restriction on [appellee's] constitutionally protected expression." We find it unnecessary to pass on the "symbolic speech" issue. We note [however] that appellees' claim of symbolic expression is substantially undermined by their prayer in the District Court for issuance of special license plates not bearing the state motto. This is hardly consistent with the stated intent to communicate affirmative opposition to the motto. Whether or not we view appellees' present practice of covering the motto with tape as sufficiently communicative to sustain a claim of symbolic expression, display of the "expurgated" plates requested by appellees would surely not satisfy that standard.

We find more appropriate First Amendment grounds to affirm the judgment of the District Court. We turn instead to what in our view is the essence of appellees' objection to the requirement that they display the motto "Live Free or Die" on their automobile license plates. This is succinctly summarized in the statement made by Mr. Maynard in his affidavit filed with the District

Court: "I refuse to be coerced by the State into advertising a slogan which I find morally, ethically, religiously and politically abhorrent."

We are thus faced with the question of whether the State may constitutionally require an individual to participate in the dissemination of an ideological message by displaying it on his private property in a manner and for the express purpose that it be observed and read by the public. We hold that the State may not do so.

We begin with the proposition that the right of freedom of thought protected by the First Amendment against state action includes both the right to speak freely and the right to refrain from speaking at all. A system which secures the right to proselytize religious, political, and ideological causes must also guarantee the concomitant right to decline to foster such concepts. The right to speak and the right to refrain from speaking are complementary components of the broader concept of "individual freedom of mind."

The Court in *West Virginia Board of Education v. Barnette*, 319 U.S. 624 (1943), was faced with a state statute which required public school students to participate in daily public ceremonies by honoring the flag both with words and traditional salute gestures. The Court held that "a ceremony so touching matters of opinion and political attitude may [not] be imposed upon the individual by official authority under powers committed to any political organization under our Constitution." Compelling the affirmative act of a flag salute involved a more serious infringement upon personal liberties than the passive act of carrying the state motto on a license plate, but the difference is essentially one of degree. Here, as in *Barnette*, we are faced with a state measure which forces an individual, as part of his daily life—indeed constantly while his automobile is in public view—to be an instrument for fostering public adherence to an ideological point of view he finds unacceptable. In doing so, the State "invades the sphere of intellect and spirit which it is the purpose of the First Amendment to our Constitution to reserve from all official control." New Hampshire's statute in effect requires that appellees use their private property as a "mobile billboard" for the State's ideological message, or suffer a penalty, as Maynard already has. As a condition to driving an automobile—a virtual necessity for most Americans—the Maynards must display "Live Free or Die" to hundreds of people each day. The fact that most individuals agree with the thrust of New Hampshire's motto is not the test; most Americans also find the flag salute acceptable. The First Amendment protects the right of individuals to hold a point of view different from the majority and to refuse to foster, in the way New Hampshire commands, an idea they find morally objectionable.

Identifying the Maynards' interests as implicating First Amendment protections does not end our inquiry however. We must also determine whether the State's countervailing interest is sufficiently compelling to justify requiring appellees to display the state motto on their license plates. The two interests advanced by the State are that display of the motto (1) facilitates the identification of passenger vehicles, and (2) promotes appreciation of history, individualism, and state pride.

The State first points out that passenger vehicles, but not commercial, trailer, or other vehicles are required to display the state motto. Thus, the argument proceeds, officers of the law are more easily able to determine whether passenger vehicles are carrying the proper plates. However, the record here reveals that New Hampshire passenger license plates normally consist of a specific configuration of letters and numbers, which makes them readily distinguishable from other types of plates, even without reference to the state motto. Even were we to credit the State's reasons and even though the governmental purpose be legitimate and substantial, that purpose cannot be pursued by means that broadly stifle fundamental personal liberties when the end can be more narrowly achieved. The breadth of legislative abridgment must be viewed in the light of less drastic means for achieving the same basic purpose.

The State's second claimed interest is not ideologically neutral. The State is seeking to communicate to others an official view as to proper appreciation of history, state pride, and individualism. Of course, the State may legitimately pursue such interests in any number of ways. However, where the State's interest is to disseminate an ideology, no matter how acceptable to some, such interest cannot outweigh an individual's First Amendment right to avoid becoming the courier for such message.

We conclude that the State of New Hampshire may not require appellees to display the state motto upon their vehicle license plates; and, accordingly, we affirm the judgment of the District Court.

It has been suggested that today's holding will be read as sanctioning the obliteration of the national motto, "In God We Trust" from United States coins and currency. That question is not before us today but we note that currency, which is passed from hand to hand, differs in significant respects from an automobile, which is readily associated with its operator. Currency is generally carried in a purse or pocket and need not be displayed to the public. The bearer of currency is thus not required to publicly advertise the national motto.

POINTS FOR DISCUSSION

1. Should the right not to speak be dependent on how strongly one abhors the message? Suppose a Philadelphian covered up her license plate motto

("You have a friend in Pennsylvania"), not because it offends her, but because she thinks it silly? What about an Anchorage resident who thinks that the cosmos, not the state of Alaska, is "the last frontier"?
2. Suppose a state could demonstrate that its automobile license's color scheme is very similar to that of one or two other states, and that the motto therefore helps to identify the driver as a local resident. Should the Court's result have then been different?

▪ *Johanns v. Livestock Marketing Association*
544 U.S. 550 (2005)
Justice Scalia:

For the third time in eight years, we consider whether a federal program that finances generic advertising to promote an agricultural product violates the First Amendment. In these cases, unlike the previous two, the dispositive question is whether the generic advertising at issue is the Government's own speech and therefore is exempt from First Amendment scrutiny.

The Beef Promotion and Research Act of 1985 announces a federal policy of promoting the marketing and consumption of "beef and beef products," using funds raised by an assessment on cattle sales and importation. The statute directs the Secretary of Agriculture to implement this policy by issuing a Beef Promotion and Research Order. The Secretary is to impose a $1-per-head assessment (or "checkoff") on all sales or importation of cattle and a comparable assessment on imported beef products, used to fund beef-related projects, including promotional campaigns approved by the Secretary.

More than $1 billion has been collected through the checkoff, and a large fraction of that sum has been spent on promotional projects authorized by the Beef Act—many using the familiar trademarked slogan "Beef. It's What's for Dinner."[1] Many promotional messages funded by the checkoff bear the attribution "Funded by America's Beef Producers." Most print and television messages also bear a Beef Board logo, usually a check-mark with the word "BEEF."

Respondents are two associations whose members collect and pay the checkoff, and several individuals who raise and sell cattle subject to the checkoff. They sued the Secretary, the Department of Agriculture, and the Board in Federal District Court on a number of constitutional and statutory grounds.

---

1. A sample ad from the campaign is on my website. Go to www.paulsiegelcommlaw.com, and on the left side (*Communication Law in America*), click on "Images from the Book," then "Chapter 2," and then on "Beef Ad."

The District Court ruled for respondents on their First Amendment claims. The Court of Appeals for the Eighth Circuit affirmed.

While the litigation was pending, we held in *United States v. United Foods, Inc.,* 533 U.S. 405 (2001), that a mandatory checkoff for generic mushroom advertising violated the First Amendment. Noting that the mushroom program closely resembles the beef program, respondents amended their complaint to assert a First Amendment challenge to the use of the beef checkoff for promotional activity. Respondents noted that the advertising promotes beef as a generic commodity, which, they contended, impedes their efforts to promote the superiority of, *inter alia,* American beef, grain-fed beef, or certified Angus or Hereford beef.

[In *United Foods*] we sustained a compelled-subsidy challenge to an assessment very similar to the beef checkoff, imposed to fund mushroom advertising. Deciding the case on the assumption that the advertising was private speech, not government speech, we concluded that mushroom producers were [improperly] obliged to pay the checkoff. The mandatory fee would be permitted if it were germane to a broader regulatory scheme, [but] in *United Foods* the only regulatory purpose was the funding of the advertising.

In all of the cases invalidating exactions to subsidize speech, the speech was, or was presumed to be, that of an entity other than the government itself. Our compelled-subsidy cases have consistently respected the principle that compelled support of a private association is fundamentally different from compelled support of government.

Compelled support of government—even those programs of government one does not approve—is of course perfectly constitutional, as every taxpayer must attest. And some government programs involve, or entirely consist of, advocating a position. The government, as a general rule, may support valid programs and policies by taxes or other exactions binding on protesting parties. Within this broader principle it seems inevitable that funds raised by the government will be spent for speech and other expression to advocate and defend its own policies. We have generally assumed, though not yet squarely held, that compelled funding of government speech does not alone raise First Amendment concerns.

Respondents do not seriously dispute these principles, nor do they contend that, as a general matter, their First Amendment challenge requires them to show only that their checkoff dollars pay for speech with which they disagree. Rather, they assert that the challenged promotional campaigns differ dispositively from the type of government speech that, our cases suggest, is not susceptible to First Amendment challenge. They point to the role of the Beef Board and its Operating Committee in designing the promotional campaigns, and to the use of a mandatory assessment on beef producers to fund the advertising. We consider each in turn.

The Secretary of Agriculture does not write ad copy himself. Rather, the Beef Board's promotional campaigns are designed by the Beef Board's Operating Committee, only half of whose members are Beef Board members appointed by the Secretary. Respondents contend that speech whose content is effectively controlled by a nongovernmental entity—the Operating Committee—cannot be considered "government speech." We need not address this contention, because we reject its premise: The message of the promotional campaigns is effectively controlled by the Federal Government itself.

The message set out in the beef promotions is from beginning to end the message established by the Federal Government. Congress and the Secretary have set out the overarching message and some of its elements, and they have left the development of the remaining details to an entity whose members are answerable to the Secretary (and in some cases appointed by him as well). Moreover, the record demonstrates that the Secretary exercises final approval authority over every word used in every promotional campaign. All proposed promotional messages are reviewed by Department officials both for substance and for wording, and some proposals are rejected or rewritten by the Department. Nor is the Secretary's role limited to final approval or rejection: officials of the Department also attend and participate in the open meetings at which proposals are developed.

Respondents also contend that the beef program does not qualify as "government speech" because it is funded by a targeted assessment on beef producers, rather than by general revenues. This funding mechanism, they argue, has two relevant effects: it gives control over the beef program not to politically accountable legislators, but to a narrow interest group that will pay no heed to respondents' dissenting views, and it creates the perception that the advertisements speak for beef producers such as respondents.

We reject the first point. The compelled-*subsidy* analysis is altogether unaffected by whether the funds for the promotions are raised by general taxes or through a targeted assessment. Citizens may challenge compelled support of private speech, but have no First Amendment right not to fund government speech. And that is no less true when the funding is achieved through targeted assessments devoted exclusively to the program to which the assessed citizens object. The First Amendment does not confer a right to pay one's taxes into the general fund, because the injury of compelled funding (as opposed to the injury of compelled speech) does not stem from the Government's mode of accounting.

Some of our cases have justified compelled funding of government speech by pointing out that government speech is subject to democratic accountability. But [not] every instance of government speech must be funded by a line item in an appropriations bill. Here, the beef advertisements are subject to political safeguards more than adequate to set them apart from private messages. The program is authorized and the basic message prescribed by federal statute, and specific requirements for the promotions' content are imposed by federal regulations promulgated after notice and comment. The Secretary of Agriculture, a politically accountable official, oversees the program, appoints and dismisses the key personnel, and retains absolute veto power over the advertisements' content, right down to the wording. And Congress, of course, retains oversight authority, not to mention the ability to reform the program at any time. No more is required.

As to the second point, respondents' argument proceeds as follows: They contend that crediting the advertising to "America's Beef Producers" impermissibly uses not only their money but also their seeming endorsement to promote a message with which they do not agree. Communications cannot be "government speech," they argue, if they are attributed to someone other than the government; and the person to whom they are attributed, when he is, by compulsory funding, made the unwilling instrument of communication, may raise a First Amendment objection.

We need not determine the validity of this argument—which relates to compelled *speech* rather than compelled subsidy—with regard to respondents' facial challenge. Since neither the Beef Act nor the Beef Order *requires* attribution, neither can be the cause of any possible First Amendment harm. The District Court's order enjoining the enforcement of the Act and the Order thus cannot be sustained on this theory.

The judgment of the Court of Appeals is vacated.

POINTS FOR DISCUSSION

1. Earlier in this chapter you read *Wooley v. Maynard*, in which the Court held that New Hampshire residents could not be forced to espouse the state's motto—"Live Free or Die!"—on their automobile license plates. Are the beef producers who brought the case before you also being forced here to utter a message with which they disagree? In other words, do you buy Justice Scalia's argument that this is government speech, and thus unlike the *Wooley* case? Isn't a car license plate also "government speech"?
2. The Johanns decision rests on the Court's having "framed" the controversy as one of government speech rather than compelled citizen speech. And

there is a certain logic to allowing the government to say what it wants. But, as Justice Souter pointed out in dissent, the government might seem a bit confused about its own message. Is the government's case weakened at all in your judgment by the fact that the same Department of Agriculture that created the "Beef: It's What's for Dinner" campaign also publishes "Dietary Guidelines for Americans," which recommends that Americans *reduce* their intake of fats, and suggests that we also get most of our fats not from beef but from fish, nuts, and vegetable oil?

▪ U.S. v. O'Brien
391 U.S. 367 (1968)
Chief Justice Warren:

On the morning of March 31, 1966, David Paul O'Brien and three companions burned their Selective Service registration certificates on the steps of the South Boston Courthouse. A sizable crowd, including several agents of the Federal Bureau of Investigation, witnessed the event. Immediately after the burning, members of the crowd began attacking O'Brien and his companions. An FBI agent ushered O'Brien to safety inside the courthouse. After he was advised of his right to counsel and to silence, O'Brien stated to FBI agents that he had burned his registration certificate because of his beliefs, knowing that he was violating federal law. He produced the charred remains of the certificate, which, with his consent, were photographed.

For this act, O'Brien was indicted, tried, convicted, and sentenced in the United States District Court for the District of Massachusetts. He did not contest the fact that he had burned the certificate. He stated in argument to the jury that he burned the certificate publicly to influence others to adopt his antiwar beliefs, as he put it, "so that other people would reevaluate their positions with Selective Service, with the armed forces, and reevaluate their place in the culture of today, to hopefully consider my position."

The indictment upon which he was tried charged that he "willfully and knowingly did mutilate, destroy, and change by burning . . . [his] Registration Certificate (Selective Service System Form No. 2); in violation of Title 50, App., United States Code, Section 462 (b)."

Section 462 (b) is part of the Universal Military Training and Service Act of 1948. Section 462 (b)(3), one of six numbered subdivisions of Section 462 (b), was amended by Congress in 1965, so that at the time O'Brien burned his certificate an offense was committed by any person "who forges, alters, knowingly destroys, knowingly mutilates, or in any manner changes any such certificate." In the District Court, O'Brien argued that the 1965 Amendment prohibiting the knowing destruction or mutilation of certificates was unconstitutional because it was enacted to abridge free speech, and because it served no legitimate legislative purpose. The District Court rejected these arguments, holding that the statute on its face did not abridge First Amendment rights, that the court was not competent to inquire into the motives of Congress in enacting the 1965 Amendment, and that the Amendment was a reasonable exercise of the power of Congress to raise armies.

On appeal, the Court of Appeals for the First Circuit held the 1965 Amendment unconstitutional as a law abridging freedom of speech. At the time the Amendment was enacted, a regulation of the Selective Service System required registrants to keep their registration certificates in their "personal possession at all times." Wilful violations of regulations promulgated pursuant to the Universal Military Training and Service Act were made criminal by statute. The Court of Appeals, therefore, was of the opinion that conduct punishable under the 1965 Amendment was already punishable under the nonpossession regulation, and consequently that the Amendment served no valid purpose; further, that in light of the prior regulation, the Amendment must have been "directed at public as distinguished from private destruction." On this basis, the court concluded that the 1965 Amendment ran afoul of the First Amendment by singling out persons engaged in protests for special treatment. The court ruled, however, that O'Brien's conviction should be affirmed under the statutory provision, 50 U.S.C. App. Section 462 (b)(6), which in its view made violation of the nonpossession regulation a crime, because it regarded such violation to be a lesser included offense of the crime defined by the 1965 Amendment.

The Government petitioned for certiorari, arguing that the Court of Appeals erred in holding the statute unconstitutional, and that its decision conflicted with decisions by the Courts of Appeals for the Second and Eighth Circuits upholding the 1965 Amendment against identical constitutional challenges. O'Brien cross-petitioned for certiorari, arguing that the Court of Appeals erred in sustaining his conviction on the basis of a crime of which he was neither charged nor tried. We granted the Government's petition to resolve the conflict in the circuits, and we also granted O'Brien's cross-petition. We hold that the 1965 Amendment is constitutional both as enacted and as applied. We therefore vacate the judgment of the Court of Appeals and reinstate the judgment and sentence of the District Court without reaching the issue raised by O'Brien.

When a male reaches the age of 18, he is required by the Universal Military

Training and Service Act to register with a local draft board. He is assigned a Selective Service number, and within five days he is issued a registration certificate. Subsequently, and based on a questionnaire completed by the registrant, he is assigned a classification denoting his eligibility for induction, and "as soon as practicable" thereafter he is issued a Notice of Classification. This initial classification is not necessarily permanent, and if in the interim before induction the registrant's status changes in some relevant way, he may be reclassified. After such a reclassification, the local board "as soon as practicable" issues to the registrant a new Notice of Classification.

Both the registration and classification certificates are small white cards, approximately 2 by 3 inches. The registration certificate specifies the name of the registrant, the date of registration, and the number and address of the local board with which he is registered. Also inscribed upon it are the date and place of the registrant's birth, his residence at registration, his physical description, his signature, and his Selective Service number. The Selective Service number itself indicates his State of registration, his local board, his year of birth, and his chronological position in the local board's classification record.

The classification certificate shows the registrant's name, Selective Service number, signature, and eligibility classification. It specifies whether he was so classified by his local board, an appeal board, or the President. It contains the address of his local board and the date the certificate was mailed.

Both the registration and classification certificates bear notices that the registrant must notify his local board in writing of every change in address, physical condition, and occupational, marital, family, dependency, and military status, and of any other fact which might change his classification. Both also contain a notice that the registrant's Selective Service number should appear on all communications to his local board.

Congress demonstrated its concern that certificates issued by the Selective Service System might be abused well before the 1965 Amendment here challenged. Under the 1948 Act, it was unlawful (1) to transfer a certificate to aid a person in making false identification; (2) to possess a certificate not duly issued with the intent of using it for false identification; (3) to forge, alter, "or in any manner" change a certificate or any notation validly inscribed thereon; (4) to photograph or make an imitation of a certificate for the purpose of false identification; and (5) to possess a counterfeited or altered certificate. In addition, as previously mentioned, regulations of the Selective Service System required registrants to keep both their registration and classification certificates in their personal possession at all times.

By the 1965 Amendment, Congress added the provision here at issue, subjecting to criminal liability not only one who "forges, alters, or in any manner changes" but also one who "knowingly destroys, [or] knowingly mutilates" a certificate.

We note at the outset that the 1965 Amendment plainly does not abridge free speech on its face, and we do not understand O'Brien to argue otherwise. On its face [the Amendment] deals with conduct having no connection with speech. It prohibits the knowing destruction of certificates issued by the Selective Service System, and there is nothing necessarily expressive about such conduct. The Amendment does not distinguish between public and private destruction, and it does not punish only destruction engaged in for the purpose of expressing views. A law prohibiting destruction of Selective Service certificates no more abridges free speech on its face than a motor vehicle law prohibiting the destruction of drivers' licenses, or a tax law prohibiting the destruction of books and records. O'Brien nonetheless argues that the 1965 Amendment is unconstitutional in its application to him, and is unconstitutional as enacted because what he calls the "purpose" of Congress was "to suppress freedom of speech." We consider these arguments separately.

O'Brien first argues that the 1965 Amendment is unconstitutional as applied to him because his act of burning his registration certificate was protected "symbolic speech" within the First Amendment. His argument is that the freedom of expression which the First Amendment guarantees includes all modes of "communication of ideas by conduct," and that his conduct is within this definition because he did it in "demonstration against the war and against the draft." We cannot accept the view that an apparently limitless variety of conduct can be labeled "speech" whenever the person engaging in the conduct intends thereby to express an idea. However, even on the assumption that the alleged communicative element in O'Brien's conduct is sufficient to bring into play the First Amendment, it does not necessarily follow that the destruction of a registration certificate is constitutionally protected activity. This Court has held that when "speech" and "nonspeech" elements are combined in the same course of conduct, a sufficiently important governmental interest in regulating the nonspeech element can justify incidental limitations on First Amendment freedoms. To characterize the quality of the governmental interest which must appear, the Court has employed a variety of descriptive terms: compelling; substantial; subordinating; paramount; cogent; strong. Whatever imprecision inheres in these terms, we think it clear that a government regulation is sufficiently justified if it is within the constitutional power of the Government; if it furthers an important or substantial governmental interest; if the governmental interest is unrelated to the suppression of free expression; and if the incidental restriction on alleged First Amendment freedoms is no greater than is essential to the furtherance of that interest.

We find that the 1965 Amendment meets all of these requirements, and consequently that O'Brien can be constitutionally convicted for violating it.

The constitutional power of Congress to raise and support armies and to make all laws necessary and proper to that end is broad and sweeping. The power of Congress to classify and conscript manpower for military service is beyond question. Pursuant to this power, Congress may establish a system of registration for individuals liable for training and service, and may require such individuals within reason to cooperate in the registration system. The issuance of certificates indicating the registration and eligibility classification of individuals is a legitimate and substantial administrative aid in the functioning of this system. And legislation to insure the continuing availability of issued certificates serves a legitimate and substantial purpose in the system's administration.

O'Brien's argument to the contrary is necessarily premised upon his unrealistic characterization of Selective Service certificates. He essentially adopts the position that such certificates are so many pieces of paper designed to notify registrants of their registration or classification, to be retained or tossed in the wastebasket according to the convenience or taste of the registrant. Once the registrant has received notification, according to this view, there is no reason for him to retain the certificates. O'Brien notes that most of the information on a registration certificate serves no notification purpose at all; the registrant hardly needs to be told his address and physical characteristics. We agree that the registration certificate contains much information of which the registrant needs no notification. This circumstance, however, does not lead to the conclusion that the certificate serves no purpose, but that, like the classification certificate, it serves purposes in addition to initial notification. Many of these purposes would be defeated by the certificates' destruction or mutilation. Among these are:

- The registration certificate serves as proof that the individual described thereon has registered for the draft. Voluntarily displaying the two certificates is an easy and painless way for a young man to dispel a question as to whether he might be delinquent in his Selective Service obligations. Further, it is in the interest of the just and efficient administration of the system that [the certificates] be continually available, in the event, for example, of a mix-up in the registrant's file.
- The information supplied on the certificates facilitates communication between registrants and local boards, simplifying the system and benefiting all concerned. To begin with, each certificate bears the address of the registrant's local board, an item unlikely to be committed to memory. Further,

each card bears the registrant's Selective Service number, and a registrant who has his number readily available so that he can communicate it to his local board when he supplies or requests information can make simpler the board's task in locating his file. Finally, a registrant's inquiry, particularly through a local board other than his own, concerning his eligibility status is frequently answerable simply on the basis of his classification certificate; whereas, if the certificate were not reasonably available and the registrant were uncertain of his classification, the task of answering his questions would be considerably complicated.
- Both certificates carry continual reminders that the registrant must notify his local board of any change of address, and other specified changes in his status.
- The regulatory scheme involving Selective Service certificates includes clearly valid prohibitions against the alteration, forgery, or similar deceptive misuse of certificates. The destruction or mutilation of certificates obviously increases the difficulty of detecting and tracing abuses such as these. Further, a mutilated certificate might itself be used for deceptive purposes.

The many functions performed by Selective Service certificates establish beyond doubt that Congress has a legitimate and substantial interest in preventing their wanton and unrestrained destruction and assuring their continuing availability by punishing people who knowingly and wilfully destroy or mutilate them.

We think it apparent that the continuing availability to each registrant of his Selective Service certificates substantially furthers the smooth and proper functioning of the system that Congress has established to raise armies. We think it also apparent that the Nation has a vital interest in having a system for raising armies that functions with maximum efficiency and is capable of easily and quickly responding to continually changing circumstances. For these reasons, the Government has a substantial interest in assuring the continuing availability of issued Selective Service certificates.

It is equally clear that the 1965 Amendment specifically protects this substantial governmental interest. We perceive no alternative means that would more precisely and narrowly assure the continuing availability of issued Selective Service certificates than a law which prohibits their wilful mutilation or destruction. The 1965 Amendment prohibits such conduct and does nothing more. In other words, both the governmental interest and the operation of the 1965 Amendment are limited to the noncommunicative aspect of O'Brien's conduct. The governmental interest and the scope of the 1965 Amendment are limited to preventing harm to the smooth and efficient functioning of the

Selective Service System. When O'Brien deliberately rendered unavailable his registration certificate, he wilfully frustrated this governmental interest. For this noncommunicative impact of his conduct, and for nothing else, he was convicted.

In conclusion, we find that because of the Government's substantial interest in assuring the continuing availability of issued Selective Service certificates, because [the law] is an appropriately narrow means of protecting this interest and condemns only the independent noncommunicative impact of conduct within its reach, and because the noncommunicative impact of O'Brien's act of burning his registration certificate frustrated the Government's interest, a sufficient governmental interest has been shown to justify O'Brien's conviction.

POINTS FOR DISCUSSION

1. The *O'Brien* Court says it "cannot accept the view that an apparently limitless variety of conduct can be labeled 'speech' whenever the person engaging in the conduct intends thereby to express an idea." When, if ever, *should* conduct be treated the same as speech? Are you exercising your right to free speech when you walk on a picket line? What about the civil rights demonstrators of the 1960s who conducted "sit-ins" at lunch counters that refused to serve "Coloreds"?
2. O'Brien was charged with "willfully and knowingly" mutilating, destroying, and burning his draft card. Given the unlikelihood that a young man would take such actions in support of the Vietnam War, what are we to make of Chief Justice Warren's assertion that the statute at issue here was aimed at "the *noncommunicative* aspect of O'Brien's conduct?"

▪ *Morse v. Frederick*
551 U.S. 393 (2007)
Chief Justice Roberts:

On January 24, 2002, the Olympic Torch Relay passed through Juneau, Alaska, on its way to the winter games in Salt Lake City, Utah. The torchbearers were to proceed along a street in front of Juneau-Douglas High School (JDHS) while school was in session. Petitioner Deborah Morse, the school principal, decided to permit staff and students to participate in the Torch Relay as an approved social event or class trip. Students were allowed to leave class to observe the relay from either side of the street. Teachers and administrative officials monitored the students' actions.

Respondent Joseph Frederick, a JDHS senior, was late to school that day. When he arrived, he joined his friends (all but one of whom were JDHS students) across the street from the school to watch the event. Not all the students waited patiently. Some became rambunctious, throwing plastic cola bottles and snowballs and scuffling with their classmates. As the torchbearers and camera crews passed by, Frederick and his friends unfurled a 14-foot banner bearing the phrase: "BONG HITS 4 JESUS."

Principal Morse immediately crossed the street and demanded that the banner be taken down. Everyone but Frederick complied. Morse confiscated the banner and told Frederick to report to her office, where she suspended him for 10 days. Morse later explained that she told Frederick to take the banner down because she thought it encouraged illegal drug use, in violation of established school policy.

Frederick administratively appealed his suspension, but the Juneau School District Superintendent upheld it. The superintendent determined that:

> The common-sense understanding of the phrase "bong hits" is that it is a reference to a means of smoking marijuana. Given Frederick's inability or unwillingness to express any other credible meaning for the phrase, I can only agree with the principal and countless others who saw the banner as advocating the use of illegal drugs. Frederick's speech was not political. He was not advocating the legalization of marijuana or promoting a religious belief. He was displaying a fairly silly message promoting illegal drug usage in the midst of a school activity, for the benefit of television cameras covering the Torch Relay. Frederick's speech was potentially disruptive to the event and clearly disruptive of and inconsistent with the school's educational mission to educate students about the dangers of illegal drugs and to discourage their use.

The superintendent concluded that the principal's actions were permissible because Frederick's banner was "speech or action that intrudes upon the work of the schools." The Juneau School District Board of Education upheld the suspension. Frederick then filed suit, alleging that the school board and Morse had violated his First Amendment rights. The District Court granted summary judgment for the school board and Morse; the Ninth Circuit reversed. Deciding that the school punished Frederick without demonstrating that his speech gave rise to a "risk of substantial disruption."

At the outset, we reject Frederick's argument that this is not a school speech case. The event occurred during normal school hours. It was sanctioned by Principal Morse "as an approved social event or class trip," and the school district's rules expressly provide that pupils in "approved social events and class trips are subject to district rules for student conduct." Teachers and administrators were interspersed among the students and charged with supervising them. The high school band and cheerleaders performed. There is some uncertainty at the outer boundaries as to when courts should apply school-speech precedents, but not on these facts.

The message on Frederick's banner is cryptic. It is no doubt offensive to some, perhaps amusing to others. To still others, it probably means nothing at all. Frederick himself claimed "that the words were just nonsense meant to attract television cameras." But Principal Morse thought the banner would be interpreted by those viewing it as promoting illegal drug use, and that interpretation is plainly a reasonable one. We agree with Morse. At least two interpretations of the words on the banner demonstrate that the sign advocated the use of illegal drugs. First, the phrase could be interpreted as an imperative: "[Take] bong hits . . ."—a message equivalent, as Morse explained in her declaration, to "smoke marijuana" or "use an illegal drug." Alternatively, the phrase could be viewed as celebrating drug use—"bong hits [are a good thing]," or "[we take] bong hits"—and we discern no meaningful distinction between celebrating illegal drug use in the midst of fellow students and outright advocacy or promotion.

Frederick [of course, maintains that] he "just wanted to get on television." But that is a description of Frederick's *motive* for displaying the banner; it is not an interpretation of what the banner says. The *way* Frederick was going to fulfill his ambition of appearing on television was by unfurling a pro-drug banner at a school event, in the presence of teachers and fellow students. [Since] not even Frederick argues that the banner conveys any sort of political or religious message, this is plainly not a case about political debate over the criminalization of drug use or possession.

The question thus becomes whether a principal may, consistent with the First Amendment, restrict student speech at a school event, when that speech is reasonably viewed as promoting illegal drug use. We hold that she may.

[Our leading student speech case, *Tinker v. Des Moines Independent Community School District*],[2] held that student expression may not be suppressed unless school officials reasonably conclude that it will "materially and substantially disrupt the work and discipline of the school. [But our later student cases have made clear that Tinker's "disruption" standard] is not the only basis for restricting student speech [and that] "the constitutional rights of students in public school are not automatically coextensive with the rights of adults in other settings."

---

2. 393 U.S. 503 (1969).

[Moreover, our Fourth Amendment cases in school settings, governing such matters as locker searches and drug testing, have made clear that] deterring drug use by schoolchildren is an "important—indeed, perhaps compelling" interest. Drug abuse can cause severe and permanent damage to the health and well-being of young people. Congress has declared that part of a school's job is educating students about the dangers of illegal drug use. It has provided billions of dollars to support state and local drug-prevention programs. Thousands of school boards throughout the country—including JDHS—have adopted policies aimed at effectuating this message. Those school boards know that peer pressure is perhaps the single most important factor leading schoolchildren to take drugs, and that students are more likely to use drugs when the norms in school appear to tolerate such behavior. Student speech celebrating illegal drug use at a school event, in the presence of school administrators and teachers, thus poses a particular challenge.

Petitioners urge us to adopt the broader rule that Frederick's speech is proscribable because it is plainly "offensive." [But] much political and religious speech might be perceived as offensive to some. The concern here is not that Frederick's speech was offensive, but that it was reasonably viewed as promoting illegal drug use.

School principals have a difficult job, and a vitally important one. When Frederick suddenly and unexpectedly unfurled his banner, Morse had to decide to act—or not act—on the spot. It was reasonable for her to conclude that the banner promoted illegal drug use—in violation of established school policy—and that failing to act would send a powerful message to the students in her charge, including Frederick, about how serious the school was about the dangers of illegal drug use. The First Amendment does not require schools to tolerate at school events student expression that contributes to those dangers.

The judgment of the United States Court of Appeals for the Ninth Circuit is reversed, and the case is remanded for further proceedings consistent with this opinion. It is so ordered.

POINTS FOR DISCUSSION

1. Is the majority guilty of having it both ways, on the one hand infusing young Mr. Frederick's message with serious cognitive content (an incitement to illegal drug use), but also rejecting the notion that the message had any political elements (after all, he "only wanted to get on TV")?
2. Justice Stevens's dissenting opinion reminds the Court that alcohol abuse is far more dangerous than marijuana use. But what if Mr. Frederick's ban-

ner had read "Wine Sips for Jesus?" Such a message still would be arguably an incitement to illegal (for minors, anyway) drug use, but it does seem to have religious, perhaps political, overtones. What do you think of Stevens's point here (or of his additional point that almost any message regarding pot use in Alaska cannot avoid being seen as a political one, given the state's highly controversial citizen referenda legalizing private possession of small amounts of the drug, and explicitly accepting its medical uses)?

▪ *U.S. v. The Progressive*
467 F. Supp. 990 (W.D. Wisc. 1979)
Judge Warren:

On March 9, 1979, this Court, at the request of the government, but after hearing from both parties, issued a temporary restraining order enjoining defendants, their employees, and agents from publishing or otherwise communicating or disclosing in any manner any restricted data contained in the article: "The H-Bomb Secret: How We Got It, Why We're Telling It."

In keeping with the Court's order that the temporary restraining order should be in effect for the shortest time possible, a preliminary injunction hearing was scheduled for one week later, on March 16, 1979. At the request of the parties and with the Court's acquiescence, the preliminary injunction hearing was rescheduled for 10:00 A.M. today in order that both sides might have additional time to file affidavits and arguments. The Court continued the temporary restraining order until 5:00 P.M. today.

In order to grant a preliminary injunction, the Court must find that plaintiff has a reasonable likelihood of success on the merits, and that the plaintiff will suffer irreparable harm if the injunction does not issue. In addition, the Court must consider the interest of the public and the balance of the potential harm to plaintiff and defendants.

In its argument and briefs, plaintiff relies on national security, as enunciated by Congress in The Atomic Energy Act of 1954, as the basis for classification of certain documents. Plaintiff contends that, in certain areas, national preservation and self-interest permit the retention and classification of government secrets. The government argues that its national security interest also permits it to impress classification and censorship upon information originating in the public domain, if when drawn together, synthesized and collated, such information acquires the character of presenting immediate, direct and irreparable harm to the interests of the United States.

Defendants argue that freedom of expression as embodied in the First Amendment is so central to the heart of liberty that prior restraint in any form becomes anathema. They contend that this is particularly true when a nation is not at war and where the prior restraint is based on surmise or conjecture. While acknowledging that freedom of the press is not absolute, they maintain that the publication of the projected article does not rise to the level of immediate, direct and irreparable harm which could justify incursion into First Amendment freedoms.

Both parties have already marshaled impressive opinions covering all aspects of the case. The Court has read all this material and has now heard extensive argument. It is time for decision.

From the founding days of this nation, the rights to freedom of speech and of the press have held an honored place in our constitutional scheme. The establishment and nurturing of these rights is one of the true achievements of our form of government. Because of the importance of these rights, any prior restraint on publication comes into court under a heavy presumption against its constitutional validity.

However, First Amendment rights are not absolute. They are not boundless. Free speech is not so absolute or irrational a conception as to imply paralysis of the means for effective protection of all the freedoms secured by the Bill of Rights.

In *Near v. Minnesota*, 283 U.S. 697 (1931), the Supreme Court specifically recognized an extremely narrow area, involving national security, in which interference with First Amendment rights might be tolerated and a prior restraint on publication might be appropriate. The Court stated: "When a nation is at war many things that might be said in time of peace are such a hindrance to its effort that their utterance will not be endured so long as men fight and that no Court could regard them as protected by any constitutional right. No one would question but that a government might prevent actual obstruction to its recruiting service or the publication of the sailing dates of transports or the number and location of troops."

Thus, it is clear that few things, save grave national security concerns, are sufficient to override First Amendment interests. A court is well admonished to approach any requested prior restraint with a great deal of skepticism.

Juxtaposed against the right to freedom of expression is the government's contention that the national security of this country could be jeopardized by publication of the article.

The Court is convinced that the government has a right to classify certain sensitive documents to protect its national security. The problem is with the scope of the classification system.

Defendants contend that the projected article merely contains data already in the public domain and readily available to any diligent seeker. They say other nations already have the same information or the opportunity to obtain it. How then, they argue, can they be in violation of [the relevant federal laws], which purport to authorize injunctive relief against one who would disclose restricted data "with reason to believe such data will be utilized to injure the United States or to secure an advantage to any foreign nation"? Although the government states that some of the information is in the public domain, it contends that much of the data is not, and that the Morland article contains a core of information that has never before been published.

Furthermore, the government's position is that whether or not specific information is in the public domain or has been declassified at some point is not determinative. The government states that a court must look at the nature and context of prior disclosures and analyze what the practical impact of the prior disclosures are as contrasted to that of the present revelation.

The government feels that the mere fact that the author, Howard Morland, could prepare an article explaining the technical processes of thermonuclear weapons does not mean that those processes are available to everyone. They lay heavy emphasis on the argument that the danger lies in the exposition of certain concepts never heretofore disclosed in conjunction with one another.

In an impressive affidavit, Dr. Hans A. Bethe states that sizeable portions of the Morland text should be classified as restricted data because the processes outlined in the manuscript describe the essential design and operation of thermonuclear weapons. He later concludes that "the design and operational concepts described in the manuscript are not expressed or revealed in the public literature nor do I believe they are known to scientists not associated with the government weapons programs."

The Court has grappled with this difficult problem and has read and studied the affidavits and other documents on file. After all this, the Court finds concepts within the article that it does not find in the public realm, concepts that are vital to the operation of the hydrogen bomb.

Even if some of the information is in the public domain, due recognition must be given to the human skills and expertise involved in writing this article. The author needed sufficient expertise to recognize relevant, as opposed to irrelevant, information and to assimilate the information obtained. The right questions had to be asked or the correct educated guesses had to be made.

Does the article provide a "do-it-yourself" guide for the hydrogen bomb? Probably not. A number of affidavits make quite clear that a *sine qua non* to thermonuclear capability is a large, sophisticated industrial capability coupled with a coterie of imaginative, resourceful scientists and technicians. One does not build a hydrogen bomb in the basement. However, the article could possibly provide sufficient information to allow a medium-size nation to move faster in developing a hydrogen weapon. It could provide a ticket to bypass blind alleys.

Although the defendants state that the information contained in the article is relatively easy to obtain, only five countries now have a hydrogen bomb. Yet the United States first successfully exploded the hydrogen bomb some twenty-six years ago.

The point has also been made that it is only a question of time before other countries will have the hydrogen bomb. That may be true. However, there are times in the course of human history when time itself may be very important. This time factor becomes critical when considering mass annihilation weaponry. Witness the failure of Hitler to get his V-1 and V-2 bombs operational quickly enough to materially affect the outcome of World War II.

Defendants have stated that publication of the article will alert the people of this country to the false illusion of security created by the government's futile efforts at secrecy. They believe publication will provide the people with needed information to make informed decisions on an urgent issue of public concern.

However, this Court can find no plausible reason why the public needs to know the technical details about hydrogen bomb construction to carry on an informed debate on this issue. Furthermore, the Court believes that the defendants' position in favor of nuclear non-proliferation would be harmed, not aided, by the publication of this article.

The Court is of the opinion that the government has shown that the defendants had reason to believe that the data in the article, if published, would injure the United States or give an advantage to a foreign nation. Extensive reading and studying of the documents on file lead to the conclusion that not all the data is available in the public realm in the same fashion, if it is available at all.

What is involved here is information dealing with the most destructive weapon in the history of mankind, information of sufficient destructive potential to nullify the right to free speech and to endanger the right to life itself. Stripped to its essence, then, the question before the Court is a basic confrontation between the First Amendment right to freedom of the press and national security.

Our Founding Fathers believed, as we do, that one is born with certain inalienable rights which, as the Declaration of Independence intones, include the right to life, liberty and the pursuit of happiness. The Constitution, including the Bill of Rights, was enacted to make those rights operable in everyday life.

The Court believes that each of us is born seized of a panoply of basic rights, that we institute governments to secure these rights and that there is a hierarchy of values attached to these rights which is helpful in deciding the clash now before us.

Certain of these rights have an aspect of imperativeness or centrality that make them transcend other rights. Somehow it does not seem that the right to life and the right to not have soldiers quartered in your home can be of equal import in the grand scheme of things. While it may be true in the long-run, as Patrick Henry instructs us, that one would prefer death to life without liberty, nonetheless, in the short-run, one cannot enjoy freedom of speech, freedom to worship or freedom of the press unless one first enjoys the freedom to live.

Faced with a stark choice between upholding the right to continued life and the right to freedom of the press, most jurists would have no difficulty in opting for the chance to continue to breathe and function as they work to achieve perfect freedom of expression.

Is the choice here so stark? Only time can give us a definitive answer. But considering another aspect of this panoply of rights we all have is helpful in answering the question now before us. This aspect is the disparity of the risk involved.

The destruction of various human rights can come about in differing ways and at varying speeds. Freedom of the press can be obliterated overnight by some dictator's imposition of censorship or by the slow nibbling away at a free press through successive bits of repressive legislation enacted by a nation's lawmakers. Yet, even in the most drastic of such situations, it is always possible for a dictator to be overthrown, for a bad law to be repealed or for a judge's error to be subsequently rectified. Only when human life is at stake are such corrections impossible. The case at bar is so difficult precisely because the consequences of error involve human life itself and on such an awesome scale.

A mistake in ruling against *The Progressive* will seriously infringe cherished First Amendment rights. If a preliminary injunction is issued, it will constitute the first instance of prior restraint against a publication in this fashion in the history of this country, to this Court's knowledge. Such notoriety is not to be sought. It will curtail defendants' First Amendment rights in a drastic and substantial fashion. It will infringe upon our right to know and to be informed as well. A mistake in ruling against the United States could pave the way for thermonuclear annihilation for us all. In that event, our right to life is extinguished and the right to publish becomes moot.

In the *Near* case, the Supreme Court recognized that publication of troop movements in time of war would threaten national security and could therefore be restrained. Times have changed significantly since 1931 when *Near* was decided. Now war by foot soldiers has been replaced in large part by war by machines and bombs. No longer need there be any advance warning or any preparation time before a nuclear war could be commenced.

In light of these factors, this Court concludes that publication of the technical information on the hydrogen bomb contained in the article is analogous to publication of troop movements or locations in time of war and falls within the extremely narrow exception to the rule against prior restraint.

Because the government has met its heavy burden of showing justification for the imposition of a prior restraint on publication of the objected-to technical portions of the Morland article, and because the Court is unconvinced that suppression of the objected-to technical portions of the Morland article would in any plausible fashion impede the defendants in their laudable crusade to stimulate public knowledge of nuclear armament and bring about enlightened debate on national policy questions, the Court finds that the objected-to portions of the article fall within the narrow area recognized by the Court in *Near v. Minnesota* in which a prior restraint on publication is appropriate.

However, the Court is acutely aware of the old legal adage that "bad cases make bad law." This case in its present posture will undoubtedly go to the Supreme Court because it does present so starkly the clash between freedom of press and national security. Does it go there with the blessing of the entire press? The Court thinks not. Many elements of the press see grave risk of permanent damage to First Amendment freedoms if this case goes forward. They feel appellate courts will find, as this Court has, that the risk is simply too great to permit publication.

Furthermore, if there is any one inescapable conclusion that one arrives at after wading through all these experts' affidavits, it is that many wise, intelligent, patriotic individuals can hold diametrically opposite opinions on the issues before us.

The government seeks only the deletion of certain technical material and, in the Court's opinion, would have an interest in settling this case out of court. On the other hand, the Court believes that *The Progressive* does not really require the objected-to material in order to ventilate its views on government secrecy and the hydrogen bomb.

The facts and circumstances as presented here fall within the extremely narrow recognized area, involving national security, in which a prior restraint on publication is appropriate. Issuance of a preliminary injunction does not, under the circumstances presented to the Court, violate defendants' First Amendment rights.

Plaintiff has proven all necessary prerequisites for issuance of a preliminary injunction restraining defendants from publishing or disclosing any Restricted Data contained in the Morland article until a final determination in this action has been made by the Court.

[*Editor's note*: As it turns out, the *Progressive* case never went to the Supreme Court. While an appeal was pending, a number of other publications—including campus newspapers at the University of Wisconsin and Stanford University—printed essays very similar to the Morland article. The case was therefore dismissed as moot in that there was no more damage that could be done by the Morland article itself.]

POINTS FOR DISCUSSION

1. Suppose that a publication wanted to print an essay arguing that the U.S. government is inadequately preparing for the possibility of terrorism using biological weapons. Suppose further that the publisher felt that the point can only be made by showing how easy it would be to wage biologic warfare against this country. Upon the government's request, should a modern-day court do as Judge Warren did? Should publication of the article be stopped?
2. Judge Warren struggled with this case precisely because he was asked to impose a prior restraint on publication, and such restraints were viewed with special disdain by the Founders. He allows that a prior restraint is appropriate here because total annihilation of the human race may result if he permits publication and then determines if the Morland essay was in violation of the Atomic Energy Act. Are there other situations, beyond the possible end of humankind, that you think justify the use of prior restraints on communication?

▪ *U.S. v. Stevens*
130 S. Ct. 1577 (2010)
Chief Justice Roberts:

Congress enacted 18 U.S.C. § 48 to criminalize the commercial creation, sale, or possession of certain depictions of animal cruelty. The statute does not address underlying acts harmful to animals, but only portrayals of such conduct. The question presented is whether the prohibition in the statute is consistent with the freedom of speech guaranteed by the First Amendment.

Section 48 establishes a criminal penalty of up to five years in prison for anyone who knowingly "creates, sells, or possesses a depiction of animal cruelty," if done "for commercial gain" in interstate or foreign commerce. A depiction of "animal cruelty" is defined as one "in which a living animal is intentionally maimed, mutilated, tortured, wounded, or killed," if that conduct violates federal or state law where "the creation, sale, or possession takes place." In what is referred to as the "exceptions clause," the law exempts from prohibition any depiction "that has serious religious, political, scientific, educational, journalistic, historical, or artistic value."

The legislative background of § 48 focused primarily on the interstate market for "crush videos," [which] feature the intentional torture and killing of helpless animals, including cats, dogs, monkeys, mice, and hamsters. Crush videos often depict women slowly crushing animals to death with their bare feet or while wearing high heeled shoes, sometimes while talking to the animals in a kind of dominatrix patter over the cries and squeals of the animals, obviously in great pain. Apparently these depictions appeal to persons with a very specific sexual fetish who find them sexually arousing or otherwise exciting. The acts depicted in crush videos are typically prohibited by the animal cruelty laws enacted by all 50 States and the District of Columbia. But crush videos rarely disclose the participants' identities, inhibiting prosecution of the underlying conduct.

This case, however, involves an application of § 48 to depictions of animal fighting. Dogfighting, for example, is unlawful in all 50 States and the District of Columbia, and has been restricted by federal law since 1976. Respondent Robert J. Stevens ran a business, "Dogs of Velvet and Steel," and an associated Web site, through which he sold videos of pit bulls engaging in dogfights and attacking other animals. Among these videos were *Japan Pit Fights* and *Pick-A-Winna: A Pit Bull Documentary*, which include contemporary footage of dogfights in Japan (where such conduct is allegedly legal) as well as footage of American dogfights from the 1960s and 1970s. A third video, *Catch Dogs and Country Living*, depicts the use of pit bulls to hunt wild boar, as well as a gruesome scene of a pit bull attacking a domestic farm pig. On the basis of these videos, Stevens was indicted on three counts of violating § 48. Stevens moved to dismiss the indictment, arguing that § 48 is facially invalid under the First Amendment.

The Government's primary submission is that § 48 necessarily complies with the Constitution because the banned depictions of animal cruelty, as a class, are categorically unprotected by the First Amendment. We disagree.

The First Amendment provides that "Congress shall make no law . . . abridging the freedom of speech." As a general matter, the First Amendment means that government has no power to restrict expression because of its message, its ideas, its subject matter, or its content. Section 48 explicitly regulates expression based on content: The statute restricts "visual [and] auditory depiction[s]," such as photographs, videos, or sound recordings, depending on whether they depict conduct in which a living animal is intentionally harmed. As such, § 48 is presumptively invalid, and the Government bears the burden to rebut that presumption.

From 1791 to the present, however, the First Amendment has permitted restrictions upon the content of speech in a few limited areas, and has never included a freedom to disregard these traditional limitations. These historic and traditional categories include obscenity, defamation, fraud, incitement, and speech integral to criminal conduct.

The Government argues that "depictions of animal cruelty" should be added to the list. It contends that depictions of illegal acts of animal cruelty that are made, sold, or possessed for commercial gain necessarily lack expressive value, and may accordingly be regulated as *unprotected* speech. The claim is not just that Congress may regulate depictions of animal cruelty subject to the First Amendment, but that these depictions are outside the reach of that Amendment altogether.

As the Government notes, the prohibition of animal cruelty itself has a long history in American law, starting with the early settlement of the Colonies. But we are unaware of any similar tradition excluding *depictions* of animal cruelty from "the freedom of speech" codified in the First Amendment, and the Government points us to none.

The Government contends that historical evidence about the reach of the First Amendment is not a necessary prerequisite for regulation today, and that categories of speech may be exempted from the First Amendment's protection without any long-settled tradition of subjecting that speech to regulation. Instead, the Government points to Congress's legislative judgment that depictions of animals being intentionally tortured and killed are of such minimal redeeming value as to render them unworthy of First Amendment protection, and asks the Court to uphold the ban on the same basis. The Government thus proposes that a claim of categorical exclusion should be considered under a simple balancing test: "Whether a given category of speech enjoys First Amendment protection depends upon a categorical balancing of the value of the speech against its societal costs."

As a free-floating test for First Amendment coverage, that sentence is startling and dangerous. The First Amendment's guarantee of free speech does not extend only to categories of speech that survive an ad hoc balancing of relative social costs and benefits. The First Amendment itself reflects a judgment by the American people that the benefits of its restrictions on the Government outweigh the costs. Our Constitution forecloses any attempt to revise that judgment simply on the basis that some speech is not worth it. The Constitution is not a document prescribing limits, and declaring that those limits may be passed at pleasure

To be fair to the Government, its view did not emerge from a vacuum. As the Government correctly notes, this Court has often *described* historically unprotected categories of speech as being of such slight social value as a step to truth that any benefit that may be derived from them is clearly outweighed by the social interest in order and morality. But such descriptions are just that—descriptive. They do not set forth a test that may be applied as a general matter to permit the Government to imprison any speaker so long as his speech is deemed valueless or unnecessary, or so long as an ad hoc calculus of costs and benefits tilts in a statute's favor.

When we have identified categories of speech as fully outside the protection of the First Amendment, it has not been on the basis of a simple cost-benefit analysis. [When] we classified child pornography as such a category, we noted that the State has a compelling interest in protecting children from abuse, and that the value of using children in these works (as opposed to simulated conduct or adult actors) was *de minimis*. But our decision did not rest on this balance of competing interests alone. We made clear that child pornography was a special case, intrinsically related to the underlying abuse, and was therefore an integral part of the production of such materials, an activity illegal throughout the Nation.

Our decisions cannot be taken as establishing a freewheeling authority to declare new categories of speech outside the scope of the First Amendment. Maybe there are some categories of speech that have been historically unprotected, but have not yet been specifically identified or discussed as such in our case law. But if so, there is no evidence that depictions of animal cruelty is among them. Because we decline to carve out from the First Amendment any novel exception for § 48, we review Stevens's First Amendment challenge under our existing doctrine.

Stevens challenged § 48 on its face, arguing that any conviction secured under the statute would be unconstitutional. To succeed in a typical facial attack, Stevens would have to establish that no set of circumstances exists under which § 48 would be valid, or that the statute lacks any plainly legitimate sweep. Here the Government asserts that Stevens cannot prevail because § 48 is plainly legitimate as applied to crush videos and animal fighting depictions. Deciding this case through a traditional facial analysis would require us to resolve whether these applications of § 48 are in fact consistent with the Constitution.

In the First Amendment context, however, this Court recognizes a second type of facial challenge whereby a law may be invalidated as overbroad if a substantial number of its applications are unconstitutional, judged in relation to the statute's plainly legitimate sweep.

Stevens argues that § 48 applies to common depictions of ordinary and lawful activities, and that these depictions constitute the vast majority of materials subject to the statute. The Government makes no effort to defend such a broad ban as constitutional. Instead, the Government's entire defense of § 48 rests on interpreting the statute as narrowly limited to specific types of "extreme" material. As the parties have presented the issue, therefore, the constitutionality of § 48 hinges on how broadly it is construed. It is to that question that we now turn.

The first step in overbreadth analysis is to construe the challenged statute; it is impossible to determine whether a statute reaches too far without first knowing what the statute covers. We read § 48 to create a criminal prohibition of alarming breadth. To begin with, the text of the statute's ban on a "depiction of animal cruelty" nowhere requires that the depicted conduct be cruel. That text applies to "any depiction" in which "a living animal is intentionally maimed, mutilated, tortured, wounded, or killed." "Maimed, mutilated, [and] tortured" convey cruelty, but "wounded" or "killed" do not suggest any such limitation. The Government contends that the terms in the definition should be read to require the additional element of "accompanying acts of cruelty." The Government bases this argument on the [the fact that the phrase being defined is] "depiction of animal *cruelty*," and on the commonsense [notion] that an ambiguous term may be given more precise content by the neighboring words with which it is associated.

But the phrase "wounded or killed" at issue here contains little ambiguity. The Government's opening brief properly applies the ordinary meaning of these words, stating for example that to " 'kill' is 'to deprive of life.' " We agree that "wounded" and "killed" should be read according to their ordinary meaning. Nothing about that meaning requires cruelty.

While not requiring cruelty, § 48 does require that the depicted conduct be "illegal." But this requirement does not limit § 48 along the lines the Government suggests. There are myriad federal and state laws concerning the proper treatment of animals, but many of them are not designed to guard against animal cruelty. Protections of endangered species, for example, restrict even the *humane* wounding or killing of living animals. Livestock regulations are often designed to protect the health of human beings, and hunting and fishing rules (seasons, licensure, bag limits, weight requirements) can be designed to raise revenue, preserve animal populations, or prevent accidents. The text of § 48(c) draws no distinction based on the reason the intentional killing of an animal is made illegal, and includes, for example, the humane slaughter of a stolen cow.

What is more, the application of § 48 to depictions of illegal conduct extends to conduct that is illegal in only a single jurisdiction. Under subsection (c)(1), the depicted conduct need only be illegal in "the State in which the creation, sale, or possession takes place, regardless of whether the wounding or killing took place in that State." A depiction of entirely lawful conduct runs afoul of the ban if that depiction later finds its way into another State where the same conduct is unlawful. This provision greatly expands the scope of § 48, because although there may be a broad societal consensus against cruelty to animals, there is substantial disagreement on what types of conduct are properly regarded as cruel. Both views about cruelty to animals and regulations having no connection to cruelty vary widely from place to place.

In the District of Columbia, for example, all hunting is unlawful. Other jurisdictions permit or encourage hunting, and there is an enormous national market for hunting-related depictions in which a living animal is intentionally killed. Hunting periodicals have circulations in the hundreds of thousands or millions, and hunting television programs, videos, and Web sites are equally popular. The demand for hunting depictions exceeds the estimated demand for crush videos or animal fighting depictions by several orders of magnitude. Nonetheless, because the statute allows each jurisdiction to export its laws to the rest of the country, § 48(a) extends to *any* magazine or video depicting lawful hunting, so long as that depiction is sold within the Nation's Capital.

Those seeking to comply with the law thus face a bewildering maze of regulations from at least 56 separate jurisdictions. Some States permit hunting with crossbows, while others forbid it, or restrict it only to the disabled. Missouri allows the "canned" hunting of ungulates held in captivity but Montana restricts such hunting to certain bird species. The sharp-tailed grouse may be hunted in Idaho, but not in Washington.

The disagreements among the States extend well beyond hunting. State agricultural regulations permit different methods of livestock slaughter in different places or as applied to different animals. Even cockfighting, long considered immoral in much of America, is legal in Puerto Rico, and was legal in Louisiana until 2008. An otherwise-lawful image of any of these practices, if sold or possessed for commercial gain within a State that happens to forbid the practice, falls within the prohibition of § 48(a).

The only thing standing between defendants who sell such depictions and five years in federal prison—other than the mercy of a prosecutor—is the statute's exceptions clause. Subsection (b) exempts from prohibition "any depiction that has serious religious, political, scientific, educational, journalistic, historical, or artistic value." The Government argues that this clause substantially narrows the statute's reach: News reports about animal cruelty have "journalistic" value; pictures of bullfights in Spain have "historical" value; and instructional hunting videos have "educational" value. Thus, the Government argues, § 48 reaches only crush videos, depictions of animal fighting (other than Spanish bullfighting) and perhaps other depictions of "extreme acts of animal cruelty."

The Government's attempt to narrow the statutory ban, however, requires an unrealistically broad reading of the exceptions clause. As the Government reads the clause, any material with "redeeming societal value," "at least some minimal value," or anything more than "scant social value" is excluded under § 48(b). But the text says "serious" value, and "serious" should be taken seriously. We decline the Government's invitation—advanced for the first time in this Court—to regard as "serious" anything that is not "scant." "Serious" ordinarily means a good bit more.

Quite apart from the requirement of "serious" value in § 48(b), the excepted speech must also fall within one of the enumerated categories. Much speech does not. Most hunting videos, for example, are not obviously instructional in nature, except in the sense that all life is a lesson. According to Safari Club International and the Congressional Sportsmen's Foundation, many popular videos "have primarily entertainment value" and are designed to "entertain the viewer, market hunting equipment, or increase the hunting community." The Government offers no principled explanation why depictions of hunting or depictions of Spanish bullfights would be *inherently* valuable while those of Japanese dogfights are not. There is simply no adequate reading of the exceptions clause that results in the statute's banning only the depictions the Government would like to ban.

The Government explains that the language of § 48(b) was largely drawn from our opinion in *Miller v. California* (1973), which excepted from its definition of obscenity any material with "serious literary, artistic, political, or scientific value." In *Miller* we held that "serious" value shields depictions of sex from regulation as obscenity. Limiting *Miller*'s exception to "serious" value ensured that "a quotation from Voltaire in the flyleaf of a book would not constitutionally redeem an otherwise obscene publication." We did not, however, determine that serious value could be used as a general precondition to protecting *other* types of speech in the first place. *Most* of what we say to one another lacks "religious, political, scientific, educational, journalistic, historical, or artistic value" (let alone serious value), but it is still sheltered from government regulation.

Not to worry, the Government says: The Executive Branch construes § 48 to reach only "extreme" cruelty, and it neither has brought nor will bring a prosecution for anything less.

The Government hits this theme hard, invoking its prosecutorial discretion several times. But the First Amendment protects against the Government; it does not leave us at the mercy of *noblesse oblige*. We would not uphold an unconstitutional statute merely because the Government promised to use it responsibly.

This prosecution is itself evidence of the danger in putting faith in government representations of prosecutorial restraint. When this legislation was enacted, the Executive Branch announced that it would interpret § 48 as covering only depictions "of wanton cruelty to animals designed to appeal to a prurient interest in sex." No one suggests that the videos in this case fit that description. The Government's assurance that it will apply § 48 far more restrictively than its language provides is pertinent only as an implicit acknowledgment of the potential constitutional problems with a more natural reading.

Our construction of § 48 decides the constitutional question; the Government makes no effort to defend the constitutionality of § 48 as applied beyond crush videos and depictions of animal fighting. It argues that those particular depictions are intrinsically related to criminal conduct or are analogous to obscenity (if not themselves obscene), and that the ban on such speech is narrowly tailored to reinforce restrictions on the underlying conduct, prevent additional crime arising from the depictions, or safeguard public mores. But the Government nowhere attempts to extend these arguments to depictions of any other activities—depictions that are presumptively protected by the First Amendment but that remain subject to the criminal sanctions of § 48.

Nor does the Government seriously contest that the presumptively impermissible applications of § 48 (properly construed) far outnumber any permissible ones. However "growing" and "lucrative" the markets for crush videos and dogfighting depictions might be, they are dwarfed by the market for other depictions, such as hunting magazines and videos, that we have determined to be within the scope of § 48. We therefore need not and do not decide whether a statute limited to crush videos or other depictions of extreme animal cruelty would be constitutional. We hold only that § 48 is not so limited but is instead substantially overbroad, and therefore invalid under the First Amendment.

POINTS FOR DISCUSSION

1. Can you think of ways in which the law at issue here might be rewritten so as to forbid "crush videos" but not videos of hunting? Do you think your reworked statute would be found constitutional?

2. The Court's reference to *Miller v. California* reminds us that American communication law is far more concerned with sex than with violence. Hard-core sexual images can be outlawed outright, but not violent ones. What are your thoughts about this pattern? Are we more squeamish about sex than about violence in general?

3

Libel: Common Law Elements

Libel law is designed to protect individuals' interest in their reputation, permitting aggrieved parties to sue those who make false and defamatory statements of fact about them. Generally, plaintiffs must prove four things to prevail:

- **Identification** (that the utterances in question are about the plaintiff)
- **Publication** (that at least one third party has heard or read the charges)
- **Defamation** (that the utterance would tend to damage reputation)
- **Fault** (that the speaker or publisher was guilty, minimally, of negligence in disseminating the charges)

The court cases in this chapter were selected because they exemplify key principles of common law applied to libel, long before the Supreme Court ever suggested that the First Amendment itself places important limitations on the use of libel suits to squelch political debate.

In *Greenbelt Cooperative Publishing Association v. Bresler*, the Supreme Court says that language is complex, and that utterances that seem to make false factual allegations may instead be expressions only of the speaker's opinion. What does it mean, the Court had to decide, to call someone a "blackmailer"? The answer, as you will see, is that "it depends . . . upon the context." Although the case was decided a few years after the Court had applied constitutional limitations to libel law, its holding is not dependent on First Amendment doctrine.

Next comes *Nichols v. Moore*, a case right out of the headlines, in which the brother of one of the Oklahoma City bombing conspirators sued film director Michael Moore, whose *Bowling for Columbine*, he alleges, suggests that he, too, was criminally involved. You can view the relevant scenes from the film on my website, www.paulsiegelcommlaw.com.

Sexual orientation is the issue in *Amrak Productions v. Morton*, a case involving rock star Madonna, and a photo whose caption introduced some confusion into who is who in her entourage. (The relevant photo that led to the suit is also on my website.)

Stanton v. Metro Corporation serves as a cautionary tale, reminding us that we might be guilty of libeling another even if we never mention her by name. The court here tells us that we must consider the visuals as well as the text, and even take into consideration the likelihood that reasonable readers will actually see an article's disclaimers, which, if read, would make clear that there is no defamation. The case involves an illustrated *Boston* magazine article about very sexually active teens. (Again, you can visit my website to see the article.)

Next we look at a case involving Kato Kaelin, who achieved fame of sorts by dint of his status as O. J. Simpson's houseguest at the time of Simpson's murder trial (*Kaelin v. Globe Communications Corporation*). Kaelin's suit against a tabloid newspaper emphasizes that a misleading headline can be defamatory even if the article it introduces is not. (The tabloid cover is also available on my website.)

Finally we examine *Diaz v. NBC*, a fascinating case involving the film *American Gangster* and the difficulty in establishing the libel element of identification when dealing with works that, although based on true events, are somewhat fictionalized.

▪ *Greenbelt Cooperative Publishing Association v. Bresler*

398 U.S. 6 (1970)
Justice Stewart:

The petitioners are the publishers of a small weekly newspaper, the *Greenbelt News Review*, in the city of Greenbelt, Maryland. The respondent Bresler is a prominent local real estate developer and builder in Greenbelt, and was, during the period in question, a member of the Maryland House of Delegates from a neighboring district. In the autumn of 1965 Bresler was engaged in negotiations with the Greenbelt City Council to obtain certain zoning variances that would allow the construction of high-density housing on land owned by him. At the same time the city was attempting to acquire another tract of land owned by Bresler for the construction of a new high school. Extensive litigation concerning compensation for the school site seemed imminent, unless there should be an agreement on its price between Bresler and the city authorities, and the concurrent negotiations obviously provided both parties considerable bargaining leverage.

These joint negotiations evoked substantial local controversy, and several tumultuous city council meetings were held at which many members of the community freely expressed their views. The meetings were reported at length in the news columns of the *Greenbelt News Review*. Two news articles in consecutive weekly editions of the paper stated that at the public meetings some people had characterized Bresler's negotiating position as "blackmail." The word appeared several times, both with and without quotation marks, and was used once as a subheading within a news story.

Bresler reacted to these news articles by filing the present lawsuit for libel, seeking both compensatory and punitive damages. The primary thrust of his complaint was that the articles, individually and along with other items published in the petitioners' newspaper, imputed to him the crime of blackmail. The case went to trial, and the jury awarded Bresler $5,000 in compensatory damages and $12,500 in punitive damages. The Maryland Court of Appeals affirmed the judgment.

It is not disputed that the articles published in the petitioners' newspaper were accurate and truthful reports of what had been said at the public hearings before the city council. The contention is, rather, that the speakers at the meeting, in using the word "blackmail," and the petitioners in reporting the use of that word in the newspaper articles, were charging Bresler with the crime of blackmail, and that since the petitioners knew that Bresler had committed no such crime, they could be held liable for the knowing use of falsehood. It was upon this theory that the case was submitted to the jury, and upon this theory that the judgment was affirmed by the Maryland Court of Appeals. For the reasons that follow, we hold that the word "blackmail" in these circumstances was not slander when spoken, and not libel when reported in the *Greenbelt News Review*.

There can be no question that the public debates at the sessions of the city council regarding Bresler's negotiations with the city were a subject of substantial concern to all who lived in the community. The debates themselves were heated, as debates about controversial issues usually are. During the course of the arguments Bresler's opponents characterized the position he had taken in his negotiations with the city officials as "blackmail." The *Greenbelt News Review* was performing its wholly legitimate function as a community newspaper when it published full reports of these public debates in its news columns. If the reports had been truncated or distorted in such a way as to extract the word "blackmail" from the context in which it was used at the public meetings, this would be a different case. But the reports were accurate and full. Their headlines, "School Site Stirs Up Council—Rezoning Deal Offer Debated" and "Council Rejects By 4-1 High School Site Deal," made it clear to all readers that the paper was reporting the public debates on the pending land negotiations. Bresler's proposal was accurately and fully described in each article, along with the accurate statement that some people at the meetings had referred to the proposal as blackmail, and others had indicated they thought Bresler's position not unreasonable.

It is simply impossible to believe that a reader who reached the word "blackmail" in either article would not have understood exactly what was meant: it was Bresler's public and wholly legal negotiating proposals that were being criticized. No reader could have thought that either the speakers at the meetings or the newspaper articles reporting their words were charging Bresler with the commission of a criminal offense. On the contrary, even the most careless reader must have perceived that the word was no more than rhetorical hyperbole, a vigorous epithet used by those who considered Bresler's negotiating position extremely unreasonable. Indeed, the record is completely devoid of evidence that anyone in the city of Greenbelt or anywhere else thought Bresler had been charged with a crime.

To permit the infliction of financial liability upon the petitioners for publishing these two news articles would subvert the most fundamental meaning of a free press. Accordingly, we reverse the judgment and remand the case to the Court of Appeals of Maryland for further proceedings not inconsistent with this opinion.

POINTS FOR DISCUSSION

1. Does Justice Stewart's analysis suggest that readers will always "get the joke" when newspapers engage in exaggeration, irony, or "rhetorical hyperbole"? How would such an assumption square with the many times that news outlets have felt the need to apologize to individuals or to whole groups who have felt maligned by a *failed* attempt at humor?
2. The *Greenbelt News Review* escaped liability because the larger context made clear that it was not really accusing Bresler of criminal activity. What should happen in situations where the allegedly libelous words are vague on their face, but highly inflammatory if a larger context is known? For example, suppose that a state governor is accused in the press of having fashioned a "final solution" for prison unrest. If the governor sues for libel, could the media plausibly claim that very few of its readers know enough

about contemporary history to recognize the phrase as a reference to the Nazis' program of genocide, and that "final solution" could refer innocently to a solution that would not have to be revisited?

▪ *Nichols v. Moore*
477 F.3d 396 (6th Cir. 2007)
Judge Guy:

In 2002, documentary film producer Michael Moore released the movie *Bowling for Columbine*, which explored the topic of gun violence in America. As part of the movie, Moore interviewed James Nichols, the brother of convicted Oklahoma City bomber Terry Nichols and acquaintance of convicted Oklahoma City bomber Timothy McVeigh. Moore edited the three-hour interview with James Nichols and included ten minutes of this interview in the movie. Related to this interview, Moore also included a brief narration regarding the Oklahoma City bombing. James Nichols asserts that this narration was defamatory.[1]

Nichols asserts that the narration defamed him because it falsely stated that he made practice bombs before Oklahoma City and because the narration falsely implied that he was arrested and charged in connection to the Oklahoma City bombing. In contrast to Moore's narration, Nichols asserts that he did not make practice bombs and that he was never arrested or charged with a criminal offense in connection to the Oklahoma City bombing. Instead, Nichols asserts that, shortly after the Oklahoma City bombing, he was charged with an explosives offense which was not related to the Oklahoma City bombing and which was ultimately dismissed.

In October 2003, Nichols filed the present action in the Eastern District of Michigan against defendant Michael Moore; the district court granted summary judgment for defendant Michael Moore and entered a final judgment in Moore's favor. Nichols now appeals the district court's summary judgment ruling to this court.

In support of his summary judgment motion, defendant Michael Moore [asserted] that the statements regarding James Nichols in *Bowling for Columbine* were substantially true.

---

1. The relevant scenes are on my website, www.paulsiegelcommlaw.com. On the left side (*Communication Law in America*), click on "Video Clips," then "Chapter 3," then on "Bowling for Columbine."

1. *McVeigh and the Nichols brothers made practice bombs before Oklahoma City.*

Plaintiff James Nichols first argues that the district court did not draw all reasonable inferences in his favor in concluding that the "made practice bombs" statement was substantially true. Nichols asserts that the district court failed to accept as true his under-oath statements asserting that he had never experimented with explosive devices and that the only explosive device he ever made was a small pill-vial bomb made out of black powder to loosen soybeans lodged in his grain bin. Plaintiff misconstrues the appropriate legal standard.

In libel cases such as the present one, it is the plaintiff's burden to prove falsity. [Under Michigan law], "damages shall not be awarded in a libel action for the publication or broadcast of a fair and true report of matters of public record, a public and official proceeding, or of a governmental notice, announcement, written or recorded report or record generally available to the public, or act or action of a public body, or for a heading of the report which is a fair and true headnote of the report."

In its opinion, the district court reasoned that there was sufficient evidence in the public record to justify Moore's "made practice bombs" statement. The district court relied on an affidavit provided by FBI Agent Patrick W. Wease: "James Nichols further stated that he participated with McVeigh and Terry Nichols in making 'bottle bombs' in 1992, and that in 1994, he, James Nichols, has made small explosive devices using prescription vials, pyrodex, blasting caps, and safety fuse."

The district court next noted that the amended criminal complaint also referenced several sources which described plaintiff making bombs. Additionally, the district court referred to an order of detention pending trial that was entered by the magistrate against plaintiff, which found that there was clear and convincing evidence that plaintiff had experimented with explosive materials.

Nichols also argues that the second half of the "made practice bombs" statement is defamatory because there was no evidence that any practice bombs were made *in preparation for Oklahoma City*. Moore's statement merely stated, however, that "McVeigh and the Nichols brothers made practice bombs *before* Oklahoma City." There is no dispute that any practice bombs made on Nichols's property were made "before Oklahoma City." Accordingly, we agree with the district court's finding that the entire "made practice bombs before Oklahoma City" statement is substantially true.

2. *Terry and James were both arrested in connection to the bombing.*

The district court viewed the "arrested in connection to the bombing" statement as troubling because Nichols is correct in asserting that he was never arrested or charged for having committed any criminal act directly related to the Oklahoma City bombing. Nichols is also correct in asserting that Michael Moore knew this fact to be true when he published *Bowling for Columbine*. Despite the troubling nature of Moore's statement, we nevertheless agree with the district court's finding that Moore's "arrested in connection to the bombing" statement is substantially true.

Though Nichols was neither charged nor arrested regarding the Oklahoma City bombing, we believe that Nichols's arrest was sufficiently in connection to the bombing for Moore's statement to be considered "substantially true." Nichols was arrested only days after the bombing and his arrest was brought about by the FBI's investigation into Timothy McVeigh's and Terry Nichols's roles in the bombing. Additionally, Nichols was held as a material witness in connection to the Oklahoma City bombing, and Nichols himself admitted that he did not know whether this constituted an arrest in connection to the bombing.

3. *Officials charged James, who was at the hearing, and Terry, who was not, with conspiring to make and possess small bombs.*

Nichols next argues that the district court erred in finding that the "officials charged James with conspiring to make and possess small bombs" statement was substantially true. We agree with the district court's finding. In the 1995 criminal prosecution of plaintiff, the federal grand jury indictment charged plaintiff with "Conspiracy to Possess Unregistered Firearms." The indictment alleged that "the co-conspirators would manufacture destructive devices on Nichols' farm in Decker, Michigan." The "overt acts" section asserted: "In approximately 1992, James Nichols, Terry Nichols and Timothy McVeigh experimented in the manufacture and detonation of destructive devices made up of readily available materials such as brake fluid and diesel fluid."

Based on the allegations of the indictment against James Nichols, we find that Moore's statement is substantially true.

4. *But the feds didn't have the goods on James, so the charges were dropped.*

We agree with the district court's finding that this statement is "literally and substantially true." It is undisputed that the charges against James Nichols *were* dropped due to a lack of evidence against him.

Lastly, we consider whether the district court correctly rejected plaintiff's defamation by implication claim. By this claim, Nichols argues that even if Moore's statements were literally true when read in isolation, when viewed in their entirety and in proper context, they defamed plaintiff by implying that he was involved in the Oklahoma City bombing. Under Michigan law, claims of defamation by implication, which by nature present ambiguous evidence with respect to falsity, face a severe constitutional hurdle. [As Michigan] Chief Justice Cavanaugh [has written], "a defamation defendant cannot be held liable for the reader's possible inferences, speculations, or conclusions, where the defendant has not made or directly implied any provably false factual assertion, and has not, by selective omission of crucial relevant facts, misleadingly conveyed any false factual implication."

In the present case, each sentence of Moore's narration regarding James Nichols in *Bowling for Columbine* is substantially true. Though it is possible that a viewer of the movie could erroneously conclude that James Nichols made practice bombs in preparation for Oklahoma City, and was arrested and charged in the Oklahoma City bombing, the court finds that plaintiff's evidence cannot meet the high hurdle presented by a defamation by implication claim. Plaintiff has not presented any evidence indicating that Michael Moore intended to falsely implicate James Nichols in the Oklahoma City bombing. Plaintiff's claim for defamation by implication must fail.

POINTS FOR DISCUSSION

1. Moore clearly characterized Nichols's pre-Oklahoma City bomb making as "practice." Practice for what? Is not the most natural interpretation of Moore's narration that Nichols was practicing for the deadly bombing of the federal building?
2. In a similar vein, do you think the court was straining a bit in its interpretation of the assertion that Nichols had been arrested "in connection to" the bombing? Was not again the most natural interpretation that Nichols might have been as culpable as his brother and McVeigh?

Amrak Productions v. Morton

410 F.3d 69 (1st Cir. 2005)

Judge Torruella:

James Albright, a former bodyguard and lover of Madonna, and his corporate agent, Amrak Productions, Inc. appeal from the dismissal of their defamation claim stemming from the publication of a tell-all book, *Madonna*. In a nutshell, defendants-appellees author and publishers allegedly portrayed Albright as a homosexual by miscaptioning a picture of a homosexual individual with

Albright's name in a book and magazines.[2] The district court dismissed appellants' claims, finding that for the "photograph to make any kind of statement regarding Albright's sexuality requires the Court to pile inference upon innuendo, innuendo upon stereotype." The court also applied recent Federal and State Supreme Court decisions on homosexuality to hold that a statement identifying an individual as homosexual is not defamatory per se under Massachusetts law. Appellants argue otherwise, stating that continued societal and governmental acceptance of various forms of discrimination against homosexuals should lead to a presumption of injury. We affirm the dismissals, albeit on more limited grounds than the district court's holding.

Amrak employed Albright—who has been involved in the personal and professional security business for over ten years—as a professional bodyguard. From January to July 1992, Albright served as Madonna's bodyguard, during which time he became romantically involved with the artist and remained so until 1994. In December 2000, Albright entered into a contract with O'Mara Books to sell information about Madonna for an upcoming biography. The book, entitled *Madonna*, was written by author Andrew Morton and published by O'Mara Books in the United Kingdom and by St. Martin's Press in the United States in 2001. Chapter 11 of the book details Albright's relationship with Madonna.

The book also contains forty-eight pages of photographs, including one in which Madonna is accompanied by two men. The man to the left is wearing black pants, a black and white shirt, a black leather jacket, tinted sunglasses, a string necklace, and an earring. The caption states:

> Madonna attends ex-lover Prince's concert with her secret lover and one-time bodyguard Jimmy Albright (left). Albright, who bears an uncanny resemblance to Carlos Leon, the father of Madonna's daughter, enjoyed a stormy three-year relationship with the star. They planned to marry, and had even chosen names for their children.

This photograph allegedly defamed Albright because the man pictured was, in fact, Jose Guitierez, an "outspoken homosexual" who "often dressed as a woman," and engaged in what appellants describe as "homosexual, sexually graphic, lewd, lascivious, offensive, and possibly illegal" conduct. Guitierez was employed as one of Madonna's dancers.

---

2. The photo can be seen at www.paulsiegelcommlaw.com, if you click on the left side (*Communication Law in America*) on "Images from Book," then "Chapter 3," then "Madonna."

On November 12, 2001, *People* magazine, a publication of Time Inc., published the same photograph along with the erroneous caption. *News of the World*, a publication of News Group Newspapers, Ltd., published the same on March 17, 2002.

Appellants subsequently brought suit in the District of Massachusetts. On May 28, 2004, the district court granted appellees' motion to dismiss on all counts. First, the court held that no reasonable view of the photograph and text would suggest that Albright is homosexual, and thus the publication cannot be construed as defamatory. Alternatively, the court held that imputing homosexuality cannot be considered defamatory per se in Massachusetts. Given appellants' failure to state a defamation claim, the court dismissed the derivative claims of commercial use, false light invasion of privacy, emotional distress, negligence, and unfair trade practices. This appeal follows.

Appellants first argue that they have met the pleading requirements necessary to survive a motion to dismiss a defamation claim. We disagree. To prevail in a defamation claim, plaintiffs must establish that defendants were at fault for the publication of a false statement regarding the plaintiff, capable of damaging the plaintiff's reputation in the community, which either caused economic loss or is actionable without proof of economic loss. A court may dismiss written defamation claims, i.e., libel claims, if the communication is incapable of a defamatory meaning. This threshold question, whether a communication is reasonably susceptible of a defamatory meaning, is a question of law for the court.

A communication is susceptible to defamatory meaning if it would tend to hold the plaintiff up to scorn, hatred, ridicule or contempt in the minds of any considerable and respectable segment in the community. The communication must be interpreted reasonably, leading a "reasonable reader" to conclude that it conveyed a defamatory meaning. Context matters in assessing such claims: Courts must consider all the words used, not merely a particular phrase or sentence.

The miscaptioned photograph in the instant case is not reasonably susceptible of a defamatory meaning. Nothing in Guitierez's appearance, particularly given the accompanying caption stressing Albright's heterosexuality (e.g., Madonna's "secret lover"), gives any indication that Albright is homosexual. To draw such an inference, the reader—who would have to view homosexuals with "scorn, hatred, ridicule or contempt," must follow Madonna and her cohort closely enough to recognize Guitierez as a gay man, but not closely enough to know Guitierez's name or what Albright looks like. Few, if any, readers would fall into this "considerable and respectable segment in the community."

The context of the text accompanying the photograph further deflates any argument that the photo conveys a defamatory meaning. When we consider all the words used in the accompanying text—including phrases such as Albright's "long-time girlfriend," his "hot and heavy" affair with Madonna, their sexual encounters, and Albright's "fling" with a "girl at a club"—we find that no reasonable reader could conclude that Albright is homosexual. This conclusion is supported by the caption, which states that Albright was Madonna's "secret lover," that they "enjoyed a stormy three-year relationship," and that they planned to marry and "had even chosen names for their children."

Given appellants' failure to satisfy the threshold question of defamatory meaning, we affirm the court's dismissal of the defamation claim. Moreover, given the court's correct finding that the photograph and its caption make no imputation of homosexuality, we need not decide whether such an imputation constitutes defamation per se in Massachusetts.

The district court's judgments are affirmed.

POINTS FOR DISCUSSION

1. The court seems to assume that references to a person's heterosexual conduct (such as to a man's having been Madonna's secret lover, etc.) negate the possibility of that same person also engaging in homosexual behavior. Does bisexuality's being far more prevalent than a 100 percent homosexual orientation have any implications for the court's logic?
2. Unlike the district court, this appellate decision carefully sidesteps the question of whether it can ever be libelous to accuse someone of being gay. After all, the United States Supreme Court has said that sodomy laws are unconstitutional, and it is relevant, too, that the *Amrak* case was based on Massachusetts defamation law, and Massachusetts was, as of 2007, the only state in the union to recognize same-sex marriage (joined as of 2011 by Connecticut, Iowa, New Hampshire, and Vermont, as well as Washington, D.C.). Do you think, as a legal or logical matter or both, that being thought gay can diminish one's reputation in the eyes of large numbers of reasonable people?

■ *Stanton v. Metro Corporation*
438 F.3d 119 (1st Cir. 2006)
Judge DiClerico:

Stacy Stanton has appealed the dismissal of her state-law defamation action against Metro Corp., which arises out of the publication of her photograph alongside an article entitled "The Mating Habits of the Suburban High School Teenager." Metro Corporation publishes *Boston* magazine, a monthly general interest publication that ran the article in question in its May 2003 issue. The cover of the magazine refers to the article with the phrase, "Fast Times at Silver Lake High: Teen Sex in the Suburbs." Inside, Stanton is one of five young people pictured in a photograph that occupies the entire first page of the article and half of the facing page. Stanton's image occupies most of the left-hand side of the photograph, where she appears standing, with her face and most of her body fully visible.[3]

The other half of the facing page consists of a column of text of varying sizes, including the aforementioned headline, which appears in the largest font and takes up most of the column. A "superhead," appearing above the headline in a smaller font, reads: "They hook up online. They hook up in real life. With prom season looming, meet your kids—they might know more about sex than you do." Just above the byline, and just below the main article text, the following [disclaimer] appears in italicized type: "The photos on these pages are from an award-winning five-year project on teen sexuality taken by photojournalist Dan Habib. The individuals pictured are unrelated to the people or events described in this story. The names of the teenagers interviewed for this story have been changed." These words are rendered in the smallest font on the page.

The thrust of the story is that teenagers in the greater Boston area have become more sexually promiscuous over the span of the last decade. The article draws support for this thesis from both statistical and anecdotal evidence, including interviews with a number of local high school students. The story also declares that high school has replaced college as the time for sexual experimentation, describes a profound ignorance among teens about sexually transmitted diseases, and notes a related trend of increased sexual aggression among high school boys.

Stanton, who lives in Manchester, New Hampshire, responded to the appearance of her photograph with the article by filing suit against Metro, alleging that the publication was defamatory in that the juxtaposition of her photograph and the text describing suburban teenage promiscuity insinuated that she was engaged in the activity described in the article.

To succeed on a defamation claim under Massachusetts law, a plaintiff must show that the defendant was at fault for the publication of a false statement of

---

3. The most salient visual features from the article are on my website. Go to www.paulsiegelcommlaw.com, then, on the left side (*Communication Law in America*), click on "Images from the Book," then on "Chapter 3," and then on "Boston Magazine."

and concerning the plaintiff which was capable of damaging his or her reputation in the community and which either caused economic loss or is actionable without proof of economic loss.

The district court [granted the defendant's motion to dismiss], ruling that "the defamatory statements at issue are not 'of and concerning' [Stanton], and are not reasonably capable of a defamatory meaning." In reaching these conclusions, the district court relied heavily on the disclaimer appearing at the bottom of the first column of the article, i.e., "the individuals pictured are unrelated to the people or events described in this story."

We are not called upon to determine the ultimate issue of whether the article is defamatory, but to answer the threshold question of whether the communication is reasonably susceptible of a defamatory meaning. If the answer to this question is yes, then the ultimate issue of whether the article is defamatory is not the court's to decide. Where the communication is susceptible of both a defamatory and nondefamatory meaning, a question of fact exists for the jury.

The district court reasoned that, since the disclaimer *directly* contradicts the otherwise-defamatory connection between the photograph and the text, the article could be susceptible to a defamatory meaning only if a reasonable reader would overlook the disclaimer, misunderstand it, or fail to give it credence. According to the district court, no reasonable reader could do so because the disclaimer appears on the first page of the article and "certainly, the *reasonable* (or average) reader can be expected to read at least the first page of a six-page article." It was here that the district court erred.

We cannot assume, as the district court did, that placing a disclaimer on the first page of an article itself ensures that a reasonable reader will see it. Here, the disclaimer occupies the field between the body of the story and the byline, making it easy enough to overlook between the larger fonts of both. The disclaimer is also separated from the column of text by a horizontal line, accompanied by an arrow directing the reader to turn to the next page, where the story continues. We cannot say that no reasonable reader would follow this visual signal and simply flip to the next page after reading the entirety of the text on the first page, but before reaching the disclaimer.

Nor can we say that any reasonable reader who notices the disclaimer would necessarily read the crucial second sentence, i.e., "the individuals pictured are unrelated to the people or events described in this story." It is at least conceivable that a reader might take the first sentence of the disclaimer, which states that "the photos on these pages are from an award-winning five-year project on teen sexuality by photojournalist Dan Habib," as a satisfactory explanation of the photographs and therefore stop reading the disclaimer before the second sentence. Such a reader would thus remain under the impression that the teenagers depicted in the photograph have some connection to the accompanying story.

The district court appears to have reasoned that the percentage of casual readers who would disregard the disclaimer was not sizeable enough to represent what it called "the *reasonable* (or average) reader." But words may be actionable even if they do not tend to damage a plaintiff's reputation or hold him up to ridicule in the community at large or among all reasonable people; it is enough to do so among a considerable and respectable class of people.

Accordingly, in assessing whether a publication is susceptible to a defamatory meaning, it is not dispositive that a numerical majority of its audience would arrive at a non-defamatory interpretation. Metro rejoins that, given the "express disclaimer," any reading of the article as defamatory toward Stanton is necessarily incorrect, so "it does not matter whether a considerable number of people might unreasonably misunderstand the publication in such a way." But determining whether an allegedly defamatory statement can reasonably bear that construction as a matter of law should not be confused with a search for its meaning in the objective sense.

In deciding whether a statement is susceptible to a defamatory interpretation, the court must gauge the reasonableness of the interpretation based on what a considerable and respectable segment of the community would make of the statement.

Here, we cannot say as a matter of law that too few readers would overlook the disclaimer to constitute a considerable and respectable segment of the community. The article is thus reasonably susceptible to a defamatory meaning.

In reaching this conclusion, we do not mean to suggest that language in the nature of a disclaimer can never serve to render a statement incapable of conveying a defamatory meaning. We simply recognize that, given the placement of the disclaimer in the article and the nature of the publication in general, a reasonable reader could fail to notice it.

We also recognize that, as Metro argues, the article draws no literal connection between the subjects of the photograph and the subjects of its story. Under Massachusetts law, however, a statement need not explicitly refer to the plaintiff to constitute defamation. A plaintiff may establish that the defendant's words were of and concerning the plaintiff by proving at least that the defendant was negligent in publishing words which reasonably could be interpreted to refer to the plaintiff.

Defamation can arise from the publication of the plaintiff's photograph in conjunction with a defamatory statement, even in the absence of any express textual connection between the statement and the photograph.

Like the question of whether a communication can reasonably be understood to be defamatory, whether a communication can reasonably be understood to be of and concerning the plaintiff depends on the circumstances. The presence of the disclaimer does not permit the conclusion, as a matter of law, that the article is not of and concerning Stanton.

As we have explained, a reasonable reader could ignore the disclaimer, leaving the article with the impression—incorrect, but not unreasonable—that Stanton is the subject of the unflattering statements set forth in its text. [Such a reader might wonder], "Why was *this* photograph used to illustrate *this* article about sexual misconduct, if there is no connection between the two?" Once again, we do not intimate that this interpretation is the only reasonable reading of the article. We say only that at this very preliminary stage, it does not appear beyond doubt that Stanton will be unable to prove a set of facts that would support a finding that Metro's statements were of and concerning her.

In a similar vein, Metro argues that the article makes no "articulably false statement" about Stanton and thus cannot support a defamation claim. [Admittedly], certain statements about a plaintiff, though pejorative, are too vague to be cognizable as the subject of a defamation action. [But] statements that are too vague to constitute defamation generally fall into the category of epithets, such as "communist," "barbarian," "lunkhead," "meathead," and "nut." Here, in contrast, Stanton has alleged that Metro defamed her by making a statement susceptible to the interpretation that she engages in sexually promiscuous behavior. That statement is clear enough to support a defamation claim.

Finally, Metro argues that Stanton's amended complaint should have been dismissed because she failed to "allege any facts that, if true, would demonstrate that Metro acted with negligent disregard for the truth by juxtaposing the photograph and the article." We disagree.

If the recipient reasonably understood the communication to be made concerning the plaintiff, it may be inferred that the defamer was negligent in failing to realize that the communication would be so understood, provided the plaintiff can prove that a reasonable understanding on the part of the recipient that the communication referred to the plaintiff was one that the defamer was negligent in failing to anticipate.

Stanton's allegations sufficiently state a defamation claim based on the theory that Metro negligently used [her] photograph to illustrate a story describing teenagers as sexually promiscuous without realizing that the publication might therefore be reasonably understood to mean that she was sexually promiscuous.

A [libel] complaint should not be dismissed unless it is apparent beyond doubt that the plaintiff can prove no set of facts in support of his claim that would entitle him to relief.

Based on our review of the amended complaint and the article in question, we conclude that this standard has not been met. We reverse the order of the district court insofar as it dismissed Stanton's defamation claim arising out of the juxtaposition of her photograph and the text of the article.

POINTS FOR DISCUSSION

1. Here we have a case in which the plaintiff was not named in the article, and the printed disclaimer makes clear to anyone who bothers to read it that the photos in the article are not related to the debauchery described in the text. What more should the magazine have done? How important was the fact that the disclaimer was printed in the smallest font anywhere in the article?
2. Does the appellate court's assessment of what a "reasonable" reader may or may not do make sense to you? Do you believe that readers who do take note of the disclaimer's first sentence are unlikely to also read its second sentence?

■ *Kaelin v. Globe Communications Corporation*
162 F.3d 1036 (9th Cir. 1998)

Judge Silverman:

Brian "Kato" Kaelin became known to the public during the course of the criminal trial of O.J. Simpson as the houseguest at Simpson's estate. Kaelin testified to various events surrounding the killings of Nicole Brown Simpson and Ronald Goldman. Simpson was acquitted of the double murders on October 3, 1995. One week later, the *National Examiner*, a weekly newspaper published by Globe Communications Corporation, featured the following headline on its cover:[4]

---

4. The cover, including headline and photo, is on my website. Go to www.paulsiegel commlaw.com, then, on the left side (*Communication Law in America*), click on "Images from Book," then "Chapter 3," and finally on "Kato Kaelin."

COPS THINK KATO DID IT!
He fears they want him for perjury, say pals

Inside the paper, on page 17, in large, boldface, capital letters, [an almost identical] headline appeared. The first four paragraphs of the article read as follows:

> Kato Kaelin is still a suspect in the murder of Nicole Brown Simpson and Ron Goldman, friends fear.
>
> They are worried that LAPD cops are desperately looking for a way to put Kato behind bars for perjury.
>
> "We're sure the cops have been trying to prove that Kato didn't tell them everything he knows, that somehow he spoiled their case against O.J.," says one pal. "It's not true, but we think they're out to get even with Kato.
>
> "I'm worried that Kato will get a persecution complex. He'll end up looking around every corner and thinking he sees a cop."

The remainder of the article contained other comments supposedly made by Kaelin's friends regarding the Simpson case. It also contained several references to a book about Kaelin by author Marc Eliot.

In a letter dated October 12, 1995, Kaelin demanded a retraction. Globe refused. Kaelin then filed this libel action against Globe in the Superior Court of California, and Globe removed it to federal court on the basis of diversity of citizenship.

During discovery, John Garton, the news editor of the *National Examiner* and Globe's designated representative, testified at deposition as follows:

> Q. Okay. Did you have any concerns when you saw this headline of September 22nd [the deadline for the article] about the way this headline was framed?
> A. I wasn't mad about it.
> Q. What do you mean by that?
> A. Journalistically I didn't think it was the best headline in the world.
> Q. Were you concerned that it implied that Kato had committed the murders or played some role in them?
> A. No, I just didn't think it was very accurate to the story. It could have been better.
>
> ■ ■ ■
>
> Q. Other than what is actually written in Exhibit 2 [prior published articles], any of the things that are in those articles, did the National Examiner have

in its possession on September 22nd, 1995 any information that a police officer anywhere thought that Kato Kaelin was involved in Nicole Brown Simpson's and Ronald Goldman's murders?
A. No.
Q. What did you think, on September 22nd, 1995 about what the words "Cops Think He Did It" meant? What is the "it" to which this statement—
A. Perjury.
Q. Perjury?
A. Mm-hmm.
Q. Did you have any concern that a reader might connect the "Cops Think He Did It" with the other information in the article that refers to allegations that Mr. Kaelin was involved in the murders themselves?
A. I was a bit concerned about it, yes, but in fact I thought the second part of the headline coped with that. . . .

Globe filed a motion for summary judgment. Focusing its analysis on the text of the article rather than on the headline, which was the heart of Kaelin's claim, the district court ruled that Kaelin ". . . has not submitted any evidence which tends to show that Defendants actually doubted the truth of the story . . ." With respect to the headline, the district court stated, "While Globe employees might not have acted with the professionalism that would be expected at a more reputable journalistic institution before running the article about Plaintiff, the failure to act reasonably is not enough to establish malice." [The District Court granted defendant's motion for summary judgment.]

We must decide, viewing the evidence in the light most favorable to the nonmoving party, whether there are any genuine issues of material fact and whether the district court correctly applied the relevant substantive law.

We must draw all justifiable inferences in favor of Kaelin, including questions of credibility and of the weight to be accorded particular evidence. The plaintiff, to survive the defendant's motion, need only present evidence from which a jury might return a verdict in his favor. If he does so, there is a genuine issue of fact that requires a trial.

Although Kaelin complains about the first sentence of the article on page 17, we assume for the purposes of this appeal that the text of the story is not defamatory. This case is about the headlines, especially the one appearing on the cover. The first issue is whether the headlines alone are susceptible of a false and defamatory meaning and, if so, whether they can be the basis of a libel action even though the accompanying story is not defamatory.

As already seen, the front page headline consists of two sentences. The first—"COPS THINK KATO DID IT!"—states what the cops supposedly think. The second—"He fears they want him for perjury, say pals"—is what

Kato's pals supposedly said. These two sentences express two different thoughts and are not mutually exclusive. California courts in libel cases have emphasized that the publication is to be measured, not so much by its effect when subjected to the critical analysis of a mind trained in the law, but by the natural and probable effect upon the mind of the average reader. Since the publication occurred just one week after O.J. Simpson's highly publicized acquittal for murder, we believe that a reasonable person, at that time, might well have concluded that the "it" in the first sentence of the cover and internal headlines referred to the murders. Such a reading of the first sentence is not negated by or inconsistent with the second sentence as a matter of logic, grammar, or otherwise. In our view, an ordinary reader reasonably could have read the headline to mean that the cops think that Kato committed the murders and that Kato fears that he is wanted for perjury.

Globe argues that the "it" refers to perjury. Even assuming that such a reading is reasonably possible, it is not the only reading that is reasonably possible as a matter of law. So long as the publication is reasonably susceptible of a defamatory meaning, a factual question for the jury exists.

Globe argues that even if the front page headline could be found to be false and defamatory, the totality of the publication is not. Globe's position is that because the text of the accompanying story is not defamatory, the headline by itself cannot be the basis of a libel action under California law.

It is true that a defamatory meaning must be found, if at all, in a reading of the publication as a whole. This is a rule of reason. Defamation actions cannot be based on snippets taken out of context. By the same token, not every word of an allegedly defamatory publication has to be false and defamatory to sustain a libel action. The test of libel is not quantitative; a single sentence may be the basis for an action in libel even though buried in a much longer text.

Although California courts have not had occasion to opine on whether a headline alone can be the basis of a libel action, it is certainly clear under California law that headlines are not irrelevant, extraneous, or liability-free zones. They are essential elements of a publication. In *Selleck v. Globe International* (1985), for example, Globe published headlines, a caption to a photograph, and the text of an article, all of which created the false impression that the father of actor Tom Selleck had granted an interview to Globe. While not addressing whether any one element of the publication alone would support a libel claim, the court explained that "headlines and captions of an allegedly libelous article are regarded as a part of the article." The court concluded that "the article, including the headline and caption and taking into account the circumstances of its publication, is reasonably susceptible of a defamatory meaning on its face and therefore is libelous per se." In *Davis v. Hearst* (1911), the Supreme Court of California concerned itself with three headlines that read as follows:

MAYOR INVESTIGATES THE BOARD OF EDUCATION'S ACTS
EXPOSURES MADE BY 'EXAMINER' FOUND TO BE TRUE
PASADENA COUNCIL WILL ACT

Although the article explained that the mayor's investigation covered only one matter, the court found that the text did not negate the effect of the headlines, which implied that the mayor had discovered more than one impropriety. It stated that "the mere fact that in the body of the article the mayor's investigations are limited to a single charge is not controlling. The captions and headlines are themselves a part of the libel."

Globe argues that the entirety of the publication, including the story itself, clears up any false and defamatory meaning that could be found on the cover. Whether it does or not is a question of fact for the jury. The Kaelin story was located 17 pages away from the cover. In this respect, the *National Examiner*'s front page headline is unlike a conventional headline that immediately precedes a newspaper story, and nowhere does the cover headline reference the internal page where readers could locate the article. A reasonable juror could conclude that the Kaelin article was too far removed from the cover headline to have the salutary effect that Globe claims. In analyzing the totality of the circumstances of an allegedly defamatory publication, the effect of a front page headline is neither insignificant nor unprecedented. In any event, it is a fact question for a jury.

Viewing the facts in the light most favorable to Kaelin as we are required to do, we hold that Kaelin has come forward with clear and convincing evidence to get to a jury on the issue of whether the headlines are susceptible of a false and defamatory meaning.

Globe editor John Garton testified at his deposition that he saw the headline before it ran and did not think that it "was very accurate to the story." He stated that he was "a bit concerned" that readers might connect the "it" in the headline with the murders. This is direct evidence from which a reasonable juror could find that Globe knew that the headline was factually inaccurate or that Globe acted with reckless disregard for the truth. It is for a jury to decide whether, as Globe argues, it intended to clarify the sentence "COPS THINK KATO DID IT!" with the sentence that followed, ". . . he fears they want him for perjury, say pals." The editors' statements of their subjective intention are matters of credibility for a jury.

It is [also] undisputed that Globe ran the headline "COPS THINK KATO DID IT!" knowing that it had no reason to believe that Kaelin was a murder suspect. This is not a case where Globe relied in good faith on information that turned out to be false. It is undisputed that Globe never believed Kaelin to be a suspect in the murders.

Garton testified at his deposition that "the front page of the tabloid paper is what we sell the paper on, not what's inside it." That testimony permits a reasonable juror to draw the inference that Globe had a pecuniary motive for running a headline that, in Garton's words, was not "very accurate to the story."

Because the issue at this stage of the case is only whether Kaelin has come forward with evidence adequate to survive summary judgment, we analyze the facts and draw the inferences in the light most favorable to him. We hold today that a reasonable juror could find, by clear and convincing evidence, that the headlines are defamatory, and that Globe's editors acted with actual malice[5] in their decision to run a headline from which a reasonable juror could conclude that Kaelin was a murder suspect. Globe's motion for summary judgment should have been denied.

POINTS FOR DISCUSSION

1. John Garton, one of the *National Examiner*'s editors, admitted at trial that the headline at issue here was not "the best in the world," and that it may not have been 100 percent accurate. Does the way in which his words were used against the newspaper suggest that editors should be very careful about ever expressing doubts about their work product?
2. The court here makes much of the fact that the non-defamatory explanation of the headline does not show up until page 17 of the newspaper. What if the explanation appeared on the front page, but the plaintiff produced experts to show that most of these tabloids' "readers" never see much of anything beyond the headlines, because they are only glancing at the papers while standing in line at the supermarket? Could such tabloids thus be less protected from libel suits than more "serious" newspapers, not because of the papers' contents, but because of the different ways that readers consume that content?

---

5. See the excerpts from *New York Times v. Sullivan*, beginning on page 72, for an explanation of "actual malice."

▪ *Diaz v. NBC Universal, Inc.*
536 F. Supp. 2d 337 (S.D.N.Y. 2008)[6]
Judge McMahon:

The feature film *American Gangster* (the "Film"), which was produced by Universal Pictures (a division of Universal City Studios, LLP) is "based on" a true story involving a notorious heroin dealer, Frank Lucas. Lucas was a key figure in the New York City drug trade in the late 1960s and early 1970s. Eventually, Lucas joined "Team America" and cooperated in the prosecution of some high level drug dealers in New York City.

Plaintiffs Louis Diaz, Gregory Korniloff and Jack Toal have sued on behalf of themselves and as representatives of a class of "approximately 400 present and former Special Agents of the New York office of the United States Drug Enforcement Administration" (the "USDEA" or "DEA") who were employed at some time during the period from 1973 through 1985. The Complaint alleges that the three named plaintiffs and every New York City–based DEA agent during that 12-year period were defamed by an allegedly false legend that appears on screen at the end of the film. The legend says that Frank Lucas' "collaboration [with law enforcement] led to the conviction of three quarters of New York City's Drug Enforcement Agency." The statement about Lucas' cooperation leading to these convictions is not true. Nonetheless, the Complaint must be dismissed.

The Film depicts the life of Frank Lucas (played by Denzel Washington), an African American drug kingpin in New York City who was arrested in 1975 and subsequently convicted of drug trafficking. The film also includes a character identified as Richie Roberts (played by Russell Crowe), a law enforcement official in Essex County, New Jersey. As is common with motion pictures inspired by true events, the Film ends with a standard disclaimer noting that a number of the incidents are "fictionalized," and that "some of the characters have been composited or invented. . . ."

Throughout the film, there are references to corruption among some members of the local police forces in New York City and New Jersey. Several characters depict corrupt narcotics detectives employed by the New York City Police Department (NYPD)—including Josh Brolin, who plays a character identified as Detective Trupo of the NYPD's Special Investigations Narcotics Unit. At no point in the Film is any character identified as a DEA agent; neither is there any suggestion that any federal agent is corrupt.

---

6. The decision was later affirmed in a very terse opinion at 337 Fed. Appx. 94 (2nd Cir. 2009).

At one point in the film, law enforcement personnel search Lucas' home. During this scene, Lucas' wife is assaulted, his dog is shot in a vicious manner, and hundreds of thousands of dollars are stolen by corrupt law enforcement officials. The film does not identify the people who do these despicable things as DEA agents. The officer who steals the money, however, says that the Feds are going to arrive later and "take everything . . . ."[7]

After the Lucas character has been arrested by Roberts and his team, the film ends with a series of vignettes that purport to show how everything worked out: Lucas meets with Roberts; photographs of the actors who portray corrupt New York City narcotics officers are tacked to a bulletin board; and those same New York City police officers are arrested (or, in the case of the Brolin character, commit suicide). Voiceovers accompanying these scenes include "news" reports describing the arrests and prosecution of local police officers by federal authorities. There follow shots with text at the bottom. One of those texts (the "legend") refers to Lucas' cooperation with authorities, and notes that Lucas' cooperation led to "the convictions of three quarters of New York City's Drug Enforcement Agency."

[In reality], Lucas cooperated with the United States Attorney's Office and the DEA and assisted in the apprehension and convictions of numerous other narcotics traffickers. Lucas' cooperation, however, did not lead to the conviction of a single agent of the New York City office of the USDEA or any member of the NYPD, or any other law enforcement official in New York or elsewhere. There was and is no federal, state or local agency called the "New York City Drug Enforcement Agency." The federal agency is and always has been the Drug Enforcement *Administration*. NYPD has at various times had special units devoted to narcotics (e.g., the Special Investigations Narcotics Unit), none of which was called the Drug Enforcement Agency.

A former Special Agent from the New York City office of the USDEA is currently stationed in Iraq and is a member of the putative plaintiff class. Approximately 20 soldiers stationed in Iraq who saw *American Gangster* questioned him about the legend. The soldiers all thought the legend referred to Special Agents of DEA, and they asked the former DEA agent how three quarters of the USDEA agents based in New York City could be convicted criminals. Although [he] told these soldiers that no such thing happened, he felt "deeply hurt and embarrassed by the questions, even though he knew the legend was false."

Some members of the putative plaintiff class are currently employed as pri-

---

7. You can see the relevant scene at www.paulsiegelcommlaw.com, by clicking on "Video Clips," then "Chapter 3," and then on "American Gangster."

vate investigators, and many members are currently employed in law enforcement agencies (including the USDEA) and security companies. Plaintiffs contend that the erroneous legend harms their reputation and damages them in their trade and profession.

On November 23, 2007, counsel for plaintiff Gregory Korniloff wrote to Universal Studios, owned by defendant, demanding that the allegedly false legend be removed from further distribution of *American Gangster*. On December 7, 2007, David L. Burg, Senior Vice President of NBC Universal, wrote to Mr. Korniloff's counsel, rejecting this demand.

Although the Complaint contains a lengthy description of the many items in the Film with which plaintiffs are dissatisfied, the Complaint identifies only one allegedly defamatory statement: the legend that appears for a few seconds at the end of the Film, stating that Lucas' cooperation with authorities after his arrest "led to the conviction of three quarters of New York City's Drug Enforcement Agency." Plaintiffs' libel claim is barred under constitutional and common law principles, because plaintiffs cannot demonstrate that the allegedly defamatory statement is "of and concerning" any particular person.

Under the group libel doctrine, when a reference is made to a large group of people, no individual within that group can fairly say that the statement is about him, nor can the "group" as a whole state a claim for defamation. The New York Courts have not set a particular group number above which defamation of a group member is not possible. However, [there is an] absence of any cases where individual members of groups larger than sixty have been permitted to go forward with a libel claim [in this jurisdiction]. [Here,] the putative class contains approximately four hundred former and current special agents of the USDEA. Plaintiffs concede that neither the legend, nor the movie more generally, ever specifically identifies any of the named plaintiffs, or any other putative class member, by name. Thus, under New York law, they would appear to be out of court. The same results pertain if the governing law is the law of California (where Universal produced the film) or Nevada or Florida (where two named plaintiffs reside), since the law in all four states is identical.

Nonetheless, plaintiffs allege that each of them can be identified by an average viewer because the film depicts as corrupt virtually the entire New York City narcotics law enforcement community. Therefore, plaintiffs argue that the legend need not reference the plaintiffs by name.

At a minimum, plaintiffs argue that the claims of the nine DEA agents who took part in the search of Lucas' home should be permitted to go forward, because (1) that subset of the entire group is small enough to fall within the exception to the group libel doctrine, and (2) the searching officers in the Film engage in particularly despicable conduct that never happened. To support their position, plaintiffs argue that the article on which the Film is based, "Return of the Superfly," by Mark Jacobson, contains a contention by Lucas that Agent Korniloff and his DEA colleagues took nine or ten million dollars from him during this search. During the search scene in the film, a character portraying a corrupt NYPD officer tells Lucas' wife that the "Feds are going to come in and take everything, take it all, but not before I get my gratuity." (He then steals money.) Plaintiffs contend that these statements allegedly defame "the Feds" (i.e., the DEA), and so need not reference these plaintiffs by name, since an average viewer who was aware that DEA searched the house would view these DEA agents as having stolen nine or ten million dollars ("take[n] it all"). The same viewer would then assume that DEA agents were later convicted for these crimes.

The first thing to note is that the Complaint does not mention the Jacobson article, so it is of no moment what it does or does not say. Moreover, it would be improper to "bootstrap" an erroneous statement in the Jacobson article onto the movie (which does not track the article), and then to find that the movie (not the article) libels Korniloff and his companions. In the film, the nine DEA agents who participated in the search are not identifiable. The film never names the DEA agents who searched Lucas' home. Nor does the film mention that DEA agents (or anyone else) stole "nine or ten million dollars" from Lucas' home. The movie does not show a single person who is identifiable as a DEA agent. The person who steals the money is an NYPD officer. (In fact, the line quoted by plaintiffs could just as easily mean that the "Feds" would seize "all" of Lucas' money *legally,* and that the corrupt NYPD officer wanted to get his "gratuity" before the "Feds" got there.) A viewer must go beyond the movie (i.e., have read the Jacobson article) to know that Lucas alleged the theft of a much greater sum by the DEA agents ("Feds") who searched his house. Korniloff may have been libeled by Lucas' statement in the "Superfly" article (as to which the statute of limitations has long run). However, he and the eight other DEA agents were not libeled by the legend that appears onscreen at the end of *American Gangster.*

The cause of action for libel is dismissed as barred by the group libel doctrine. I need not reach defendant's alternative argument that no reasonable person could interpret the legend as referring to federal DEA agents, rather than New York City police officers.

It would behoove a major corporation like Universal (which is owned by a major news organization, NBC) not to put inaccurate statements at the end of popular films. However, nothing in this particular untrue statement is actionable. The Complaint is dismissed.

POINTS FOR DISCUSSION

1. After viewing the scene from *American Gangster* on my website, consider whether you think the court's suggestion that the line about the Feds' impending visit could reasonably be interpreted to mean that they would only engage in quite legal behavior when they show up.
2. How important to the decision do you think it is that there is no "Drug Enforcement *Agency*."

4

Libel: Constitutional Considerations

For most of this country's history, the existence of libel law was not seen as at all inconsistent with the First Amendment's promise that "no law" should abridge freedom of the press. A dramatic change came in 1964, in *New York Times v. Sullivan*, when the U.S. Supreme Court concluded that to permit public officials to sue citizens who criticize their performance in office is hauntingly reminiscent of sedition laws that criminalized antigovernment speech. The Supreme Court's *New York Times* ruling, which begins this chapter, did not prohibit public officials from bringing suit for libel, but it did make such suits far more difficult to prove.

Ten years later, in *Gertz v. Welch*, the Supreme Court fine-tunes its evolving libel doctrine, and creates important new law. No longer would libel plaintiffs be able to prevail without proving that they were harmed in some way by a defendant's utterance; moreover, any plaintiff seeking punitive damages—those designed to punish the press more than to compensate for reputational harm—would have to overcome the same obstacles constitutionally mandated for public officials.

In the traditional common law of libel, plaintiffs did not have to prove that the defamations hurled against them were false. They were presumed false, in that citizens' reputations were presumed unsullied until proven otherwise. In *Philadelphia Newspapers, Inc. v. Hepps*, the Court considers whether this tradition rule can survive the application of First Amendment principles to libel law.

Next, *Peterson v. Grisham* is a ringing endorsement of the public policy reasoning behind making it very difficult for public officials to win libel suits. I admit I chose the case in part because of the celebrity of defendant John Grisham.

Finally, *Brock v. Viacom*, where the defendants are distributors of the popular cable series *Bullshit!* hosted by Penn and Teller, makes clear that expressions of even the most pointed opinions are constitutionally protected. (The relevant scene is on my website.)

■ *New York Times v. Sullivan*

376 U.S. 254 (1964)

Justice Brennan:

We are required in this case to determine for the first time the extent to which the constitutional protections for speech and press limit a State's power to award damages in a libel action brought by a public official against critics of his official conduct. L. B. Sullivan is one of the three elected Commissioners of the City of Montgomery, Alabama. He brought this civil libel action against the four individual petitioners, who are Negroes and Alabama clergymen, and against petitioner the New York Times Company. A jury in the Circuit Court of Montgomery County awarded him damages of $500,000, the full amount claimed, against all the petitioners, and the Supreme Court of Alabama affirmed.

Respondent's complaint alleged that he had been libeled by statements in a full-page advertisement that was carried in the *New York Times* on March 29, 1960. Entitled "Heed Their Rising Voices," the advertisement began by stating that "As the whole world knows by now, thousands of Southern Negro students are engaged in widespread non-violent demonstrations in positive affirmation of the right to live in human dignity as guaranteed by the U.S. Constitution and the Bill of Rights." It went on to charge that "in their efforts to uphold these guarantees, they are being met by an unprecedented wave of terror by those who would deny and negate that document which the whole world looks upon as setting the pattern for modern freedom. . . ." Succeeding paragraphs purported to illustrate the "wave of terror" by describing certain alleged events. The text concluded with an appeal for funds for three purposes: support of the student movement, "the struggle for the right-to-vote," and the legal defense of Dr. Martin Luther King, Jr., leader of the movement, against a perjury indictment then pending in Montgomery.

The text appeared over the names of 64 persons, many widely known for their activities in public affairs, religion, trade unions, and the performing arts. Below these names, and under a line reading "We in the south who are struggling daily for dignity and freedom warmly endorse this appeal," appeared the names of the four individual petitioners and of 16 other persons, all but two of whom were identified as clergymen in various Southern cities. The advertisement was signed at the bottom of the page by the "Committee to Defend Martin Luther King and the Struggle for Freedom in the South," and the officers of the Committee were listed.

Of the 10 paragraphs of text in the advertisement, the third and a portion of the sixth were the basis of respondent's claim of libel. The third paragraph read:

> In Montgomery, Alabama, after students sang "My Country, 'Tis of Thee" on the State Capitol steps, their leaders were expelled from school, and truckloads of police armed with shotguns and tear-gas ringed the Alabama State College Campus. When the entire student body protested to state authorities by refusing to re-register, their dining hall was padlocked in an attempt to starve them into submission.

The sixth paragraph read:

> Again and again the Southern violators have answered Dr. King's peaceful protests with intimidation and violence. They have bombed his home almost killing his wife and child. They have assaulted his person. They have arrested him seven times—for "speeding," "loitering" and similar "offenses." And now they have charged him with "perjury"—a felony under which they could imprison him for ten years....

Although neither of these statements mentions respondent by name, respondent contended that the word "police" in the third paragraph referred to him as the Montgomery Commissioner who supervised the Police Department, so that he was being accused of "ringing" the campus with police. He further claimed that the paragraph would be read as imputing to the police, and hence to him, the padlocking of the dining hall in order to starve the students into submission. As to the sixth paragraph, he contended that it [accused] the Montgomery police, and hence him, of answering Dr. King's protests with "intimidation and violence," bombing his home, assaulting his person, and charging him with perjury.

It is uncontroverted that some of the statements contained in the two paragraphs were not accurate descriptions of events which occurred in Montgomery. Although nine students were expelled by the State Board of Education, this was not for leading the demonstration at the Capitol, but for demanding service at a lunch counter in the Montgomery County Courthouse on another day. Not the entire student body, but most of it, had protested the expulsion, not by refusing to register, but by boycotting classes on a single day; virtually all the students did register for the ensuing semester. The campus dining hall was not padlocked on any occasion, and the only students who may have been barred from eating there were the few who had neither signed a preregistration application nor requested temporary meal tickets. Although the police were deployed near the campus in large numbers on three occasions, they did not at any time "ring" the campus, and they were not called to the campus in connection with the demonstration on the State Capitol steps, as the third paragraph implied. Dr. King had not been arrested seven times, but only four; and although he claimed to have been assaulted some years earlier in connection with his arrest for loitering outside a courtroom, one of the officers who made the arrest denied that there was such an assault.

On the premise that the charges in the sixth paragraph could be read as referring to him, respondent was allowed to prove that he had not participated in the events described. Although Dr. King's home had in fact been bombed twice when his wife and child were there, both of these occasions antedated respondent's tenure as Commissioner, and the police were not only not implicated in the bombings, but had made every effort to apprehend those who were. Three of Dr. King's four arrests took place before respondent became Commissioner. Although Dr. King had in fact been indicted (he was subsequently acquitted) on two counts of perjury, each of which carried a possible five-year sentence, respondent had nothing to do with procuring the indictment.

Respondent relies heavily, as did the Alabama courts, on statements of this Court to the effect that the Constitution does not protect libelous publications. Those statements do not foreclose our inquiry here. None of the cases sustained the use of libel laws to impose sanctions upon expression critical of the official conduct of public officials.

The general proposition that freedom of expression upon public questions is secured by the First Amendment has long been settled by our decisions. Thus we consider this case against the background of a profound national commitment to the principle that debate on public issues should be uninhibited, robust, and wide-open, and that it may well include vehement, caustic, and sometimes unpleasantly sharp attacks on government and public officials. The present advertisement, as an expression of grievance and protest on one of the major public issues of our time, would seem clearly to qualify for the constitutional protection. The question is whether it forfeits that protection by the falsity of some of its factual statements and by its alleged defamation of respondent. Authoritative interpretations of the First Amendment guarantees have consistently refused to recognize an exception for any test of truth— whether administered by judges, juries, or administrative officials—and especially one that puts the burden of proving truth on the speaker. Erroneous statement is inevitable in free debate, and it must be protected if the freedoms of expression are to have the breathing space that they need to survive.

Injury to official reputation affords no more warrant for repressing speech that would otherwise be free than does factual error. Where judicial officers are involved, this Court has held that concern for the dignity and reputation of the courts does not justify the punishment as criminal contempt of criticism of the judge or his decision. This is true even though the utterance contains half-truths and misinformation. Such repression can be justified, if at all, only by a clear and present danger of the obstruction of justice. If judges are to be treated as men of fortitude, able to thrive in a hardy climate, surely the same must be true of other government officials, such as elected city commissioners. Criticism of their official conduct does not lose its constitutional protection merely because it is effective criticism and hence diminishes their official reputations.

If neither factual error nor defamatory content suffices to remove the constitutional shield from criticism of official conduct, the combination of the two elements is no less inadequate. This is the lesson to be drawn from the great controversy over the Sedition Act of 1798, which first crystallized a national awareness of the central meaning of the First Amendment. Although the Sedition Act was never tested in this Court, the attack upon its validity has carried the day in the court of history. Fines levied in its prosecution were repaid by Act of Congress on the ground that it was unconstitutional. Jefferson, as President, pardoned those who had been convicted and sentenced under the Act and remitted their fines.

What a State may not constitutionally bring about by means of a criminal statute is likewise beyond the reach of its civil law of libel. The fear of damage awards under a rule such as that invoked by the Alabama courts here may be markedly more inhibiting than the fear of prosecution under a criminal statute. Alabama, for example, has a criminal libel law. Presumably a person charged with violation of this statute enjoys ordinary criminal-law safeguards such as the requirements of an indictment and of proof beyond a reasonable doubt. These safeguards are not available to the defendant in a civil action. The judgment awarded in this case—without the need for any proof of actual pecuniary loss—was one thousand times greater than the maximum fine provided by the Alabama criminal statute, and one hundred times greater than that provided by the Sedition Act. Whether or not a newspaper can survive a succession of such judgments, the pall of fear and timidity imposed upon those who would give voice to public criticism is an atmosphere in which the First Amendment freedoms cannot survive.

The state rule of law is not saved by its allowance of the defense of truth. A rule compelling the critic of official conduct to guarantee the truth of all his factual assertions—and to do so on pain of libel judgments virtually unlimited in amount—leads to self-censorship. Allowance of the defense of truth, with the burden of proving it on the defendant, does not mean that only false speech will be deterred. Under such a rule, would-be critics of official conduct may be deterred from voicing their criticism, even though it is believed to be true and even though it is in fact true, because of doubt whether it can be proved in court or fear of the expense of having to do so. The rule thus dampens the vigor and limits the variety of public debate.

The constitutional guarantees require, we think, a federal rule that prohibits a public official from recovering damages for a defamatory falsehood relating to his official conduct unless he proves that the statement was made with "actual malice"—that is, with knowledge that it was false or with reckless disregard of whether it was false or not. Such a privilege for criticism of official conduct is appropriately analogous to the protection accorded a public official when he is sued for libel by a private citizen. The reason for the official privilege is said to be that the threat of damage suits would otherwise inhibit the fearless, vigorous, and effective administration of policies of government and dampen the ardor of all but the most resolute, or the most irresponsible, in the unflinching discharge of their duties. Analogous considerations support the privilege for the citizen-critic of government. It is as much his duty to criticize as it is the official's duty to administer.

We have no occasion here to determine how far down into the lower ranks of government employees the "public official" designation would extend for purposes of this rule, or otherwise to specify categories of persons who would or would not be included. Nor need we here determine the boundaries of the "official conduct" concept. It is enough for the present case that respondent's position as an elected city commissioner clearly made him a public official, and that the allegations in the advertisement concerned what was allegedly his official conduct as Commissioner in charge of the Police Department.

We hold today that the Constitution delimits a State's power to award damages for libel in actions brought by public officials against critics of their official conduct. Since this is such an action, the rule requiring proof of actual malice is applicable. While Alabama law apparently requires proof of actual malice for an award of punitive damages, where general damages are concerned malice is "presumed." Such a presumption is inconsistent with the federal rule.

We consider that the proof presented to show actual malice lacks the convincing clarity which the constitutional standard demands, and hence that it would not constitutionally sustain the judgment for respondent under the proper rule of law. The case of the individual petitioners requires little discussion. Even assuming that they could constitutionally be found to have authorized the use of their names on the advertisement, there was no evidence whatever that they were aware of any erroneous statements or were in any way reckless in that regard. The judgment against them is thus without constitutional support. As to the *Times*, we similarly conclude that the facts do not support a finding of actual malice.

There is evidence that the *Times* published the advertisement without checking its accuracy against the news stories in the *Times'* own files. The mere presence of the stories in the files does not, of course, establish that the *Times* "knew" the advertisement was false, since the state of mind required for actual malice would have to be brought home to the persons in the *Times'* organization having responsibility for the publication of the advertisement. With respect to the failure of those persons to make the check, the record shows that they relied upon their knowledge of the good reputation of many of those whose names were listed as sponsors of the advertisement. There was testimony that the persons handling the advertisement saw nothing in it that would render it unacceptable under the *Times'* policy of rejecting advertisements containing "attacks of a personal character"; their failure to reject it on this ground was not unreasonable.

We think the evidence against the *Times* supports at most a finding of negligence in failing to discover the misstatements, and is constitutionally insufficient to show the recklessness that is required for a finding of actual malice.

We also think the evidence was constitutionally defective in another respect: it was incapable of supporting the jury's finding that the allegedly libelous statements were made "of and concerning" respondent. There was no reference to respondent in the advertisement, either by name or official position. A number of the allegedly libelous statements—the charges that the dining hall was padlocked and that Dr. King's home was bombed, his person assaulted, and a perjury prosecution instituted against him—did not even concern the police.

The judgment of the Supreme Court of Alabama is reversed and the case is remanded to that court for further proceedings not inconsistent with this opinion.

POINTS FOR DISCUSSION

1. Since very few libel defendants will ever admit that they went to press knowing that they would be printing falsehoods, public officials will need

to prove that the defendant published with "reckless disregard of truth or falsity." What kinds of behaviors would or should constitute proof of such reckless disregard?
2. There is much talk these days about the importance of political candidates' "character." If the citizenry has a legitimate interest in their representatives' character, can there ever be criticisms of public officials that do *not* at least have important implications for their "official conduct"?

▪ *Gertz v. Welch*
418 U.S. 323 (1974)
Justice Powell:

In 1968 a Chicago policeman named Nuccio shot and killed a youth named Nelson. The state authorities prosecuted Nuccio for the homicide and ultimately obtained a conviction for murder in the second degree. The Nelson family retained petitioner Elmer Gertz, a reputable attorney, to represent them in civil litigation against Nuccio.

Respondent publishes *American Opinion*, a monthly outlet for the views of the John Birch Society. In March 1969 respondent published [an] article under the title "FRAME-UP: Richard Nuccio And The War On Police." The article purports to demonstrate that the testimony against Nuccio at his criminal trial was false and that his prosecution was part of the Communist campaign against the police.

In his capacity as counsel for the Nelson family in the civil litigation, petitioner attended the coroner's inquest into the boy's death and initiated actions for damages, but he neither discussed Officer Nuccio with the press nor played any part in the criminal proceeding. Notwithstanding petitioner's remote connection with the prosecution of Nuccio, respondent's magazine portrayed him as an architect of the "frame-up." According to the article, the police file on petitioner took "a big, Irish cop to lift." The article stated that petitioner had been an official of the "Marxist League for Industrial Democracy, originally known as the Intercollegiate Socialist Society, which has advocated the violent seizure of our government." It labeled Gertz a "Leninist" and a "Communist-fronter." It also stated that Gertz had been an officer of the National Lawyers Guild, described as a Communist organization that "probably did more than any other outfit to plan the Communist attack on the Chicago police during the 1968 Democratic Convention."

These statements contained serious inaccuracies. The implication that petitioner had a criminal record was false. There was also no basis for the charge that petitioner was a "Leninist" or a "Communist-fronter." And he had never been a member of the "Marxist League for Industrial Democracy" or the "Intercollegiate Socialist Society."

Petitioner claimed that the falsehoods published by respondent injured his reputation as a lawyer and a citizen. Respondent asserted that petitioner was a public official or a public figure and that the article concerned an issue of public interest and concern. For these reasons, respondent argued, it was entitled to invoke the privilege enunciated in *New York Times Co. v. Sullivan*, under [which] respondent would escape liability unless petitioner could prove publication of defamatory falsehood with actual malice—that is, with knowledge that it was false or with reckless disregard of whether it was false or not.

The principal issue in this case is whether a newspaper or broadcaster that publishes defamatory falsehoods about an individual who is neither a public official nor a public figure may claim a constitutional privilege against liability for the injury inflicted by those statements.

We begin with the common ground. Under the First Amendment there is no such thing as a false idea. However pernicious an opinion may seem, we depend for its correction not on the conscience of judges and juries but on the competition of other ideas. But there is no constitutional value in false statements of fact. Neither the intentional lie nor the careless error materially advances society's interest in uninhibited, robust, and wide-open debate on public issues.

Although the erroneous statement of fact is not worthy of constitutional protection, it is nevertheless inevitable in free debate. And punishment of error runs the risk of inducing a cautious and restrictive exercise of the constitutionally guaranteed freedoms of speech and press. The need to avoid self-censorship by the news media is, however, not the only societal value at issue. If it were, this Court would have embraced long ago the view that publishers and broadcasters enjoy an unconditional and indefeasible immunity from liability for defamation. Such a rule would, indeed, obviate the fear that the prospect of civil liability for injurious falsehood might dissuade a timorous press from the effective exercise of First Amendment freedoms. Yet absolute protection for the communications media requires a total sacrifice of the competing value served by the law of defamation. The legitimate state interest underlying the law of libel is the compensation of individuals for the harm inflicted on them by defamatory falsehood. We would not lightly require the State to abandon this purpose.

Some tension necessarily exists between the need for a vigorous and uninhibited press and the legitimate interest in redressing wrongful injury. This

Court has extended a measure of strategic protection to defamatory falsehood. The *New York Times* standard defines the level of constitutional protection appropriate to the context of defamation of a public person. Those who, by reason of the notoriety of their achievements or the vigor and success with which they seek the public's attention, are properly classed as public figures and those who hold governmental office may recover for injury to reputation only on clear and convincing proof that the defamatory falsehood was made with knowledge of its falsity or with reckless disregard for the truth. For the reasons stated below, we conclude that the state interest in compensating injury to the reputation of private individuals requires that a different rule should obtain with respect to them.

The first remedy of any victim of defamation is self-help—using available opportunities to contradict the lie or correct the error and thereby to minimize its adverse impact on reputation. Public officials and public figures usually enjoy significantly greater access to the channels of effective communication and hence have a more realistic opportunity to counteract false statements than private individuals normally enjoy. Private individuals are therefore more vulnerable to injury, and the state interest in protecting them is correspondingly greater.

More important than the likelihood that private individuals will lack effective opportunities for rebuttal, there is a compelling normative consideration underlying the distinction between public and private defamation plaintiffs. An individual who decides to seek governmental office must accept certain necessary consequences of that involvement in public affairs. He runs the risk of closer public scrutiny than might otherwise be the case. Those classed as public figures stand in a similar position. Hypothetically, it may be possible for someone to become a public figure through no purposeful action of his own, but the instances of truly involuntary public figures must be exceedingly rare. For the most part those who attain this status have assumed roles of special prominence in the affairs of society. Some occupy positions of such persuasive power and influence that they are deemed public figures for all purposes. More commonly, those classed as public figures have thrust themselves to the forefront of particular public controversies in order to influence the resolution of the issues involved. In either event, they invite attention and comment.

A private individual has not accepted public office or assumed an influential role in ordering society, has relinquished no part of his interest in the protection of his own good name, and consequently he has a more compelling call on the courts for redress of injury inflicted by defamatory falsehood. Thus, private individuals are not only more vulnerable to injury than public officials and public figures; they are also more deserving of recovery.

For these reasons we conclude that the States should retain substantial latitude in their efforts to enforce a legal remedy for defamatory falsehood injurious to the reputation of a private individual. We hold that, so long as they do not impose liability without fault, the States may define for themselves the appropriate standard of liability for a publisher or broadcaster of defamatory falsehood injurious to a private individual.

The *New York Times* privilege [is not] wholly inapplicable to the context of private individuals. We hold that the States may not permit recovery of presumed or punitive damages, at least when liability is not based on a showing of knowledge of falsity or reckless disregard for the truth. The common law of defamation is an oddity of tort law, for it allows recovery of purportedly compensatory damages without evidence of actual loss. Under the traditional rules pertaining to actions for libel, the existence of injury is presumed from the fact of publication. Juries may award substantial sums as compensation for supposed damage to reputation without any proof that such harm actually occurred. The largely uncontrolled discretion of juries to award damages where there is no loss unnecessarily compounds the potential of any system of liability for defamatory falsehood to inhibit the vigorous exercise of First Amendment freedoms. Additionally, the doctrine of presumed damages invites juries to punish unpopular opinion rather than to compensate individuals for injury sustained by the publication of a false fact. More to the point, the States have no substantial interest in securing for plaintiffs such as this petitioner gratuitous awards of money damages far in excess of any actual injury.

It is necessary to restrict defamation plaintiffs who do not prove knowledge of falsity or reckless disregard for the truth to compensation for actual injury. We need not define "actual injury," as trial courts have wide experience in framing appropriate jury instructions in tort actions. Suffice it to say that actual injury is not limited to out-of-pocket loss. Indeed, the more customary types of actual harm inflicted by defamatory falsehood include impairment of reputation and standing in the community, personal humiliation, and mental anguish and suffering. There need be no evidence which assigns an actual dollar value to the injury.

We also find no justification for allowing awards of punitive damages against publishers and broadcasters held liable under state-defined standards of liability for defamation. In most jurisdictions jury discretion over the amounts awarded is limited only by the gentle rule that they not be excessive. Consequently, juries assess punitive damages in wholly unpredictable amounts bearing no necessary relation to the actual harm caused. And they remain free to use their discretion selectively to punish expressions of unpopular views. Punitive damages are not compensation for injury. Instead, they are private fines levied by civil juries to punish reprehensible conduct and to deter its future occurrence. In short, the private defamation plaintiff who establishes liability under a less demanding standard than that stated by *New York Times* may recover only such damages as are sufficient to compensate him for actual injury.

Notwithstanding our refusal to extend the *New York Times* privilege to defamation of private individuals, respondent contends that we should affirm the judgment below on the ground that petitioner is either a public official or a public figure. There is little basis for the former assertion. Several years prior to the present incident, petitioner had served briefly on housing committees appointed by the mayor of Chicago, but at the time of publication he had never held any remunerative governmental position. [The public figure] designation may rest on either of two alternative bases. In some instances an individual may achieve such pervasive fame or notoriety that he becomes a public figure for all purposes and in all contexts. More commonly, an individual voluntarily injects himself or is drawn into a particular public controversy and thereby becomes a public figure for a limited range of issues. In either case such persons assume special prominence in the resolution of public questions. Petitioner has long been active in community and professional affairs. He has served as an officer of local civic groups and of various professional organizations, and he has published several books and articles on legal subjects. Although petitioner was consequently well known in some circles, he had achieved no general fame or notoriety in the community. None of the prospective jurors called at the trial had ever heard of petitioner prior to this litigation, and respondent offered no proof that this response was atypical of the local population. We would not lightly assume that a citizen's participation in community and professional affairs rendered him a public figure for all purposes. Absent clear evidence of general fame or notoriety in the community, and pervasive involvement in the affairs of society, an individual should not be deemed a public personality for all aspects of his life. It is preferable to reduce the public-figure question to a more meaningful context by looking to the nature and extent of an individual's participation in the particular controversy giving rise to the defamation. In this context it is plain that petitioner was not a public figure. He played a minimal role at the coroner's inquest, and his participation related solely to his representation of a private client. He took no part in the criminal prosecution of Officer Nuccio. Moreover, he never discussed either the criminal or civil litigation with the press and was never quoted as having done so. He plainly did not thrust himself into the vortex of this public issue, nor did he engage the public's attention in an attempt to influence its outcome. We therefore conclude that the *New York Times* standard is inapplicable to this case.

POINTS FOR DISCUSSION

1. Justice Powell provides two reasons in support of making it very hard for public officials and public figures to win libel suits. One reason is that people choose to be public officials and typically become public figures as a result of their own actions. Clearly one cannot become a public official involuntarily. But are instances of involuntary public figures as "exceedingly rare" as Justice Powell suggests?
2. The second reason Justice Powell offers for setting up obstacles to libel suits by public officials and public figures is that such persons have access to "self-help," that they can always call a press conference, and the press will come. From the viewers' perspective, however, is there not a world of difference between seeing a public official's self-serving response to an allegedly defamatory article, and learning that a neutral jury found that the article was libelous?

▪ *Philadelphia Newspapers, Inc. v. Hepps*
475 U.S. 767 (1986)
Justice O'Connor:

This case requires us once more to struggle to define the proper accommodation between the law of defamation and the freedoms of speech and press protected by the First Amendment. In *Gertz v. Robert Welch, Inc.* the Court held that a private figure who brings a suit for defamation cannot recover without some showing that the media defendant was at fault in publishing the statements at issue. Here, we hold that, at least where a newspaper publishes speech of public concern, a private-figure plaintiff cannot recover damages without also showing that the statements at issue are false.

Maurice S. Hepps is the principal stockholder of General Programming, Inc. (GPI), a corporation that franchises a chain of stores—known at the relevant time as "Thrifty" stores—selling beer, soft drinks, and snacks. Mr. Hepps, GPI, and a number of its franchisees are the appellees here. Appellant Philadelphia Newspapers, Inc., owns the *Philadelphia Inquirer*. The *Inquirer* published a series of articles containing the statements at issue here. The general theme of the five articles, which appeared in the *Inquirer* between May 1975 and May 1976, was that appellees had links to organized crime and used some of those links to influence the State's governmental processes, both legislative and administrative. The articles discussed a state legislator, described as "a Pittsburgh Democrat and convicted felon," whose actions displayed "a clear pattern of interference in state government by [the legislator] on behalf of Hepps and Thrifty." The stories reported that federal "investigators have found connections between Thrifty and underworld figures," that "the Thrifty Beverage beer chain . . . had connections . . . with organized crime," and that Thrifty had "won a series of competitive advantages through rulings by the State Liquor Control Board." A grand jury was said to be investigating the "alleged relationship between the Thrifty chain and known Mafia figures," and "[whether] the chain received special treatment from the [state Governor's] administration and the Liquor Control Board."

Appellees brought suit for defamation against appellants in a Pennsylvania state court. Consistent with *Gertz*, Pennsylvania requires a private figure who brings a suit for defamation to bear the burden of proving negligence or malice by the defendant in publishing the statements at issue. As to falsity, Pennsylvania follows the common law's presumption that an individual's reputation is a good one. Statements defaming that person are therefore presumptively false, although a publisher who bears the burden of proving the truth of the statements has an absolute defense.

The parties first raised the issue of burden of proof as to falsity before trial, but the trial court reserved its ruling on the matter. Appellee Hepps testified at length that the statements at issue were false, and he extensively cross-examined the author of the stories as to the veracity of the statements at issue. After all the evidence had been presented by both sides, the trial court concluded that Pennsylvania's statute giving the defendant the burden of proving the truth of the statements violated the Federal Constitution. The trial court therefore instructed the jury that the plaintiffs bore the burden of proving falsity.

The Pennsylvania Supreme Court viewed *Gertz* as simply requiring the plaintiff to show fault in actions for defamation. It concluded that a showing of fault did not require a showing of falsity. We noted probable jurisdiction, and now reverse.

One can discern [from our prior decisions] two forces that may reshape the common-law landscape to conform to the First Amendment. The first is whether the plaintiff is a public official or figure, or is instead a private figure. The second is whether the speech at issue is of public concern. When the speech is of public concern and the plaintiff is a public official or public figure, the Constitution clearly requires the plaintiff to surmount a much higher barrier before recovering damages from a media defendant than is raised by the common law. When the speech is of public concern but the plaintiff is a private figure, as in *Gertz*, the Constitution still supplants the standards of the common law, but the constitutional requirements are, in at least some of their range, less forbidding than when the plaintiff is a public figure and the speech is of public concern. When the speech is of exclusively private concern and the plaintiff is a private figure, the constitutional requirements do not necessarily force any change in at least some of the features of the common-law landscape.

Here, as in *Gertz*, the plaintiff is a private figure and the newspaper articles are of public concern. In *Gertz*, as in *New York Times*, the common-law rule was superseded by a constitutional rule. We believe that the common law's rule on falsity—that the defendant must bear the burden of proving truth—must similarly fall here to a constitutional requirement that the plaintiff bear the burden of showing falsity, as well as fault, before recovering damages.

There will always be instances when the fact finding process will be unable to resolve conclusively whether the speech is true or false; it is in those cases that the burden of proof is dispositive. Under a rule forcing the plaintiff to bear the burden of showing falsity, there will be some cases in which plaintiffs cannot meet their burden despite the fact that the speech is in fact false. The plaintiff's suit will fail despite the fact that, in some abstract sense, the suit is meritorious. Similarly, under an alternative rule placing the burden of showing truth on defendants, there would be some cases in which defendants could not bear their burden despite the fact that the speech is in fact true. Those suits would succeed despite the fact that, in some abstract sense, those suits are unmeritorious. Under either rule, then, the outcome of the suit will sometimes be at variance with the outcome that we would desire if all speech were either demonstrably true or demonstrably false.

This dilemma stems from the fact that the allocation of the burden of proof will determine liability for some speech that is true and some that is false, but all of such speech is unknowably true or false. Because the burden of proof is the deciding factor only when the evidence is ambiguous, we cannot know how much of the speech affected by the allocation of the burden of proof is true and how much is false. In a case presenting a configuration of speech and plaintiff like the one we face here, and where the scales are in such an uncertain balance, we believe that the Constitution requires us to tip them in favor of protecting true speech. To ensure that true speech on matters of public concern is not deterred, we hold that the common-law presumption that defamatory speech is false cannot stand when a plaintiff seeks damages against a media defendant for speech of public concern. We note that our decision adds only marginally to the burdens that the plaintiff must already bear as a result of our earlier decisions in the law of defamation. The plaintiff must show fault. A jury is obviously more likely to accept a plaintiff's contention that the defendant was at fault in publishing the statements at issue if convinced that the relevant statements were false. As a practical matter, then, evidence offered by plaintiffs on the publisher's fault in adequately investigating the truth of the published statements will generally encompass evidence of the falsity of the matters asserted.

We have no occasion to consider the quantity of proof of falsity that a private-figure plaintiff must present to recover damages. Nor need we consider what standards would apply if the plaintiff sues a nonmedia defendant, or if a State were to provide a plaintiff with the opportunity to obtain a judgment that declared the speech at issue to be false but did not give rise to liability for damages.

For the reasons stated above, the judgment of the Pennsylvania Supreme Court is reversed, and the case is remanded for further proceedings not inconsistent with this opinion.

POINTS FOR DISCUSSION

1. The *Hepps* case tells us that three variables determine much of the First Amendment's impact on libel law: Who is the plaintiff (public official/figure or private citizen)? Who is the defendant (media or nonmedia)? And what was the topic of the allegedly libelous remark (a topic of public, or private, interest)? These variables create a 2 x 2 x 2 matrix of sorts, as if all libel scenarios can be sorted into eight "boxes." Which one of those eight boxes is most directly affected by the *Hepps* ruling itself?
2. Justice O'Connor suggests that libel plaintiffs who are already required to prove actual malice must thus surely also have proven falsity. After all, it makes no sense to publish the *truth* "with reckless disregard for truth or falsity." But can't the same be said of the lesser burden of proof demanded of private plaintiffs? Does it make sense to be punished for "negligently" publishing the truth?

▪ *Peterson v. Grisham*

594 F.3d 723 (10th Cir. 2010)
Judge Lucero:

In 1988, Ronald Williamson and Dennis Fritz were wrongly convicted of the rape and murder of Debra Sue Carter. Both men were later exonerated after spending over a decade in jail. Their painful story caught the attention of renowned legal-fiction author John Grisham, who wrote a book about Williamson appropriately titled *The Innocent Man*. Fritz also wrote a book, *Journey Toward Justice*, detailing the horror of his years of unjust confinement.

Each of the plaintiffs in this case—Oklahoma District Attorney William Peterson; former Shawnee police officer Gary Rogers; and former Oklahoma state criminologist Melvin Hett—played a role in the investigation or prosecution and conviction of Williamson and Fritz. Neither *The Innocent Man* nor *Journey Toward Justice* paints the plaintiffs in a positive light. Following the release of these books, plaintiffs filed suit in Oklahoma district court seeking relief for defamation. They named Grisham, Fritz, anti–death penalty advocate Barry Scheck, and author Robert Mayer—along with their respective publishers—as defendants. The district court dismissed the suit for failure to state a claim upon which relief can be granted. We affirm.

On the morning of December 8, 1982, Carter was found dead in her garage apartment in the small town of Ada, Oklahoma. She had been raped and suffocated by her assailant. Four years later, Rogers and his fellow officers arrested Williamson and Fritz for Carter's murder. Peterson prosecuted the case.

The evidence against Williamson and Fritz consisted of hair samples, Williamson's statement to police about a dream in which he had committed the murder, and the testimony of jailhouse informants. Hett testified that hairs recovered from the crime scene belonged to Williamson and Fritz. Based on this evidence, the jury convicted Williamson and Fritz of rape and murder. Williamson was sentenced to death, and Fritz received life in prison.

Following a grant of habeas relief by the Eastern District of Oklahoma, DNA testing was ordered in 1999. That testing revealed that hair and semen samples taken from the crime scene could not have come from Williamson and Fritz. Both men had been wrongfully convicted. Another man was eventually found guilty of Carter's murder.

Grisham published *The Innocent Man* in 2006. It tells Williamson's life story and explores the circumstances leading to his wrongful conviction, imprisonment, and subsequent exoneration. Grisham depicts Peterson, Rogers, and Hett as particularly responsible for the plight of Williamson and Fritz. He also faults what he describes as a broken criminal justice system that condones "bad police work, junk science, faulty eyewitness identifications, bad defense lawyers, lazy prosecutors, and arrogant prosecutors." In *Journey Toward Justice*, Fritz speaks in equally harsh tones about the public officials who put him behind bars. As the title suggests, the book describes Fritz's agonizing trail from wrongful imprisonment to exoneration. Fritz recounts in vivid detail his fears and frustrations as a wrongfully accused murder suspect and convict, and his eventual elation upon release.

Barry Scheck, Fritz's former attorney and a prominent anti–death penalty advocate, wrote the foreword to *Journey Toward Justice*. In that foreword, Scheck commends Fritz for having the courage to write his personal story, and praises Fritz for his recent work in the anti–death penalty movement. Both Fritz and Scheck were interviewed by Grisham for *The Innocent Man*. Scheck ultimately devoted a chapter of his 2003 book, *Actual Innocence*, to the wrongful convictions of Williamson and Fritz. Lastly, Robert Mayer's book, *The Dreams of Ada*, explores the 1985 convictions of Tommy Ward and Karl Fontenot for the death of Denice Haraway. The Haraway case shared many parallels with the Carter case, including minimal physical evidence, the use of "dream" confessions, and reliance on testimony by jailhouse informants. That case also involved a similar cast of characters: Peterson was the prosecutor and Rogers was the investigator. Grisham used *The Dreams of Ada*—and found it to be particularly helpful—in his research for *The Innocent Man*. Shortly after Grisham's book was published, Broadway Books reissued *The Dreams of Ada* with a new afterword written by Mayer.

With the exception of *Actual Innocence*, all these books were released (or, in the case of *The Dreams of Ada*, re-released) in October 2006. One year later, Peterson and Rogers filed suit.

After defendants filed motions to dismiss, the district court directed plaintiffs to file a second amended complaint specifying the alleged defamatory statements.

In their 116-page second amended complaint, plaintiffs claimed that defendants engaged in "a massive joint defamatory attack" against them. This attack was motivated in part by defendants' shared desire "to further efforts to abolish the death penalty." The district court dismissed the second amended complaint for failure to state a claim upon which relief can be granted. This appeal ensued.

Plaintiffs contend that the district court "failed to take into consideration any of the one-hundred and three pages of specific factual allegations" in their second amended complaint. According to plaintiffs, the court sweepingly concluded that statements by authors regarding government officials and public figures could never be considered defamatory or otherwise actionable. They further accuse the district court of neglecting to analyze each of the factual allegations in their complaint on the basis that the district court noted that such a task would be "boring" and "repetitive."

Plaintiffs mischaracterize the district court's statements. The court did not rule that defamation claims against authors writing about public officials are never plausible. Instead, it dismissed plaintiffs' complaint only "after review of each of the statements alleged." Though we encourage district courts to more fully articulate their reasoning [in granting motions to dismiss], the court was not required to engage in a detailed written analysis of each of dozens of allegedly defamatory statements. The district court concluded the statements shared common characteristics that preclude relief, and the record on appeal provides this court with an adequate basis for reviewing each statement.

Turning to plaintiffs' individual claims, we agree with the district court that each cause of action fails to state a claim upon which relief can be granted. Taking as true the facts plaintiffs allege in their second amended complaint, we conclude that defendants are statutorily protected from suit. Oklahoma law defines libel as "a false or malicious unprivileged publication . . . which exposes any person to public hatred, contempt, ridicule or obloquy, or which tends to deprive him of public confidence, or to injure him in his occupation." To state a claim for libel, a plaintiff must allege that a defendant made: "(1) a false and defamatory statement concerning [plaintiff]; (2) an unprivileged publication to a third party; and (3) fault amounting to at least negligence on the part of the publisher." Unless a plaintiff demonstrates that a defendant committed libel per se, she must also plead and prove special damages caused by publication.

Because plaintiffs in this case concede that they alleged no special damages, they must prove libel per se, which requires a statement that is "clearly defamatory on its face." In contrast, statements that are reasonably susceptible of both a defamatory and innocent meaning are not libelous per se.

Given that plaintiffs are public officials, they face an especially heavy burden in attempting to demonstrate libel per se. Under the Oklahoma Statutes, "any and all criticisms upon the official acts of any and all public officers" are privileged and cannot be considered libelous, unless a defendant makes a false allegation that the official engaged in criminal behavior. The [publication] must obviously import the commission of crime punishable by indictment.

Plaintiffs have not carried their burden. Several of the statements included in plaintiffs' second amended complaint do not concern plaintiffs and therefore would not constitute libel against them regardless of their status as public officials or whether they had pled special damages. As to those that do, we agree with the district court that plaintiffs point to no statement in which defendants directly accuse any plaintiff of a crime.

Plaintiffs expect us to scale a mountain of inferences in order to reach the conclusion that defendants' statements impute criminal acts to plaintiffs and render the statutory privilege inapplicable. We decline to engage in such inferential analysis, or to take a myriad of other analytical leaps plaintiffs ask us to make. Any connection between defendants' statements and an accusation of criminal activity is far too tenuous for us to declare them as unprivileged.

Because Oklahoma law is dispositive in this case, we need not engage in a constitutional analysis. But we note that, at a minimum, allowing the plaintiffs to recover would offend the spirit of the First Amendment. Defendants wrote about a miscarriage of justice and attempted to encourage political and social change. To the extent their perceptions of the affair were erroneous, we depend on the marketplace of ideas—not the whim of the bench—to correct insidious opinions.

Affirmed.

POINTS FOR DISCUSSION

1. Notice that in Oklahoma, public officials have a more difficult time winning libel suits than even *New York Times v. Sullivan* demands. Such plaintiffs, when suing about a publication on a matter of public concern, have to show not only actual malice, but also that they are being accused of criminal wrongdoing. Do you think this strikes the right balance?
2. At the federal district court level, Judge White suggests that courts should be especially forgiving of most factual errors from an author like Dennis Fritz, who "spent eleven years in prison falsely convicted of murder." Readers are or should be wise enough to expect a "tone of moral outrage, a biased account based on conjecture and passion." Is it proper for courts to take into account how justified a libel defendant's outrage might be?

▪ *Brock v. Viacom International, Inc.*

2005 U.S. Dist. LEXIS 12217 (N.D. Ga. 2005)

Judge Pannell:

On March 14, 2003, the premium television network Showtime exhibited an episode of the "*Penn & Teller: Bullshit!*" television series. The Episode, entitled "Creationism," concerned an ongoing public debate before the Cobb County, Georgia, School Board regarding creationism versus evolution and whether either or both should be taught in Cobb County's public schools. The debate before the Cobb County School Board received widespread local and national media attention.[1]

---

1. The relevant scene from the episode is on my website. Go to www.paulsiegelcommlaw.com; on the left side (*Communication Law in America*), click on "Video Clips," then on "Chapter 4," and finally on "Penn and Teller's B.S. on Creationism."

As the material for the Episode was being gathered, the plaintiffs were contacted and offered the opportunity to give an interview to explain their positions in favor of the teaching of creationism. One of the plaintiffs, Russ Brock, had already appeared before the School Board at its public hearing to advocate for the teaching of creationism. According to the plaintiffs, when they met with the defendants to discuss the television series and consider the interviews, the defendants represented that the series had not yet been named and that it was a program about topics that Americans are passionate about. After agreeing to sit for the interviews, the defendants asked the plaintiffs to sign releases. While reviewing the releases, the plaintiffs noticed language indicating that the taped interviews might be used for satirical or humorous purposes. The plaintiffs requested an explanation of this language from the defendants, and the defendants responded by saying that the releases were a standard form that is used for all types of television programs. The defendants then told the plaintiffs "not to worry" because the television program was "not that kind of show." The defendants assured the plaintiffs that the television series was not a satirical show and that the interviews would not be used for satirical or humorous purposes. Based on these representations, the plaintiffs agreed to sit for the taped interviews. Plaintiff Russ Brock was paid $300 for the interview, but none of the other plaintiffs were paid.

As it turned out, the show was already entitled "Bullshit!" and the content of the Episode was a combination of interviews and film clips from the media's coverage of the public hearings before the Cobb County School Board, together with acerbic commentary by Penn & Teller. Penn & Teller's commentary was highly critical of the plaintiffs' views on the teaching of creationism in public schools. Penn & Teller, in an often harsh and sarcastic manner, repeatedly voiced their opinion that the teaching of creationism in public schools would violate the United States Constitution's mandate of the separation of church and state. The plaintiffs complain that, instead of being a program about things that Americans are passionate about, as represented by the defendants, "the program was an aggressive, irreverent exposé of the beliefs of Christianity and Creationism, and a personal attack on Plaintiffs for their desire to have both Creationism and Evolution taught as alternate theories in the Public School System of Cobb County."

A year after the Episode initially aired, the plaintiffs brought this action, complaining that the broadcast placed the plaintiffs in an unfavorable light and that the plaintiffs were misled as to the content of the Episode at the time that they agreed to be interviewed. The plaintiffs' nine-count complaint asserts a variety of claims including libel. The plaintiffs particularly bemoan Penn & Teller's comments ridiculing plaintiff Myrna Feldman's wig and the fact that it was on in a crooked manner, as well as Penn & Teller's comments claiming, according to the plaintiffs, that the plaintiffs were "un-American" and "mentally unsound, infirm and/or unwise." The plaintiffs further claim that, as a result of the airing of the Episode, the plaintiffs "have each been embarrassed and suffered public ridicule and humiliation."

Though they couch their claims in terms of, among other things, fraud in the inducement, breach of contract, and promissory estoppel, the gravamen of the plaintiffs' cause of action is defamation.

In paragraph 36 of their complaint, the plaintiffs state, "As a result of the broadcast of episode 8 of the 'Bullshit' series, Plaintiffs have each been embarrassed and suffered public ridicule and humiliation. Additionally, each Plaintiff has endured emotional distress and damage to their personal relationships as a result of the broadcast." This paragraph makes it clear that the plaintiffs are seeking damages due to the harm that the broadcast of the Episode caused to their respective reputations and states of mind. In each of their claims, the plaintiffs incorporate paragraph 36 and then merely state, "Plaintiffs have each been damaged." Finally, in paragraph 70, the plaintiffs state that they "have been injured as a proximate result of Defendants' actions and are entitled to recover money damages from them." Other than these paragraphs, the plaintiffs make no other mention of any damages they have suffered. At no point in their complaint do the plaintiffs allege that they suffered any non-reputational economic damages, such as those associated with lost wages or lost employment opportunities. Clearly, then, the plaintiffs are complaining of what amounts to damages to reputation or state of mind, and, therefore, they must meet the constitutional requirements of a defamation claim in order to survive the defendants' motion to dismiss.

In *New York Times Co. v. Sullivan*, the Supreme Court held that the First Amendment prohibits a public official from recovering damages for defamatory statements regarding matters of public concern unless he shows that the statements were false and that they were made with actual malice, that is, with knowledge that the statements were false or with reckless disregard of whether they were false or not. Three years later, the Court extended the *New York Times* rule to plaintiffs who are not public officials but are nevertheless public figures.

The court notes that the defendants argue that the plaintiffs are public figures because they injected themselves into the public controversy concerning the place of creationism and evolution in public school curriculum. Without ruling on this issue, the court will assume for the purposes of this order that the plaintiffs are private-figure citizens and will apply the less forbidding standard regarding what the plaintiffs must demonstrate in order to make a defamation-type claim for damages to reputation and state of mind.

As an initial matter, the court finds that the speech at issue is clearly of public concern. The debate regarding the teaching of creationism alongside evolution in public schools implicates the Establishment Clause of the First Amendment's requirement of the separation of church and state, a fact demonstrated by the recent litigation of the Cobb County School Board's placement of stickers commenting on evolution in certain science textbooks. This debate concerns the boundaries of the federal, state, and local governments' power and the rights of all citizens of the United States, and, therefore, it is an issue that affects each citizen of this country. It is hard for this court to imagine a subject matter that would be of more public concern than the one at issue in this case. Thus, the court finds that the speech at issue, i.e., the opinions expressed regarding the teaching of creationism alongside evolution in public schools, to be of public concern.

When the speech at issue is of public concern, it is a constitutional requirement that the private citizen plaintiff bear the burden of showing falsity, as well as fault, before recovering damages. The determination of whether a defendant was at fault in publishing the statements at issue is closely connected to demonstrating that the statements were false: The crucial burden on a plaintiff in making a defamation or defamation-type claim is to show the falsity of the statements made.

In this case, the plaintiffs have failed to state a claim upon which relief can be granted because they have failed to allege in their complaint that any of the statements pertaining to the plaintiffs made during the episode were false. Even liberally construing their complaint in the best possible light for purposes of the defendants' motion to dismiss, the court can find no set of facts that the plaintiffs could prove that would demonstrate that the statements made during the Episode were false.

The episode consists of essentially two kinds of statements. The first type are those made by the plaintiffs themselves during the Episode. The second type are those statements made by the people, including Mr. Jillette, criticizing the plaintiffs' views. As to the first type, the statements made by the plaintiffs during the Episode cannot form the basis of a defamation claim because the plaintiffs actually made those statements. The Episode shows a portion of Mr. Brock's speech made during the Cobb County School Board's public hearings on whether it should permit the teaching of creationism. There is no dispute that Mr. Brock made these statements during the hearing. The Episode also shows portions of interviews with the plaintiffs in which the plaintiffs stated their support for the teaching of creationism alongside the teaching of biology in public schools. There is no dispute that the plaintiffs made these statements during their interviews. Furthermore, the plaintiffs do not allege that the depictions of their statements were in any way inaccurate or false. Thus, the plaintiffs' claims cannot be premised upon the statements that they made since these statements reflect their own opinion.

As to the second type, the nonverbal gestures of Mr. Teller and the statements by Mr. Jillette and the others featured on the show who oppose the teaching of creationism are opinions, which constitute the core of the type of speech that is to be protected under the First Amendment. Furthermore, opinions cannot be proven false for purposes of defamation. In order for an alleged defamatory statement to be actionable, it must express or imply a statement of fact that is capable of being proven false.

In this case, Mr. Jillette and the others on the show simply expressed their opinions regarding the views of the plaintiffs, though the court recognizes that these opinions were sometimes harsh. But just as the plaintiffs are entitled to express their beliefs regarding Christianity and their opinion that creationism should be taught in public schools, Mr. Jillette, Mr. Teller, and the others on the Episode are entitled to express their beliefs that the plaintiffs' views are wrong. The emphatic and often mocking manner in which Mr. Jillette and the others criticized the plaintiffs' views did not transform these protected opinions into actionable defamation.

The plaintiffs' primary complaint is not that any of the statements made in the Episode were false, but that the show advocated a viewpoint different from theirs and, in doing so, criticized their position in an "aggressive" and "irreverent" manner. But the Supreme Court has rejected the notion that harsh criticism of a viewpoint can constitute actionable defamation.

Because the plaintiffs have failed to allege that any of the statements contained in the Episode are false and because the plaintiffs cannot prove the falsity of the complained of statements given that those statements are opinions, the plaintiffs' defamation-type claims fail as a matter of law, and their complaint fails to state a claim for which relief can be granted. For all of these reasons, the court grants the defendants' motion to dismiss.

POINTS FOR DISCUSSION

1. If plaintiffs' assertion that Penn and Teller's producers misled them about the nature of the program is credible, should that deception count in consideration of the libel claim?
2. After viewing the relevant scene from the episode on my website, consider whether the show treats creationism as an important political issue, or as merely a vehicle for making a personal attack on the plaintiff. Should your answer make a difference on the libel claim?

5

Invasion of Privacy

Compared with libel, invasion of privacy cases are relative newcomers to the American scene. Their birth is often attributed to an 1890 *Harvard Law Review* article written by Boston attorney Samuel Warren and his law partner Louis Brandeis (later to achieve fame as a U.S. Supreme Court justice). Seventy years later, Dean William Prosser of the University of California Law School reviewed the development of privacy law, and determined that it had grown into four distinct civil actions, or torts.

- The **false light** tort is highly similar to libel, except that the revelation about the plaintiff need not be defamatory. The first case in this chapter—*Time v. Hill*, a 1967 Supreme Court decision—emphasizes this feature of the tort. And *Solano v. Playgirl* offers an unusual variation on the theme.
- The **public disclosure** tort is distinguishable from libel, in that the revelations are true (although embarrassing). The plaintiff in *Neff v. Time, Inc.* complains of being "revealed" not through prose but through a candid photograph of him in a state of partial undress. The case also involves elements of the misappropriation tort, described below.
- The **intrusion** tort is the only one of the four that does not require publication to be actionable. The action, similar to trespass, typically alleges that the defendant has intruded on the plaintiff's personal space, her zone of privacy (such as in following her around incessantly, camera in hand). The radio news reporter in *Holman v. Central Arkansas Broadcasting Company* did not use a roving microphone. He did not need to, because his subject, being held in jail on a DUI charge, could not escape. And *Boring v. Google* seems to combine intrusion and public disclosure elements, as the plaintiffs alleged that the folks compiling Google Maps might not only be publicizing their private goings-on but also may have trespassed in the production of their images.

- The **misappropriation** tort involves the unauthorized use of another's name or "likeness" (e.g., his or her voice or photo) for commercial purposes. When the plaintiff's main grievance is not having been paid for the use, the tort is sometimes referred to as the **right of publicity**. *Zacchini v. Scripps Howard Broadcasting Company* is the Supreme Court's only foray into this area of law, and commentators have generally agreed that the unusual facts of the case make its precedential value limited.

Our final case, *Owasso Independent School District v. Falvo*, deals with a whimsical privacy issue apart from the four torts, but most closely paralleling the public disclosure category of actions.

Time, Inc. v. Hill
385 U.S. 374 (1967)
Justice Brennan:

The question in this case is whether appellant, publisher of *Life* Magazine, was denied constitutional protections of speech and press by the application of the New York Civil Rights Law to award appellee damages on allegations that *Life* falsely reported that a new play portrayed an experience suffered by appellee and his family.

The article appeared in *Life* in February 1955. It was entitled "True Crime Inspires Tense Play," with the subtitle, "The ordeal of a family trapped by convicts gives Broadway a new thriller, '*The Desperate Hours*.'" The text of the article reads as follows:

> Three years ago Americans all over the country read about the desperate ordeal of the James Hill family, who were held prisoners in their home outside Philadelphia by three escaped convicts. Later they read about it in Joseph Hayes's novel, *The Desperate Hours*, inspired by the family's experience. Now they can see the story re-enacted in Hayes's Broadway play based on the book, and next year will see it in his movie, which has been filmed but is being held up until the play has a chance to pay off.
>
> The play, directed by Robert Montgomery and expertly acted, is a heart-stopping account of how a family rose to heroism in a crisis. *LIFE* photographed the play during its Philadelphia tryout, transported some of the actors to the actual house where the Hills were besieged.

The pictures on the ensuing two pages included an enactment of the son being "roughed up" by one of the convicts, entitled "brutish convict," a picture of the daughter biting the hand of a convict to make him drop a gun, entitled "daring daughter," and one of the father throwing his gun through the door after a "brave try" to save his family is foiled.[1]

The James Hill referred to in the article is the appellee. He and his wife and five children involuntarily became the subjects of a front-page news story after being held hostage by three escaped convicts in their suburban, Whitemarsh, Pennsylvania, home for 19 hours on September 11–12, 1952. The family was released unharmed. In an interview with newsmen after the convicts departed, appellee stressed that the convicts had treated the family courteously, had not molested them, and had not been at all violent. The convicts were thereafter apprehended in a widely publicized encounter with the police which resulted in the killing of two of the convicts. Shortly thereafter the family moved to Connecticut. The appellee discouraged all efforts to keep them in the public spotlight through magazine articles or appearances on television.

In the spring of 1953, Joseph Hayes' novel, *The Desperate Hours*, was published. The story depicted the experience of a family of four held hostage by three escaped convicts in the family's suburban home. But, unlike Hill's experience, the family of the story suffer violence at the hands of the convicts; the father and son are beaten and the daughter subjected to a verbal sexual insult. The book was made into a play, also entitled *The Desperate Hours*, and it is *Life*'s article about the play which is the subject of appellee's action. The complaint sought damages on allegations that the *Life* article was intended to, and did, give the impression that the play mirrored the Hill family's experience, which, to the knowledge of defendant "was false and untrue." Appellant's defense was that the article was "a subject of legitimate news interest." [Hill was awarded $30,000 in compensatory damages.]

In *New York Times v. Sullivan*, we held that the Constitution delimits a State's power to award damages for libel in actions brought by public officials against critics of their official conduct. Factual error, content defamatory of official reputation, or both, are insufficient for an award of damages for false statements unless actual malice—knowledge that the statements are false or in reckless disregard of the truth—is alleged and proved. We hold that the constitutional protections for speech and press preclude the application of the New York statute to redress false reports of matters of public interest in the absence of proof that the defendant published the report with knowledge of its falsity or in reckless disregard of the truth. The guarantees for speech and

---

1. The photo layout is available in PowerPoint at www.paulsiegelcommlaw.com; on the left-hand side (*Communication Law in America*), click on "Additional Images," then "Chapter 5," then "Additional Time v. Hill pictures," and "click to enlarge."

press are not the preserve of political expression or comment upon public affairs, essential as those are to healthy government. One need only pick up any newspaper or magazine to comprehend the vast range of published matter which exposes persons to public view, both private citizens and public officials. Exposure of the self to others in varying degrees is a concomitant of life in a civilized community. The risk of this exposure is an essential incident of life in a society which places a primary value on freedom of speech and of press.

We have no doubt that the subject of the *Life* article, the opening of a new play linked to an actual incident, is a matter of public interest. The line between the informing and the entertaining is too elusive for the protection of freedom of the press. Erroneous statement is no less inevitable in such a case than in the case of comment upon public affairs, and in both, if innocent or merely negligent, it must be protected if the freedoms of expression are to have the breathing space that they need to survive. We held in *New York Times* that calculated falsehood enjoyed no immunity in the case of alleged defamation of a public official concerning his official conduct. Similarly, calculated falsehood should enjoy no immunity in the situation here presented us. This is neither a libel action by a private individual nor a statutory action by a public official. Therefore, although the First Amendment principles pronounced in *New York Times* guide our conclusion, we reach that conclusion only by applying these principles in this discrete context.

Turning to the facts of the present case, the proofs reasonably would support either a jury finding of innocent or merely negligent misstatement by *Life*, or a finding that *Life* portrayed the play as a re-enactment of the Hill family's experience reckless of the truth or with actual knowledge that the portrayal was false.

Joseph Hayes, author of the book, also wrote the play. His story was not shaped by any single incident, but by several, including incidents which occurred in California, New York, and Detroit. [Still], the Hill family's experience "triggered" the writing of the book and the play.

The *Life* article was prepared at the direction and under the supervision of its entertainment editor (Prideaux), who learned of the production of the play from a news story. The play's director, Robert Montgomery, later suggested to him that its interesting stage setting would make the play a worthwhile subject for an article in *Life*. Hayes [told Prideaux] that an incident somewhat similar to the play had occurred in Philadelphia, and agreed to find out whether the former Hill residence would be available for the shooting of pictures for a *Life* article. Prideaux drove with Hayes to the former Hill residence to test its suitability for a picture story.

Prideaux's first draft made no mention of the Hill name except for the caption of one of the photographs. The text related that the play was a "somewhat fictionalized" account of the family's heroism in time of crisis. Prideaux's research assistant, whose task it was to check the draft for accuracy, put a question mark over the words "somewhat fictionalized." Prideaux testified that the question mark "must have been" brought to his attention, although he did not recollect having seen it. The draft was also brought before the copy editor, who, in the presence of Prideaux, made several changes in emphasis and substance. The first sentence was changed to focus on the Hill incident, using the family's name; the novel was said to have been "inspired" by that incident, and the play was referred to as a "re-enactment." The words "somewhat fictionalized" were deleted.

The jury might reasonably conclude from this evidence—particularly that the *New York Times* article was in the story file—that the copy editor deleted "somewhat fictionalized" after the research assistant questioned its accuracy, and that Prideaux admitted that he knew the play was "between a little bit and moderately fictionalized"—that *Life* knew the falsity of, or was reckless of the truth in, stating in the article that "the story re-enacted" the Hill family's experience. On the other hand, the jury might reasonably predicate a finding of innocent or only negligent misstatement on the testimony that a statement was made to Prideaux by the free-lance photographer that linked the play to an incident in Philadelphia, that the author Hayes cooperated in arranging for the availability of the former Hill home, and that Prideaux thought beyond doubt that the "heart and soul" of the play was the Hill incident.

We do not think, however, that the instructions confined the jury to a verdict of liability based on a finding that the statements in the article were made with knowledge of their falsity or in reckless disregard of the truth. The jury was instructed that liability could rest only on findings that (1) *Life* published the article, "not to disseminate news, but was using plaintiffs' names, in connection with a fictionalized episode as to plaintiffs' relationship to *The Desperate Hours*"; and that (2) the article was published to advertise the play or "for trade purposes." The court also instructed the jury that an award of punitive damages was justified if the jury found that the appellant falsely connected appellee to the play "knowingly or through failure to make a reasonable investigation," if you find "a reckless or wanton disregard of the plaintiffs' rights."

We [note] the marked contrast in the instructions on compensatory and punitive damages. The element of "knowingly" is mentioned only in the instruction that punitive damages must be supported by a finding that *Life* falsely connected the Hill family with the play "knowingly or through failure to make a reasonable investigation." Moreover, even as to punitive damages, the instruction that such damages were justified on the basis of "failure to make a reasonable investigation" is an instruction that proof of negligent misstatement is enough, and we have rejected the test of negligent misstatement as inadequate.

The requirement that the jury also find that the article was published "for trade purposes," as defined in the charge, cannot save the charge from constitutional infirmity. That books, newspapers, and magazines are published and sold for profit does not prevent them from being a form of expression whose liberty is safeguarded by the First Amendment.

The judgment of the Court of Appeals is set aside and the case is remanded for further proceedings not inconsistent with this opinion. It is so ordered.

POINTS FOR DISCUSSION

1. The main difference between libel and false light privacy cases is that, in the latter, plaintiffs need not prove that the falsehoods were defamatory. Presuming that Hill could prove the requisite degree of fault (the "actual malice" test from *New York Times v. Sullivan*), could the facts of *Time v. Hill* have produced a libel suit? Were the falsehoods defamatory?
2. The Court's holding, requiring application of the "actual malice" test to false light privacy cases, is limited to "false reports *of matters of public interest.*" This case involved a popular magazine—likely better known for its photography than for its prose—not a serious newspaper with a tight deadline. The article itself dealt with the arts (the opening of a play), not political events; and the Hill family's ordeal had been years ago. With that in mind, what likelihood is there that the Court would ever find an article that appears in a mainstream media outlet to be *not* "of public interest"?

▪ *Solano v. Playgirl, Inc.*

292 F.3d 1078 (9th Cir. 2002)
Judge Fisher:

The January 1999 issue of *Playgirl* magazine featured a cover photograph of actor José Solano, Jr., best known for his role as Manny Gutierrez on the syndicated television program *Baywatch*. Solano was shown shirtless and wearing his red lifeguard trunks, the uniform of his *Baywatch* character, under a heading reading: TV Guys. PRIMETIME'S SEXY YOUNG STARS EXPOSED. *Playgirl*, ostensibly focused on a female readership, typically contains nude photographs of men in various poses emphasizing their genitalia, including some showing them engaged in simulated sex acts. Although Solano, who did not pose for or give an interview to *Playgirl*, did not in fact appear nude in the magazine, he sued *Playgirl*, alleging it deliberately created the false impression that he did so, making it appear he was willing to degrade himself and endorse such a magazine.[2]

The district court granted *Playgirl* summary judgment. We reverse for a trial.

Because this case concerns the magazine cover, we describe it in some detail. As indicated above, Solano appeared bare-chested wearing his red trunks, dominating the cover. In the upper left corner was a red circle containing the words, "TV Guys," followed by the headline, "Primetime's Sexy Young Stars Exposed," which ran across the top of Solano's head. Immediately to the left of Solano's picture, the magazine proclaimed, "12 Sizzling Centerfolds Ready to Score With You." The "s" in "Centerfolds" was superimposed on Solano's right shoulder. Also placed to the left of Solano, running down the left margin, the cover touted "Countdown to Climax: Naughty Ways to Ring in the New Year," "Toyz in the Hood: The Best in Erotic Home Shopping" and "Bottoms Up: Hot Celebrity Buns." In the cover's lower right hand corner was the headline, "Baywatch's Best Body, José Solano."

Solano's sole appearance inside the magazine was on page 21, in a quarter-page, head-and-shoulders photograph showing him fully dressed in a tee shirt and sweater alongside a brief, quarter-page profile of the actor. Solano's profile included information about his *Baywatch* character, facts about his life before he began acting and a quote in which he says that with two younger brothers he strives to be a positive role model and hopes to encourage others to pursue their dreams. Significantly, *Playgirl* issues are displayed on newsstands packaged in plastic wrap to prevent potential customers from flipping through the pages to view the magazine's contents.

Solano filed suit alleging *Playgirl* invaded his privacy by portraying him in a false light. [*Editor's note*: Solano also made misappropriation claims, which have been deleted from this excerpt.] He claimed he was humiliated and embarrassed when he learned of the use of his photograph on the cover of *Playgirl* and that he suffered a decline in job offers, invitations to charity events and social contacts with others in the entertainment industry following the publication of the January 1999 issue.

---

2. The cover and inside photos are on my website. Go to www.paulsiegelcommlaw.com, and on the left side (*Communication Law in America*), click on "Images from Book," then "Chapter 5," where you can view "Solano cover" and "Solano actual."

Solano contends that there is a triable issue of fact regarding the falsity of the message conveyed by *Playgirl*. We agree. He contends that his bare-chested, three-quarter-length photograph alongside the suggestive headlines on the *Playgirl* cover created the false impression that readers could expect to find more photographs of him inside the magazine, nude, exposed in *Playgirl*'s typical sexually explicit and revealing mode of depicting its sexy male subjects. It is well-established that a defendant is liable for what is insinuated as well as for what is stated explicitly.

That Solano's profile inside the magazine was of a relatively innocent and nonsexual nature is of little significance. The profile appeared 21 pages away from the cover with plenty of graphic frontal male nudity to traverse before reaching "TV Guys" and Solano's tame profile.

Given the record before us, especially when we recall that the magazine is displayed for sale in plastic wrapping, making the cover the key to what a reader can expect to find inside the magazine, a jury reasonably could find that the *Playgirl* cover conveyed the message that Solano was not the wholesome person he claimed to be, that he was willing to or was washed up and had to sell himself naked to a women's sex magazine. To survive summary judgment Solano must, as a public figure, also establish by clear and convincing evidence that *Playgirl*'s editors knowingly or recklessly created this false impression. We now turn to the conflicting evidence regarding the existence of actual malice on the part of *Playgirl* editors in assembling the January 1999 issue.

Playgirl associate editor Theresa O'Rourke testified in her deposition that at an October 1998 meeting to discuss the January 1999 cover, *Playgirl* senior vice president Carmine Bellucci generally instructed the editorial staff to sex up the magazine to imply that there was more nudity in the magazine than actually was there. She stated that Bellucci wanted to "bang [readers] over the head with something like, 'hey, this is sexy young stars exposed' so that people are going to want to pick up the magazine more." According to O'Rourke, "we definitely weren't trying to be subtle, and we knew it." She stated that there had been discussion in the cover meetings that the cover layout implied Solano appeared nude in a centerfold inside the magazine. She said the "Primetime's Sexy Young Stars Exposed" headline specifically sparked debate at the meetings because "some of us did not feel like it was fair to do that." Editor-in-chief Claire Viguerie Harth testified that the magazine's intent with the headline was "to make a line that was sexy enough [that] people would be intrigued and want to look inside, but not to say something that the magazine was showing something that it didn't have."

Playgirl art director Joanne Chiaramonte emphasized that if the magazine had contained a nude photograph of Solano, the cover explicitly would have said so. She stated that she never thought readers would expect to see Solano in a centerfold photograph because the headline, "Baywatch's Best Body, José Solano," clearly referred to Solano's *presence* in the magazine. Additionally, she explained that exposed and nude are really two different things.

Associate art director Serena Spiezio disagreed. She testified that she thought it would be reasonable for a reader to expect to see Solano nude inside the magazine because it says "TV Guys" and "they're being exposed." And it's *Playgirl* Magazine. What *else* would they be exposing but their bodies?

O'Rourke also recalled that someone raised a concern about the "12 Sizzling Centerfolds: Ready to Score with You" headline because it occupied the space where the headline relating to the cover subject often is placed. She believed "someone's going to think that he's naked in there." O'Rourke said that Bellucci tended to "just blow off such comments and concerns." Bellucci agreed in his deposition that Solano was a "primetime sexy young star" as those words were used in the cover headline, but denied that the editors used Solano's photograph and the cover headlines falsely to imply that Solano appeared nude in the magazine.

The testimony of O'Rourke and Spiezio serve to prove that during the editorial process someone raised concerns about the use of Solano's photograph alongside the suggestive headlines; both Bellucci and Chiaramonte were aware of some staffers' concerns that the cover might falsely imply that Solano appeared nude inside the magazine. Given that awareness and the evidence that Bellucci wanted to "sex up" the magazine to imply nudity, plainly to promote magazine sales, a jury could conclude *Playgirl*'s editors knowingly or recklessly published the misleading cover. Such evidence is sufficient to satisfy the actual malice standard.

It is neither surprising nor fatal to Solano's case that there is conflicting, circumstantial evidence that *Playgirl* entertained serious doubt whether the magazine cover would create the false impression that Solano appeared nude inside the magazine. As we have yet to see a defendant who admits to entertaining serious subjective doubt about the authenticity of an article it published, we must be guided by circumstantial evidence. By examining the editors' actions we try to understand their motives.

The final element necessary to prove a case for false light is damages. *Playgirl* argues that Solano cannot prove any damages. Solano admitted in his deposition that he did not seek therapy or any other type of treatment from any medical professional, although he did seek spiritual counseling from his father, a minister. He testified to both personal and familial humiliation and embarrassment because of the publication of his picture in the magazine. He claimed that several possibilities for appearing on various television programs failed to materialize after the publication of the *Playgirl* issue, yet he was unable to provide evidence that any lost job was related to his appearance in the magazine. Solano's current and previous agent and previous manager all stated that no one ever has mentioned the *Playgirl* issue to them, especially in relation to a job for Solano. Solano also argues that his invitations to charity events declined after the publication of the *Playgirl* issue, but again he admitted that he could only speculate and had no proof that there is a connection between the two events.

Solano's testimony regarding his humiliation and embarrassment is sufficient to establish a genuine issue with respect to damages and precludes summary judgment. (We make no predictions about whether this evidence alone will suffice to sustain the damages element at trial.)

For the reasons stated, we reverse the district court's grant of summary judgment to *Playgirl* and remand for further proceedings.

POINTS FOR DISCUSSION

1. The court makes much of the fact that *Playgirl* is typically displayed at newsstands in a plastic wrapping, thus in this case preventing potential purchasers from seeing that Solano's actual appearance in the magazine was quite innocent. But those plastic wrappers are not used to tease, they are used to avoid criminal liability for making pornographic images too accessible to minors. Should such a prophylactic measure used by publishers to avoid one kind of legal liability open them up to other kinds of liability?
2. Do you think it was fair for the court to take into account the magazine's overall cover design, or should Judge Fisher have restricted himself only to those elements clearly referring to the Solano feature? What difference should it make, for example, that this particular issue also includes an article about sex toys (or "toyz")?

▪ *Neff v. Time, Inc.*

406 F. Supp. 858 (W.D. Pa. 1976)
Judge Marsh:

A complaint filed by John W. Neff, the plaintiff, against Time, Inc., the defendant, alleging that the defendant is the owner of a magazine known as *Sports Illustrated*, that in its issue of August 5, 1974, the defendant's magazine used Neff's picture without his prior knowledge and consent to illustrate an article entitled "A Strange Kind of Love"; that the photograph[3] shows Neff with the front zipper of his trousers completely opened implying that he is a "crazy, drunken slob," and combined with the title of the article, "a sexual deviate." Neff alleges that the unauthorized publication and circulation of his picture to illustrate the article invaded his right of privacy and subjected him to public ridicule and contempt.

The undenied facts contained in affidavits filed by defendant establish beyond peradventure that the picture was taken with Neff's knowledge and with his encouragement; that he knew he was being photographed by a photographer for *Sports Illustrated* and thereby impliedly consented to its publication.

The photograph was taken about 1:00 o'clock P.M. November 25, 1973, while Neff was present on a dugout with a group of fans prior to a professional football game at Cleveland between the Cleveland Browns and the Pittsburgh Steelers. The photographer was on the field intending to take pictures of the Steeler players as they entered the field from the dugout. Neff and the others were jumping up and down in full view of the fans in the stadium; they were waving Steeler banners and drinking beer; they all seemed to be slightly inebriated. One of the group asked the photographer for whom he was working and was told *Sports Illustrated*, whereupon the group began to act as if a television camera had been put on them; as the pictures were taken they began to react even more, screaming and howling and imploring the photographer to take more pictures. The more pictures taken of the group, the more they hammed it up.

During the period from July through December, 1973, this photographer took 7,200 pictures pursuant to his assignment to cover the Steelers. As part of his duty he edited the pictures and submitted one hundred to the magazine for selection by a committee of five employees. After several screenings of the thirty pictures of the group on the dugout, the committee selected Neff's picture with his fly open. Although Neff's fly was not open to the point of being revealing, the selection was deliberate and surely in utmost bad taste; subjectively, as to Neff, the published picture could have been embarrassing, humiliating and offensive to his sensibilities. Without doubt the magazine deliberately exhibited Neff in an embarrassing manner.

It appears that the pictures were taken to illustrate a book being written by one Blount about the Steeler fans, and three excerpts from the book were published in the magazine. Only three pictures, including Neff's, accompanied the

---

3. The photo can be seen at www.paulsiegelcommlaw.com. On the left side of the site (*Communication Law in America*), click on "Images from Book," then "Chapter 5," and finally on "Neff photo."

article of August 5, 1974. The title to this article "A Strange Kind of Love" could convey to some readers a derogatory connotation. Neff is not mentioned by name in the article; the Steeler-Cleveland game of November 1974 is not mentioned in the article; Neff's photograph was not selected on the basis of its relationship to that game. The caption appearing adjacent to the photograph reads: "In the fading autumn Sundays at Three Rivers, the fans joined the players in mean pro dreams." Three Rivers is the name of the stadium in Pittsburgh. Neff's photograph was selected because "it represented the typical Steeler fan: a rowdy, strong rooter, much behind his team, having a good time at the game," and "it fitted in perfectly with the text of the story."

It seems to us that art directors and editors should hesitate to deliberately publish a picture which most likely would be offensive and cause embarrassment to the subject when many other pictures of the same variety are available. Notwithstanding, the courts are not concerned with establishing canons of good taste for the press or the public.

The right of privacy is firmly established in Pennsylvania despite the fact that its perimeter is not yet clearly defined and its contours remain amorphous. In Pennsylvania, invasion of privacy is actionable under any one of four distinct, but coordinate, torts.

Plaintiff's claim is based on "appropriation of name or likeness" and "publicity given to private life." [An appropriation suit cannot stand] when a person's picture is used in a non-commercial article dealing with an accident, or the picture of a bystander at a political convention, or parade, or generally in the reporting of news. We think actions of excited fans at a football game are news as is a story about the fans of a professional football team. The fact that *Sports Illustrated* is a magazine published for profit does not constitute a "commercial appropriation of Neff's likeness." The fact that Neff was photographed in a public place for a newsworthy article entitles the defendant to the protection of the First Amendment.

[As to Neff's "publicity" action,] the article about Pittsburgh Steeler fans was of legitimate public interest; the football game in Cleveland was of legitimate public interest; Neff's picture was taken in a public place with his knowledge and with his encouragement; he was catapulted into the news by his own actions; nothing was falsified; a photograph taken at a public event which everyone present could see, with the knowledge and implied consent of the subject, is not a matter concerning a private fact. A factually accurate public disclosure is not tortious when connected with a newsworthy event even though offensive to ordinary sensibilities. The constitutional privilege protects all truthful publications relevant to matters of public interest.

Of course, we are concerned that Neff's picture was deliberately selected by an editorial committee from a number of similar pictures and segregated and published alone. If his picture had appeared as part of the general crowd scene of fans at a game, even though embarrassing, there would be no problem. Although we have some misgivings, it is our opinion that the publication of Neff's photograph taken with his active encouragement and participation, and with knowledge that the photographer was connected with a publication, even though taken without his express consent, is protected by the Constitution.

POINTS FOR DISCUSSION

1. Judge Marsh makes much of the fact that Neff and his friends were keenly aware of the *Sports Illustrated* photographer's presence. But what if Neff and company were acting drunk and rowdy only for their own pleasure, completely unaware that they were being photographed. Should the judgment be different?
2. Suppose that the offensive photo were more revealing, at least partially exposing Neff's genitalia. Would the added degree of offensiveness inherent in publishing such a photo in a popular magazine outweigh the publisher's First Amendment interests?

Holman v. Central Arkansas Broadcasting Company
610 F.2d 542 (8th Circ. 1979)
Judge Lay:

Summary judgment was granted defendants Central Arkansas Broadcasting Company, Inc. [and news reporter] Carl Connerton, in a suit brought by Marvin Holman for alleged invasion of Holman's right of privacy. We affirm.

On November 20, 1975, Holman and his wife were stopped on the highway at approximately 3:56 A.M., and taken to the Russellville, Arkansas police station. Holman was charged with the offense of driving while intoxicated, second offense, and using profane and abusive language; Mrs. Holman was charged with public drunkenness. Holman, an attorney, had formerly served as municipal judge.

Holman was allowed to privately confer with his retained counsel, Robert Hays Williams, at 4:30 A.M. in a private lounge. Williams later represented Holman at his trial in municipal court. Holman's young associate, an attorney named Roderick Weaver, came to the jail shortly after 5:30 A.M. to secure the release of Holman and his wife on bond. The police informed him they would not release the Holmans until 9:00 A.M. Upon his return he observed at least two persons who were not police officers, one of whom he later learned was Mr. Connerton, a news reporter. When he went to Holman's cell he noticed Connerton was in the cell block a short distance behind him and had a tape recorder in his hand. Weaver told Connerton not to record any conversation between himself and Holman. According to Weaver, Connerton appeared to walk away. At this time, Holman's wife was taken from her cell for fingerprinting and photographing. According to the affidavits of three police officers, Holman was hitting and banging on his cell door, hollering and cursing from the time of his arrest until his release at approximately 9:00 A.M. The police communications operator stated Holman became abusive and refused to cooperate when she tried to give him a gas chromatograph test. When placed in the holding cell, he started hollering, cussing and screaming.

No credible evidence appears in the record that Connerton recorded any confidential information. It is obvious that the words broadcast could be heard by others in the police station. Holman argues the Fourth and Sixth Amendments create a "zone" of privacy which was violated by Connerton's recording and publishing of Holman's statements. The simple answer to this contention is that the boisterous complaints which were recorded were not made with the expectation of privacy or confidentiality. Neither Weaver nor Holman asserts confidential legal advice was given. The evidence demonstrates unequivocally that Holman was simply complaining loudly while Weaver tried to quiet him down in order to arrange his release.

Even assuming the police called the news reporter to the station and allowed him to enter the cell block, no right to privacy is invaded when state officials allow or facilitate publication of an official act such as an arrest. Although Weaver asked Connerton not to record Holman's statements, they were made loudly and in such a manner as to attract attention. Connerton could not be prevented from reporting the statements he could so easily overhear aurally; use of a device to record them cannot create a claim for invasion of privacy when one would not otherwise exist.

We recognize the important and vital right to private consultation that is basic to effective representation by counsel flows from the confidential relationship between an accused and his counsel. However, the undisputed facts distinguish this case from those in which that right is protected. Here there was no attempt to record or overhear statements made with an expectation of privacy. Holman's boisterous complaints were obviously not intended for Weaver's ears alone. The tape demonstrates this.

POINTS FOR DISCUSSION

1. The reporter, we learn here, "appeared to walk away" when instructed by Holman's attorney not to record his conversations with his client. Might the case have come out differently if the reporter had explicitly *promised* not to record the conversation?
2. As you likely know, conversations between attorney and client generally enjoy a great deal of confidentiality in the U.S. legal system. Attorneys can almost never be compelled to testify as to what their clients have told them, and the American Bar Association's code of ethics makes clear that attorneys must keep to themselves that which they learn from their clients. Should the client's loudness (because he is drunk and presumably not thinking clearly) be sufficient to waive any rights to confidentiality?

Boring v. Google, Inc.
362 F. Appx. 273 (3rd Cir. 2010)
Judge Jordan:

On April 2, 2008, Aaron C. Boring and Christine Boring commenced an action in the Court of Common Pleas of Allegheny County, Pennsylvania against Google, Inc., asserting claims for invasion of privacy, trespass, injunctive relief, negligence, and conversion. The Borings' claims arise from Google's "Street View" program, a feature on Google Maps that offers free access on the Internet to panoramic, navigable views of streets in and around major cities across the United States. To create the Street View program, representatives of Google attach panoramic digital cameras to passenger cars and drive around cities photographing the areas along the street. Google allows individuals to report and request the removal of inappropriate images that they find on Street View.

The Borings, who live on a private road in Pittsburgh, discovered that Google had taken colored imagery of their residence, including the swimming pool, from a vehicle in their residence driveway months earlier without obtaining any privacy waiver or authorization. They allege that their road is clearly marked with a "Private Road, No Trespassing" sign and they contend that, in driving up their road to take photographs for Street View and in making those photographs available to the public, Google "disregarded their privacy interest."

The District Court granted Google's motion to dismiss as to all of the Borings' claims. The Court dismissed the invasion of privacy claim because the

Borings were unable to show that Google's conduct was highly offensive to a person of ordinary sensibilities. Pennsylvania law recognizes four torts under the umbrella of invasion of privacy: [1] unreasonable intrusion upon the seclusion of another; [2] appropriation of another's name or likeness; [3] unreasonable publicity given to another's private life; and [4] publicity that unreasonably places the other in a false light before the public.

The District Court treated the Borings' complaint as asserting claims for both intrusion upon seclusion and publicity to private life, and it held that the complaint failed to state a claim for either, focusing on the lack of facts in the complaint to support a conclusion that the Street View images would be highly offensive to a reasonable person.

To state a claim for intrusion upon seclusion, plaintiffs must allege conduct demonstrating "an intentional intrusion upon the seclusion of their private concerns which was substantial and highly offensive to a reasonable person, and aver sufficient facts to establish that the information disclosed would have caused mental suffering, shame or humiliation to a person of ordinary sensibilities." Publication is not an element of the claim, and thus we must examine the harm caused by the intrusion itself.

No person of ordinary sensibilities would be shamed, humiliated, or have suffered mentally as a result of a vehicle entering into his or her ungated driveway and photographing the view from there. Indeed, the privacy allegedly intruded upon was the external view of the Borings' house, garage, and pool—a view that would be seen by any person who entered onto their driveway, including a visitor or a delivery man. Thus, what really seems to be at the heart of the complaint is not Google's fleeting presence in the driveway, but the photographic image captured at that time. The existence of that image, though, does not in itself rise to the level of an intrusion that could reasonably be called highly offensive. Significantly, the Borings do not allege that they themselves were viewed inside their home, which is a relevant factor in analyzing intrusion upon seclusion claims.

Google spends much time arguing that the Borings' driveway was not actually a private place sufficient to sustain an invasion of privacy claim. It notes that numerous courts have found no intrusion upon seclusion based upon a view that can be seen from the outside of the home, and points to the fact that images of the Borings' home were already available on the Internet. Because we conclude that the alleged conduct would not be highly offensive to a person of ordinary sensibilities, we need not decide whether the Borings' driveway was a "private place" for purposes of an invasion of privacy claim.

In sum, accepting the Borings' allegations as true, their claim for intrusion upon seclusion fails as a matter of law, because the alleged conduct would not be highly offensive to a person of ordinary sensibilities.

To state a claim for publicity given to private life, a plaintiff must allege that the matter publicized is "(1) publicity, given to (2) private facts, (3) which would be highly offensive to a reasonable person, and (4) is not of legitimate concern to the public." For the reasons just described with respect to the intrusion upon seclusion claim, we agree with the District Court that the Borings have failed to allege facts sufficient to establish the third element of a publicity to private life claim, i.e., that the publicity would be highly offensive to a reasonable person. It is therefore unnecessary to address the other three prongs. (We note, however, that the facts revealed may not actually be "private facts," as required by prong 2, because the Borings' property allegedly is or recently was available to public view by virtue of tax records and maps on other Internet sites.)

Accepting the Borings' allegations as true, their claim for publicity given to private life fails as a matter of law, because the alleged conduct would not be highly offensive to a person of ordinary sensibilities.

For the foregoing reasons, we will affirm the District Court's grant of Google's motion to dismiss the Borings' claims for invasion of privacy.

POINTS FOR DISCUSSION

1. The Borings also claimed that Google's van trespassed on their private land. (I did not reprint that part of the case here, in that simple trespass is not really a communication law issue.) Google denies the charge. Suppose it turns out that Google did trespass on the Borings' lot. Should the court's view of the privacy claims be affected by such a conclusion?
2. The court makes much of the fact that the cat is already out of the bag, that even without Google, images of our property are already easily available on the Internet. Suppose this case came about earlier in the history of cyberspace, and that Google Maps would be the very first such alleged intrusion on our sense of privacy or seclusion. Should that make a difference to the outcome of the case?

Zacchini v. Scripps-Howard Broadcasting Company
433 U.S. 562 (1977)
Justice White:

Petitioner, Hugo Zacchini, is an entertainer. He performs a "human cannonball" act in which he is shot from a cannon into a net some 200 feet away.[4] Each performance occupies some 15 seconds. In August and September 1972, petitioner was engaged to perform his act on a regular basis at the Geauga County Fair in Burton, Ohio. Members of the public attending the fair were not charged a separate admission fee to observe his act.

On August 30, a free-lance reporter for Scripps-Howard Broadcasting Co., the operator of a television broadcasting station, attended the fair. He carried a small movie camera. Petitioner noticed the reporter and asked him not to film the performance. The reporter did not do so on that day; but on the instructions of the producer of his daily newscast, returned the following day and videotaped the entire act. This film clip, approximately 15 seconds in length, was shown on the 11 o'clock news program that night, together with favorable commentary ("The great Zacchini is about the only human cannonball around, these days. Although it's not a long act, it's a thriller, and you really need to see it in person to appreciate it.")

Petitioner then brought this action for damages, alleging that respondent showed and commercialized the film of his act without his consent, and that such conduct was an unlawful appropriation of plaintiff's professional property. Respondent answered and moved for summary judgment, which was granted by the trial court.

The Court of Appeals of Ohio reversed. The Supreme Court of Ohio [reinstated the granting of summary judgment]. We granted certiorari to consider whether the First and Fourteenth Amendments immunized respondent from damages for its alleged infringement of petitioner's state-law right of publicity. Insofar as the Ohio Supreme Court held that the First and Fourteenth Amendments of the United States Constitution required judgment for respondent, we reverse the judgment of that court.

The Ohio Supreme Court held that respondent is constitutionally privileged to include in its newscasts matters of public interest that would otherwise be

---

4. A photo of Mr. Zacchini in action is there for you at www.paulsiegelcommlaw.com. On the left side of the site (*Communication Law in America*), click on "Images from Book," then "Chapter 5," and finally on "Human Cannonball."

protected by the right of publicity, absent an intent to injure or to appropriate for some nonprivileged purpose. If under this standard respondent had merely reported that petitioner was performing at the fair and described or commented on his act, with or without showing his picture on television, we would have a very different case. But petitioner is not contending that his appearance at the fair and his performance could not be reported by the press as newsworthy items. His complaint is that respondent filmed his entire act and displayed that film on television for the public to see and enjoy. This, he claimed, was an appropriation of his professional property.

The Ohio Supreme Court held that the challenged invasion was privileged, that the press "must be accorded broad latitude in its choice of how much it presents of each story or incident, and of the emphasis to be given to such presentation." Under this view, respondent was thus constitutionally free to film and display petitioner's entire act. The Ohio Supreme Court relied heavily on *Time, Inc. v. Hill*, but that case does not mandate a media privilege to televise a performer's entire act without his consent. It is also abundantly clear that *Time, Inc. v. Hill*, [a "false light" privacy case], did not involve a performer, a person with a name having commercial value, or any claim to a "right of publicity."

The differences between these two torts are important. First, the State's interests in providing a cause of action in each instance are different. The interest protected in permitting recovery for placing the plaintiff in a false light is clearly that of reputation, with the same overtones of mental distress as in defamation. By contrast, the State's interest in permitting a right of publicity is in protecting the proprietary interest of the individual in his act in part to encourage such entertainment.

Second, the two torts differ in the degree to which they intrude on dissemination of information to the public. In "false light" cases the only way to protect the interests involved is to attempt to minimize publication of the damaging matter, while in "right of publicity" cases the only question is who gets to do the publishing. An entertainer such as petitioner usually has no objection to the widespread publication of his act as long as he gets the commercial benefit of such publication. Indeed, in the present case petitioner did not seek to enjoin the broadcast of his act; he simply sought compensation for the broadcast in the form of damages.

Wherever the line in particular situations is to be drawn between media reports that are protected and those that are not, we are quite sure that the First and Fourteenth Amendments do not immunize the media when they broadcast a performer's entire act without his consent. The Constitution no more prevents a State from requiring respondent to compensate petitioner for broadcasting his act on television than it would privilege respondent to film and broadcast a copyrighted dramatic work without liability to the copyright owner.

The broadcast of a film of petitioner's entire act poses a substantial threat to the economic value of that performance. [Zacchini's] act is the product of his own talents and energy, the end result of much time, effort, and expense. Much of its economic value lies in the right of exclusive control over the publicity given to his performance; if the public can see the act free on television, it will be less willing to pay to see it at the fair. The effect of a public broadcast of the performance is similar to preventing petitioner from charging an admission fee. Moreover, the broadcast of petitioner's entire performance, unlike the unauthorized use of another's name for purposes of trade or the incidental use of a name or picture by the press, goes to the heart of petitioner's ability to earn a living as an entertainer.

Of course, [there is more involved here] than a desire to compensate the performer for the time and effort invested in his act; the protection provides an economic incentive for him to make the investment required to produce a performance of interest to the public. This same consideration underlies the patent and copyright laws long enforced by this Court.

There is no doubt that entertainment, as well as news, enjoys First Amendment protection. It is also true that entertainment itself can be important news. But it is important to note that neither the public nor respondent will be deprived of the benefit of petitioner's performance as long as his commercial stake in his act is appropriately recognized. Petitioner does not seek to enjoin the broadcast of his performance; he simply wants to be paid for it. Respondent knew that petitioner objected to televising his act but nevertheless displayed the entire film. We conclude that although the State of Ohio may as a matter of its own law privilege the press in the circumstances of this case, the First and Fourteenth Amendments do not require it to do so.

Reversed.

POINTS FOR DISCUSSION

1. Justice White's opinion makes much of the fact that the TV station broadcast Zacchini's "entire act." But did it really? Do not carnival stunts such as this one usually begin with some fanfare (introduction of the performer, description of the uniqueness and danger of that which is to come, perhaps a last-minute check of the equipment) designed to heighten the audience's anticipation? If Zacchini's "act" included such moments, which were not broadcast, is doubt cast on White's analysis?

2. Was Zacchini really hurt by the station's conduct? Note that the commentator went out of his way to advise viewers that to really appreciate the act, they should see it *in person*. Is it not at least, therefore, arguable that the TV story increased the live attendance?

▪ *Owasso Independent School District v. Falvo*
534 U.S. 426 (2002)
Justice Kennedy:

Teachers sometimes ask students to score each other's tests, papers, and assignments as the teacher explains the correct answers to the entire class. Respondent contends this practice, which the parties refer to as peer grading, violates the Family Educational Rights and Privacy Act of 1974 (FERPA). We took this case to resolve the issue.

Under FERPA, schools and educational agencies receiving federal financial assistance must comply with certain conditions. One condition specified in the Act is that sensitive information about students may not be released without parental consent. The Act states that federal funds are to be withheld from school districts that have "a policy or practice of permitting the release of education records (or personally identifiable information contained therein . . .) of students without the written consent of their parents." The phrase "education records" is defined, under the Act, as "records, files, documents, and other materials" containing information directly related to a student, which "are maintained by an educational agency or institution or by a person acting for such agency or institution." The definition of education records contains an exception for "records of instructional, supervisory, and administrative personnel . . . which are in the sole possession of the maker thereof and which are not accessible or revealed to any other person except a substitute." The precise question for us is whether peer-graded classroom work and assignments are education records.

Three of respondent Kristja J. Falvo's children are enrolled in Owasso Independent School District No. I-011, in a suburb of Tulsa, Oklahoma. The children's teachers, like many teachers in this country, use peer grading. In a typical case, the students exchange papers with each other and score them according to the teacher's instructions, then return the work to the student who prepared it. The teacher may ask the students to report their own scores. In this case it appears the student could either call out the score or walk to the teacher's desk and reveal it in confidence, though by that stage, of course, the score was known at least to the one other student who did the grading. Both the grading and the system of calling out the scores are in contention here.

Respondent claimed the peer grading embarrassed her children. She asked the school district to adopt a uniform policy banning peer grading and requiring teachers either to grade assignments themselves or at least to forbid students from grading papers other than their own. The school district declined to do so, and respondent brought a class action against the school district, Superintendent Dale Johnson, Assistant Superintendent Lynn Johnson, and Principal Rick Thomas. Respondent alleged the school district's grading policy violated FERPA and other laws not relevant here. The United States District Court for the Northern District of Oklahoma granted summary judgment in favor of the school district's position. The court held that grades put on papers by another student are not, at that stage, records "maintained by an educational agency or institution or by a person acting for such agency or institution," and thus do not constitute "education records" under the Act. On this reasoning it ruled that peer grading does not violate FERPA.

The Court of Appeals for the Tenth Circuit reversed, holding that peer grading violates the Act. The grades marked by students on each other's work, it held, are education records protected by the statute, so the very act of grading was an impermissible release of the information to the student grader. We granted certiorari to decide whether peer grading violates FERPA. Finding no violation of the Act, we reverse.

The parties appear to agree that if an assignment becomes an education record the moment a peer grades it, then the grading, or at least the practice of asking students to call out their grades in class, would be an impermissible release of the records. Without deciding the point, we assume for the purposes of our analysis that they are correct. The parties disagree, however, whether peer-graded assignments constitute education records at all. The papers do contain information directly related to a student, but they are records under the Act only when and if they "are maintained by an educational agency or institution or by a person acting for such agency or institution."

Petitioners contend the definition covers only institutional records—namely, those materials retained in a permanent file as a matter of course. They argue that records "maintained by an educational agency or institution" generally would include final course grades, student grade point averages, standardized test scores, attendance records, counseling records, and records of disciplinary actions—but not student homework or classroom work. Respondent, adopting the reasoning of the Court of Appeals, contends student-graded assignments fall within the definition of education records. That definition contains an exception for "records of instructional, supervisory, and administrative personnel ... which are in the sole possession of the maker thereof and which are not accessible or revealed to any other person except a substitute." The Court of Appeals reasoned that if grade books are not education records, then it would have been unnecessary for Congress to enact the exception. Grade books and the grades within, the court concluded, are "maintained" by a teacher and so are covered by FERPA. The court recognized that teachers do not maintain the grades on individual student assignments until they have recorded the result in the grade books. It reasoned, however, that if Congress forbids teachers to disclose students' grades once written in a grade book, it makes no sense to permit the disclosure immediately beforehand. The court thus held that student graders maintain the grades until they are reported to the teacher.

The Court of Appeals' logic does not withstand scrutiny. Its interpretation, furthermore, would effect a drastic alteration of the existing allocation of responsibilities between States and the National Government in the operation of the Nation's schools. We would hesitate before interpreting the statute to effect such a substantial change in the balance of federalism unless that is the manifest purpose of the legislation. This principle guides our decision.

Two statutory indicators tell us that the Court of Appeals erred in concluding that an assignment satisfies the definition of education records as soon as it is graded by another student. First, the student papers are not, at that stage, "maintained" within the meaning of [the Act]. The ordinary meaning of the word "maintain" is "to keep in existence or continuance; preserve; retain." Even assuming the teacher's grade book is an education record—a point the parties contest and one we do not decide here—the score on a student-graded assignment is not "contained therein," until the teacher records it. The teacher does not maintain the grade while students correct their peers' assignments or call out their own marks. Nor do the student graders maintain the grades within the meaning of [the Act]. The word "maintain" suggests FERPA records will be kept in a filing cabinet in a records room at the school or on a permanent secure database, perhaps even after the student is no longer enrolled. The student graders only handle assignments for a few moments as the teacher calls out the answers. It is fanciful to say they maintain the papers in the same way the registrar maintains a student's folder in a permanent file.

The Court of Appeals was further mistaken in concluding that each student grader is "a person acting for" an educational institution. The phrase "acting for" connotes agents of the school, such as teachers, administrators, and other school employees. Just as it does not accord with our usual understanding to say students are "acting for" an educational institution when they follow their teacher's direction to take a quiz, it is equally awkward to say students are "acting for" an educational institution when they follow their teacher's direction to score it. Correcting a classmate's work can be as much a part of the assignment as taking the test itself. It is a way to teach material again in a new context, and it helps show students how to assist and respect fellow pupils. By explaining the answers to the class as the students correct the papers, the teacher not only reinforces the lesson but also discovers whether the students have understood the material and are ready to move on. We do not think FERPA prohibits these educational techniques. We also must not lose sight of the fact that the phrase "by a person acting for [an educational] institution" modifies "maintain." Even if one were to agree students are acting for the teacher when they correct the assignment, that is different from saying they are acting for the educational institution in maintaining it.

Other sections of the statute support our interpretation. It is a fundamental canon of statutory construction that the words of a statute must be read in their context and with a view to their place in the overall statutory scheme. FERPA, for example, requires educational institutions to "maintain a record, kept with the education records of each student." This record must list those who have requested access to a student's education records and their reasons for doing so. The record of access "shall be available only to parents, [and] to the school official and his assistants who are responsible for the custody of such records."

Under the Court of Appeals' broad interpretation of education records, every teacher would have an obligation to keep a separate record of access for each student's assignments. Indeed, by that court's logic, even students who grade their own papers would bear the burden of maintaining records of access until they turned in the assignments. We doubt Congress would have imposed such a weighty administrative burden on every teacher, and certainly it would not have extended the mandate to students.

Also FERPA requires "a record" of access for each pupil. This single record must be kept "with the education records." This suggests Congress contemplated that education records would be kept in one place with a single record of access. By describing a "school official" and "his assistants" as the personnel responsible for the custody of the records, FERPA implies that education records are institutional records kept by a single central custodian, such as a registrar, not individual assignments handled by many student graders in their separate classrooms.

FERPA also requires recipients of federal funds to provide parents with a hearing at which they may contest the accuracy of their child's education records. The hearings must be conducted "in accordance with regulations of the Secretary," which in turn require adjudication by a disinterested official and the opportunity for parents to be represented by an attorney. It is doubtful Congress would have provided parents with this elaborate procedural machinery to challenge the accuracy of the grade on every spelling test and art project the child completes.

Respondent's construction of the term "education records" to cover student homework or classroom work would impose substantial burdens on teachers across the country. It would force all instructors to take time, which otherwise could be spent teaching and in preparation, to correct an assortment of daily student assignments. Respondent's view would make it much more difficult for teachers to give students immediate guidance. The interpretation respondent urges would force teachers to abandon other customary practices, such as group grading of team assignments. Indeed, the logical consequences of respondent's view are all but unbounded. At argument, counsel for respondent seemed to agree that if a teacher in any of the thousands of covered classrooms in the Nation puts a happy face, a gold star, or a disapproving remark on a classroom assignment, federal law does not allow other students to see it.

We doubt Congress meant to intervene in this drastic fashion with traditional state functions. Under the Court of Appeals' interpretation of FERPA, the federal power would exercise minute control over specific teaching methods and instructional dynamics in classrooms throughout the country. The Congress is not likely to have mandated this result, and we do not interpret the statute to require it.

For these reasons, even assuming a teacher's grade book is an education record, the Court of Appeals erred, for in all events the grades on students' papers would not be covered under FERPA at least until the teacher has collected them and recorded them in his or her grade book. We limit our holding to this narrow point, and do not decide the broader question whether the grades on individual student assignments, once they are turned in to teachers, are protected by the Act.

The judgment of the Court of Appeals is reversed, and the case is remanded for further proceedings consistent with this opinion.

POINTS FOR DISCUSSION

1. Wholly apart from the provisions of the federal law at issue in this case, do you think that parents should have *any* legal recourse against the perceived privacy invasions inherent in peer grading? Peer grading is almost never used in higher educational settings. Is this a function of enhanced respect for adult students' privacy interests, or to the belief (cited, if not explicitly

embraced, by the Court) that peer grading in the K–12 context carries its own pedagogic value, that it reinforces the day's lesson?

2. The Court sidesteps the issue of whether teachers' grade books are "educational records," as defined by FERPA. Where would you come down on this definitional issue?

6

Copyright and Trademark

The constitutional basis for federal copyright law is found in Article I, Section 8, which tells Congress that it may create laws to protect "for limited times to authors . . . the exclusive right to their respective writings and discoveries." Under current law, individuals who create literary, musical, or similar works will enjoy the exclusive right to profit from their creations throughout their lives, after which their heirs may inherit that protection for an additional seventy years. In our first case, *Eldred v. Ashcroft*, unsuccessful litigants challenged Congress's right to extend the duration of copyright yet again.

Not every taking of another's work is an actionable infringement. Section 107 of the Copyright Act, the text of which you likely have seen reproduced above self-service copy machines at commercial shops such as Kinko's, seeks to establish a balance between the interests of the original author and those who wish to comment on, or otherwise build on, the original. One often-litigated issue has been the special role of the parodist in the context of fair use analysis. The Supreme Court's 1994 decision in *Campbell v. Acuff-Rose Music* tells us what it means to be a parodist, and *Bourne Company v. Twentieth Century Fox Corporation* is a more recent application of copyright law to parody. Also within this grouping, *ProtectMarriage.com v. Courage Campaign* shows us that the parody defense is available in trademark cases, too.

One need not produce a parody to be protected by the Fair Use doctrine. The lesson of cases such as *Tillman v. New Line Cinema Corporation* and *The Sheldon Abend Revocable Trust v. Spielberg* is that storytelling often involves highly predictable elements, the copying of which might not be actionable.

▪ *Eldred v. Ashcroft*
537 U.S. 186 (2003)
Justice Ginsburg:

This case concerns the authority the Constitution assigns to Congress to prescribe the duration of copyrights. The Copyright and Patent Clause of the

Constitution provides as to copyrights: "Congress shall have Power . . . to promote the Progress of Science . . . by securing [to Authors] for limited Times . . . the exclusive Right to their . . . Writings." In 1998, in the measure here under inspection [The Copyright Term Extension Act, or CTEA], Congress enlarged the duration of copyrights by 20 years. As in the case of prior extensions, principally in 1831, 1909, and 1976, Congress provided for application of the enlarged terms to existing and future copyrights alike.

Petitioners are individuals and businesses whose products or services build on copyrighted works that have gone into the public domain. They seek a determination that the CTEA fails constitutional review under both the Copyright Clause's "limited Times" prescription and the First Amendment's free speech guarantee. Under the 1976 Copyright Act, copyright protection generally lasted from the work's creation until 50 years after the author's death. Under the CTEA, most copyrights now run from creation until 70 years after the author's death. Petitioners do not challenge the "life-plus-70-years" time span itself. "Whether 50 years is enough, or 70 years too much," they acknowledge, "is not a judgment meet for this Court." Congress went awry, petitioners maintain, not with respect to newly created works, but in enlarging the term for published works with existing copyrights. The "limited Time" in effect when a copyright is secured, petitioners urge, becomes the constitutional boundary, a clear line beyond the power of Congress to extend. As to the First Amendment, petitioners contend that the CTEA is a content-neutral regulation of speech that fails inspection under the heightened judicial scrutiny appropriate for such regulations.

We evaluate petitioners' challenge to the constitutionality of the CTEA against the backdrop of Congress' previous exercises of its authority under the Copyright Clause. The Nation's first copyright statute, enacted in 1790, provided a federal copyright term of 14 years from the date of publication, renewable for an additional 14 years if the author survived the first term. The 1790 Act's renewable 14-year term applied to existing works (*i.e.*, works already published and works created but not yet published) and future works alike. Congress expanded the federal copyright term to 42 years in 1831 (28 years from publication, renewable for an additional 14 years), and to 56 years in 1909 (28 years from publication, renewable for an additional 28 years). Both times, Congress applied the new copyright term to existing and future works.

In 1976, Congress altered the method for computing federal copyright terms. For works created by identified natural persons, the 1976 Act provided that federal copyright protection would run from the work's creation, not—as in the 1790, 1831, and 1909 Acts—its publication; protection would last until 50 years after the author's death. In these respects, the 1976 Act aligned United

States copyright terms with the then-dominant international standard adopted under the Berne Convention for the Protection of Literary and Artistic Works. For anonymous works, pseudonymous works, and works made for hire, the 1976 Act provided a term of 75 years from publication or 100 years from creation, whichever expired first. These new copyright terms, the 1976 Act instructed, governed all works not published by its effective date of January 1, 1978, regardless of when the works were created. For published works with existing copyrights as of that date, the 1976 Act granted a copyright term of 75 years from the date of publication, a 19-year increase over the 56-year term applicable under the 1909 Act.

The measure at issue here, the CTEA, installed the fourth major duration extension of federal copyrights. Retaining the general structure of the 1976 Act, the CTEA enlarges the terms of all existing and future copyrights by 20 years. For works created by identified natural persons, the term now lasts from creation until 70 years after the author's death. This standard harmonizes the baseline United States copyright term with the term adopted by the European Union in 1993. For anonymous works, pseudonymous works, and works made for hire, the term is 95 years from publication or 120 years from creation, whichever expires first. In common with the 1831, 1909, and 1976 Acts, the CTEA's new terms apply to both future and existing copyrights.

Petitioners' suit challenges the CTEA's constitutionality under both the Copyright Clause and the First Amendment. On cross-motions for judgment on the pleadings, the District Court entered judgment for the Attorney General (respondent here). The Court of Appeals for the District of Columbia Circuit affirmed. We granted certiorari to address two questions: whether the CTEA's extension of existing copyrights exceeds Congress' power under the Copyright Clause; and whether the CTEA's extension of existing and future copyrights violates the First Amendment. We now answer those two questions in the negative and affirm.

We address first the determination of the courts below that Congress has authority under the Copyright Clause to extend the terms of existing copyrights. Text, history, and precedent, we conclude, confirm that the Copyright Clause empowers Congress to prescribe "limited Times" for copyright protection and to secure the same level and duration of protection for all copyright holders, present and future. The CTEA's baseline term of life plus 70 years, petitioners concede, qualifies as a "limited Time" as applied to future copyrights. Petitioners contend, however, that existing copyrights extended to endure for that same term are not "limited." Petitioners' argument essentially reads into the text of the Copyright Clause the command that a time prescription, once set, becomes forever "fixed" or "inalterable." The word "limited," however, does not convey a meaning so constricted. At the time of the Framing, that word meant what it means today: "confined within certain bounds," "restrained," or "circumscribed." Thus understood, a time span appropriately "limited" as applied to future copyrights does not automatically cease to be "limited" when applied to existing copyrights.

History reveals an unbroken congressional practice of granting to authors of works with existing copyrights the benefit of term extensions so that all under copyright protection will be governed evenhandedly under the same regime. As earlier recounted, the First Congress accorded the protections of the Nation's first federal copyright statute to existing and future works alike. Since then, Congress has regularly applied duration extensions to both existing and future copyrights.

Because the Clause empowering Congress to confer copyrights also authorizes patents, congressional practice with respect to patents informs our inquiry. We count it significant that early Congresses extended the duration of numerous individual patents as well as copyrights.

The courts saw no "limited Times" impediment to such extensions; renewed or extended terms were upheld in the early days, for example, by Chief Justice Marshall and Justice Story sitting as circuit justices. Further, although prior to the instant case this Court did not have occasion to decide whether extending the duration of existing copyrights complies with the "limited Times" prescription, the Court has found no constitutional barrier to the legislative expansion of existing patents. Congress' consistent historical practice of applying newly enacted copyright terms to future and existing copyrights reflects a judgment that the author of yesterday's work should not get a lesser reward than the author of tomorrow's work just because Congress passed a statute lengthening the term today. The CTEA follows this historical practice by keeping the duration provisions of the 1976 Act largely in place and simply adding 20 years to each of them. Guided by text, history, and precedent, we cannot agree with petitioners' submission that extending the duration of existing copyrights is categorically beyond Congress' authority under the Copyright Clause.

Satisfied that the CTEA complies with the "limited Times" prescription, we turn now to whether it is a rational exercise of the legislative authority conferred by the Copyright Clause. On that point, we defer substantially to Congress. The CTEA reflects judgments of a kind Congress typically makes, judgments we cannot dismiss as outside the Legislature's domain.

A key factor in the CTEA's passage was a 1993 European Union (EU) directive instructing EU members to establish a copyright term of life plus 70 years. Consistent with the Berne Convention, the EU directed its members to deny this longer term to the works of any non-EU country whose laws did not secure the same extended term. By extending the baseline United States copyright term to life plus 70 years, Congress sought to ensure that American authors would receive the same copyright protection in Europe as their European counterparts. The CTEA may also provide greater incentive for American and other authors to create and disseminate their work in the United States. Matching the level of copyright protection in the United States to that in the EU can ensure stronger protection for U.S. works abroad and avoid competitive disadvantages vis-à-vis foreign rightholders. The United States could not play a leadership role in the give-and-take evolution of the international copyright system, indeed it would lose all flexibility, if the only way to promote the progress of science were to provide incentives to create new works.

In addition to international concerns, Congress passed the CTEA in light of demographic, economic, and technological changes, and rationally credited projections that longer terms would encourage copyright holders to invest in the restoration and public distribution of their works. Members of Congress expressed the view that, as a result of increases in human longevity and in parents' average age when their children are born, the pre-CTEA term did not adequately secure the right to profit from licensing one's work during one's lifetime and to take pride and comfort in knowing that one's children—and perhaps their children—might also benefit from one's posthumous popularity.

In sum, we find that the CTEA is a rational enactment; we are not at liberty to second-guess congressional determinations and policy judgments of this order, however debatable or arguably unwise they may be. Accordingly, we cannot conclude that the CTEA is an impermissible exercise of Congress' power under the Copyright Clause.

Petitioners' Copyright Clause arguments rely on several novel readings of the Clause. We next address these arguments and explain why we find them unpersuasive.

Petitioners contend that even if the CTEA's 20-year term extension is literally a "limited Time," permitting Congress to extend existing copyrights allows it to evade the "limited Times" constraint by creating effectively perpetual copyrights through repeated extensions. We disagree.

As the Court of Appeals observed, a regime of perpetual copyrights "clearly is not the situation before us." Nothing before this Court warrants construction of the CTEA's 20-year term extension as a congressional attempt to evade or override the "limited Times" constraint.

Critically, we again emphasize, petitioners fail to show how the CTEA crosses a constitutionally significant threshold with respect to "limited Times" that the 1831, 1909, and 1976 Acts did not. Those earlier Acts did not create perpetual copyrights, and neither does the CTEA.

Petitioners advance a series of arguments all premised on the proposition that Congress may not extend an existing copyright absent new consideration from the author. They pursue this main theme under three headings. Petitioners contend that the CTEA's extension of existing copyrights (1) overlooks the requirement of "originality," (2) fails to "promote the Progress of Science," and (3) ignores copyright's *quid pro quo*. Petitioners' "originality" argument draws on *Feist Publications*, in which we observed that "the *sine qua non* of copyright is originality," and held that copyright protection is unavailable to "a narrow category of works in which the creative spark is utterly lacking or so trivial as to be virtually nonexistent." Relying on *Feist*, petitioners urge that even if a work is sufficiently "original" to qualify for copyright protection in the first instance, any extension of the copyright's duration is impermissible because, once published, a work is no longer original. *Feist*, however, did not touch on the duration of copyright protection. Rather, the decision addressed the core question of copyrightability, *i.e.*, the "creative spark" a work must have to be eligible for copyright protection at all. Explaining the originality requirement, *Feist* trained on the Copyright Clause words "Authors" and "Writings." The decision did not construe the "limited Times" for which a work may be protected, and the originality requirement has no bearing on that prescription.

More forcibly, petitioners contend that the CTEA's extension of existing copyrights does not "promote the Progress of Science" as contemplated by the preambular language of the Copyright Clause. To sustain this objection, petitioners do not argue that the Clause's preamble is an independently enforceable limit on Congress' power. Rather, they maintain that the preambular language identifies the sole end to which Congress may legislate; accordingly, they conclude, the meaning of "limited Times" must be "determined in light of that specified end." The CTEA's extension of existing copyrights categorically fails to "promote the Progress of Science," petitioners argue, because it does not stimulate the creation of new works but merely adds value to works already created.

[In previous cases], we have described the Copyright Clause as "both a grant of power and a limitation," and have said that "the primary objective of copyright" is "to promote the Progress of Science." The "constitutional command," we have recognized, is that Congress, to the extent it enacts copyright laws at all, create a "system" that "promotes the Progress of Science." We have also stressed, however, that it is generally for Congress, not the courts, to decide how best to pursue the Copyright Clause's objectives. The justifications we earlier set out for Congress' enactment of the CTEA provide a rational basis for the conclusion that the CTEA "promotes the Progress of Science." On the issue of copyright duration, Congress, from the start, has routinely applied new definitions or adjustments of the copyright term to both future works and existing works not yet in the public domain. Such consistent congressional practice is entitled to very great weight, and when it is remembered that the rights thus established have not been disputed during a period of over two centuries, it is almost conclusive.

Closely related to petitioners' preambular argument, or a variant of it, is their assertion that the Copyright Clause "imbeds a quid pro quo." They contend, in this regard, that Congress may grant to an "Author" an "exclusive Right" for a "limited Time," but only in exchange for a "Writing." Congress' power to confer copyright protection, petitioners argue, is thus contingent upon an exchange: The author of an original work receives an "exclusive Right" for a "limited Time" in exchange for a dedication to the public thereafter. Extending an existing copyright without demanding additional consideration, petitioners maintain, bestows an unpaid-for benefit on copyright holders and their heirs, in violation of the *quid pro quo* requirement.

We can demur to petitioners' description of the Copyright Clause as a grant of legislative authority empowering Congress "to secure a bargain—this for that." But the legislative evolution earlier recalled demonstrates what the bargain entails. Given the consistent placement of existing copyright holders in parity with future holders, the author of a work created in the last 170 years would reasonably comprehend, as the "this" offered her, a copyright not only for the time in place when protection is gained, but also for any renewal or extension legislated during that time. Congress could rationally seek to "promote . . . Progress" by including in every copyright statute an express guarantee that authors would receive the benefit of any later legislative extension of the copyright term. Nothing in the Copyright Clause bars Congress from creating the same incentive by adopting the same position as a matter of unbroken practice.

For the several reasons stated, we find no Copyright Clause impediment to the CTEA's extension of existing copyrights.

Petitioners separately argue that the CTEA is a content-neutral regulation of speech that fails heightened judicial review under the First Amendment. We reject petitioners' plea for imposition of uncommonly strict scrutiny on a copyright scheme that incorporates its own speech-protective purposes and safeguards. The Copyright Clause and First Amendment were adopted close in time. This proximity indicates that, in the Framers' view, copyright's limited monopolies are compatible with free speech principles. Indeed, copyright's purpose is to *promote* the creation and publication of free expression. The Framers intended copyright itself to be the engine of free expression. By establishing a marketable right to the use of one's expression, copyright supplies the economic incentive to create and disseminate ideas.

In addition to spurring the creation and publication of new expression, copyright law contains built-in First Amendment accommodations. First, it distinguishes between ideas and expression and makes only the latter eligible for copyright protection. Specifically, [the law] provides: "In no case does copyright protection for an original work of authorship extend to any idea, procedure, process, system, method of operation, concept, principle, or discovery, regardless of the form in which it is described, explained, illustrated, or embodied in such work." This "idea/expression dichotomy" strikes a definitional balance between the First Amendment and the Copyright Act by permitting free communication of facts while still protecting an author's expression. Due to this distinction, every idea, theory, and fact in a copyrighted work becomes instantly available for public exploitation at the moment of publication.

Second, the "fair use" defense allows the public to use not only facts and ideas contained in a copyrighted work, but also expression itself in certain circumstances. The defense provides: "The fair use of a copyrighted work, including such use by reproduction in copies for purposes such as criticism, comment, news reporting, teaching (including multiple copies for classroom use), scholarship, or research, is not an infringement of copyright." The fair use defense affords considerable latitude for scholarship and comment, and even for parody.

The CTEA itself supplements these traditional First Amendment safeguards. First, it allows libraries, archives, and similar institutions to "reproduce" and "distribute, display, or perform in facsimile or digital form" copies of certain published works "during the last 20 years of any term of copyright . . . for purposes of preservation, scholarship, or research" if the work is not already being exploited commercially and further copies are unavailable at a reasonable price. Second, Title II of the CTEA, known as the Fairness in Music Licensing Act of 1998, exempts small businesses, restaurants, and like entities from having to pay performance royalties on music played from licensed radio, television, and similar facilities.

As we read the Framers' instruction, the Copyright Clause empowers Congress to determine the intellectual property regimes that, overall, in that body's judgment, will serve the ends of the Clause. Beneath the facade of their inventive constitutional interpretation, petitioners forcefully urge that Congress pursued very bad policy in prescribing the CTEA's long terms. The wisdom of

Congress' action, however, is not within our province to second guess. Satisfied that the legislation before us remains inside the domain the Constitution assigns to the First Branch, we affirm the judgment of the Court of Appeals. It is so ordered.

POINTS FOR DISCUSSION

1. The majority seems to be saying that any individual extension of copyright's duration is not a negation of the Constitution's requirement that protection will last only for "limited" times. But does extension after extension, such that nothing has entered the public domain in several decades, not amount, practically speaking, to perpetual copyright? Would your answer be affected at all if you knew that the CTEA was passed in large part as a result of a huge lobbying effort from the Disney Corporation, out of fear that some early Mickey Mouse films were about to enter the public domain?
2. As Justice Ginsburg points out, the CTEA was not unique in extending copyright's duration retroactively to already-existing works. Imagine for a moment that the CTEA represents the very first time that Congress extended copyright retroactively (not just to works created after the law was to take effect). Can a retroactive extension, logically, satisfy the spirit of the relevant constitutional provision, telling us that copyright is supposed to "promote the progress" of the arts? How can you encourage the creation of that which has already been created?

▪ *Campbell v. Acuff-Rose Music*
510 U.S. 569 (1994)
Justice Souter:

In 1964, Roy Orbison and William Dees wrote a rock ballad called "Oh, Pretty Woman" and assigned their rights in it to respondent Acuff-Rose Music, Inc. Acuff-Rose registered the song for copyright protection. Petitioners Luther R. Campbell, Christopher Wongwon, Mark Ross, and David Hobbs are collectively known as 2 Live Crew, a popular rap music group. In 1989, Campbell wrote a song entitled "Pretty Woman," which he later described in an affidavit as intended, "through comical lyrics, to satirize the original work." In June or July 1989, 2 Live Crew released records, cassette tapes, and compact discs of "Pretty Woman" in a collection of songs entitled "As Clean As They Wanna Be." Almost a year later, after nearly a quarter of a million copies of the recording had been sold, Acuff-Rose sued 2 Live Crew and its record company, Luke Skyywalker Records, for copyright infringement. The District Court granted summary judgment for 2 Live Crew, reasoning that the commercial purpose of 2 Live Crew's song was no bar to fair use; that 2 Live Crew's version was a parody, which "quickly degenerates into a play on words, substituting predictable lyrics with shocking ones" to show "how bland and banal the Orbison song" is; that 2 Live Crew had taken no more than was necessary to "conjure up" the original in order to parody it; and that it was "extremely unlikely that 2 Live Crew's song could adversely affect the market for the original." The Court of Appeals for the Sixth Circuit reversed; concluding that its "blatantly commercial purpose" prevents [2 Live Crew's] parody from being a fair use. We granted certiorari to determine whether 2 Live Crew's commercial parody could be a fair use.

The first factor in a fair use enquiry is "the purpose and character of the use, including whether such use is of a commercial nature or is for nonprofit educational purposes." The enquiry here looks to whether the use is for criticism, or comment, or news reporting, and the like. The central purpose of this investigation is to see whether the new work merely supersedes the objects of the original creation or instead adds something new, with a further purpose or different character, altering the first with new expression, meaning, or message; it asks, in other words, whether and to what extent the new work is "transformative." Parody has an obvious claim to transformative value, by shedding light on an earlier work, and, in the process, creating a new one. The heart of any parodist's claim to quote from existing material is the use of some elements of a prior author's composition to create a new one that, at least in part, comments on that author's works. If, on the contrary, the commentary has no critical bearing on the substance or style of the original composition, which the alleged infringer merely uses to get attention or to avoid the drudgery in working up something fresh, the claim to fairness in borrowing from another's work diminishes accordingly (if it does not vanish).

The fact that parody can claim legitimacy for some appropriation does not, of course, tell either parodist or judge much about where to draw the line. Like a book review quoting the copyrighted material criticized, parody may or may not be fair use, and petitioners' suggestion that any parodic use is presumptively fair has no more justification in law or fact than the equally hopeful claim that any use for news reporting should be presumed fair

Here, the District Court held, and the Court of Appeals assumed, that 2 Live Crew's "Pretty Woman" contains parody, commenting on and criticizing the original work, whatever it may have to say about society at large. As the District Court remarked, the words of 2 Live Crew's song copy the original's first line, but then "quickly degenerate into a play on words, substituting predictable lyrics with shocking ones that derisively demonstrate how bland and banal the Orbison song seems to them." The 2 Live Crew song "was clearly intended to ridicule the white-bread original" and "reminds us that sexual congress with nameless streetwalkers is not necessarily the stuff of romance and is not necessarily without its consequences. The singers (there are several) have the same thing on their minds as did the lonely man with the nasal voice, but here there is no hint of wine and roses." While we might not assign a high rank to the parodic element here, we think it fair to say that 2 Live Crew's song reasonably could be perceived as commenting on the original or criticizing it, to some degree.

The Court of Appeals, however, immediately cut short the enquiry into 2 Live Crew's fair use claim by confining its treatment of the first factor essentially to one relevant fact, the commercial nature of the use. The court then inflated the significance of this fact by applying a presumption ostensibly that "every commercial use of copyrighted material is presumptively . . . unfair." In giving virtually dispositive weight to the commercial nature of the parody, the Court of Appeals erred.

The language of the statute makes clear that the commercial or nonprofit educational purpose of a work is only one element of the first factor enquiry into its purpose and character. Accordingly, the mere fact that a use is educational and not for profit does not insulate it from a finding of infringement, any more than the commercial character of a use bars a finding of fairness. If, indeed, commerciality carried presumptive force against a finding of fairness, the presumption would swallow nearly all of the illustrative uses listed in the [Copyright Act], including news reporting, comment, criticism, teaching, scholarship, and research, since these activities are generally conducted for profit in this country.

The second statutory factor, "the nature of the copyrighted work," calls for recognition that some works are closer to the core of intended copyright protection than others, with the consequence that fair use is more difficult to establish when the former works are copied. We agree with both the District Court and the Court of Appeals that the Orbison original's creative expression for public dissemination falls within the core of the copyright's protective purposes. This fact, however, is not much help in this case, or ever likely to help much in separating the fair use sheep from the infringing goats in a parody case, since parodies almost invariably copy publicly known, expressive works.

The third factor asks whether "the amount and substantiality of the portion used in relation to the copyrighted work as a whole" are reasonable in relation to the purpose of the copying. Here, attention turns to the persuasiveness of a parodist's justification for the particular copying done, and the enquiry will harken back to the first of the statutory factors, for we recognize that the extent of permissible copying varies with the purpose and character of the use. The facts bearing on this factor will also tend to address the fourth, by revealing the degree to which the parody may serve as a market substitute for the original or potentially licensed derivatives.

The District Court considered the song's parodic purpose in finding that 2 Live Crew had not helped themselves overmuch. The Court of Appeals disagreed, stating that "while it may not be inappropriate to find that no more was taken than necessary, the copying was qualitatively substantial. Taking the heart of the original and making it the heart of a new work was to purloin a substantial portion of the essence of the original." The Court of Appeals is of course correct that this factor calls for thought not only about the quantity of the materials used, but about their quality and importance, too. Where we part company with the court below is in applying this guide to parody, and in particular to parody in the song before us. Parody presents a difficult case. Parody's humor, or in any event its comment, necessarily springs from recognizable allusion to its object through distorted imitation. Its art lies in the tension between a known original and its parodic twin. When parody takes aim at a particular original work, the parody must be able to "conjure up" at least enough of that original to make the object of its critical wit recognizable. What makes for this recognition is quotation of the original's most distinctive or memorable features, which the parodist can be sure the audience will know. Once enough has been taken to assure identification, how much more is reasonable will depend, say, on the extent to which the song's overriding purpose and character is to parody the original or, in contrast, the likelihood that the parody may serve as a market substitute for the original. But using some characteristic features cannot be avoided.

We think the Court of Appeals was insufficiently appreciative of parody's need for the recognizable sight or sound when it ruled 2 Live Crew's use unreasonable as a matter of law. It is true, of course, that 2 Live Crew copied the characteristic opening bass riff (or musical phrase) of the original, and true that the words of the first line copy the Orbison lyrics. But if quotation of the opening riff and the first line may be said to go to the "heart" of the original, the heart is also what most readily conjures up the song for parody, and it is the heart at which parody takes aim. Copying does not become excessive in relation to parodic purpose merely because the portion taken was the original's heart. If 2 Live Crew had copied a significantly less memorable part of the original, it is difficult to see how its parodic character would have come through.

This is not, of course, to say that anyone who calls himself a parodist can skim the cream and get away scot free. Context is everything, and the question of fairness asks what else the parodist did besides go to the heart of the original. It is significant that 2 Live Crew not only copied the first line of the original, but thereafter departed markedly from the Orbison lyrics for its own ends. 2 Live Crew not only copied the bass riff and repeated it, but also produced otherwise distinctive sounds, interposing "scraper" noise, overlaying the music with solos in different keys, and altering the drum beat. This is not a case, then, where "a substantial portion" of the parody itself is composed of a "verbatim" copying of the original. It is not, that is, a case where the parody is so insubstantial, as compared to the copying, that the third factor must be resolved as a matter of law against the parodists. Suffice it to say here that, as to the lyrics, we think the Court of Appeals correctly suggested that "no more was taken than necessary," but just for that reason, we fail to see how the copying can be excessive in relation to its parodic purpose, even if the portion taken is the original's "heart." As to the music, we express no opinion whether repetition of the bass riff is excessive copying, and we remand to permit evaluation of the amount taken, in light of the song's parodic purpose and character, its transformative elements, and considerations of the potential for market substitution sketched more fully below.

The fourth fair use factor is "the effect of the use upon the potential market for or value of the copyrighted work." It requires courts to consider not only the extent of market harm caused by the particular actions of the alleged infringer, but also "whether unrestricted and widespread conduct of the sort engaged in by the defendant would result in a substantially adverse impact on the potential market" for the original. The enquiry "must take account not only of harm to the original but also of harm to the market for derivative works." Since fair use is an affirmative defense, its proponent would have difficulty carrying the burden of demonstrating fair use without favorable evidence about relevant markets. In moving for summary judgment, 2 Live Crew left themselves at just such a disadvantage when they failed to address the effect on the market for rap derivatives, and confined themselves to uncontroverted submissions that there was no likely effect on the market for the original. The [appellate] court resolved the fourth factor against 2 Live Crew, just as it had the first, by applying a presumption about the effect of commercial use, a presumption which as applied here we hold to be error. As to parody pure and simple, it is likely that the new work will not affect the market for the original in a way cognizable under this factor, that is, by acting as a substitute for it. This is so because the parody and the original usually serve different market functions. We do not, of course, suggest that a parody may not harm the market at all, but when a lethal parody, like a scathing theater review, kills demand for the original, it does not produce a harm cognizable under the Copyright Act. The role of the courts is to distinguish between biting criticism that merely suppresses demand and copyright infringement, which usurps it.

2 Live Crew's song comprises not only parody but also rap music, and the derivative market for rap music is a proper focus of enquiry. Evidence of substantial harm to it would weigh against a finding of fair use, because the licensing of derivatives is an important economic incentive to the creation of originals. Of course, the only harm to derivatives that need concern us, as discussed above, is the harm of market substitution. The fact that a parody may impair the market for derivative uses by the very effectiveness of its critical commentary is no more relevant under copyright than the like threat to the original market. Although 2 Live Crew submitted uncontroverted affidavits on the question of market harm to the original, neither they, nor Acuff-Rose, introduced evidence or affidavits addressing the likely effect of 2 Live Crew's parodic rap song on the market for a nonparody, rap version of "Oh, Pretty Woman." The District Court essentially passed on this issue, observing that Acuff-Rose is free to record "whatever version of the original it desires," and the Court of Appeals went the other way by erroneous presumption. Contrary to each treatment, it is impossible to deal with the fourth factor except by recognizing that a silent record on an important factor bearing on fair use disentitled the proponent of the defense, 2 Live Crew, to summary judgment. The evidentiary hole will doubtless be plugged on remand.

We reverse the judgment of the Court of Appeals and remand the case for further proceedings consistent with this opinion.

POINTS FOR DISCUSSION

1. Justice Souter makes clear that parodies enjoy special protection only when they make fun of the original, but do most artists we think of as musical parodists—from Mark Russell to the Capitol Steps to the late Alan Sherman—really accomplish that? The Capitol Steps' "Breaking Knees Is Hard to Do" is aimed straight at controversial ice skater Tonya Harding, not at songwriter Neil Sedaka ("Breaking Up Is Hard to Do"), and their "The Fools on the Hill" is a critique of Congress, not of the similarly titled Lennon-McCartney tune. With these examples in mind, how much protection does the *Campbell* decision really provide to such parodists?
2. What do you think *should* be the proper balance between the interests of the original artists and those of parodists? The typical musical parodist

takes an entire melody from a familiar tune, and writes comedic lyrics for the tune. If audiences appreciate the new work, and if that new work will not by its very structure dampen the market for the original, what harm is there in protecting the parodist? On the other hand, why should parodists have the right to borrow others' melodies without permission?

▪ *Bourne Company v. Twentieth Century Fox Film Corporation*
602 F. Supp. 2d 499 (S.D.N.Y. 2009)
Judge Batts:

Bourne is the sole owner of the copyright to the popular song "When You Wish Upon a Star." Defendants Seth MacFarlane, Fuzzy Door Productions Inc., Twentieth Century Fox Film Corporation, and Twentieth Century Fox Television (a unit of Defendant Fox Broadcasting Company) create and produce an animated television series called *Family Guy*, including an episode entitled "When You Wish Upon a Weinstein." Defendant Cartoon Network, Inc. aired the Episode in November 2003 and has telecast it no fewer than thirty-six times. Defendant Walter Murphy is a composer of television film scores for *Family Guy* and wrote at least part of a song entitled "I Need a Jew" that appears in the episode.

Plaintiff has sued Defendants for copyright infringement, alleging that "I Need a Jew" "consists of a thinly-veiled copy of the music from 'When You Wish Upon a Star' coupled with new anti-Semitic lyrics." This matter is before the Court on the Parties' cross-motions for summary judgment.

"When You Wish Upon a Star" is a popular song by Leigh Harline and Ned Washington originally written for the classic Walt Disney film *Pinocchio*, in which it was sung by Cliff Edwards as the voice of the character Jiminy Cricket. Bourne owns the copyright registrations for the unpublished version of the song, the published version as included in *Pinocchio*, the published sheet music, and other arrangements of the song. Over 100 performing artists and orchestras have recorded the song, and it has also been used extensively in commercials, television and film. The song has also been used in the opening sequences of the Disney anthology television series, "The Wonderful World of Disney," in Walt Disney Pictures' opening logos, and in television advertisements for its Disneyland theme park. Defendants argue, and Plaintiff disputes, that the song is "an integral part of Walt Disney's and the Walt Disney Company's personality and reputation" and is "associated with Walt Disney in the public mind." *Family Guy*, which airs on the Fox Network and the Cartoon Network, among other networks, frequently pokes fun at popular TV shows, movies, songs and celebrities. The show regularly contains irreverent, iconoclastic plotlines and pop-cultural references. The subject of this suit is a half-hour episode entitled "When You Wish Upon a Weinstein" which was produced in 2000. The Episode is centered around the show's father character, Peter, and his inability to manage his family's finances. After hearing his friends talk about how men with Jewish-sounding names have helped them to achieve financial success, Peter decides that he "needs a Jew" to help him with his finances. The overall theme of the Episode is that Peter's beliefs based upon racial stereotypes, even potentially "positive" ones, are ridiculous. At the end of the Episode, Peter says to his wife, Lois, "I see what you're saying. The Jewish are just like us. No better, no worse." According to Defendants, "one of the comedic values present is that although this is an obvious concept, it was not obvious to Peter."

The scene at issue in this litigation depicts Peter looking out of a window up at the night sky in a manner similar to that of the toymaker Gepetto in Walt Disney's *Pinocchio* when Gepetto is wishing for a "real boy."[1] The cartoon accompanying the song further depicts "Jews as magical creatures that come to Peter in the form of a magical spaceship that turns into a flying dreidel."

The Parties agree that the song was created in a manner intended to evoke "When You Wish Upon a Star." The tune of "I Need a Jew" is similar to "When You Wish Upon a Star" and the first four melody notes of "I Need a Jew" are identical to the first four melody notes of "When You Wish Upon a Star."

Defendants initially sought a license from Plaintiff to use "When You Wish Upon a Star" for their song, but Plaintiff refused. After permission was denied, MacFarlane and co-Producer David Zuckerman asked Murphy to write music that would evoke "When You Wish Upon a Star" to go with lyrics that had already been written. With "When You Wish Upon a Star" in mind, Murphy wrote a version of "I Need a Jew"; later, either MacFarlane or Zuckerman mentioned to him "that they would like the melody to be even closer to the Disney song" and "changed a few notes here and there" "to make the average person realize that this was going to be a parody."

---

1. You can see the relevant scenes from *Family Guy* and *Pinocchio* at www.paulsiegelcommlaw.com. On the left side of the site (*Communication Law in America*), click on "Video Clips, then "Chapter 6," then "Family Guy and Pinocchio combined."

Fox Broadcasting initially decided not to televise the Episode as part of Season Two of *Family Guy* due to concerns about the potentially controversial religious content of the Episode. The Episode, including the song "I Need a Jew," was first distributed on home video by Fox Home Entertainment on or about September 9, 2003 as part of the *Family Guy* "Volume 2, Season 3" DVD box set, which has remained on sale since that time. The Episode was first telecast by the Cartoon Network's Adult Swim programming service on November 9, 2003 and was repeatedly telecast thereafter. The Episode was ultimately televised by Fox Broadcasting on December 10, 2004. The Episode was also distributed on DVD by Fox Home Entertainment on or about December 14, 2004 as part of the "*Family Guy*—The Freakin' Sweet Collection" DVD, which has also been on sale since that time.

Bourne did not discover the use of "When You Wish Upon a Star" in the Episode until March 2007 when a Bourne employee found a clip on YouTube. Bourne filed this action within seven months of learning of the alleged infringement.

The major facts at issue in this litigation are not in dispute. For the purposes of this motion, the Parties agree that Defendants' use of the song "When You Wish Upon a Star" would be an infringement of Bourne's rights under the Copyright Act but for a finding of fair use. The Parties agree that "When You Wish Upon a Weinstein" incorporates musical elements from "When You Wish Upon a Star" and was created in a manner intended to evoke that song. The Parties also agree that at least one of the purposes of the song used in the Episode was to hold bigotry and people like Peter Griffin up to ridicule.

The Parties disagree, however, on certain other facts including: whether "When You Wish Upon a Star" is associated either with the Walt Disney Company or with Walt Disney himself, and whether Disney's purported anti-Semitism is a part of the popular lore surrounding the person of Walt Disney. However, even after resolving all ambiguities and drawing all reasonable inferences in favor of the Plaintiff, Defendants are nevertheless entitled to Summary Judgment.

The starting point of the Court's analysis is determining whether the Defendants' use of "When You Wish Upon a Star" is properly considered satire, parody, or neither, as those terms have come to be defined by fair use caselaw. The distinction between parody and satire turns on the object of the "comment" made by the allegedly infringing work. The nub of the definitions, and the heart of any parodist's claim to quote from existing material, is the use of some elements of a prior author's composition to create a new one that, at least in part, comments on that author's works. If, on the contrary, the commentary has no critical bearing on the substance or style of the original composition, which the alleged infringer merely uses to get attention or to avoid the drudgery in working up something fresh, the claim to fairness in borrowing from another's work diminishes accordingly (if it does not vanish), and other factors, like the extent of its commerciality, loom larger. Parody needs to mimic an original to make its point, and so has some claim to use the creation of its victim's (or collective victims') imagination, whereas satire can stand on its own two feet and so requires justification for the very act of borrowing.

The Defendants in this case have sought to justify their use of Plaintiff's copyrighted material as parody in two ways: 1) as a comment on the "saccharine sweet," "innocent" and "wholesome" worldview presented in and represented by "When You Wish Upon a Star," and 2) by evoking "the song most associated with Walt Disney and his company" commenting "on the song while simultaneously making a sharp point about Walt Disney's reputed anti-Semitism." Defendants argue that their song works to "lampoon the 'purity' and 'wholesome' values expressed in 'Wish Upon a Star'"; the song "turns the sweetness of this idyllic message on its head by having Peter ignorantly sing about stereotypes of Jewish people, while at the same time earnestly, and innocently, wishing for a Jew, as if they were some kind of mystical beings who, naturally, could help him solve his financial problems."

Plaintiff argues that Defendants' song "I Need a Jew" does not criticize, ridicule, or in any way comment upon its song but rather "ridicules anti-Semitism and Jewish stereotypes." It argues "there is absolutely nothing about 'I Need a Jew' that overtly comments on or criticizes the subject matter, quality or style of 'When You Wish Upon a Star.'"

The Court finds that by juxtaposing the "saccharin sweet" song "When You Wish Upon a Star" with "I Need a Jew" the Defendants do more than just comment on racism and bigotry generally, as Plaintiff contends. Rather, Defendants' use of "When You Wish Upon a Star" calls to mind a warm and fuzzy view of the world that is ultimately nonsense; wishing upon a star does not, in fact, make one's dreams come true. By pairing Peter's "positive," though racist, stereotypes of Jewish people with that fairy tale world-view, "I Need a Jew" comments both on the original work's fantasy of stardust and magic, as well as Peter's fantasy of the "superiority" of Jews. The song can be "reasonably perceived" to be commenting that any categorical view of a race of people is childish and simplistic, just like wishing upon a star.

This interpretation of "I Need a Jew" is supported by the visual elements on screen at the time the song is being sung by Peter in the Episode. The visual elements, depicting Peter staring out a window at a starry night, echo the equivalent scene in *Pinocchio* in which Gepetto is wishing for a real boy. It is undisputed that *Pinocchio* is the original context of the song "When You Wish Upon a Star." The visual reference to *Pinocchio* makes plain that this is not a case in which the creators simply substituted new lyrics for a known song to get attention or to avoid the drudgery in working up something fresh. The creators of the Episode were clearly attempting to comment in some way on the wishful, hopeful scene in *Pinocchio* with which the song is associated. Consequently, "I Need a Jew" is properly understood as a parody of "When You Wish Upon a Star."

The Court's finding is further supported by Defendants' proffered evidence that the song in the Episode makes an additional comment, or "inside joke," about the "widespread belief" that Walt Disney was anti-Semitic. Defendants argue that, "the creators of the *Family Guy* Song thought it would be the perfect, cutting commentary to use the iconic song most closely-associated with Walt Disney, 'Wish Upon a Star,' in a parodic reverie where the main character 'wishes upon a star' for, of all things, a Jew." Defendants have offered deposition testimony of the show's creator, MacFarlane, and Executive Producer, Zuckerman, who both testified that one of the song's intentions was to make a point about Disney's alleged anti-Semitism.

(The show has made this same joke, more recently, but before the suit was filed against Defendants, in a 2005 *Family Guy* movie, "Family Guy Presents Stewie Griffin: The Untold Story" which at one point depicts Walt Disney emerging from a cryogenic chamber and asking "Are the Jews gone yet?"; when the scientist in the cartoon tells him no, Disney replies, "Put me back in!")

Plaintiff argues that, although "When You Wish Upon a Star" "was sometimes used as a theme song by the Walt Disney Company," Bourne "specifically refused to admit that their song was associated in the minds of the public with the Disney Company or was in any way associated with Walt Disney individually or personally, and further refused to admit that the public associates the Disney Company with Walt Disney personally." Further, Plaintiff argues that Defendants have provided "no admissible evidence that the public actually believes Mr. Disney was an anti-Semite." However, Plaintiff misapprehends the nature of the inquiry in making both of these arguments. Defendants need to prove neither that the public associates the song with Walt Disney individually or personally nor "actually believes" Walt Disney was an anti-Semite; Defendants need only demonstrate that a parodic character may be reasonably perceived. Further, the law protects parodies even when they fail to speak clearly. Therefore, even if Defendants intended to make an "inside joke" about Walt Disney's alleged anti-Semitism but that joke failed, it can still support a finding of fair use. Although this joke may not be an obvious one,

Defendants have established sufficient facts for the Court to find that one of their intended comments in parodying "When You Wish Upon a Star" related to the reputation of Walt Disney as an anti-Semite and that such a comment may be reasonably perceived. Here Defendants have produced uncontroverted evidence that a parallel joke about Walt Disney was discussed in the writers' room prior to the recording of the song. What's more, the fact that Defendants have attempted to make the same joke, subsequent to their creation of the Episode, but prior to this litigation, lends credence to their claim that such an inside joke was intended and further demonstrates that the creators expected their viewership to understand the joke. The Court takes judicial notice of the fact that the internet contains many references to the claim that Walt Disney was an anti-Semite. The Court further notes that Defendants have proffered, in addition to other evidence, a *Los Angeles Times* Book Prize–winning biography of Walt Disney which notes that "it was no secret that Walt Disney was a fervent anti-Communist" but "another question—one that would haunt him for the rest of his life and even haunt his reputation decades after he died—was whether he was also an anti-Semite." Further, the Court finds that it may be reasonably perceived that Walt Disney is associated with the Walt Disney Company. Therefore, the Court finds that it may be reasonably perceived that "I Need a Jew" was commenting on Walt Disney's alleged anti-Semitism. Consequently, Defendants have established that their song, "I Need a Jew" contains several layers of parody of Plaintiff's copyrighted work "When You Wish Upon a Star."

FAIR USE Question #1: The Nature of the Use

Having already found that Defendants' work "I Need a Jew" comments on "When You Wish Upon a Star" the Court must now turn to the question of whether it adds something new to the original song and qualifies as "transformative." The central purpose of this investigation is to see whether the new work adds something new, with a further purpose or different character. It is clear that the song "I Need a Jew" is transformative of the original work here. The lyrics of "I Need a Jew" are almost entirely different from those of "When You Wish Upon a Star"—and are strikingly different in tone and message. In addition, the tune of the song, though very similar to the original, is at least somewhat different. And, although they are both songs written for cartoons to express the wish of the singer, the wishes, and indeed the cartoons themselves, could not be more different. The Court finds that the new work is transformative; consequently, the first factor weighs in favor of a finding of fair use.

Question #2: The Nature of the Work

There is no question that in this case, the original song ("When You Wish Upon a Star") is a creative expression for public dissemination which falls within the core of the copyright's protective purposes. But this fact is not much help in this case, or ever likely to help much in separating the fair use sheep from the infringing goats in a parody case, since parodies almost invariably copy publicly known, expressive works. Consequently, the Court affords little weight to this second prong of the analysis.

Question #3: The Amount Taken

When the use at issue is a parody, it is undisputed that the parody must be able to conjure up at least enough of that original to make the object of its critical wit recognizable. The facts in this case make clear that the Defendants thought about how much of the original song was necessary to make the object of their parody recognizable. While Murphy originally wrote a new song that evoked the original, MacFarlane or Zuckerman asked him to make changes in order to make the allusion clearer. Indeed, Murphy expressed concern that by making changes to bring the song closer to the original, he would no longer be creating a "unique" song, as he is required to do under his contract with Fox. MacFarlane nevertheless insisted that a few notes be changed to make the reference to "When You Wish Upon a Star" apparent to the ordinary listener. The internal, creative dispute over how much of the original to use demonstrates that Defendants were concerned about taking just enough of the original to make their point clear. Therefore, even assuming that Defendants took substantially all of the song, that borrowing was necessary to allow the parodic character of their work to come through. Consequently, the Court finds the third factor weighs in favor of Defendants.

Question #4: The Effect of the Use Upon the Potential Market for or Value of the Copyrighted Work

Plaintiff makes two arguments that market harm exists here. First, Plaintiff argues that widespread, similar unlicensed uses (including other irreverent comedic uses) "would substitute for and compete with licensed comedic programs, in addition to depriving Bourne of significant licensing revenue." Second, it argues that "I Need a Jew" harms the value of its song because it is "unquestionable" that it "would be highly offensive to a significant number of people," harming the original song by association. Both arguments rely on a misconception of the fourth factor analysis. In considering the fourth factor, our concern is not whether the secondary use suppresses or even destroys the market for the original work or its potential derivatives, but whether the secondary use usurps the market of the original work. The market for potential derivative uses includes only those that creators of original works would in general develop or license others to develop. In this case, there can be no question that "I Need a Jew" does not usurp the market for "When You Wish Upon a Star." As the Supreme Court predicted, the parody and the original here serve different market functions. Even Plaintiff admits that its song is known for its wholesomeness and sweetness, where *Family Guy*'s parody of it is so different as to be (they argue) offensive. Plaintiff does not even make the contention that "I Need a Jew" could in any way substitute for "When You Wish Upon a Star." Indeed, Plaintiff argues for a reading of the fourth factor that would swallow the rule entirely. All uses of copyrighted work under a fair use rationale deprive the owner of licensing fees. If a parody of the original work would usurp the market for licensing other comedic uses of the original work, then all parodies would fail under this prong of the analysis. The Supreme Court clearly intended otherwise as did Congress in creating an opportunity for fair use.

Neither can Plaintiff succeed on its theory that their song is harmed by association with "I Need a Jew." It was the Supreme Court's intention for the parody doctrine to protect new works that have reason to fear they will be unable to obtain a license from copyright holders who wish to shield their works from criticism. Any harm [brought] to the original by association is likely to be the exact use of the original material that the law aims to protect. Therefore, the Court finds that the fourth factor mitigates in favor of the Defendants.

The owner of the rights to a well-known work must expect, or at least tolerate, a parodist's deflating ridicule. Plaintiff reaps the benefit of their song's association with *Pinocchio* and Disney, and enjoys its reputation for wholesomeness; it is precisely that beneficial association that opens the song up to ridicule by parodists seeking to take the wind out of such lofty, magical, or pure associations. Such deflating uses serve the important social function of shedding light on the earlier work. Transformative uses of a copyrighted work, such as the *Family Guy* parody here, lie at the heart of the fair use doctrine's guarantee of breathing space within the confines of copyright.

Defendants' Motion for Summary Judgment is GRANTED.

POINTS FOR DISCUSSION

1. Should parodies that are merely "inside jokes," which might be understood only by the artists themselves rather than by a general audience, be protected by Fair Use analysis?

2. After going to the website (www.paulsiegelcommlaw.com), consider whether you agree with the court that "I Need a Jew" is making a comment on "When You Wish Upon a Star," or whether it is rather commenting on anti-Semitism in general.

■ *ProtectMarriage.com v. Courage Campaign*
680 F. Supp. 2d 1225 (E.D. Ca. 2010)
Judge Karlton:

This is a trademark dispute. Plaintiff seeks a temporary restraining order enjoining defendant from using the allegedly infringing mark. For the reasons stated below, the court concludes that plaintiff is unlikely to overcome the conclusion that defendant's use of the mark is protected under the First Amendment, in that the use is relevant to an expressive parody and the use is not explicitly misleading. Plaintiff's motion is therefore denied.

In 2008, the California Electorate passed Proposition 8, which amended the state constitution to provide that "Only marriage between a man and a woman is valid or recognized in California." Plaintiff California Renewal is a nonprofit corporation which operates "ProtectMarriage.com—Yes on 8." Plaintiff helped place Proposition 8 on the ballot, campaigned for Proposition 8's passage, and has since informed the public about challenges to Proposition 8 and raised funds to defend against such challenges.

In all of the above activities, plaintiff has used a logo it refers to as the "ProtectMarriage Trademark." This logo depicts four stylized silhouettes: two larger figures, one in pants and one in a dress, standing on either side of two smaller figures, also one in pants and one in a dress. Thus, the logo represents a heterosexual family. All four figures have their arms raised. This graphic is often, but not always, presented in blue, under an arcing banner reading "Yes on 8 Protect Marriage." In this banner, the 8 is centered and in larger type.

Defendant is a nonprofit organization that supports a right to homosexual marriage. Thus, plaintiff and defendant have opposing views on Proposition 8. When trial in *Perry v. Schwarzenegger* [challenging the constitutionality of the same-sex marriage ban] began on January 11, 2010, defendant began operating a website dedicated to providing coverage of the trial, prop8trialtracker.com. Prop8trialtracker.com uses a logo admittedly derived from the "ProtectMarriage" logo. The prop8trialtracker logo also features four stylized silhouettes. While plaintiff's logo depicts the "parent" figures in pants and a dress, both "parent" figures in defendant's logo wear dresses, suggesting same-sex parents. The text in the banner in defendant's logo has been replaced to read "Prop 8 Trial Tracker."[2] Defendant has filed an opposition to plaintiff's motion. The court concludes that no hearing on the matter is necessary, and resolves the motion on the papers.

Ordinarily, a plaintiff seeking a preliminary injunction must demonstrate that he is [1] likely to succeed on the merits, [2] likely to suffer irreparable harm in the absence of preliminary relief, [3] that the balance of equities tips in his favor, and [4] that an injunction is in the public interest. In the trademark context, however, the likelihood of success on the merits largely determines the remaining factors. Irreparable injury may be presumed from a showing of likelihood of success on the merits. This presumption in turn influences the balancing of hardships. Finally, "avoiding confusion to consumers," the goal of trademark protection, is itself a public interest that is often demonstrated by likelihood of success. Accordingly, the court's analysis is limited to the first [likely to succeed on the merits] factor.

Plaintiff's complaint alleges claims under section 43(a) of the Lanham Act and under California unfair competition and common law trademark infringement. Plaintiff's motion for a temporary restraining order refers only to the Lanham Act trademark claim.

Trademark law aims to protect trademark owners from a false perception that they are associated with or endorse a product. The traditional elements of a claim for trademark infringement are ownership of a protectable mark and likelihood of confusion arising from defendant's use of the mark. In this case, the mark is protectable in that it is suggestive and thus inherently distinctive. While the mark is unregistered, registration is not a prerequisite to suit. Plaintiff's prior public use of the mark indicates plaintiff's ownership thereof.

The second element of a claim for infringement is the likelihood of confusion as to the source, sponsorship, or approval of the allegedly infringing product. One way to negate the element of confusion is to show that the allegedly infringing mark is a parody of the original mark, and that this parody is unlikely to show confusion.

The Ninth Circuit cases on the issue concern "artistic" parodies of trademarks. Under a test borrowed from the Second Circuit, an artistic work's use of a mark does not violate the Lanham Act unless the use "has no artistic relevance to the underlying work whatsoever" or the use "explicitly misleads as to the source or the content of the work." The Ninth Circuit has taken "no rele-

---

2. The two logos can be seen on my website, www.paulsiegelcommlaw.com. On the left-hand of the site (*Communication Law in America*), click on "Additional Images," then "Chapter 6," and then on "Proposition 8."

vance" literally. Thus, a video game's use of a strip club's trademark logo was entitled to First Amendment protection even though the video game was not primarily "about" the club, and was instead "about," at most, the club's neighborhood.

In this case, the logo itself is artistic. Moreover, the broader website, while perhaps not artistic, is undeniably expressive of a political idea, and both political and artistic expression are protected by the First Amendment. Defendant's use of the mark has relevance to the expressive message, namely, support for homosexual marriages, and specifically, opposition to recent California efforts to limit the right to such marriages. This support is expressed by the modification of the "father" figure in the original mark to depict a second "mother." Further, the mark does not explicitly mislead as to the source of the work. Any potential for confusion or misdirection is obviated by the images and text that uniformly accompany defendant's use of the mark, namely, photos of homosexual couples together with text explicitly endorsing homosexual marriage. Plaintiff is unlikely to succeed in showing that a visitor to the prop8trialtracker website is likely to be confused as to whether plaintiff is affiliated with the site.

When use of a trademark is a protected parody, further analysis of the trademark infringement is unnecessary. Alternatively, it appears that the text and images that uniformly accompany defendant's use of the mark are sufficient to dispel any possible consumer confusion. For these reasons, plaintiff is unlikely to succeed on the merits of its trademark infringement claim.

POINTS FOR DISCUSSION

1. Is "parody" really the most apt concept here? Is the defendant's goal to make fun of the plaintiff's logo?
2. A whimsical notion—in times in the not very distant past, when it was constitutional to treat homosexuals as criminals, when the very thought of same-sex marriage would have been preposterous, might the owner of a trademark pursue anyone who dared to associate that mark in any way with homosexuality, with a plausible claim that the use "tarnished" the reputation of plaintiff's goods and services?

▪ *Tillman v. New Line Cinema Corporation*
295 Fed. Appx. 840 (7th Cir. 2008)
Order by the court:

In this action for copyright infringement, Chitunda Tillman claims that New Line Cinema Corporation and its parent company produced the Denzel Washington movie *John Q.* from a script filched from Tillman's own screenplay, *Kharisma Heart of Gold*. The district court granted summary judgment for the defendants, and Tillman appeals. Like the district court, we detect no pertinent similarities between the screenplays, which should not be surprising because New Line's undisputed evidence establishes that *John Q.* was written five years before Tillman's work. Accordingly, we affirm the judgment.

Tillman's screenplay, written and copyrighted in 1998, is based in part on his own struggle to secure medical care for his son. The script tells the story of Tune Love, a millionaire whose assets are frozen by the IRS just when he needs $600,000 to pay for critical heart surgeries for his newborn daughter, Kharisma. When all seems lost, Tune happens to be eating lunch at the mall food court and witnesses a robbery in progress. Tune intervenes and knocks the two robbers unconscious, but not until they have shot his sandwich out of his hands. During this interlude Tune devises a plan: he will insure his life for $3.5 million and then commit suicide so that his family can pay for Kharisma's surgery with the proceeds. After securing his life insurance policy and saying goodbye to his family, Tune drives off a cliff while R. Kelly's "Trade in My Life" plays in the background. The script closes with Tune's spirit visiting a healthy Kharisma five years after her successful surgeries.

In 2002 New Line released *John Q.*, the tale of factory laborer John Q. Archibald who is struggling to make ends meet when tragedy strikes and his son, Mikey, collapses from a heart disorder requiring a transplant. The hospital refuses to perform Mikey's transplant because the family's health insurance will not cover the procedure, and John cannot afford to pay out of pocket. Hopeless, John takes everyone in the hospital waiting room hostage in an effort to force the hospital to perform Mikey's surgery. The story reaches its climax as John turns his gun on himself in a selfless attempt to give his own heart to Mikey, but—as so often happens in the movies—John's gun jams and he is apprehended by authorities. Although the hospital saves Mikey's life by agreeing to perform the surgery, the law holds John accountable and the movie ends with John being driven off to prison as his young son looks on.

Tillman saw the movie and believed it was copied from *Kharisma Heart of Gold*. He investigated the production of *John Q.* and concluded that screenwriter James Kearns, a member of the Writers Guild of America West, had read and stolen *Kharisma Heart of Gold* after Tillman registered it with the Guild. In February 2005 Tillman filed a complaint in district court for copyright infringement against New Line, parent company Time Warner Inc., employees of both companies, and Kearns.

For purposes here we refer to the surviving defendants as New Line. New Line moved for summary judgment, arguing that the scripts are not alike and that Kearns could not have stolen Tillman's script because he wrote *John Q.* in 1993—five years before *Kharisma Heart of Gold.* Along with the two scripts, New Line submitted a declaration from Kearns stating that he wrote *John Q.* in 1993 and then sold the script to Island World Productions. New Line also submitted the purchase contract and the declaration of Island World's senior vice-president confirming that the company bought Kearns's screenplay in 1993. Finally, New Line submitted several articles published in 1993 discussing Kearns's screenplay, *John Q.* Tillman responded not with contrary evidence, but by accusing New Line of falsifying its documentary evidence. The district court sided with New Line and specifically noted that Tillman's claim rests on similarities between unprotected ideas rather than expressions.

To sustain a claim of copyright infringement, the plaintiff must prove (1) ownership of a valid copyright, and (2) copying of constituent elements of the work that are original. The parties agree that Tillman holds a valid copyright in *Kharisma Heart of Gold.* Therefore, the key inquiry is whether Tillman could establish that *John Q.* was copied from his work. Copying may be established via direct evidence, or may be inferred where the defendant had access to the copyrighted work and the accused work is substantially similar to the copyrighted work.

Where no reasonable juror could find that two works are substantially similar, summary judgment in favor of the alleged infringer is appropriate. That is the situation here. Tillman lists perceived similarities between the two scripts. For example, he notes that both scripts include sick children, caring fathers, hospital nurses, a beeping heart monitor, the lack of health insurance, praying, crying, and expressions such as "Don't Shoot!" and "It's a miracle." But these are generic similarities far removed from the realm of protected expression. The central characters, theme, and plot in *John Q.* differ markedly from those in *Kharisma Heart of Gold,* and thus the district court properly reasoned that the scripts are not substantially similar. And any similarities between the two scripts, such as the leading character being a concerned father willing to do anything for his sick child, are standard elements known as *scenes à faire* that are unprotected under copyright law.

That the two scripts are dissimilar is not surprising given the uncontroverted evidence that Kearns *could not* have copied Tillman's script because *John Q.* was written *five years* before *Kharisma Heart of Gold.* The district court reasoned that this evidence established that *John Q.* was independently created and rebutted an inference of copying. But here Tillman has not established an inference of copying, and really this is just further proof that Kearns did not copy Tillman's script. Tillman's unsubstantiated assertions that New Line fabricated testimony, legal documents, and news articles showing that *John Q.*

predates his own screenplay are not sufficient to create a triable issue of material fact. And therefore the district court properly granted summary judgment in favor of New Line.

POINTS FOR DISCUSSION

1. Clearly the plots of the plaintiff's and defendant's works here are quite different. But how much similarity would you require? Suppose plaintiff's work more closely paralleled *John Q.*, except for one crucial plot element, such as the hostage taking?[3]
2. The issue of access is always of concern in these kinds of cases. If you were in the movie business, how much would you adjust your life to avoid the possibility of potential plaintiffs being able to prove access? Would you, for example, never open mail from someone you don't know, for fear that it might include a portion of a screenplay?

■ *The Sheldon Abend Revocable Trust v. Spielberg*

2010 U.S. Dist. LEXIS 99080 (S.D.N.Y. 2010)

Judge Swain:

The Sheldon Abend Revocable Trust brings this action asserting copyright infringement, contributory infringement, and vicarious copyright infringement as well as common law breach of contract claims alleging that the motion picture *Disturbia*—a film produced by Spielberg, owner of DW Studios, LLC, which is in turn a wholly-owned subsidiary of Paramount Pictures Corporation and its parent company, Viacom, Inc.—infringed upon Plaintiff's copyright in the short story *Rear Window* and upon the derivative Alfred Hitchcock film of the same name. The case is now before the Court on Defendants' motion for partial summary judgment dismissing Plaintiff's copyright infringement claims. For the reasons discussed below, Defendants' motion for partial summary judgment is granted.

In 1942, Cornell Woolrich wrote the short story *Rear Window* which was published in the *Dime Detective Magazine*. Plaintiff currently holds the copy-

---

3. The scene in which the hostage taking element begins can be seen on my website. Go to www.paulsiegelcommlaw.com, on the left side of the site (*Communication Law in America*) click on "Video Clips," then on "Chapter 6," and then on "John Q."

right in the short story. In 1953, a predecessor to Defendant Paramount Pictures obtained the motion picture rights to the short story, which was subsequently made into a film of the same title, directed by Alfred Hitchcock, in 1954. Plaintiff relies heavily on the film in its claims of substantial similarity and copyright infringement.

Defendants produced and distributed the motion picture *Disturbia*; distribution began in April 2007. The record before the Court includes a published version of the short story and a DVD copy of *Disturbia*.

Plaintiff has also submitted thousands of pages of exhibits, including: expert reports; previous drafts of the screenplay; references to and copies of media articles and film critics' reviews likening *Disturbia* to the *Rear Window* film; and many lists, charts and DVDs purporting to identify similarities among the short story, the *Rear Window* film, and *Disturbia*. Defendants have proffered copies of numerous published works predating the short story, in support of their contention that various elements of the short story are not protectable and/or not original.

For a plaintiff to prevail in a copyright infringement case, two elements must be proved: (1) ownership of a valid copyright, and (2) copying of constituent elements of the work that are original. The second criterion, copying of original constituent elements, may be proven with either direct or indirect evidence: to prove copying via indirect evidence, a plaintiff must show (1) defendant's access to the allegedly infringed work; (2) actual copying; and (3) unlawful appropriation of copyrightable materials. For purposes of the instant motion, Defendants have conceded access and actual copying. Thus, the only questions for resolution are whether there is a genuine dispute of material fact as to whether Defendants unlawfully appropriated copyrightable (that is, protectable) elements from Plaintiff's short story, and, if there is no such appropriation, whether Defendants are entitled to judgment dismissing Plaintiff's copyright infringement claims as a matter of law.

To prove unlawful appropriation of protectible elements, a plaintiff must show that there is substantial similarity between protectible elements in the two disputed works. The appropriate test for substantial similarity is whether an ordinary observer, unless he set out to detect the disparities, would be disposed to overlook them, and regard the aesthetic appeal as the same.

Where, as here, a work is an amalgamation of protectible and unprotectible elements, a "more discerning" ordinary observer test is employed, which requires that the court first filter out from consideration any non-protectible elements. The remaining, protectible elements are then analyzed for substantial similarity.

Because questions of substantial similarity often present close questions of fact, courts have historically been hesitant to grant summary judgment on copyright infringement claims. However, the question of substantial similarity is by no means exclusively reserved for resolution by a jury; in certain circumstances, it is entirely appropriate for a district court to resolve that question as a matter of law, either because the similarity between two works concerns only non-copyrightable elements of the plaintiff's work, or because no reasonable jury, properly instructed, could find that the two works are substantially similar.

A determination of copyright infringement requires a side-by-side comparison of the disputed works themselves. The elements that should be considered in analyzing two works for substantial similarity include such aspects as the total concept and feel, theme, characters, plot, sequence, pace, and setting of the plaintiff's and the defendants' works. The Court has reviewed both works carefully.

Cornell Woolrich's *Rear Window*

The short story spans four days and depicts, through first-person narrative, protagonist Hal Jeffries' observations of his neighbors' activities which eventually lead him to discover and solve a crime through deductive logic. It is set in New York City.

At the opening of the short story, the reader learns that Jeffries is incapacitated such that he can only move from his bed to a chair near the window of his second floor bedroom. The reader learns little of Jeffries' background and personality, as the character is minimally developed.

To pass the time, Jeffries observes from his window the goings-on in several of his neighbors' homes. He watches a young couple with an active social life, a young widow and her child, and a couple whom he later learns are the Thorwalds.

Mrs. Thorwald, he notices, is in chronic poor health. At first, her husband, Lars Thorwald, appears concerned about her health but, as Jeffries observes the Thorwalds over a period of days, he notices that Mrs. Thorwald has disappeared. Jeffries speculates that Thorwald has murdered her. He phones his old friend, Detective Boyne, to report his suspicion, and Boyne institutes an investigation. Following a lead that Mrs. Thorwald's belongings had been shipped to the countryside, the police encounter a woman who identifies herself as Mrs. Thorwald. Boyne then stops the investigation, to Jeffries' dismay.

Undeterred from the belief that Thorwald murdered his wife, Jeffries enlists the assistance of his faithful servant, Sam, in obtaining proof of the murder. Sam's character is also minimally developed. Jeffries instructs Sam to slip a note that reads "What have you done with her?" beneath Thorwald's door. Upon receiving the note, Thorwald becomes agitated, and paces his apartment nervously. His pacing closely parallels that of a realtor showing a newly renovated apartment two floors above Thorwald, but Jeffries does not immediately recognize the significance of this coincidence. Thorwald's reaction to the note, however, convinces Jeffries that Thorwald is, in fact, guilty of murder.

To obtain more concrete evidence of murder, Jeffries phones Thorwald, pretending to be a blackmailer, and convinces Thorwald to meet him in a local park. When Thorwald sets out to pay off his blackmailer, Jeffries dispatches Sam to Thorwald's apartment with instructions to make it appear as if the apartment has been searched, in order to make Thorwald believe that his blackmailer has obtained concrete evidence of the murder. Sam does as he is told. When Thorwald returns, Jeffries immediately phones him, pretending to have discovered evidence, but Thorwald does not believe him.

Thorwald then unexpectedly phones Jeffries, and, hearing his voice, deduces that Jeffries is his blackmailer. After this phone call, Jeffries suddenly recalls the mirrored movements of Thorwald and the realtor two floors above. He realizes that, when passing from the kitchen to the living room, the realtor's height relative to the window changed while Thorwald's remained the same because, as part of the ongoing renovations to the building, a raised kitchen floor had been poured in concrete for decorative effect. Jeffries deduces that Thorwald buried his wife's body in the still-wet concrete of the fifth floor apartment, which was under renovation.

Jeffries attempts to phone Inspector Boyne, but the line goes dead: Thorwald has entered Jeffries' building and severed the telephone line. Jeffries realizes Thorwald is coming to kill him. Rendered unable to escape by his cast, Jeffries conceals himself with a rug, and places a bust sculpture upon his shoulder, hoping that in the dark Thorwald would be tricked by the ruse. As Thorwald enters and shoots the bust, Inspector Boyne arrives. Thorwald escapes out the window, climbs to the roof of his own building, then shoots into Jeffries' apartment. Inspector Boyne returns fire and strikes Thorwald, causing him to fall to his death.

From the available information, Jeffries completes his theory of the case for the reader: Thorwald had been poisoning his wife for some time, but killed her outright when she discovered what he was doing; and he concocted a scheme with another woman, likely his lover, to suggest that his wife had gone upstate. The other woman impersonated Mrs. Thorwald when the police investigated, and was going to stage her suicide. In the closing lines of the story, a doctor arrives to remove the cast and notes, ironically, that Jeffries must have been bored while sitting around.

Disturbia

The events depicted in *Disturbia* span more than a year. The story's chief protagonist is Kale Brecht, a troubled teenager who, sentenced to house arrest, spies on neighbors to stave off boredom and, after learning of the disappearance of several women in the area, discovers that his neighbor may be to blame.

Kale is introduced to the viewer while on a fishing trip with his father. In a picturesque wilderness setting, Kale and his father joke and bond. On the trip home, however, while Kale is driving, a horrific accident occurs and his father is killed. A year later, Kale has become a troubled and depressed teenager. After assaulting a teacher, Kale goes to court and is sentenced to three months of house arrest in suburban California. His probation officer outfits him with an ankle bracelet that confines him to a 100-yard radius from the receiver in his kitchen.

Kale begins to entertain himself by watching his neighbors live their unrestricted lives. He observes his new neighbors moving in, and takes particular note of their attractive teenage daughter, Ashley. Among other things, he notices, almost in passing, Robert Turner, a neighbor who constantly mows his lawn. After hearing news reports about a missing woman, and of a string of missing women in Texas, Kale recalls that Turner's car matches the description of the suspect's vehicle, right down to a dented fender. Venturing outside, Kale spies on Turner.[4]

Kale's friend Ronnie joins Kale in his surveillance of Turner and in spying on Ashley. Eventually, Ashley catches them watching her and confronts them. Ronnie explains their interest in Turner, and she joins them in the stake-out. During their stake-outs, a romance develops between Kale and Ashley.

One night, Kale observes Turner escorting a red-haired woman to his home, and then later sees her panicked and trying to escape the house. A reflection of Kale's video camera alerts Turner to the fact that Kale is watching. Kale later sees a redhead leaving Turner's house, and reasons that he may have been mistaken (although the viewer later learns that it was, in fact, Turner wearing a wig). Some time later, at Turner's house, there is a scream and blood spatters across the inside of a window.

Ashley later notices Turner dragging a blood-covered blue bag into his garage. Kale, Ashley, and Ronnie decide to investigate Turner's garage. With Ashley acting as a look-out and Kale watching via live-feed video camera, Ron-

---

4. The scene in which Kale and Turner first speak to each other is on my website, www.paulsiegelcommlaw.com; on the left side of the site (*Communication Law in America*), click on "Video Clips," then "Chapter 6," and then on "Disturbia."

nie finds the blue bag, in which he sees something decomposing. Ronnie panics, and, fearing for his friend, Kale rushes to Turner's house wielding a baseball bat, triggering his ankle bracelet, and summoning the police. He tells the police about the blue bag, in which they discover the decomposing carcass of a deer.

Upon reviewing the footage that Ronnie shot while sneaking about Turner's house, Kale notices the face of a dead woman, visible in the basement through a heating grate. At the same time, Kale's mother is attacked by Turner in Turner's home. Turner then comes to Kale's house and attacks Ronnie and Kale, rendering them unconscious. Kale awakens, bound with tape. Turner informs Kale of his plan to frame Kale for murdering his own mother and to stage Kale's suicide. Ashley arrives at the last moment, however, and in the course of a struggle, Kale and Ashley escape to safety by jumping off Kale's roof and into Ashley's pool.

Kale then returns to Turner's house, armed with hedge clippers, to rescue his mother. He discovers the body of the dead woman he had seen in Ronnie's video, as well as an operating room filled with gruesome mementos. Summoned by Kale's ankle bracelet, a police officer arrives at Turner's house, but is killed by Turner. Meanwhile, while searching the basement of Turner's house for his mother, Kale falls into a pool of water filled with the dead bodies of Turner's previous victims. Kale locates his mother just as Turner arrives. Kale, his mother, and Turner fight, culminating in Turner being stabbed and falling into the pool.

The next day, Kale's parole officer removes his ankle bracelet, releasing him from house arrest early for good behavior. The film ends with Kale and Ashley kissing while Ronnie attempts to videotape them.

Comparison of the Works

It cannot be disputed that both works tell the story of a male protagonist, confined to his home, who spies on neighbors to stave off boredom and, in so doing, discovers that one of his neighbors is a murderer. The voyeur is himself discovered by the suspected murderer, is attacked by the murderer, and is ultimately vindicated. Although it is possible to characterize the plots of both works so they appear indistinguishable, such similarity is not, standing alone, indicative of substantial similarity. The law of copyright only protects an author's particular expression of an idea, not the idea itself. Here, as will be explained in the analysis that follows, the expression of the voyeur-suspicion-peril-vindication plot idea is quite different in the two works. This broad plot idea, or premise, is not a protectible element. Similarity at this level of generality is not probative of the question of infringement.

Plaintiff contends that character elements of *Disturbia* are derivative of (i.e. substantially similar to) *Rear Window*, notwithstanding some differences. The bar for substantial similarity in a character is set quite high. Because substantial similarity should be determined based on the Court's considered impressions, a comparison of some of the disputed characters is warranted. The protagonists of the respective disputed works at issue here are not substantially similar. While Plaintiff correctly points out that both Kale and Jeffries are confined, single men, such generalized similarities are not protectible. Furthermore, Jeffries' character is far less developed than the Kale character in *Disturbia*. Kale Brecht is a troubled teen, struggling to cope with the loss of his father, and is confined to his house on house arrest. Hal Jeffries is a male of indeterminate age. Kale has, at least initially, other pastimes to stave off boredom—television, video games, and music—while Jeffries has none. While Kale consistently finds himself in trouble with a police officer, Jeffries' close friend is a detective. Any similarities between Kale and Jeffries are too general to be afforded protection under copyright law.

Nor are the antagonists in Plaintiff's short story and Defendants' *Disturbia* substantially similar. Turner is a single middle aged man who is suspected—and later is confirmed—to be a serial killer. Thorwald is a married man, who kills his wife—apparently the first and only woman he murders—to be with another woman. Plaintiff attempts to demonstrate substantial similarity between the antagonists by characterizing Turner as a neighbor suspected of killing women and Thorwald as a neighbor who murders a woman. The similarity between these two characters ends, however, with their middle age and their position as the protagonist's neighbor: a serial killer is distinguishable from a one-time killer. These similarities amount to nothing more than age, sex, and status as a personification of evil living next door—a basic character type—and therefore do not rise to the level of protectible expression of an idea.

Plaintiff also asserts that the supporting characters in each work are substantially similar. Notwithstanding the fact that Ronnie and Ashley are, in fact two people, and Sam is but one, Plaintiff attempts to demonstrate substantial similarity by designating their character types as "the Assistant(s)." The characters of Ronnie and Ashley however, bear no resemblance to Sam, beyond the most generalized level of supporting characters. Such a basic character type and functional role warrants no copyright protection.

Plaintiff contends that there is substantial similarity between settings in the short story and *Disturbia*. Plaintiff's position cannot withstand scrutiny. *Disturbia* is set in a house in suburban California while the short story is set in an apartment in New York City. The setting of the short story is Jeffries' bedroom, and more specifically, his chair within that bedroom and the view from that chair. In contrast, *Disturbia*'s setting encompasses all of Kale's house and much of his yard, as well as a shopping center, a parking garage, Ashley's house and yard, a courthouse, the wilderness, a classroom, and Turner's home. Furthermore, where Jeffries' room is impersonal—the only detail the author provides is that the books and sculpture in Jeffries' room were left by a previous tenant—Kale's room reflects his personality, and his house is furnished and decorated with personal items and photographs. Jeffries' world, as expressed in the short story, consists of what he can see from his single bedroom window. Kale, on the other hand, roams from room to room, utilizes windows throughout his home, and goes outside. The role of the windows is similar only at a high level of generalization, and thus is not protectible.

For the foregoing reasons, the Defendants' motion for partial summary judgment is granted. Plaintiff's claims of copyright infringement, vicarious infringement, and contributory infringement are dismissed.

POINTS FOR DISCUSSION

1. Does the very fact that Judge Swain needed to invent a clever shorthand for describing the narrative similarities between the two works ("voyeur-suspicion-peril-vindication") suggest that there is more in common here than she allows?
2. Should the fact that so very many professional film critics found it helpful to put *Disturbia* in context by mentioning *Rear Window* also suggest that the similarities between the two works might be more than superficial?

7

Access to Government Information

The U.S. Supreme Court has occasionally remarked that the First Amendment provides at least some measure of protection for the process of news gathering. Still, it is clear that the First Amendment deals mostly with the media's right to report information they already know, and does not create a right to *learn* that information in the first place. The legislative branch has filled much of the vacuum, however, through federal and state laws governing access to publicly held information, and creating a presumption that official meetings of government agencies will be conducted in public view.

The first case in this chapter, *Saxbe v. Washington Post*, is one of several Supreme Court decisions from the 1970s putting the press on notice that they are granted no special rights of access to sensitive government property (here, a jail) than that granted to the general public. Then, we see how a federal appellate court, in *Baltimore Sun v. Ehrlich*, held that public officials have no obligation to return reporters' calls, and indeed can formally "blackball" disfavored media representatives, just so long as they are at least invited to regularly scheduled press conferences and the like.

The federal Freedom of Information Act (FOIA) is the impetus for hundreds of court cases annually. In many of these cases, courts are called on to determine whether one of the statute's exemptions from the presumption of disclosure is implicated by the specific information sought by a requestor. *National Archives and Records Administration v. Favish* is one such case. It involves a portion of the FOIA's law enforcement exemption, and asks whether the portion of the exemption referring to "unwarranted privacy invasions" applies only to the subject of a file, or can be extended to cover the (deceased) subject's survivors.

Next we examine a case from the Texas Supreme Court—*Acker v. Texas*

Water Commission—that interprets that state's Open Meetings Act, warning public officials that even the most casual exchange of views in the most informal of settings might constitute a "meeting."

Finally we look at a U.S. Supreme Court case (*Doe v. Reed*) asking whether the state of Washington's open records law, if used to reveal the names and addresses of persons who signed a petition to get a controversial issue on a referendum ballot, would violate those signatories' First Amendment rights.

▪ *Saxbe v. Washington Post*
417 U.S. 843 (1974)
Justice Stewart:

In March 1972, the respondents requested permission from the petitioners, the officials responsible for administering federal prisons, to conduct several interviews with specific inmates in the prisons at Lewisburg, Pennsylvania, and Danbury, Connecticut. The petitioners denied permission for such interviews on the authority of Policy Statement 1220.1A, prohibiting any personal interviews between newsmen and individually designated federal prison inmates. [Respondents contend] that the prohibition of all press interviews with prison inmates abridges the protection that the First Amendment accords the news gathering activity of a free press.

The District Court agreed with this contention and held that the Policy Statement, insofar as it totally prohibited all press interviews at the institutions involved, violated the First Amendment. The Court of Appeals affirmed, holding that press interviews with prison inmates could not be totally prohibited as the Policy Statement purported to do, but may "be denied only where it is the judgment of the administrator directly concerned, based on either the demonstrated behavior of the inmate, or special conditions existing at the institution at the time the interview is requested, or both, that the interview presents a serious risk of administrative or disciplinary problems."

The policies of the Federal Bureau of Prisons regarding visitations to prison inmates accord liberal visitation privileges to inmates' families, their attorneys, and religious counsel. Even friends of inmates are allowed to visit, although their privileges appear to be somewhat more limited. Other than members of these limited groups with personal and professional ties to the inmates, members of the general public are not permitted under the Bureau's policy to enter the prisons and interview consenting inmates. This policy is applied with an even hand to all prospective visitors, including newsmen, who, like other members of the public, may enter the prisons to visit friends or family members. But, again like members of the general public, they may not enter the prison and insist on visiting an inmate with whom they have no such relationship.

Except for the limitation in Policy Statement 1220.1A on face-to-face press-inmate interviews, members of the press are accorded substantial access to the federal prisons in order to observe and report the conditions they find there. Indeed, journalists are given access to the prisons and to prison inmates that in significant respects exceeds that afforded to members of the general public. For example, Policy Statement 1220.1A permits press representatives to tour the prisons and to photograph any prison facilities. During such tours a newsman is permitted to conduct brief interviews with any inmates he might encounter. In addition, newsmen and inmates are permitted virtually unlimited written correspondence with each other. Outgoing correspondence from inmates to press representatives is neither censored nor inspected. Incoming mail from press representatives is inspected only for contraband or statements inciting illegal action. Moreover, prison officials are available to the press and are required by Policy Statement 1220.1A to "give all possible assistance" to press representatives "in providing background and a specific report" concerning any inmate complaints.

The respondents have also conceded in their brief that Policy Statement 1220.1A "has been interpreted by the Bureau to permit a newsman to interview a randomly selected group of inmates." As a result, the reporter respondent in this case was permitted to interview a randomly selected group of inmates at the Lewisburg prison. Finally, in light of the constant turnover in the prison population, it is clear that there is always a large group of recently released prisoners who are available to both the press and the general public as a source of information about conditions in the federal prisons.

Thus, it is clear that Policy Statement 1220.1A is not part of any attempt by the Federal Bureau of Prisons to conceal from the public the conditions prevailing in federal prisons. This limitation on prearranged press interviews with individually designated inmates was motivated by disciplinary and administrative considerations. The interest of the press is often concentrated on a relatively small number of inmates who, as a result, become virtual "public figures" within the prison society and gain a disproportionate degree of notoriety and influence among their fellow inmates. As a result those inmates who are conspicuously publicized tend to become the source of substantial disciplinary problems that can engulf a large portion of the population at a prison.

It is unnecessary to engage in any delicate balancing of such penal considerations against the legitimate demands of the First Amendment. For it is apparent that the sole limitation imposed on news gathering by Policy Statement

1220.1A is no more than a particularized application of the general rule that nobody may enter the prison and designate an inmate whom he would like to visit, unless the prospective visitor is a lawyer, clergyman, relative, or friend of that inmate. This limitation on visitations is justified by the truism that prisons are institutions where public access is generally limited. In this regard, the Bureau of Prisons visitation policy does not place the press in any less advantageous position than the public generally. Indeed, the total access to federal prisons and prison inmates that the Bureau of Prisons accords to the press far surpasses that available to other members of the public.

Newsmen have no constitutional right of access to prisons or their inmates beyond that afforded the general public. The proposition that the Constitution imposes upon government the affirmative duty to make available to journalists sources of information not available to members of the public generally finds no support in the words of the Constitution or in any decision of this Court. Thus, since Policy Statement 1220.1A does not deny the press access to sources of information available to members of the general public, we hold that it does not abridge the freedom that the First Amendment guarantees. Accordingly, the judgment of the Court of Appeals is reversed and the case is remanded to the District Court for further proceedings consistent with this opinion. It is so ordered.

POINTS FOR DISCUSSION

1. Is there a danger that the Bureau of Prisons policy will prevent those interviews most likely to be of public interest? Suppose, for example, that a specific inmate complains of a guard's act of brutality, or that the press wishes to confirm reports that a particular inmate of some notoriety is being given special treatment.
2. Justice Stewart emphasizes the many alternative means by which reporters can gather information about the penal system without having to conduct targeted interviews. Do you think that those alternatives are satisfactory? Why or why not, and under what circumstances?

• *Baltimore Sun v. Ehrlich*

437 F.3d 410 (4th Cir. 2006)
Judge Niemeyer:

The Press Office of Maryland Governor Robert L. Ehrlich, Jr. issued the following directive on November 18, 2004:

Effective immediately, no one in the Executive Department or Agencies is to speak with [*Baltimore Sun* reporter] David Nitkin or [*Baltimore Sun* columnist] Michael Olesker until further notice. Do not return calls or comply with any requests. The Governor's Press Office feels that currently both are failing to objectively report on any issue dealing with the Ehrlich-Steele Administration. Please relay this information to your respective department heads.

The Sun is Maryland's largest newspaper with more than one million readers each week. David Nitkin, a reporter for the Baltimore Sun Company, was the State House Bureau Chief, and Michael Olesker was a columnist for the Baltimore Sun Company, who wrote a weekly opinion column.

These plaintiffs allege in their complaint that the Governor issued his November 18, 2004 directive "for the express purpose of punishing and retaliating against *The Sun* for the exercise of its First Amendment rights." They also allege that the directive "was intended to have and has had an impermissible chilling effect on *The Sun*'s right to free expression."

In support of *The Sun*'s motion for a preliminary injunction, Nitkin testified by affidavit about the effect that the Governor's directive had on him. He stated that on November 22, 2004, he called the Governor's Press Secretary, Henry Fawell, to seek comment on statements made by legislators calling for a constitutional amendment to give lawmakers a greater say in selling state-owned land. Fawell's response was that "the ban is still in effect." Nitkin also stated that on the same day he left a message for Budget Secretary James DiPaula and that DiPaula's secretary informed him that Nitkin would have to speak to the Governor's Press Office. Nitkin stated that on November 23, 2004, he called Anne Hubbard, a spokeswoman for the Department of General Services, inquiring about a contract between a private consulting firm and the Department of General Services, and Hubbard replied, "David, I can't talk to you." Nitkin related that "numerous [other] state government representatives and employees also have not returned my telephone calls." And in a second affidavit, Nitkin stated that he was excluded from a "press briefing" conducted in the Governor's conference room on December 30, 2004, and that he was not invited to one on January 4, 2005. He acknowledged that other reporters from *The Sun* attended both briefings.

On the same day that the Governor's directive was issued, Nitkin e-mailed the Governor's Press Office to learn if the directive applied to his requests for information made pursuant to Maryland's Public Information Act. The Press Office responded to Nitkin, advising him that executive officials would continue to answer those requests "as legally required."

Finally, invitations were extended to Nitkin for public press conferences, and he attended three of them during the two months following the issuance of the directive. He also continued to receive public press releases.

In his affidavit in support of *The Sun*'s motion for preliminary injunction, Olesker testified that "since the ban was enacted, several state government representatives and employees have not returned my telephone calls." He stated that on November 29, 2004, he made three telephone calls to the Governor's Press Office that were not returned.

The Baltimore Sun Company itself has apparently not been denied any access by the directive except insofar as Nitkin and Olesker have been denied access. Other reporters for *The Sun* have had their phone messages and e-mails returned, and they attended and reported on both press briefings from which Nitkin was excluded or not invited.

In affidavits filed in opposition to *The Sun*'s motion for a preliminary injunction, [members of the Ehrlich administration] explained the reach of the Governor's directive. [They] testified that both before the directive and after it, the Governor interacted with members of the media in a variety of ways, including "press conferences, press briefings, and exclusive interviews which may be limited in scope, participants, or forum." [They] observed that these practices were "consistent with well established custom within the broadcast industry, and have not changed during this administration, except to the extent that Mr. Nitkin and Mr. Olesker are not granted the special access they once enjoyed."

[Ehrlich's aides] testified that the Governor determines whether to hold a public press conference or a press briefing of a limited number of reporters, that public press conferences were held in the Governor's reception room, which has a capacity for 80 persons, and the media could request to be included on the e-mail notification list. Because Nitkin had requested to be on the notification list, he was notified of and invited to public press conferences. Olesker never requested to be on the notification list. Press briefings were held in the Governor's conference room, a private area "protected by a guard and a door with keypad access" and with the capacity to hold 10 to 12 people. The persons invited to press briefings were called by telephone or invited in person.

The Sun has not maintained—and so confirmed at oral argument—that the Governor's directive actually chilled its reporting on state government matters. The Governor pointed out that during the eight weeks before the directive, Nitkin wrote 45 articles related to state government and Olesker 1, and during the eight weeks after the directive, Nitkin wrote 43 and Olesker 1.

We address the single issue whether the issuance of the Governor's November 18, 2004 directive in response to The Sun's exercise of its First Amendment rights gives rise to an actionable claim for retaliation.

Because government retaliation tends to chill an individual's exercise of his First Amendment rights, public officials may not, as a general rule, respond to an individual's protected activity with conduct or speech even though that conduct or speech would otherwise be a lawful exercise of public authority. A retaliation claim must establish that the government responded to the plaintiff's constitutionally protected activity with conduct or speech that would chill or adversely affect his protected activity.

Not every government restriction, however, is sufficient to chill the exercise of First Amendment rights, nor is every restriction actionable, even if retaliatory. We have recognized a distinction between an adverse impact that is actionable, on the one hand, and a *de minimis* inconvenience, on the other. Some government actions, due to their nature, are not actionable even if they satisfy all the generally articulated elements of a retaliation claim. When the challenged government action is government speech, there is no retaliation liability—even if the plaintiff can demonstrate a substantial adverse impact—unless the government speech concerns private information about an individual or unless it was threatening, coercive, or intimidating so as to intimate that punishment, sanction, or adverse regulatory action will imminently follow.

This limitation on the retaliation cause of action based on government speech is necessary to balance the government's speech interests with the plaintiff's speech interests. In this case, the Governor does not dispute that Nitkin and Olesker engaged in constitutionally protected speech and that he issued the November 18, 2004 directive in response to their speech. The directive itself states that the Governor and his Press Office believed that Nitkin and Olesker had failed to be objective in their reporting. The issues not conceded by the Governor center on the remaining elements of a retaliation claim, requiring us to determine in the context of this case (1) whether making issuance of the directive actionable would tend to constitutionalize virtually every day-to-day interchange between the press and the Governor; (2) whether the directive effected a substantial adverse impact or chill on *The Sun*'s exercise of its First Amendment rights or simply created a *de minimis* inconvenience; and (3) whether the Governor's response was protected government speech.

On these issues, *The Sun* contends that the directive was not an everyday interchange but specifically targeted two reporters, denying them rights given to all other reporters. *The Sun* argues that Nitkin and Olesker are relatively and significantly worse off than other reporters because executive officials no longer can comment to them. Although the reporters would not concede at oral argument that their speech has *actually* been chilled, they argue that as a matter of law the speech of *a reasonable reporter of ordinary firmness* would be chilled by being subjected to a no-comment policy that does not apply to every reporter. In addition, *The Sun* contends that the Governor intended his order to coerce Nitkin and Olesker to conform their speech to his understanding of objective reporting. Thus, *The Sun* argues that from the moment the order issued and regardless of its effectiveness in foreclosing their access to official sources of information, a reasonable reporter's speech would be chilled by the Governor's manifest and expressed purpose.

It is common knowledge—and the parties so concede—that reporting is highly competitive, and reporters cultivate access—sometimes exclusive access—to sources, including government officials. Public officials routinely select among reporters when granting interviews or providing access to nonpublic information. They evaluate reporters and choose to communicate with those who they believe will deliver their desired messages to the public. By giving one reporter or a small group of reporters information or access, the official simultaneously makes other reporters, who do not receive discretionary access, worse off. These other reporters are sometimes denied access because an official believes them to be unobjective.

At oral argument, *The Sun* conceded that a public official's selective preferential communication to his favorite reporter or reporters would not give the much larger class of unrewarded reporters retaliation claims. This concession acknowledges that government officials frequently and without liability evaluate reporters and reward them with advantages of access—i.e., that government officials regularly subject all reporters to some form of differential treatment based on whether they approve of the reporters' expression. *The Sun* nonetheless claims that this concession is not incompatible with affording it the relief requested in this case of enjoining the enforcement of the Governor's November 18, 2004 directive.

We, however, find the scenario conceded by *The Sun* and the facts of this case to be materially indistinguishable. Both the hypothetical and this case are merely two different ways of describing the same pervasive and everyday relationship between government officials and the press, and retaliation liability cannot hinge on the conclusory statements with which a plaintiff frames a complaint about a single example of how that relationship has played out. Both the hypothetical and the facts of this case present instances in which government officials disadvantage some reporters because of their reporting and simultaneously advantage others by granting them unequal access to nonpublic information. Thus, whether the disfavored reporters number two or two million, they are still denied access to discretionarily afforded information on account of their reporting. The facts of this case and the hypothetical stand or fall together, so *The Sun*'s concession forecloses its requested relief.

We conclude that, in the circumstances of this case, no actionable retaliation claim arises when a government official denies a reporter access to discretionarily afforded information or refuses to answer questions. We also conclude that the adverse impact of such conduct [by the government] is objectively *de minimis*. It would be inconsistent with the journalist's accepted role in the "rough and tumble" political arena to accept that a reporter of ordinary firmness can be chilled by a politician's refusal to comment or answer questions on account of the reporter's previous reporting.

[Nitkin and Olesker], as typical reporters, are used to currying their sources' favors, and even though they may have been foreclosed from directly accessing sources when the sources became unhappy with how their information was being reported, they have not been chilled to any substantial degree in their reporting, as they have continued to write stories for *The Sun*, to comment, to criticize, and otherwise to speak with the full protection of the First Amendment.

The Sun argues that it is not seeking to change the competition for access, in which it is daily favored and disfavored by government officials' decisions to give access to a particular reporter. It accepts that competition and its daily successes and failures as inherent in the journalistic terrain. It seeks *only* and "simply" to "lift the retaliatory ban"—the November 18, 2004 directive. But the November 18, 2004 directive, which is no more than a formalization of the Governor's decision not to give Nitkin and Olesker access, has no greater impact than would the same decision made daily by the Governor on an *ad hoc* basis.

While Nitkin and Olesker might now be disfavored, they are no more disfavored than the many reporters without access to the Governor. Accordingly, we conclude that in the ongoing intercourse of government and press, a reporter endures only *de minimis* inconvenience when a government official denies the reporter access to discretionary information or refuses to answer the reporter's questions because the official disagrees with the substance or manner of the reporter's previous expression in reporting.

For all of the reasons given, the judgment of the district court is affirmed.

POINTS FOR DISCUSSION

1. Suppose the facts were a bit different, and that these two reporters were systematically excluded from press conferences that were otherwise open to all the local media. Would that constitute First Amendment retaliation?
2. Now suppose that the two *Sun* reporters write a series of articles maligning the governor's thin-skinned response to criticism, accusing him of being a

coward for refusing to take their calls. Would the governor have a valid claim in a defamation action against the reporters? Why or why not?

▪ *National Archives and Records Administration v. Favish*

541 U.S. 157 (2004)
Justice Kennedy:

This case requires us to interpret the Freedom of Information Act (FOIA), which does not apply if the requested data fall within one or more exemptions. Exemption 7(C) excuses from disclosure "records or information compiled for law enforcement purposes" if their production "could reasonably be expected to constitute an unwarranted invasion of personal privacy." Here, the information pertains to an official investigation into the circumstances surrounding an apparent suicide. The initial question is whether the exemption extends to the decedent's family when the family objects to the release of photographs showing the condition of the body at the scene of death. If we find the decedent's family does have a personal privacy interest recognized by the statute, we must then consider whether that privacy claim is outweighed by the public interest in disclosure.

Vincent Foster, Jr., deputy counsel to President Clinton, was found dead in Fort Marcy Park, located just outside Washington, D.C. The United States Park Police conducted the initial investigation and took color photographs of the death scene, including 10 pictures of Foster's body. The investigation concluded that Foster committed suicide by shooting himself with a revolver. Subsequent investigations by the Federal Bureau of Investigation, committees of the Senate and the House of Representatives, and independent counsels Robert Fiske and Kenneth Starr reached the same conclusion. Despite the unanimous finding of these five investigations, a citizen interested in the matter, Allan Favish, remained skeptical. Favish is now a respondent in this proceeding. In an earlier proceeding, Favish was the associate counsel for Accuracy in Media (AIM), which applied under FOIA for Foster's death-scene photographs. After the National Park Service, which then maintained custody of the pictures, resisted disclosure, Favish filed suit on behalf of AIM in the District Court for the District of Columbia to compel production. The District Court granted summary judgment against AIM. The Court of Appeals for the District of Columbia unanimously affirmed. Still convinced that the Government's investigations were "grossly incomplete and untrustworthy," Favish filed the present

FOIA request in his own name, seeking, among other things, 11 pictures, 1 showing Foster's eyeglasses and 10 depicting various parts of Foster's body. The only documents at issue in this case are the four photographs [of the 11 requested by Favish] the Court of Appeals ordered released in its 2002 unpublished opinion. We reverse.

It is common ground among the parties that the death-scene photographs in OIC's possession are "records or information compiled for law enforcement purposes" as that phrase is used in Exemption 7(C). This leads to the question whether disclosure of the four photographs "could reasonably be expected to constitute an unwarranted invasion of personal privacy."

Favish contends the family has no personal privacy interest covered by Exemption 7(C). His argument rests on the proposition that the information is only about the decedent, not his family. FOIA's right to personal privacy, in his view, means only "the right to control information about oneself." He quotes from [one of our earlier FOIA decisions] where, in holding that a person has a privacy interest sufficient to prevent disclosure of his own rap sheet, we said "the common law and the literal understandings of privacy encompass the individual's control of information concerning his or her person." This means, Favish says, that the individual who is the subject of the information is the only one with a privacy interest.

We disagree. The right to personal privacy is not confined, as Favish argues, to the "right to control information about oneself." Favish misreads [our precedents]. To say that the concept of personal privacy must "encompass" the individual's control of information about himself does not mean it cannot encompass other personal privacy interests as well.

The concept of personal privacy under Exemption 7(C) is not some limited or "cramped notion" of that idea. Records or information are not to be released under the Act if disclosure "could reasonably be expected to constitute an unwarranted invasion of personal privacy." This provision is in marked contrast to the language in Exemption 6, pertaining to "personnel and medical files," where withholding is required only if disclosure "would constitute a clearly unwarranted invasion of personal privacy." The adverb "clearly," found in Exemption 6, is not used in Exemption 7(C). In addition, whereas Exemption 6 refers to disclosures that "would constitute" an invasion of privacy, Exemption 7(C) encompasses any disclosure that "could reasonably be expected to constitute" such an invasion. Exemption 7(C)'s comparative breadth is no mere accident in drafting. We know Congress gave special consideration to the language in Exemption 7(C) because it was the result of specific amendments to an existing statute.

Law enforcement documents obtained by Government investigators often contain information about persons interviewed as witnesses or initial suspects but whose link to the official inquiry may be the result of mere happenstance. There is special reason, therefore, to give protection to this intimate personal data, to which the public does not have a general right of access in the ordinary course. In this class of cases where the subject of the documents is a private citizen, the privacy interest is at its apex.

Certain *amici* in support of Favish rely on the modifier "personal" before the word "privacy" to bolster their view that the family has no privacy interest in the pictures of the decedent. This, too, misapprehends the family's position and the scope of protection the exemption provides. The family does not invoke Exemption 7(C) on behalf of Vincent Foster in its capacity as his next friend for fear that the pictures may reveal private information about Foster to the detriment of his own posthumous reputation or some other interest personal to him. If that were the case, a different set of considerations would control. Foster's relatives instead invoke their own right and interest to personal privacy. They seek to be shielded by the exemption to secure their own refuge from a sensation-seeking culture for their own peace of mind and tranquility, not for the sake of the deceased.

In a sworn declaration filed with the District Court, Foster's sister, Sheila Foster Anthony, stated that the family had been harassed by, and deluged with requests from, "[p]olitical and commercial opportunists" who sought to profit from Foster's suicide. In particular, she was "horrified and devastated by [a] photograph [already] leaked to the press." Every time I see it, I have nightmares and heart-pounding insomnia as I visualize how he must have spent his last few minutes and seconds of his life." She opposed the disclosure of the disputed pictures because "I fear that the release of [additional] photographs certainly would set off another round of intense scrutiny by the media. Undoubtedly, the photographs would be placed on the Internet for world consumption. Once again my family would be the focus of conceivably unsavory and distasteful media coverage." "[R]eleasing any photographs," Sheila Foster Anthony continued, "would constitute a painful unwarranted invasion of my privacy, my mother's privacy, my sister's privacy, and the privacy of Lisa Foster Moody (Vince's widow), her three children, and other members of the Foster family."

As we shall explain below, we think it proper to conclude from Congress' use of the term "personal privacy" that it intended to permit family members to assert their own privacy rights against public intrusions long deemed impermissible under the common law and in our cultural traditions. This does not mean that the family is in the same position as the individual who is the subject of the disclosure. We have little difficulty, however, in finding in our case law and traditions the right of family members to direct and control disposition of the body of the deceased and to limit attempts to exploit pictures of the deceased family member's remains for public purposes.

Burial rites or their counterparts have been respected in almost all civilizations from time immemorial. They are a sign of the respect a society shows for the deceased and for the surviving family members. The power of Sophocles' story in *Antigone* maintains its hold to this day because of the universal acceptance of the heroine's right to insist on respect for the body of her brother. The outrage at seeing the bodies of American soldiers mutilated and dragged through the streets is but a modern instance of the same understanding of the interests decent people have for those whom they have lost. Family members have a personal stake in honoring and mourning their dead and objecting to unwarranted public exploitation that, by intruding upon their own grief, tends to degrade the rites and respect they seek to accord to the deceased person who was once their own.

In addition this well-established cultural tradition acknowledging a family's control over the body and death images of the deceased has long been recognized at common law. An early decision by the New York Court of Appeals [said]: "A privilege may be given the surviving relatives of a deceased person to protect his memory, but the privilege exists for the benefit of the living, to protect their feelings, and to prevent a violation of their own rights in the character and memory of the deceased." [*Editor's note*: Justice Kennedy adds short quotes from a handful of other lower-court decisions.]

We can assume Congress legislated against this background of law, scholarship, and history when it enacted FOIA and when it amended Exemption 7(C) to extend its terms. Those enactments were also against the background of the Attorney General's consistent interpretation of the exemption to protect "members of the family of the person to whom the information pertains," and to require consideration of the privacy of "relatives or descendants" and the "possible adverse effects [from disclosure] upon [the individual] or his family."

We have observed that the statutory privacy right protected by Exemption 7(C) goes beyond the common law and the Constitution. It would be anomalous to hold in the instant case that the statute provides even less protection than does the common law.

The statutory scheme must be understood, moreover, in light of the consequences that would follow were we to adopt Favish's position. As a general rule, withholding information under FOIA cannot be predicated on the identity of the requester. We are advised by the Government that child molesters, rapists, murderers, and other violent criminals often make FOIA requests for autopsies, photographs, and records of their deceased victims. Our holding ensures that the privacy interests of surviving family members would allow the Government to deny these gruesome requests in appropriate cases. We find it inconceivable that Congress could have intended a definition of "personal privacy" so narrow that it would allow convicted felons to obtain these materials without limitations at the expense of surviving family members' personal privacy.

For these reasons, we hold that FOIA recognizes surviving family members' right to personal privacy with respect to their close relative's death-scene images. Our holding is consistent with the unanimous view of the Courts of Appeals and other lower courts that have addressed the question. Neither the deceased's former status as a public official, nor the fact that other pictures had been made public, detracts from the weighty privacy interests involved.

Our ruling that the personal privacy protected by Exemption 7(C) extends to family members who object to the disclosure of graphic details surrounding their relative's death does not end the case. Although this privacy interest is within the terms of the exemption, the statute directs nondisclosure only where the information "could reasonably be expected to constitute an unwarranted invasion" of the family's personal privacy. The term "unwarranted" requires us to balance the family's privacy interest against the public interest in disclosure.

FOIA is often explained as a means for citizens to know "what the Government is up to." This phrase should not be dismissed as a convenient formalism. It defines a structural necessity in a real democracy. The statement confirms that, as a general rule, when documents are within FOIA's disclosure provisions, citizens should not be required to explain why they seek the information. A person requesting the information needs no preconceived idea of the uses the data might serve. The information belongs to citizens to do with as they choose. Furthermore, as we have noted, the disclosure does not depend on the identity of the requester. As a general rule, if the information is subject to disclosure, it belongs to all.

When disclosure touches upon certain areas defined in the exemptions, however, the statute recognizes limitations that compete with the general interest in disclosure, and that, in appropriate cases, can overcome it. In the case of Exemption 7(C), the statute requires us to protect, in the proper degree, the personal privacy of citizens against the uncontrolled release of information compiled through the power of the state. The statutory direction that the information not be released if the invasion of personal privacy could reasonably be expected to be unwarranted requires the courts to balance the competing interests in privacy and disclosure. To effect this balance and to give practical meaning to the exemption, the usual rule that the citizen need not offer a reason for requesting the information must be inapplicable.

Where the privacy concerns addressed by Exemption 7(C) are present, the exemption requires the person requesting the information to establish a sufficient reason for the disclosure. First, the citizen must show that the public interest sought to be advanced is a significant one, an interest more specific than having the information for its own sake. Second, the citizen must show the information is likely to advance that interest. Otherwise, the invasion of privacy is unwarranted.

We do not in this single decision attempt to define the reasons that will suffice, or the necessary nexus between the requested information and the asserted public interest that would be advanced by disclosure. On the other hand, there must be some stability with respect to both the specific category of personal privacy interests protected by the statute and the specific category of public interests that could outweigh the privacy claim. Otherwise, courts will be left to balance in an ad hoc manner with little or no real guidance. In the case of photographic images and other data pertaining to an individual who died under mysterious circumstances, the justification most likely to satisfy Exemption 7(C)'s public interest requirement is that the information is necessary to show the investigative agency or other responsible officials acted negligently or otherwise improperly in the performance of their duties.

The Court of Appeals was correct to rule that the family has a privacy interest protected by the statute and to recognize as significant the asserted public interest in uncovering deficiencies or misfeasance in the Government's investigations into Foster's death. It erred, however, in defining the showing Favish must make to substantiate his public interest claim. It stated that "[n]othing in the statutory command conditions [disclosure] on the requesting party showing that he has knowledge of misfeasance by the agency" and that "[n]othing in the statutory command shields an agency from disclosing its records because other agencies have engaged in similar investigations." The court went on to hold that, because Favish has "tender[ed] evidence and argument which, if believed, would justify his doubts," the FOIA request "is in complete conformity with the statutory purpose that the public know what its government is up to." This was insufficient. The Court of Appeals required no particular showing that any evidence points with credibility to some actual misfeasance or other impropriety. The court's holding leaves Exemption 7(C) with little force or content. By requiring courts to engage in a state of suspended disbelief with regard to even the most incredible allegations, the panel transformed Exemption 7(C) into nothing more than a rule of pleading. The invasion of privacy under its rationale would be extensive. It must be remembered that once there is disclosure, the information belongs to the general public. There is no mechanism under FOIA for a protective order allowing only the requester to see whether the information bears out his theory, or for proscribing its general dissemination.

We hold that, where there is a privacy interest protected by Exemption 7(C) and the public interest being asserted is to show that responsible officials acted negligently or otherwise improperly in the performance of their duties, the requester must establish more than a bare suspicion in order to obtain disclosure. Rather, the requester must produce evidence that would warrant a belief by a reasonable person that the alleged Government impropriety might have occurred. It would be quite extraordinary to say we must ignore the fact that five different inquiries into the Foster matter reached the same conclusion. As we have noted, the balancing exercise in some other case might require us to make a somewhat more precise determination regarding the significance of the public interest and the historical importance of the events in question. We might need to consider the nexus required between the requested documents and the purported public interest served by disclosure. We need not do so here, however. Favish has not produced any evidence that would warrant a belief by a reasonable person that the alleged Government impropriety might have occurred to put the balance into play.

The judgment of the Court of Appeals is reversed, and the case is remanded with instructions to grant OIC's motion for summary judgment with respect to the four photographs in dispute.

POINTS FOR DISCUSSION

1. As a general principle, does the *Favish* decision require too much of FOIA requestors? The Court seems to be saying, does it not, that a requestor who seeks specific information in order to confirm or lay to rest suspicions of government wrongdoing must be able to prove, in advance, that there is good reason to believe the wrongdoing has occurred? A bit circular, isn't it, asking requestors to prove precisely that which they hope the information they are requesting will prove?
2. Should a privacy right under exemption 7(C) apply to others, beyond family members? What of coworkers? What about same-sex partners in states (almost all of them) that do not recognize gay marriages?

Acker v. Texas Water Commission

790 S.W. 2d 299 (Texas 1990)

Justice Doggett:

The vital issue in this case is whether the decision making of a state agency in a contested administrative case should be done openly or secretly. We believe the law requires openness.

Charles M. Acker received a favorable recommendation from the hearings examiner at the Texas Water Commission on a requested permit for a wastewater treatment plant. Thereafter, during a recess of a public hearing conducted by the three-member Commission, Commissioners Hopkins and Roming were allegedly overheard conversing about this application in a restroom. This purported discussion concerned Acker's costs in complying with a city subdivision ordinance. When the public meeting reconvened, Commissioners Hopkins and Houchins voted to deny the application, and Commissioner Roming voted to grant it. Claiming a violation of the Texas Open Meetings Act, Acker brought suit seeking to set aside this order. The trial court granted Acker summary judgment based upon this asserted violation, but was reversed by the court of appeals on grounds that section 17 of the Texas Administrative Procedure and Texas Register Act [TAPTRA] allows private communications between agency members. We affirm the judgment, although not the reasoning, of the court of appeals and remand to the trial court for further proceedings.

The Open Meetings Act, enacted in 1967, [provides that] executive and legislative decisions of our governmental officials as well as the underlying reasoning must be discussed openly before the public rather than secretly behind closed doors. In order to effect this policy, this statute requires that "every regular, special, or called meeting or session of every governmental body shall be open to the public." A "meeting" includes any deliberation involving a "quorum" or majority of the members of a governing body at which they act on or discuss any public business or policy over which they have control. Any verbal exchange between a majority of the members concerning any issue within their jurisdiction constitutes a "deliberation." When a majority of a public decision making body is considering a pending issue, there can be no "informal" discussion. There is either formal consideration of a matter in compliance with the Open Meetings Act or an illegal meeting. Our citizens are entitled to more than a result. They are entitled not only to know what government decides but to observe how and why every decision is reached. The explicit command of the statute is for openness at every stage of the deliberations.

The court of appeals created a gaping hole in the Open Meetings Act through the meaning accorded to the subsequent enactment of section 17 of TAPTRA. That court held that TAPTRA authorizes a quorum of a state commission without any prior notice to meet and deliberate privately about any aspect of a pending contested proceeding. This holding effectively eviscerates the Open Meetings Act for application to the executive branch of our government. In administrative review of contested issues from a to z—from alcoholic beverages to zoos—secrecy would suddenly be authorized. This serious circumvention of open government is not warranted under the rules of statutory construction. A statute is presumed to have been enacted by the legislature with complete knowledge of the existing law and with reference to it. TAPTRA was enacted in 1975 to "afford minimum standards of uniform practice and procedure for state agencies." A subsequent amendment to section 17 of TAPTRA provided that "an agency member may communicate ex parte with other members of the agency." Without attempting to reconcile the Open Meetings Act with this provision, the court of appeals considered the latter impliedly to have repealed the former for purposes of all administrative agency consideration of contested cases.

Such statutory repeals by implication are not favored. A legislative enactment covering a subject dealt with by an older law, but not repealing that law, should be harmonized whenever possible with its predecessor in such a manner as to give effect to both. Accordingly, section 17 of TAPTRA can be harmonized with the Open Meetings Act by allowing a state commission's members to confer ex parte, but only when less than a quorum is present. Such coordinating preserves both TAPTRA and the objective of the Open Meetings Act to forbid ex parte deliberations.

Since the two statutes in question can be harmonized in a manner not compelling implicit revocation of the Open Meetings Act, we now consider whether the Commission violated the Act as a matter of law. In the review of a summary judgment, the movant has the burden of showing that there is no genuine issue of material fact and that it is entitled to judgment as a matter of law. Evidence favorable to the non-movant will be taken as true when deciding whether a material fact issue exists. All reasonable inferences must be indulged in favor of the non-movant and any doubts resolved in its favor.

The trial court's finding of an improper, closed meeting by two of the three members of the Commission is supported by the affidavit of Andrew M. Taylor who overheard the Roming/Hopkins conversation. As one of Acker's attorneys in the proceedings before the Commission, Taylor was an interested witness. His relationship with Acker, however, is not enough to defeat the motion.

Both Commissioners Roming and Hopkins testified by affidavit that they had no recollection of any conversation outside the hearing, and that considering their past behavior and habit at the Texas Water Commission, the occurrence of such a conversation was highly unlikely. The habit or custom of a person doing a particular act is relevant in determining his conduct on the occasion in question. These affidavits are sufficient to controvert the summary judgment evidence of Taylor, thereby raising a fact question and defeating Acker's motion.

We hold that a meeting between a majority of the Commissioners to discuss among themselves contested issues outside a public hearing violates section 2 of the Open Meetings Act. We further hold that in this case the Commissioners' affidavits raised a material fact issue precluding summary judgment. We affirm the judgment, although not the reasoning, of the court of appeals and remand this case to the trial court for further proceedings consistent with this opinion.

POINTS FOR DISCUSSION

1. The Texas Open Meetings Act defines a "deliberation" as "any verbal exchange between a majority of the members concerning any issue within their jurisdiction." Would there have been a violation of law had Commissioners Hopkins and Roming's men's room conversation consisted of no more than, "That Acker sure is an ugly SOB, don't you think?" and, "Yup. And his mother dresses him funny, too"?
2. The court reconciles the Open Meetings Act with TAPTRA by permitting nonpublic, *ex parte* meetings to take place, as long as a quorum is not present. At least this way, any such nonpublic meetings will not result in a final decision. What happens, though, in the case of a commission consisting only of three members? Two is a quorum, but two is also the minimum number of participants in a discussion. Can members of such a commission therefore never have a nonpublic discussion?

▪ *Doe v. Reed*

130 S. Ct. 2811 (2010)
Chief Justice Roberts:

The State of Washington allows its citizens to challenge state laws by referendum. Roughly four percent of Washington voters must sign a petition to place such a referendum on the ballot. That petition, which by law must include the names and addresses of the signers, is then submitted to the government for verification and canvassing, to ensure that only lawful signatures are counted. The Washington Public Records Act (PRA) authorizes private parties to obtain copies of government documents, and the State construes the PRA to cover submitted referendum petitions.

This case arises out of a state law extending certain benefits to same-sex couples, and a corresponding referendum petition to put that law to a popular vote. Respondent intervenors invoked the PRA to obtain copies of the petition, with the names and addresses of the signers. Certain petition signers and the petition sponsor objected, arguing that such public disclosure would violate their rights under the First Amendment.

The course of this litigation, however, has framed the legal question before us more broadly. The issue at this stage of the case is not whether disclosure of this particular petition would violate the First Amendment, but whether disclosure of referendum petitions in general would do so. We conclude that such disclosure does not as a general matter violate the First Amendment, and we therefore affirm the judgment of the Court of Appeals. We leave it to the lower courts to consider in the first instance the signers' more focused claim concerning disclosure of the information on this particular petition, which is pending before the District Court.

The Washington Constitution reserves to the people the power to reject any bill, with a few limited exceptions not relevant here, through the referendum process. To initiate a referendum, proponents must file a petition with the secretary of state that contains valid signatures of registered Washington voters equal to or exceeding four percent of the votes cast for the office of Governor at the last gubernatorial election. A valid submission requires not only a signature, but also the signer's address and the county in which he is registered to vote.

In May 2009, Washington Governor Christine Gregoire signed into law Senate Bill 5688, which expanded the rights and responsibilities of state-registered domestic partners, including same-sex domestic partners. That same month, Protect Marriage Washington, one of the petitioners here, was organized as a "State Political Committee" for the purpose of collecting the petition signatures necessary to place a referendum on the ballot, which would give the voters themselves an opportunity to vote on SB 5688. If the referendum made it onto the ballot, Protect Marriage Washington planned to encourage voters to reject SB 5688.

On July 25, 2009, Protect Marriage Washington submitted to the secretary of state a petition containing over 137,000 signatures. The secretary of state then began the verification and canvassing process, as required by Washington law, to ensure that only legal signatures were counted. Some 120,000 valid signatures were required to place the referendum on the ballot. The secretary of state determined that the petition contained a sufficient number of valid signatures, and the referendum (R-71) appeared on the November 2009 ballot. The voters approved SB 5688 by a margin of 53% to 47%.

The PRA makes all "public records" available for public inspection and copying. The Act defines "public record" as "any writing containing information relating to the conduct of government or the performance of any governmental or proprietary function prepared, owned, used, or retained by any state or local agency." Washington takes the position that referendum petitions are "public records."

By August 20, 2009, the secretary had received requests for copies of the R-71 petition from an individual and four entities, including Washington Coalition for Open Government (WCOG) and Washington Families Standing Together (WFST), two of the respondents here. Two entities, WhoSigned.org and KnowThyNeighbor.org, issued a joint press release stating their intention to post the names of the R-71 petition signers online, in a searchable format.

The referendum petition sponsor and certain signers filed a complaint and a motion for a preliminary injunction in the United States District Court for the Western District of Washington, seeking to enjoin the secretary of state from publicly releasing any documents that would reveal the names and contact information of the R-71 petition signers. Count I of the complaint alleges that the Public Records Act is unconstitutional as applied to referendum petitions. Count II of the complaint alleges that the Public Records Act is unconstitutional as applied to the Referendum 71 petition because there is a reasonable probability that the signatories of the Referendum 71 petition will be subjected to threats, harassment, and reprisals. Determining that the PRA burdened core political speech, the District Court held that plaintiffs were likely to succeed on the merits of Count I and granted them a preliminary injunction on that count, enjoining release of the information on the petition. The United States Court of Appeals for the Ninth Circuit reversed. Reviewing only Count I of the complaint, the Court of Appeals held that plaintiffs were unlikely to succeed on their claim that the PRA is unconstitutional as applied to referendum petitions generally. It therefore reversed the District Court's grant of the preliminary injunction.

It is important at the outset to define the scope of the challenge before us. The District Court decision was based solely on Count I; the Court of Appeals decision reversing the District Court was similarly limited. Neither court addressed Count II.

The parties disagree about whether Count I is properly viewed as a facial or as-applied challenge. It obviously has characteristics of both: The claim is "as applied" in the sense that it does not seek to strike the PRA in all its applications, but only to the extent it covers referendum petitions. The claim is "facial" in that it is not limited to plaintiffs' particular case, but challenges application of the law more broadly to all referendum petitions.

The label is not what matters. The important point is that plaintiffs' claim and the relief that would follow—an injunction barring the secretary of state from making referendum petitions available to the public—reach beyond the particular circumstances of these plaintiffs. They must therefore satisfy our standards for a facial challenge to the extent of that reach.

The compelled disclosure of signatory information on referendum petitions is subject to review under the First Amendment. An individual expresses a view on a political matter when he signs a petition under Washington's referendum procedure. In most cases, the individual's signature will express the view that the law subject to the petition should be overturned. Even if the signer is agnostic as to the merits of the underlying law, his signature still expresses the political view that the question should be considered by the whole electorate. In either case, the expression of a political view implicates a First Amendment right. The State, having chosen to tap the energy and the legitimizing power of the democratic process, must accord the participants in that process the First Amendment rights that attach to their roles.

Respondents counter that signing a petition is a legally operative legislative act and therefore does not involve any significant expressive element. It is true that signing a referendum petition may ultimately have the legal consequence of requiring the secretary of state to place the referendum on the ballot. But we do not see how adding such legal effect to an expressive activity somehow deprives that activity of its expressive component, taking it outside the scope of the First Amendment. Respondents themselves implicitly recognize that the signature expresses a particular viewpoint, arguing that one purpose served by disclosure is to allow the public to engage signers in a debate on the merits of the underlying law.

Petition signing remains expressive even when it has legal effect in the electoral process. But that is not to say that the electoral context is irrelevant to the nature of our First Amendment review. We allow States significant flexibility in implementing their own voting systems. To the extent a regulation concerns the legal effect of a particular activity in that process, the government will be afforded substantial latitude to enforce that regulation. Also pertinent to our analysis is the fact that the PRA is not a prohibition on speech, but instead a *disclosure* requirement. Disclosure requirements may burden the ability to speak, but they do not prevent anyone from speaking.

[Our precedents demand that] First Amendment challenges to disclosure requirements in the electoral context [be] reviewed under what has been termed "exacting scrutiny." That standard requires a substantial relation between the disclosure requirement and a sufficiently important governmental interest. To withstand this scrutiny, the strength of the governmental interest must reflect the seriousness of the actual burden on First Amendment rights.

Respondents assert two interests to justify the burdens of compelled disclosure under the PRA on First Amendment rights: (1) preserving the integrity of the electoral process by combating fraud, detecting invalid signatures, and fostering government transparency and accountability; and (2) providing information to the electorate about who supports the petition. Because we determine that the State's interest in preserving the integrity of the electoral process suffices to defeat the argument that the PRA is unconstitutional with respect to referendum petitions in general, we need not, and do not, address the State's "informational" interest.

The State's interest in preserving the integrity of the electoral process is undoubtedly important. States allowing ballot initiatives have considerable leeway to protect the integrity and reliability of the initiative process, as they have with respect to election processes generally. The State's interest is particularly strong with respect to efforts to root out fraud, which not only may produce fraudulent outcomes, but has a systemic effect as well: It drives honest citizens out of the democratic process and breeds distrust of our government. The threat of fraud in this context is not merely hypothetical; respondents and their *amici* cite a number of cases of petition-related fraud across the country to support the point.

But the State's interest in preserving electoral integrity is not limited to combating fraud. That interest extends to efforts to ferret out invalid signatures caused not by fraud but by simple mistake, such as duplicate signatures or signatures of individuals who are not registered to vote in the State. That interest also extends more generally to promoting transparency and accountability in the electoral process, which the State argues is essential to the proper functioning of a democracy.

Plaintiffs contend that the disclosure requirements of the PRA are not sufficiently related to the interest of protecting the integrity of the electoral process. They argue that disclosure is not necessary because the secretary of state is already charged with verifying and canvassing the names on a petition, advocates and opponents of a measure can observe that process, and any citizen can challenge the secretary's actions in court. They also stress that existing criminal penalties reduce the danger of fraud in the petition process.

But the secretary's verification and canvassing will not catch all invalid signatures: The job is large and difficult (the secretary ordinarily checks only 3 to 5% of signatures), and the secretary can make mistakes, too. Public disclosure can help cure the inadequacies of the verification and canvassing process.

Disclosure also helps prevent certain types of petition fraud otherwise difficult to detect, such as outright forgery and "bait and switch" fraud, in which an individual signs the petition based on a misrepresentation of the underlying issue. The signer is in the best position to detect these types of fraud, and public disclosure can bring the issue to the signer's attention.

Public disclosure thus helps ensure that the only signatures counted are those that should be, and that the only referenda placed on the ballot are those that garner enough valid signatures. Public disclosure also promotes transparency and accountability in the electoral process to an extent other measures cannot. In light of the foregoing, we reject plaintiffs' argument and conclude that public disclosure of referendum petitions in general is substantially related to the important interest of preserving the integrity of the electoral process.

Plaintiffs' more significant objection is that the strength of the governmental interest does not reflect the seriousness of the actual burden on First Amendment rights. According to plaintiffs, the objective of those seeking disclosure of the R-71 petition is not to prevent fraud, but to publicly identify those who had validly signed and to broadcast the signers' political views on the subject of the petition. Plaintiffs allege, for example, that several groups plan to post the petitions in searchable form on the Internet, and then encourage other citizens to seek out the R-71 signers.

Plaintiffs explain that once on the Internet, the petition signers' names and addresses can be combined with publicly available phone numbers and maps, in what will effectively become a blueprint for harassment and intimidation. To support their claim that they will be subject to reprisals, plaintiffs cite examples from the history of a similar proposition in California, and from the experience of one of the petition sponsors in this case.

In related contexts, we have explained that those resisting disclosure can prevail under the First Amendment if they can show a reasonable probability that the compelled disclosure of personal information will subject them to threats, harassment, or reprisals from either Government officials or private parties. The question before us, however, is not whether PRA disclosure violates the First Amendment with respect to those who signed the R-71 petition, or other particularly controversial petitions. The question instead is whether such disclosure in general violates the First Amendment rights of those who sign referendum petitions.

The problem for plaintiffs is that their argument rests almost entirely on the specific harm they say would attend disclosure of the information on the R-71 petition, or on similarly controversial ones. But typical referendum petitions concern tax policy, revenue, budget, or other state law issues. Voters care about such issues, some quite deeply—but there is no reason to assume that any burdens imposed by disclosure of typical referendum petitions would be remotely like the burdens plaintiffs fear in this case.

Faced with the State's unrebutted arguments that only modest burdens attend the disclosure of a typical petition, we must reject plaintiffs' broad challenge to the PRA. In doing so, we note—as we have in other election law disclosure cases—that upholding the law against a broad-based challenge does not foreclose a litigant's success in a narrower one. The secretary of state acknowledges that plaintiffs may press the narrower challenge in Count II of their complaint in proceedings pending before the District Court.

We conclude that disclosure under the PRA would not violate the First Amendment with respect to referendum petitions in general and therefore affirm the judgment of the Court of Appeals.

POINTS FOR DISCUSSION

1. At its core, *Doe v. Reed* is about balancing "access to government information" and privacy interests. In general, do you think that the fact that you have signed a petition to place an issue on a ballot should be considered a public record? Why or why not?
2. Media coverage of this litigation included quotes to the effect that the organizations seeking disclosure wanted to make possible "uncomfortable conversations" with anti-same-sex marriage signatories. To some the phrase suggested the possibility of threats of violence or at least of economic retribution (e.g., boycotts), while to others it meant only that public disclosure of the signatories' names could permit their closeted gay friends and family members to "come out" to them in hopes of swaying them to the other side of this divisive political issue. Should signatories have a right to avoid even "uncomfortable conversations" of the second kind?

8

Covering the Judiciary

There is a certain tension between the First Amendment's free speech and free press guarantees and the Sixth Amendment, which promises criminal defendants that their juries will be impartial. Might not certain kinds of media coverage, especially of sensational crimes, make it difficult to find jurors who can render a judgment solely on the evidence to be presented to them in the courtroom? The cases in this chapter offer a glimpse into how courts have addressed this difficult question.

We begin with *Sheppard v. Maxwell*, a 1966 U.S. Supreme Court case dealing with the trial of Dr. Sam Sheppard for the murder of his wife. You may recognize this case as the basis for the TV series and motion picture *The Fugitive*. In the course of overturning Sheppard's conviction, the Supreme Court tells trial judges that they have to do a better job than done here of keeping the press (and trial participants) in line.

In *Nebraska Press Association v. Stuart*, the Supreme Court tells trial judges under what circumstances they may impose a "gag order," prohibiting the media from publishing certain categories of information about a pending criminal investigation or an ongoing trial.

In addition to their name—*Press-Enterprise v. Superior Court*—two additional cases in this chapter have in common the question as to when trial judges will be permitted to close the courtroom to the press and public. The first case deals with the First Amendment interests raised by closure of a voir dire (jury selection) hearing.

Following immediately is *Presley v. Georgia*, in which the Supreme Court tells us that the accused separately has a constitutional right to an open voir dire hearing.

The second *Press-Enterprise* case finishes off this chapter. It involves closure of an elaborate "preliminary hearing" as conducted in California.

■ *Sheppard v. Maxwell*

384 U.S. 333 (1966)

Justice Clark:

This federal habeas corpus application involves the question whether Sheppard was deprived of a fair trial in his state conviction for the second-degree murder of his wife because of the trial judge's failure to protect Sheppard sufficiently from the massive, pervasive and prejudicial publicity that attended his prosecution. Marilyn Sheppard, petitioner's pregnant wife, was bludgeoned to death in the upstairs bedroom of their lakeshore home in Bay Village, Ohio, a suburb of Cleveland.

Sheppard was not granted a change of venue to a locale away from where the publicity originated; nor was his jury sequestered. The Sheppard jurors were subjected to newspaper, radio and television coverage of the trial while not taking part in the proceedings. They were allowed to go their separate ways outside of the courtroom, without adequate directions not to read or listen to anything concerning the case. Moreover, the jurors were thrust into the role of celebrities by the judge's failure to insulate them from reporters and photographers. The numerous pictures of the jurors, with their addresses, which appeared in the newspapers before and during the trial itself exposed them to expressions of opinion from both cranks and friends. The fact that anonymous letters had been received by prospective jurors should have made the judge aware that this publicity seriously threatened the jurors' privacy.

Sheppard stood indicted for the murder of his wife; the State was demanding the death penalty. For months the virulent publicity about Sheppard and the murder had made the case notorious. Charges and countercharges were aired in the news media besides those for which Sheppard was called to trial. In addition, only three months before trial, Sheppard was examined for more than five hours without counsel during a three-day inquest which ended in a public brawl. The inquest was televised live from a high school gymnasium seating hundreds of people. Furthermore, the trial began two weeks before a hotly contested election at which both Chief Prosecutor Mahon and Judge Blythin were candidates for judgeships.

While we cannot say that Sheppard was denied due process by the judge's refusal to take precautions against the influence of pretrial publicity alone, the court's later rulings must be considered against the setting in which the trial was held. In light of this background, we believe that the arrangements made by the judge with the news media caused Sheppard to be deprived of that judicial serenity and calm to which he was entitled. The fact is that bedlam reigned at the courthouse during the trial and newsmen took over practically the entire courtroom, hounding most of the participants in the trial, especially Sheppard. At a temporary table within a few feet of the jury box and counsel table sat some 20 reporters staring at Sheppard and taking notes. The erection of a press table for reporters inside the bar is unprecedented. The bar of the court is reserved for counsel, providing them a safe place in which to keep papers and exhibits, and to confer privately with client and co-counsel. It is designed to protect the witness and the jury from any distractions, intrusions or influences, and to permit bench discussions of the judge's rulings away from the hearing of the public and the jury. Having assigned almost all of the available seats in the courtroom to the news media the judge lost his ability to supervise that environment. The movement of the reporters in and out of the courtroom caused frequent confusion and disruption of the trial. And the record reveals constant commotion within the bar. Moreover, the judge gave the throng of newsmen gathered in the corridors of the courthouse absolute free rein. Participants in the trial, including the jury, were forced to run a gauntlet of reporters and photographers each time they entered or left the courtroom. The total lack of consideration for the privacy of the jury was demonstrated by the assignment to a broadcasting station of space next to the jury room on the floor above the courtroom, as well as the fact that jurors were allowed to make telephone calls during their five-day deliberation.

There can be no question about the nature of the publicity which surrounded Sheppard's trial. As the trial progressed, the newspapers summarized and interpreted the evidence, devoting particular attention to the material that incriminated Sheppard, and often drew unwarranted inferences from testimony. Nor is there doubt that this deluge of publicity reached at least some of the jury. Despite the extent and nature of the publicity to which the jury was exposed during trial, the judge refused defense counsel's other requests that the jurors be asked whether they had read or heard specific prejudicial comment about the case. In these circumstances, we can assume that some of this material reached members of the jury.

The court's fundamental error is compounded by the holding that it lacked power to control the publicity about the trial. From the very inception of the proceedings the judge announced that neither he nor anyone else could restrict prejudicial news accounts. And he reiterated this view on numerous occasions. Since he viewed the news media as his target, the judge never considered other means that are often utilized to reduce the appearance of prejudicial material and to protect the jury from outside influence. We conclude that these procedures would have been sufficient to guarantee Sheppard a fair trial and so do not consider what sanctions might be available against a recalcitrant press nor the charges of bias now made against the state trial judge.

The carnival atmosphere at trial could easily have been avoided since the courtroom and courthouse premises are subject to the control of the court. The judge should have adopted stricter rules governing the use of the courtroom by newsmen, as Sheppard's counsel requested. The number of reporters in the courtroom itself could have been limited at the first sign that their presence would disrupt the trial. They certainly should not have been placed inside the bar. Furthermore, the judge should have more closely regulated the conduct of newsmen in the courtroom. For instance, the judge belatedly asked them not to handle and photograph trial exhibits lying on the counsel table during recesses.

Secondly, the court should have insulated the witnesses. All of the newspapers and radio stations apparently interviewed prospective witnesses at will, and in many instances disclosed their testimony. Although the witnesses were barred from the courtroom during the trial the full verbatim testimony was available to them in the press. This completely nullified the judge's imposition of the rule.

Thirdly, the court should have made some effort to control the release of leads, information, and gossip to the press by police officers, witnesses, and the counsel for both sides. Much of the information thus disclosed was inaccurate, leading to groundless rumors and confusion. Defense counsel immediately brought to the court's attention the tremendous amount of publicity in the Cleveland press that "misrepresented entirely the testimony" in the case. Under such circumstances, the judge should have at least warned the newspapers to check the accuracy of their accounts. And it is obvious that the judge should have further sought to alleviate this problem by imposing control over the statements made to the news media by counsel, witnesses, and especially the Coroner and police officers. The prosecution repeatedly made evidence available to the news media which was never offered in the trial. Much of the "evidence" disseminated in this fashion was clearly inadmissible. The exclusion of such evidence in court is rendered meaningless when news media make it available to the public. The trial court might well have proscribed extrajudicial statements by any lawyer, party, witness, or court official which divulged prejudicial matters, such as the refusal of Sheppard to submit to interrogation or take any lie detector tests; any statement made by Sheppard to officials; the identity of prospective witnesses or their probable testimony; any belief in guilt or innocence; or like statements concerning the merits of the case. The court could also have requested the appropriate city and county officials to promulgate a regulation with respect to dissemination of information about the case by their employees. In addition reporters who wrote or broadcast prejudicial stories could have been warned as to the impropriety of publishing material not introduced in the proceedings.

Due process requires that the accused receive a trial by an impartial jury free from outside influences. Given the pervasiveness of modern communications and the difficulty of effacing prejudicial publicity from the minds of the jurors, the trial courts must take strong measures to ensure that the balance is never weighed against the accused. Of course, there is nothing that proscribes the press from reporting events that transpire in the courtroom. But where there is a reasonable likelihood that prejudicial news prior to trial will prevent a fair trial, the judge should continue the case until the threat abates, or transfer it to another county not so permeated with publicity. In addition, sequestration of the jury was something the judge should have raised *sua ponte* with counsel. If publicity during the proceedings threatens the fairness of the trial, a new trial should be ordered.

Since the state trial judge did not fulfill his duty to protect Sheppard from the inherently prejudicial publicity which saturated the community and to control disruptive influences in the courtroom, the case is remanded to the District Court with instructions to order that Sheppard be released from custody unless the State puts him to its charges again within a reasonable time. It is so ordered.

POINTS FOR DISCUSSION

1. Justice Clark makes much of the fact that jurors "were subjected to newspaper, radio and television coverage of the trial." That cannot constitute an argument, however, for *always* taking the extreme step of sequestering juries (putting them up at a hotel, cutting off virtually all contact with the outside world, during the trial and their deliberations). In what circumstances do you think it is appropriate to sequester a jury?
2. The trial judge is criticized for permitting police officers, witnesses, and attorneys to provide "information" and "gossip" to the press. Clearly Justice Clark thinks the trial judge should have imposed some kind of a gag order on these media sources. What should be the outer limits of such gag orders? Would it seem a bit silly, for example, for a prosecutor to be prohibited from telling the press that he thinks the defendant is guilty? Why *else* would he be prosecuting the case?

Nebraska Press Association v. Stuart
427 U.S. 539 (1976)
Chief Justice Burger:

On the evening of October 18, 1975, local police found the six members of the Henry Kellie family murdered in their home in Sutherland, Neb., a town of about 850 people. Police released the description of a suspect, Erwin Charles Simants, to the reporters who had hastened to the scene of the crime. Simants was arrested and arraigned in Lincoln County Court the following morning, ending a tense night for this small rural community.

The crime immediately attracted widespread news coverage, by local, regional, and national newspapers, radio and television stations. Three days after the crime, the County Attorney and Simants' attorney joined in asking the County Court to enter a restrictive order, because of the reasonable likelihood of prejudicial news. The County Court granted the prosecutor's motion for a restrictive order; [as later modified by the Nebraska Supreme Court, it] prohibited reporting of three matters: (a) the existence and nature of any confessions or admissions made by the defendant to law enforcement officers, (b) any confessions or admissions made to any third parties, except members of the press, and (c) other facts "strongly implicative" of the accused. The court noted that Nebraska statutes required the District Court to try Simants within six months of his arrest, and that a change of venue could move the trial only to adjoining counties, which had been subject to essentially the same publicity as Lincoln County. The order at issue in this case expired by its own terms when the jury was impaneled. There were no restraints on publication once the jury was selected, and there are now no restrictions on what may be spoken or written about the Simants case.

The problems presented by this case are almost as old as the Republic. Neither in the Constitution nor in contemporaneous writings do we find that the conflict between these two important rights was anticipated, yet it is inconceivable that the authors of the Constitution were unaware of the potential conflicts between the right to an unbiased jury and the guarantee of freedom of the press. The speed of communication and the pervasiveness of the modern news media have exacerbated these problems, however, as numerous appeals demonstrate. The excesses of press and radio and lack of responsibility of those in authority in the Bruno Hauptmann case and others led to efforts to develop voluntary guidelines for courts, lawyers, press, and broadcasters. The effort was renewed in 1965 when the American Bar Association embarked on a project to develop standards for all aspects of criminal justice, including guidelines to accommodate the right to a fair trial and the rights of a free press. Other groups have undertaken similar studies. In the wake of these efforts, the cooperation between bar associations and members of the press led to the adoption of voluntary guidelines like Nebraska's.

In practice, of course, even the most ideal guidelines are subjected to powerful strains when a case such as Simants' arises, with reporters from many parts of the country on the scene. Reporters from distant places are unlikely to consider themselves bound by local standards. They report to editors outside the area covered by the guidelines, and their editors are likely to be guided only by their own standards. To contemplate how a state court can control acts of a newspaper or broadcaster outside its jurisdiction, even though the newspapers and broadcasts reach the very community from which jurors are to be selected, suggests something of the practical difficulties of managing such guidelines.

The Sixth Amendment guarantees "trial, by an impartial jury..." in federal criminal prosecutions; the Due Process Clause of the Fourteenth Amendment guarantees the same right in state criminal prosecutions. In the overwhelming majority of criminal trials, pre-trial publicity presents few unmanageable threats to this important right. But when the case is a "sensational" one tensions develop between the right of the accused to trial by an impartial jury and the rights guaranteed others by the First Amendment.

Pre-trial publicity—even pervasive, adverse publicity—does not inevitably lead to an unfair trial. The capacity of the jury eventually impaneled to decide the case fairly is influenced by the tone and extent of the publicity, which is in part, and often in large part, shaped by what attorneys, police, and other officials do to precipitate news coverage. The trial judge has a major responsibility. What the judge says about a case, in or out of the courtroom, is likely to appear in newspapers and broadcasts. More important, the measures a judge takes or fails to take to mitigate the effects of pre-trial publicity may well determine whether the defendant receives a trial consistent with the requirements of due process.

The costs of failure to afford a fair trial are high. In the most extreme cases, the risk of injustice [is] avoided when convictions were reversed. But a reversal means that justice has been delayed for both the defendant and the State; in some cases, because of lapse of time retrial is impossible or further prosecution is gravely handicapped. Moreover, in borderline cases in which the conviction is not reversed, there is some possibility of an injustice unredressed.

The state trial judge in the case before us acted responsibly, out of a legitimate concern, in an effort to protect the defendant's right to a fair trial. What we must decide is not simply whether the Nebraska courts erred in seeing the possibility of real danger to the defendant's rights, but whether in the circumstances of this case the means employed were foreclosed by another provision of the Constitution.

None of our decided cases on prior restraint [of speech] involved restrictive orders entered to protect a defendant's right to a fair and impartial jury. Prior restraints on speech and publication are the most serious and the least tolerable infringement on First Amendment rights. The damage can be particularly great when the prior restraint falls upon the communication of news and commentary on current events. The protection against prior restraint should have particular force as applied to reporting of criminal proceedings, whether the crime in question is a single isolated act or a pattern of criminal conduct. The press does not simply publish information about trials but guards against the miscarriage of justice by subjecting the police, prosecutors, and judicial processes to extensive public scrutiny and criticism. The extraordinary protections afforded by the First Amendment carry with them something in the nature of a fiduciary duty to exercise the protected rights responsibly—a duty widely acknowledged but not always observed by editors and publishers. It is not asking too much to suggest that those who exercise First Amendment rights in newspapers or broadcasting enterprises direct some effort to protect the rights of an accused to a fair trial by unbiased jurors.

Of course, the order at issue does not prohibit but only postpones publication. Some news can be delayed and most commentary can even more readily be delayed without serious injury, and there often is a self-imposed delay when responsible editors call for verification of information. But such delays are normally slight and they are self-imposed. Delays imposed by governmental authority are a different matter.

The authors of the Bill of Rights did not undertake to assign priorities as between First Amendment and Sixth Amendment rights, ranking one as superior to the other. In this case, the petitioners would have us declare the right of an accused subordinate to their right to publish in all circumstances. But if the authors of these guarantees, fully aware of the potential conflicts between them, were unwilling or unable to resolve the issue by assigning to one priority over the other, it is not for us to rewrite the Constitution by undertaking what they declined to do. It is unnecessary, after nearly two centuries, to establish a priority applicable in all circumstances.

The Nebraska courts in this case enjoined the publication of certain kinds of information about the Simants case. Our review of the pre-trial record persuades us that the trial judge was justified in concluding that there would be intense and pervasive pre-trial publicity concerning this case. He could also reasonably conclude, based on common human experience, that publicity might impair the defendant's right to a fair trial. His conclusion as to the impact of such publicity on prospective jurors was of necessity speculative, dealing as he was with factors unknown and unknowable.

We find little in the record [to help us determine] whether measures short of an order restraining all publication would have insured the defendant a fair trial. [Such measures include] change of trial venue to a place less exposed to the intense publicity that seemed imminent in Lincoln County; postponement of the trial to allow public attention to subside; searching questioning of prospective jurors, to screen out those with fixed opinions as to guilt or innocence; and the use of emphatic and clear instructions on the sworn duty of each juror to decide the issues only on evidence presented in open court. Sequestration of jurors is, of course, always available. Although that measure insulates jurors only after they are sworn, it also enhances the likelihood of dissipating the impact of pre-trial publicity and emphasizes the elements of the jurors' oaths.

We have examined this record to determine the probable efficacy of the measures short of prior restraint on the press and speech. There is no finding that alternative measures would not have protected Simants' rights, and the Nebraska Supreme Court did no more than imply that such measures might not be adequate. Moreover, the record is lacking in evidence to support such a finding.

We must also assess the probable efficacy of prior restraint on publication as a workable method of protecting Simants' right to a fair trial, and we cannot ignore the reality of the problems of managing and enforcing pre-trial restraining orders. Finally, we note that the events disclosed by the record took place in a community of 850 people. It is reasonable to assume that, without any news accounts being printed or broadcast, rumors would travel swiftly by word of mouth. One can only speculate on the accuracy of such reports, given the generative propensities of rumors; they could well be more damaging than reasonably accurate news accounts. But plainly a whole community cannot be restrained from discussing a subject intimately affecting life within it. Given these practical problems, it is far from clear that prior restraint on publication would have protected Simants' rights.

The record demonstrates, as the Nebraska courts held, that there was indeed a risk that pretrial news accounts, true or false, would have some adverse impact on the attitudes of those who might be called as jurors. But on the record now before us it is not clear that further publicity, unchecked, would so distort the views of potential jurors that 12 could not be found who would, under proper instructions, fulfill their sworn duty to render a just verdict exclusively on the evidence presented in open court.

Of necessity our holding is confined to the record before us. However difficult it may be, we need not rule out the possibility of showing the kind of threat to fair trial rights that would possess the requisite degree of certainty to justify restraint. Our analysis ends as it began, with a confrontation between prior restraint imposed to protect one vital constitutional guarantee and the explicit command of another that the freedom to speak and publish shall not be abridged. We reaffirm that the guarantees of freedom of expression are not an absolute prohibition under all circumstances, but the barriers to prior restraint remain high and the presumption against its use continues intact. We hold that, with respect to the order entered in this case prohibiting reporting or commentary on judicial proceedings held in public, the barriers have not been overcome; to the extent that this order restrained publication of such material, it is clearly invalid. To the extent that it prohibited publication based on information gained from other sources, we conclude that the heavy burden imposed as a condition to securing a prior restraint was not met and the judgment of the Nebraska Supreme Court is therefore reversed.

POINTS FOR DISCUSSION

1. Chief Justice Burger admits that trial judges can only speculate about the likely impact of prejudicial pre-trial publicity on potential jurors. Yet he insists that trial judges demonstrate "findings" that remedies less restrictive on First Amendment values than imposing a gag order on the press would not succeed in remedying any such effect. How might trial judges go about gathering such elusive data?
2. Trial judges very rarely impose gag orders; they do so only in the most "sensational" cases. But does not media coverage of sensational trials often carry important life lessons? The "preppy murder" case from New York City in the 1980s, for example—where the accused claimed that he killed his victim accidentally, during "rough" but consensual sex—served as a clarion call for more effective parenting, especially among the wealthy classes from which both victim and accused came. Can you think of other such "sensational" crime stories that prompted you to do some deep thinking about your own life?

▪ *Press-Enterprise v. Superior Court (I)*
464 U.S. 501 (1984)
Chief Justice Burger:

Albert Greenwood Brown, Jr., was tried and convicted of the rape and murder of a teenage girl, and sentenced to death in California Superior Court. Before the voir dire examination of prospective jurors began, petitioner, Press-Enterprise Co., moved that the voir dire be open to the public and the press. Petitioner contended that the public had an absolute right to attend the trial, and asserted that the trial commenced with the voir dire proceedings. The State opposed petitioner's motion, arguing that if the press were present, juror responses would lack the candor necessary to assure a fair trial. The trial judge agreed; the voir dire consumed six weeks and all but approximately three days was closed to the public.

After the jury was empaneled, petitioner moved the trial court to release a complete transcript of the voir dire proceedings. Counsel for Brown argued that release of the transcript would violate the jurors' right of privacy. The prosecutor agreed, adding that the prospective jurors had answered questions under an implied promise of confidentiality. The court denied petitioner's motion. After Brown had been convicted and sentenced to death, petitioner again applied for release of the transcript. In denying this application, the judge stated: "The jurors were questioned in private relating to past experiences, and some of the jurors had some special experiences in sensitive areas that do not appear to be appropriate for public discussion." The California Supreme Court denied petitioner's request for a hearing.

The process of juror selection is itself a matter of importance, not simply to the adversaries but to the criminal justice system. A review of the historical evidence reveals that, since the development of trial by jury, the process of selection of jurors has presumptively been a public process with exceptions only for good cause shown. The roots of open trials reach back to the days before the Norman Conquest when cases in England were brought before "moots," a town meeting kind of body such as the local court of the hundred or the county court. Attendance was virtually compulsory on the part of the freemen of the community, who represented the "patria," or the "country," in rendering judgment. The public aspect thus was almost a necessary incident of jury trials, since the presence of a jury already insured the presence of a large part of the public.

As the jury system evolved in the years after the Norman Conquest, and the jury came to be but a small segment representing the community, the obligation of all freemen to attend criminal trials was relaxed; however, the public character of the proceedings, including jury selection, remained unchanged.

The presumptive openness of the jury selection process in England, not surprisingly, carried over into proceedings in colonial America. Public jury selection was the common practice in America when the Constitution was adopted.

For present purposes, how we allocate the "right" to openness as between the accused and the public, or whether we view it as a component inherent in the system benefitting both, is not crucial. No right ranks higher than the right of the accused to a fair trial. But the primacy of the accused's right is difficult to separate from the right of everyone in the community to attend the voir dire which promotes fairness.

The open trial thus plays as important a role in the administration of justice today as it did for centuries before our separation from England. The value of openness lies in the fact that people not actually attending trials can have confidence that standards of fairness are being observed; the sure knowledge that anyone is free to attend gives assurance that established procedures are being followed and that deviations will become known. Openness thus enhances both the basic fairness of the criminal trial and the appearance of fairness so essential to public confidence in the system. This openness has what is sometimes described as a "community therapeutic value." Criminal acts, especially violent crimes, often provoke public concern, even outrage and hostility; this in turn generates a community urge to retaliate and desire to have justice done. Whether this is viewed as retribution or otherwise is irrelevant. When the public is aware that the law is being enforced and the criminal justice system is functioning, an outlet is provided for these understandable reactions and emotions. Proceedings held in secret would deny this outlet and frustrate the broad public interest; by contrast, public proceedings vindicate the concerns of the victims and the community in knowing that offenders are being brought to account for their criminal conduct by jurors fairly and openly selected.

The presumption of openness may be overcome only by an overriding interest based on findings that closure is essential to preserve higher values and is narrowly tailored to serve that interest. The interest is to be articulated along with findings specific enough that a reviewing court can determine whether the closure order was properly entered. We now turn to whether the presumption of openness has been rebutted in this case.

Although three days of voir dire in this case were open to the public, six weeks of the proceedings were closed, and media requests for the transcript were denied. The Superior Court asserted two interests in support of its closure order and orders denying a transcript: the right of the defendant to a fair trial, and the right to privacy of the prospective jurors. Of course the right of an accused to fundamental fairness in the jury selection process is a compelling interest. But the California court's conclusion that Sixth Amendment and privacy interests were sufficient to warrant prolonged closure was unsupported by findings showing that an open proceeding in fact threatened those interests; hence it is not possible to conclude that closure was warranted. Even with findings adequate to support closure, the trial court's orders denying access to voir dire testimony failed to consider whether alternatives were available to protect the interests of the prospective jurors that the trial court's orders sought to guard. Absent consideration of alternatives to closure, the trial court could not constitutionally close the voir dire.

The jury selection process may, in some circumstances, give rise to a compelling interest of a prospective juror when interrogation touches on deeply personal matters that person has legitimate reasons for keeping out of the public domain. The trial involved testimony concerning an alleged rape of a teenage girl. Some questions may have been appropriate to prospective jurors that would give rise to legitimate privacy interests of those persons. For example, a prospective juror might privately inform the judge that she, or a member of her family, had been raped but had declined to seek prosecution because of the embarrassment and emotional trauma from the very disclosure of the episode. The privacy interests of such a prospective juror must be balanced against the historic values we have discussed and the need for openness of the process. To preserve fairness and at the same time protect legitimate privacy, a trial judge must at all times maintain control of the process of jury selection and should inform the array of prospective jurors, once the general nature of sensitive questions is made known to them, that those individuals believing public questioning will prove damaging because of embarrassment, may properly request an opportunity to present the problem to the judge in camera but with counsel present and on the record.

By requiring the prospective juror to make an affirmative request, the trial judge can ensure that there is in fact a valid basis for a belief that disclosure infringes a significant interest in privacy. This process will minimize the risk of unnecessary closure. The exercise of sound discretion by the court may lead to excusing such a person from jury service. When limited closure is ordered, the constitutional values sought to be protected by holding open proceedings may be satisfied later by making a transcript of the closed proceedings available within a reasonable time, if the judge determines that disclosure can be accomplished while safeguarding the juror's valid privacy interests. Even then a valid privacy right may rise to a level that part of the transcript should be sealed, or the name of a juror withheld, to protect the person from embarrassment.

The judge at this trial closed an incredible six weeks of voir dire without considering alternatives to closure. Later the court declined to release a transcript of the voir dire even while stating that "most of the information" in the transcript was "dull and boring." Those parts of the transcript reasonably entitled to privacy could have been sealed without such a sweeping order; a trial judge should explain why the material is entitled to privacy.

Assuming that some jurors had protectible privacy interests in some of their answers, the trial judge provided no explanation as to why his broad order denying access to information at the voir dire was not limited to information that was actually sensitive and deserving of privacy protection. Nor did he consider whether he could disclose the substance of the sensitive answers while preserving the anonymity of the jurors involved. Thus not only was there a failure to articulate findings with the requisite specificity but there was also a failure to consider alternatives to closure and to total suppression of the transcript. The trial judge should seal only such parts of the transcript as necessary to preserve the anonymity of the individuals sought to be protected.

The judgment of the Court of Appeal is vacated, and the case is remanded for proceedings not inconsistent with this opinion. It is so ordered.

POINTS FOR DISCUSSION

1. Chief Justice Burger emphasizes that the juror selection process has traditionally been considered a public event, and that this openness serves important societal functions. Does that mean that prospective jurors must expect that everything they say in the courtroom can be made public?
2. There is an unavoidable tension between jurors' argued privacy rights and the right of the accused to be judged by impartial peers. In a murder case such as this one, involving both rape and race (the defendant was black, the victims white), the kinds of questions most likely to be "sensitive" from the jurors' perspective (Are you a rape victim? What kinds of racially prejudiced attitudes do you harbor?) are precisely the ones that the defendant will want to have answered. How should this tension be resolved?

▪ *Presley v. Georgia*

130 S. Ct. 721 (2010)
Per Curiam:

After a jury trial in the Superior Court of DeKalb County, Georgia, petitioner Eric Presley was convicted of a cocaine trafficking offense. The conviction was affirmed by the Supreme Court of Georgia. Presley claims his Sixth and Fourteenth Amendment right to a public trial was violated when the trial court excluded the public from the *voir dire* of prospective jurors.

Before selecting a jury in Presley's trial, the trial court noticed a lone courtroom observer. The court explained that prospective jurors were about to enter and instructed the man that he was not allowed in the courtroom and had to leave that floor of the courthouse entirely. The court then questioned the man and learned he was Presley's uncle. The court reiterated its instruction:

> Well, you still can't sit out in the audience with the jurors. You know, most of the afternoon actually we're going to be picking a jury. And we may have a couple of pre-trial matters, so you're welcome to come in after we complete selecting the jury this afternoon. But, otherwise, you would have to leave the sixth floor, because jurors will be all out in the hallway in a few moments. That applies to everybody who's got a case.

Presley's counsel objected to "the exclusion of the public from the courtroom," but the court explained, "there just isn't space for them to sit in the audience." When Presley's counsel requested "some accommodation," the court explained its ruling further:

> Well, the uncle can certainly come back in once the trial starts. There's really no need for the uncle to be present during jury selection. We have 42 jurors coming up. Each of those rows will be occupied by jurors. And his uncle cannot sit and intermingle with members of the jury panel. But, when the trial starts, the opening statements and other matters, he can certainly come back into the courtroom.

After Presley was convicted, he moved for a new trial based on the exclusion of the public from the juror *voir dire*. At a hearing on the motion, Presley presented evidence showing that 14 prospective jurors could have fit in the jury box and the remaining 28 could have fit entirely on one side of the courtroom, leaving adequate room for the public. The trial court denied the motion, commenting that it preferred to seat jurors throughout the entirety of the courtroom, and "it's up to the individual judge to decide what's comfortable." The court continued: "It's totally up to my discretion whether or not I want family members in the courtroom to intermingle with the jurors and sit directly behind the jurors where they might overhear some inadvertent comment or conversation." On appeal, the Court of Appeals of Georgia agreed, finding "there was no abuse of discretion here, when the trial court explained the need to exclude spectators at the voir dire stage of the proceedings and when members of the public were invited to return afterward."

The Supreme Court of Georgia affirmed. After finding "the trial court certainly had an overriding interest in ensuring that potential jurors heard no inherently prejudicial remarks from observers during voir dire," the Supreme Court of Georgia rejected Presley's argument that the trial court was required to consider alternatives to closing the courtroom, [holding instead that Presley himself] "was obliged to present the court with any alternatives that he wished the court to consider."

This Court's rulings with respect to the public trial right rest upon two different provisions of the Bill of Rights. The Sixth Amendment directs, in relevant part, that "in all criminal prosecutions, the accused shall enjoy the right to a speedy and public trial."

The Sixth Amendment right, as the quoted language makes explicit, is the right of the accused. The Court has further held that the public trial right extends beyond the accused and can be invoked under the First Amendment.

The case now before the Court is brought under the Sixth Amendment, for it is the accused who invoked his right to a public trial. An initial question is whether the right to a public trial in criminal cases extends to the jury selection phase of trial, and in particular the *voir dire* of prospective jurors. In the First Amendment context that question was answered in *Press-Enterprise v. Superior Court I*. The Court there held that the *voir dire* of prospective jurors must be open to the public under the First Amendment. Later in the same Term as *Press-Enterprise I*, the Court considered a Sixth Amendment case (*Waller v. Georgia*, 1984) concerning whether the public trial right extends to a pretrial hearing on a motion to suppress certain evidence. The *Waller* Court relied heavily upon *Press-Enterprise I* in finding that the Sixth Amendment right to a public trial extends beyond the actual proof at trial. It ruled that the pretrial suppression hearing must be open to the public because "there can be little doubt that the explicit Sixth Amendment right of the accused is no less protective of a public trial than the implicit First Amendment right of the press and public." While *Press-Enterprise I* was heavily relied upon in *Waller*, the jury selection issue in the former case was resolved under the First, not the Sixth, Amendment. In the instant case, the question then arises whether it is so well settled that the Sixth Amendment right extends to jury *voir dire* that this Court may proceed by summary disposition.

The point is well settled under *Press-Enterprise I* and *Waller*. The extent to which the First and Sixth Amendment public trial rights are coextensive is an open question, and it is not necessary here to speculate whether or in what circumstances the reach or protections of one might be greater than the other.

Still, there is no legitimate reason, at least in the context of juror selection proceedings, to give one who asserts a First Amendment privilege greater rights to insist on public proceedings than the accused has.

While the accused does have a right to insist that the *voir dire* of the jurors be public, there are exceptions to this general rule. The right to an open trial may give way in certain cases to other rights or interests, such as the defendant's right to a fair trial or the government's interest in inhibiting disclosure of sensitive information. Such circumstances will be rare, however, and the balance of interests must be struck with special care. The party seeking to close the hearing must advance an overriding interest that is likely to be prejudiced, the closure must be no broader than necessary to protect that interest, the trial court must consider reasonable alternatives to closing the proceeding, and it must make findings adequate to support the closure.

In upholding exclusion of the public at juror *voir dire* in the instant case, the Supreme Court of Georgia concluded, despite our explicit statements to the contrary, that trial courts need not consider alternatives to closure absent an opposing party's proffer of some alternatives. While the Supreme Court of Georgia concluded this was an open question under this Court's precedents, the statement in *Waller* that "the trial court must consider reasonable alternatives to closing the proceeding" settles the point. If that statement leaves any room for doubt, the Court was more explicit in *Press-Enterprise I*:

> Even with findings adequate to support closure, the trial court's orders denying access to voir dire testimony failed to consider whether alternatives were available to protect the interests of the prospective jurors that the trial court's orders sought to guard. Absent consideration of alternatives to closure, the trial court could not constitutionally close the voir dire.

That trial courts are required to consider alternatives to closure even when they are not offered by the parties is clear not only from this Court's precedents but also from the premise that the process of juror selection is itself a matter of importance, not simply to the adversaries but to the criminal justice system. The public has a right to be present whether or not any party has asserted the right. In *Press-Enterprise I*, for instance, neither the defendant nor the prosecution requested an open courtroom during juror *voir dire* proceedings; in fact, both specifically argued in favor of keeping the transcript of the proceedings confidential. The Court, nonetheless, found it was error to close the courtroom.

Trial courts are obligated to take every reasonable measure to accommodate public attendance at criminal trials. Nothing in the record shows that the trial court could not have accommodated the public at Presley's trial. Without knowing the precise circumstances, some possibilities include reserving one or more rows for the public; dividing the jury venire panel to reduce courtroom congestion; or instructing prospective jurors not to engage or interact with audience members.

Petitioner also argues that, apart from failing to consider alternatives to closure, the trial court erred because it did not even identify any overriding interest likely to be prejudiced absent the closure of *voir dire*. There is some merit to this complaint. The generic risk of jurors overhearing prejudicial remarks, unsubstantiated by any specific threat or incident, is inherent whenever members of the public are present during the selection of jurors. If broad concerns of this sort were sufficient to override a defendant's constitutional right to a public trial, a court could exclude the public from jury selection almost as a matter of course.

There are no doubt circumstances where a judge could conclude that threats of improper communications with jurors or safety concerns are concrete enough to warrant closing *voir dire*. But in those cases, the particular interest, and threat to that interest, must be articulated along with findings specific enough that a reviewing court can determine whether the closure order was properly entered.

We need not rule on this second claim of error, because even assuming, *arguendo*, that the trial court had an overriding interest in closing *voir dire*, it was still incumbent upon it to consider all reasonable alternatives to closure. It did not, and that is all this Court needs to decide. The Supreme Court of Georgia's judgment is reversed, and the case is remanded for further proceedings not inconsistent with this opinion.

POINTS FOR DISCUSSION

1. If you were a trial judge, would you feel that the *Presley* case gives you sufficient guidance? What does it mean to "consider" all alternatives before closing voir dire to the press and the public?
2. The two precedents cited in *Presley* (*Waller* and *Press-Enterprise*) determined, respectively, that there is a Sixth Amendment right to a public suppression hearing (voir dire hearings were not at issue in *Waller*) and a First Amendment right to a public voir dire hearing. How then can the Court here conclude it is "well settled" that the accused has a Sixth Amendment right to a public voir dire hearing, when this is the first time the Court has addressed that specific issue?

Press-Enterprise v. Superior Court (II)
478 U.S. 1 (1986)
Chief Justice Burger:

We granted certiorari to decide whether petitioner has a First Amendment right of access to the transcript of a preliminary hearing growing out of a criminal prosecution. On December 23, 1981, the State of California charged Robert Diaz with murder, alleging that Diaz, a nurse, murdered 12 patients by administering massive doses of the heart drug lidocaine. The preliminary hearing on the complaint commenced on July 6, 1982. Diaz moved to exclude the public from the proceedings under Cal. Penal Code Ann. § 868, which requires such proceedings to be open unless "exclusion of the public is necessary in order to protect the defendant's right to a fair and impartial trial." The Magistrate granted the unopposed motion, finding that closure was necessary because the case had attracted national publicity.

The preliminary hearing continued for 41 days. At the conclusion of the hearing, petitioner Press-Enterprise asked that the transcript of the proceedings be released. The Magistrate refused and sealed the record. On January 21, 1983, the State moved in Superior Court to have the transcript of the preliminary hearing released to the public; petitioner later joined in support of the motion. Diaz opposed the motion, contending that release of the transcript would result in prejudicial pretrial publicity.

The Superior Court found that there was "a reasonable likelihood that release of all or any part of the transcripts might prejudice defendant's right to a fair and impartial trial."

Diaz waived his right to a jury trial and the Superior Court released the transcript.

In this Court, petitioner challenges the Superior Court's original refusal to release the transcript of the preliminary hearing. The specific relief petitioner seeks has already been granted—the transcript of the preliminary hearing was released after Diaz waived his right to a jury trial. However, this controversy is capable of repetition, yet evading review. It can reasonably be assumed that petitioner will be subjected to a similar closure order and, because criminal proceedings are typically of short duration, such an order will likely evade review.

The California Supreme Court decided that [preliminary hearings may be closed]: upon finding a reasonable likelihood of substantial prejudice which would impinge upon the right to a fair trial. It is difficult to disagree in the abstract with that court's analysis balancing the defendant's right to a fair trial against the public right of access. It is also important to remember that these interests are not necessarily inconsistent. Plainly, the defendant has a right to a fair trial but one of the important means of assuring a fair trial is that the process be open to neutral observers. The right to an open public trial is a shared right of the accused and the public, the common concern being the assurance of fairness.

The right asserted here is that of the public under the First Amendment. The California Supreme Court concluded that the First Amendment was not implicated because the proceeding was not a criminal trial, but a preliminary hearing. However, the First Amendment question cannot be resolved solely on the label we give the event, i.e., "trial" or otherwise, particularly where the preliminary hearing functions much like a full-scale trial.

In cases dealing with the claim of a First Amendment right of access to criminal proceedings, our decisions have emphasized two complementary considerations. First, we have considered whether the place and process have historically been open to the press and general public. The public trial, one of the essential qualities of a court of justice in England, was recognized early on in the Colonies. Second, the Court has traditionally considered whether public access plays a significant positive role in the functioning of the particular process in question. Although many governmental processes operate best under public scrutiny, it takes little imagination to recognize that there are some kinds of government operations that would be totally frustrated if conducted openly. A classic example is our grand jury system. Other proceedings plainly require public access.

The considerations that led the Court to [find a] First Amendment right of access to criminal trials and the selection of jurors lead us to conclude that the right of access applies to preliminary hearings as conducted in California.

First, there has been a tradition of accessibility to preliminary hearings of the type conducted in California. Although grand jury proceedings have traditionally been closed to the public and the accused, preliminary hearings conducted before neutral and detached magistrates have been open to the public. Long ago in the celebrated trial of Aaron Burr for treason, for example, with Chief Justice Marshall sitting as trial judge, the probable-cause hearing was held in the Hall of the House of Delegates in Virginia, the courtroom being too small to accommodate the crush of interested citizens. From Burr until the present day, the near uniform practice of state and federal courts has been to conduct preliminary hearings in open court.

The second question is whether public access to preliminary hearings as they are conducted in California plays a particularly significant positive role in the actual functioning of the process. Public access to criminal trials and the selection of jurors is essential to the proper functioning of the criminal justice system. California preliminary hearings are sufficiently like a trial to justify the same conclusion. In California, to bring a felon to trial, the prosecutor has a choice of securing a grand jury indictment or a finding of probable cause following a preliminary hearing. Even when the accused has been indicted by a grand jury, however, he has an absolute right to an elaborate preliminary hearing before a neutral magistrate. The accused has the right to personally appear at the hearing, to be represented by counsel, to cross-examine hostile witnesses, to present exculpatory evidence, and to exclude illegally obtained evidence. If the magistrate determines that probable cause exists, the accused is bound over for trial; such a finding leads to a guilty plea in the majority of cases.

It is true that unlike a criminal trial, the California preliminary hearing cannot result in the conviction of the accused and the adjudication is before a magistrate or other judicial officer without a jury. But these features, standing alone, do not make public access any less essential to the proper functioning of the proceedings in the overall criminal justice process. Because of its extensive scope, the preliminary hearing is often the final and most important step in the criminal proceeding. Similarly, the absence of a jury, long recognized as an inestimable safeguard against the corrupt or overzealous prosecutor and against the compliant, biased, or eccentric judge, makes the importance of public access to a preliminary hearing even more significant.

Denying the transcript of a 41-day preliminary hearing would frustrate what we have characterized as the community therapeutic value of openness. Criminal acts, especially certain violent crimes, provoke public concern, outrage, and hostility. When the public is aware that the law is being enforced and the criminal justice system is functioning, an outlet is provided for these understandable reactions and emotions.

We therefore conclude that the qualified First Amendment right of access to criminal proceedings applies to preliminary hearings as they are conducted in California.

Since a qualified First Amendment right of access attaches to preliminary hearings in California, the proceedings cannot be closed unless specific, on-the-record findings are made demonstrating that closure is essential to preserve higher values and is narrowly tailored to serve that interest. If the interest asserted is the right of the accused to a fair trial, the preliminary hearing shall be closed only if specific findings are made demonstrating that, first, there is a substantial probability that the defendant's right to a fair trial will be prejudiced by publicity that closure would prevent and, second, reasonable alternatives to closure cannot adequately protect the defendant's fair trial rights.

The California Supreme Court, interpreting its access statute, concluded that "the magistrate shall close the preliminary hearing upon finding a reasonable likelihood of substantial prejudice." As the court itself acknowledged, the "reasonable likelihood" test places a lesser burden on the defendant than the "substantial probability" test which we hold is called for by the First Amendment. Moreover, that court failed to consider whether alternatives short of complete closure would have protected the interests of the accused. The standard applied by the California Supreme Court failed to consider the First Amendment right of access to criminal proceedings. Accordingly, the judgment of the California Supreme Court is reversed.

POINTS FOR DISCUSSION

1. At this preliminary hearing, defendant Diaz called no witnesses. As such, the thousands of pages of transcripts necessarily contained a rather one-sided picture of the accused. Should this fact properly be considered by a magistrate trying to determine whether to close a hearing, and whether and when to release the transcripts to the press?
2. Chief Justice Burger notes that the preliminary hearing often is the only trial, in that a ruling to bind the defendant over for trial often leads to a plea bargain. To the extent that this counts as an argument for openness, might it not also suggest that grand jury proceedings—which have traditionally been conducted in secrecy—should be open, because they too often are the "only" trial a defendant will see?

9

Protecting News Sources

Read the first few paragraphs of the front-page stories in a newspaper known for investigative journalism and you will see how, for better or worse, American journalists rely frequently on confidential sources. Whistle-blowers are afraid of losing their jobs; political dissidents are afraid of violent reprisals. Scores of journalists over the years have gone to jail rather than reveal the identity of their sources.

In this chapter we look at cases in which the government wants a reporter to reveal information. Our first case is the landmark *Branzburg v. Hayes*, in which the Supreme Court tells us that reporters enjoy no special constitutional immunity from the obligation to testify when called in front of a grand jury. Interestingly, although reporter Paul Branzburg lost, the test his attorneys put before the court—that a reporter could be compelled to testify only if there is strong reason to believe she is the only logical source of information needed by the government—has since been accepted and applied by lower courts in a variety of situations.

We next look at a more contemporary application of the *Branzburg* holding to the subpoena issued against *New York Times* reporter Judith Miller, who was jailed for about three months for refusing to disclose that former vice presidential chief of staff Lewis Libby had revealed the name of a CIA operative to her.

Our next case, *Zurcher v. Stanford Daily*, tells law enforcement agencies that they may not only subpoena reporters for relevant information, but may also conduct a search of the newsroom itself (presuming they first obtain a valid search warrant). So outraged was the press by this decision that Congress was persuaded to pass the Privacy Protection Act of 1980, which greatly limits the circumstances in which newsrooms can be searched.

Next, *Cohen v. Cowles Media Company* is a case in which the media did not valiantly try to protect a source, but rather violated their promise not to publish the source's name. The Supreme Court reasons in much the same way it did in the earlier *Branzburg* case, concluding that the media enjoy no special immunity from liability for breaking promises.

Finally, in *Chevron Corporation v. Berlinger*, we see that it can be very hard for documentary filmmakers to qualify for a "reporter's privilege."

▪ *Branzburg v. Hayes*

408 U.S. 665 (1972)

Justice White:

The issue in these cases is whether requiring newsmen to appear and testify before state or federal grand juries abridges the freedom of speech and press guaranteed by the First Amendment. We hold that it does not.

Petitioner [Paul] Branzburg [is] a staff reporter for the *Courier-Journal*, a daily newspaper published in Louisville, Kentucky. On November 15, 1969, the *Courier-Journal* carried a story under petitioner's by-line describing in detail his observations of two young residents of Jefferson County synthesizing hashish from marijuana. The article stated that petitioner had promised not to reveal the identity of the two hashish makers. Petitioner was shortly subpoenaed by the Jefferson County grand jury; he appeared, but refused to identify the individuals he had seen possessing marijuana or the persons he had seen making hashish from marijuana. A state trial court judge ordered petitioner to answer these questions and rejected his contention that the Kentucky reporters' privilege statute the First Amendment of the United States Constitution, or §§ 1, 2, and 8 of the Kentucky Constitution authorized his refusal to answer. The Kentucky Court of Appeals construed [the reporters' privilege statute] as affording a newsman the privilege of refusing to divulge the identity of an informant who supplied him with information, but held that the statute did not permit a reporter to refuse to testify about events he had observed personally, including the identities of those persons he had observed.

Although he does not claim an absolute privilege against official interrogation in all circumstances, [Branzburg] asserts that the reporter should not be forced either to appear or to testify before a grand jury or at trial until and unless sufficient grounds are shown for believing that the reporter possesses information relevant to a crime the grand jury is investigating, that the information the reporter has is unavailable from other sources, and that the need for the information is sufficiently compelling to override the claimed invasion of First Amendment interests occasioned by the disclosure. The heart of the claim is that the burden on news gathering resulting from compelling reporters to disclose confidential information outweighs any public interest in obtaining the information.

We do not question the significance of free speech, press, or assembly to the country's welfare. Nor is it suggested that news gathering does not qualify for First Amendment protection; without some protection for seeking out the news, freedom of the press could be eviscerated. But this case involves no prior restraint or restriction on what the press may publish, and no express or implied command that the press publish what it prefers to withhold. The use of confidential sources by the press is not forbidden or restricted; reporters remain free to seek news from any source by means within the law. The sole issue before us is the obligation of reporters to respond to grand jury subpoenas as other citizens do and to answer questions relevant to an investigation into the commission of crime. Citizens generally are not constitutionally immune from grand jury subpoenas; and neither the First Amendment nor any other constitutional provision protects the average citizen from disclosing to a grand jury information that he has received in confidence. The claim is, however, that reporters are exempt from these obligations because if forced to respond to subpoenas and identify their sources or disclose other confidences, their informants will refuse or be reluctant to furnish newsworthy information in the future. This asserted burden on news gathering is said to make compelled testimony from newsmen constitutionally suspect and to require a privileged position for them.

It is clear that the First Amendment does not invalidate every incidental burdening of the press that may result from the enforcement of civil or criminal statutes of general applicability. Otherwise valid laws serving substantial public interests may be enforced against the press as against others, despite the possible burden that may be imposed.

The prevailing constitutional view of the newsman's privilege is very much rooted in the ancient role of the grand jury that has the dual function of determining if there is probable cause to believe that a crime has been committed and of protecting citizens against unfounded criminal prosecutions. Grand jury proceedings are constitutionally mandated for the institution of federal criminal prosecutions for capital or other serious crimes, and its constitutional prerogatives are rooted in long centuries of Anglo-American history. The Fifth Amendment provides that "no person shall be held to answer for a capital, or otherwise infamous crime, unless on a presentment or indictment of a Grand Jury." The adoption of the grand jury in our Constitution as the sole method for preferring charges in serious criminal cases shows the high place it held as an instrument of justice. The grand jury is similarly guaranteed by many state constitutions and plays an important role in fair and effective law enforcement in the overwhelming majority of the States. Because its task is to inquire into the existence of possible criminal conduct and to return only well-founded indictments, its investigative powers are necessarily broad. The grand jury's authority to subpoena witnesses is not only historic, but essential to its task.

A number of States have provided newsmen a statutory privilege of varying breadth, but the majority have not done so, and none has been provided by federal statute. Until now the only testimonial privilege for unofficial witnesses that is rooted in the Federal Constitution is the Fifth Amendment privilege against compelled self-incrimination. We are asked to create another by interpreting the First Amendment to grant newsmen a testimonial privilege that other citizens do not enjoy. This we decline to do. We perceive no basis for holding that the public interest in law enforcement and in ensuring effective grand jury proceedings is insufficient to override the consequential, but uncertain, burden on news gathering that is said to result from insisting that reporters, like other citizens, respond to relevant questions put to them in the course of a valid grand jury investigation or criminal trial.

We cannot seriously entertain the notion that the First Amendment protects a newsman's agreement to conceal the criminal conduct of his source, or evidence thereof, on the theory that it is better to write about crime than to do something about it.

The argument that the flow of news will be diminished by compelling reporters to aid the grand jury in a criminal investigation is not irrational, nor are the records before us silent on the matter. But we remain unclear how often and to what extent informers are actually deterred from furnishing information when newsmen are forced to testify before a grand jury.

Reliance by the press on confidential informants does not mean that all such sources will in fact dry up because of the later possible appearance of the newsman before a grand jury. The reporter may never be called and if he objects to testifying, the prosecution may not insist. Also, the relationship of many informants to the press is a symbiotic one which is unlikely to be greatly inhibited by the threat of subpoena: quite often, such informants are members of a minority political or cultural group that relies heavily on the media to propagate its views, publicize its aims, and magnify its exposure to the public.

It is obvious that agreements to conceal information relevant to commission of crime have very little to recommend them from the standpoint of public policy. Concealment of crime and agreements to do so are not looked upon with favor. Such conduct deserves no encomium, and we decline now to afford it First Amendment protection by denigrating the duty of a citizen, whether reporter or informer, to respond to a grand jury subpoena and answer relevant questions put to him.

From the beginning of our country the press has operated without constitutional protection for press informants, and the press has flourished. The existing constitutional rules have not been a serious obstacle to either the development or retention of confidential news sources by the press.

We do not deal [here] with a governmental institution that has abused its proper function, as a legislative committee does when it exposes for the sake of exposure. Nothing in the record indicates that these grand juries were probing at will and without relation to existing need. Nor did the grand juries attempt to invade protected First Amendment rights by forcing wholesale disclosure of names and organizational affiliations for a purpose that was not germane to the determination of whether crime has been committed.

The administration of a constitutional newsman's privilege would present practical and conceptual difficulties of a high order. Sooner or later, it would be necessary to define those categories of newsmen who qualified for the privilege, a questionable procedure in light of the traditional doctrine that liberty of the press is the right of the lonely pamphleteer who uses carbon paper or a mimeograph just as much as of the large metropolitan publisher who utilizes the latest photo composition methods. The informative function asserted by representatives of the organized press in the present cases is also performed by lecturers, political pollsters, novelists, academic researchers, and dramatists. Almost any author may quite accurately assert that he is contributing to the flow of information to the public, that he relies on confidential sources of information, and that these sources will be silenced if he is forced to make disclosures before a grand jury.

At the federal level, Congress has freedom to determine whether a statutory newsman's privilege is necessary and desirable and to fashion standards and rules as narrow or broad as deemed necessary to deal with the evil discerned and, equally important, to refashion those rules as experience from time to time may dictate. There is also merit in leaving state legislatures free, within First Amendment limits, to fashion their own standards in light of the conditions and problems with respect to the relations between law enforcement officials and press in their own areas. It goes without saying, of course, that we are powerless to bar state courts from responding in their own way and construing their own constitutions so as to recognize a newsman's privilege, either qualified or absolute.

In addition, there is much force in the pragmatic view that the press has at its disposal powerful mechanisms of communication and is far from helpless to protect itself from harassment or substantial harm.

Finally, as we have earlier indicated, news gathering is not without its First Amendment protections, and grand jury investigations if instituted or conducted other than in good faith, would pose wholly different issues for resolution under the First Amendment. Official harassment of the press undertaken not for purposes of law enforcement but to disrupt a reporter's relationship with his news sources would have no justification. Grand juries are subject to judicial control and subpoenas to motions to quash. We do not expect courts will forget that grand juries must operate within the limits of the First Amendment as well as the Fifth.

We turn, therefore, to the disposition of the case before us. Petitioner refused to answer questions that directly related to criminal conduct that he had observed and written about. Petitioner saw the commission of the statutory felonies of unlawful possession of marijuana and the unlawful conversion of it into hashish. If what petitioner wrote was true, he had direct information to provide the grand jury concerning the commission of serious crimes.

POINTS FOR DISCUSSION

1. Branzburg's informants were clearly engaged in criminal acts; thus it is equally clear why they wanted to stay anonymous. What other categories of noncriminal informants does the Court recognize, and what motivations would such informants have for seeking anonymity from reporters?
2. Justice White refuses to create a "reporter's privilege" in part because he is unclear as to how one might go about defining who is and is not a reporter. Pretend you are a state legislator drafting a reporter's privilege statute. How will you define "reporter" in your state's law?

▪ *In re Grand Jury Subpoena, Judith Miller*

397 F.3d 964 (D.C. Cir. 2005)

Judge Sentelle:

An investigative reporter for the *New York Times*; the White House correspondent for the weekly news magazine *Time*; and Time, Inc., the publisher of *Time*, appeal from orders of the District Court for the District of Columbia finding all three appellants in civil contempt for refusing to give evidence in response to grand jury subpoenas served by Special Counsel Patrick J. Fitzgerald. Appellants assert that the information concealed by them, specifically the identity of confidential sources, is protected by a reporter's privilege arising from the First Amendment, or failing that, by federal common law privilege. The District Court held that neither the First Amendment nor the federal common law provides protection for journalists' confidential sources in the context of a grand jury investigation. For the reasons set forth below, we agree with the District Court that there is no First Amendment privilege protecting the evidence sought. We further conclude that if any such common law privilege exists, it is not absolute, and in this case has been overcome by the filings of the Special Counsel with the District Court. We further conclude that other assignments of error raised by appellants are without merit. We therefore affirm the decision of the District Court.

The controversy giving rise to this litigation began with a political and news media controversy over a sixteen-word sentence in the State of the Union Address of President George W. Bush on January 28, 2003. In that address, President Bush stated: "The British government has learned that Saddam Hussein recently sought significant quantities of uranium from Africa." The ensuing public controversy focused not on the British source of the alleged information, but rather on the accuracy of the proposition that Saddam Hussein had sought uranium, a key ingredient in the development of nuclear weaponry, from Africa. Many publications on the subject followed. On July 6, 2003, the *New York Times* published an op-ed piece by former Ambassador Joseph Wilson, in which he claimed to have been sent to Niger in 2002 by the CIA in response to inquiries from Vice President Cheney to investigate whether Iraq had been seeking to purchase uranium from Niger. Wilson claimed that he had conducted the requested investigation and reported on his return that there was no credible evidence that any such effort had been made.

On July 14, 2003, columnist Robert Novak published a column in the *Chicago Sun-Times* in which he asserted that the decision to send Wilson to Niger had been made "routinely without Director George Tenet's knowledge," and, most significant to the present litigation, that "two senior administration officials" told him that Wilson's selection was at the suggestion of Wilson's wife, Valerie Plame, whom Novak described as a CIA "operative on weapons of mass destruction." After Novak's column was published, various media accounts reported that other reporters had been told by government officials that Wilson's wife worked at the CIA monitoring weapons of mass destruction, and that she was involved in her husband's selection for the mission to Niger. One such article, published by Time.com on July 17, 2003, was authored in part by appellant Matthew Cooper. That article stated that "some government officials have noted to Time in interviews that Wilson's wife, Valerie Plame, is a CIA official." Other media accounts reported that "two top White House officials called at least six Washington journalists and disclosed the identity and occupation of Wilson's wife." The Department of Justice undertook an investigation into whether government employees had violated federal law by the unauthorized disclosure of the identity of a CIA agent. As the investigation proceeded the Deputy Attorney General appointed Patrick J. Fitzgerald, United States Attorney for the Northern District of Illinois, as Special Counsel and delegated full authority concerning the investigation to him. As part of the ongoing investigation, a grand jury investigation began in January of 2004.

In cooperation with Special Counsel Fitzgerald, the grand jury conducted an extensive investigation. On May 21, 2004, a grand jury subpoena was issued to appellant Matthew Cooper, seeking testimony and documents related to two specific articles to which Cooper had contributed. Cooper refused to comply with the subpoena, even after the Special Counsel offered to narrow its scope to cover only conversations between Cooper and a specific individual identified by the Special Counsel. Instead, Cooper moved to quash the subpoena. The Chief Judge of the United States District Court for the District of Columbia denied Cooper's motion.

A further grand jury subpoena was issued to Time, Inc., seeking the same documents requested in the subpoena to Cooper. Time also moved to quash its subpoena. The District Court denied Time's motion. Both Cooper and Time refused to comply with the subpoenas despite the District Court's denial of their motions to quash. The District Court thereafter held them in civil contempt of court. After both Cooper and Time had filed appeals, and further negotiations between Special Counsel and the two had proceeded, Cooper agreed to provide testimony and documents relevant to a specific source who had stated that he had no objection to their release. Cooper and Time fulfilled their obligations under the agreement, the Special Counsel moved to vacate the District Court's contempt order, and the notices of appeal were voluntarily dismissed.

The grand jury issued a further subpoena to Cooper seeking "any and all documents relating to conversations between Matthew Cooper and official source(s) prior to July 14, 2003, concerning in any way: former Ambassador Joseph Wilson; the 2002 trip by former Ambassador Wilson to Niger; Valerie Wilson Plame, a/k/a Valerie Wilson, a/k/a Valerie Plame (the wife of former Ambassador Wilson); and/or any affiliation between Valerie Wilson Plame and the CIA."

An August 2, 2004 subpoena to Time requested "all notes, tape recordings, e-mails, or other documents of Matthew Cooper relating to the July 17, 2003, Time.com article entitled 'A War on Wilson?' and the July 21, 2003 *Time* Magazine article entitled, 'A Question of Trust.'" Cooper and Time again moved to quash the subpoenas, and on October 7, 2004, the District Court denied the motion. The two refused to comply with the subpoenas, and the District Court held both in contempt.

In the meantime, on August 12 and August 14, grand jury subpoenas were issued to Judith Miller, seeking documents and testimony related to conversations between her and a specified government official "occurring from on or about July 6, 2003, to on or about July 13, 2003, concerning Valerie Plame Wilson (whether referred to by name or by description as the wife of Ambassador Wilson) or concerning Iraqi efforts to obtain uranium." Miller refused to comply with the subpoenas and moved to quash them. The District Court denied Miller's motion to quash. The court held her in civil contempt of court also. She has appealed.

The appellants have proceeded with common counsel and common briefing in a consolidated proceeding before this court. Their first claim is that the First Amendment affords journalists a constitutional right to conceal their confidential sources even against the subpoenas of grand juries. Secondly, they claim that reporters enjoy an evidentiary privilege under the common law to conceal confidential sources. Adjunct to this claim, while denying that the privilege is less than absolute, they argue that if the privilege is in fact qualified, the United States has not overcome the privilege. We affirm the judgment of the District Court for the reasons set out more fully below.

In his opinion below, the Chief District Judge held that "a reporter called to testify before a grand jury regarding confidential information enjoys no First Amendment protection." Appellants argue that "this proposition of law is flatly contrary to the great weight of authority in this and other circuits." Appellants are wrong. The governing authority in this case, as the District Court correctly held, comes not from this or any other circuit, but the Supreme Court of the United States. In *Branzburg v. Hayes*, the Highest Court considered and rejected the same claim of First Amendment privilege on facts materially indistinguishable from those at bar. [Reporter Paul] Branzburg claimed to have received communications from sources in confidence, just as the journalists before us claimed to have done. At least one of the [co-defendants] in *Branzburg* had witnessed the commission of crimes. On the record before us, there is at least sufficient allegation to warrant grand jury inquiry that one or both journalists received information concerning the identity of a covert operative of the United States from government employees acting in violation of the law by making the disclosure. Each petitioner in *Branzburg* and each journalist before us claimed or claims the protection of a First Amendment reporter's privilege. The Supreme Court in no uncertain terms rejected the existence of such a privilege. The Supreme Court has already decided the First Amendment issue before us today.

In rejecting the claim of privilege, the Supreme Court made its reasoning transparent and forceful. The High Court recognized that "the grand jury's authority to subpoena witnesses is not only historic, but essential to its task." The grand juries and the courts operate under the "longstanding principle that 'the public has a right to every man's evidence,' except for those persons protected by constitutional, common law, or statutory privilege." The Court then noted that "the only testimonial privilege for unofficial witnesses that is rooted in the Federal Constitution is the Fifth Amendment privilege against compelled self-incrimination." The Court then expressly declined "to create another by interpreting the First Amendment to grant newsmen a testimonial privilege that other citizens do not enjoy."

We have pressed appellants for some distinction between the facts before the Supreme Court in *Branzburg* and those before us today. They have offered none, nor have we independently found any. Unquestionably, the Supreme Court decided in *Branzburg* that there is no First Amendment privilege protecting journalists from appearing before a grand jury or from testifying before a grand jury or otherwise providing evidence to a grand jury regardless of any confidence promised by the reporter to any source. The Highest Court has spoken and never revisited the question. Without doubt, that is the end of the matter.

Appellants argue that even if there is no First Amendment privilege protecting their confidential source information, we should recognize a privilege under federal common law, arguing that regardless of whether a federal common law privilege protecting reporters existed in 1972 when *Branzburg* was decided, in the intervening years much has changed. While appellants argue for an absolute privilege under the common law, they wisely recognize the possibility that a court not recognizing such an absolute privilege might nonetheless find a qualified privilege. They therefore also argue that if there is a qualified privilege, then the government has not overcome that qualified privilege. The Court is not of one mind on the existence of a common law privilege. Judge Sentelle would hold that there is no such common law privilege for reasons set forth in a separate opinion. Judge Tatel would hold that there is such a common law privilege. Judge Henderson believes that we need not, and therefore should not, reach that question. However, all believe that if there is any such privilege, it is not absolute and may be overcome by an appropriate showing. All further believe, for the reasons set forth in the separate opinion of Judge Tatel, that if such a privilege applies here, it has been overcome. Therefore, the common law privilege, even if one exists, does not warrant reversal.

For the reasons set forth above, the judgment of the District Court is affirmed.

POINTS FOR DISCUSSION

1. As you already knew from *Branzburg v. Hayes*, there is no First Amendment right for reporters to refuse to testify in front of grand juries. Congress has flirted with passing a law that creates such a reporters' privilege. What would be your best arguments for and against such a law?
2. Judge Sentelle's opinion for the court reminds us that whoever leaked the information to Judith Miller may have violated a federal law against blowing the cover of CIA operatives. Yet we now know that Miller's source was Lewis "Scooter" Libby, former chief of staff to Vice President Cheney, who was never tried for violation of that law. (He was tried instead for having allegedly lied to the FBI, and otherwise obstructing the government's investigation of the leak.) If a grand jury is given the power to compel testimony in order to investigate crimes, what should we make of the special prosecutor's decision not to prosecute Libby for the underlying offense? Does such a state of affairs affect whether you think that Judith Miller's eventual eighty-five-day jail sentence was excessive?

▪ *Zurcher v. Stanford Daily*
436 U.S. 547 (1978)
Justice White:

Late in the day on Friday, April 9, 1971, officers of the Palo Alto Police Department and of the Santa Clara County Sheriff's Department responded to a call from the director of the Stanford University Hospital requesting the removal of a large group of demonstrators who had seized the hospital's administrative offices and occupied them since the previous afternoon. After several futile efforts to persuade the demonstrators to leave peacefully, more drastic measures were employed. The demonstrators had barricaded the doors at both ends of a hall adjacent to the administrative offices. The police chose to force their way in at the west end of the corridor. As they did so, a group of demonstrators emerged through the doors at the east end and, armed with sticks and clubs, attacked the group of nine police officers stationed there. One officer was knocked to the floor and struck repeatedly on the head; another suffered a broken shoulder. All nine were injured. There were no police photographers at the east doors, and most bystanders and reporters were on the west side. The officers themselves were able to identify only two of their assailants, but one of them did see at least one person photographing the assault at the east doors.

On Sunday, April 11, a special edition of the *Stanford Daily* (Daily), a student newspaper published at Stanford University, carried articles and photographs devoted to the hospital protest and the violent clash between demonstrators and police. The photographs carried the byline of a *Daily* staff member and indicated that he had been at the east end of the hospital hallway where he could have photographed the assault on the nine officers. The next day, the Santa Clara County District Attorney's Office secured a warrant from the Municipal Court for an immediate search of the *Daily*'s offices for negatives, film, and pictures showing the events and occurrences at the hospital on the evening of April 9. The warrant affidavit contained no allegation or indication that members of the *Daily* staff were in any way involved in unlawful acts at the hospital.

The search pursuant to the warrant was conducted later that day by four police officers and took place in the presence of some members of the *Daily* staff. The *Daily*'s photographic laboratories, filing cabinets, desks, and wastepaper baskets were searched. Locked drawers and rooms were not opened. The officers apparently had opportunity to read notes and correspondence during the search. The search revealed only the photographs that had already been published on April 11, and no materials were removed from the *Daily*'s office.

A month later the *Daily* and various members of its staff, respondents here, brought a civil action in the United States District Court for the Northern District of California seeking declaratory and injunctive relief. The complaint alleged that the search of the *Daily*'s office had deprived respondents under color of state law of rights secured to them by the First, Fourth, and Fourteenth Amendments of the United States Constitution. The District Court denied the request for an injunction but, on respondents' motion for summary judgment, granted declaratory relief. The Court of Appeals affirmed. We reverse.

Under existing law, valid warrants may be issued to search any property, whether or not occupied by a third party, at which there is probable cause to believe that fruits, instrumentalities, or evidence of a crime will be found. Nothing on the face of the Amendment suggests that a third-party search warrant should not normally issue. The Warrant Clause speaks of search warrants issued on "probable cause" and "particularly describing the place to be searched, and the persons or things to be seized." In situations where the State does not seek to seize "persons" but only those "things" which there is probable cause to believe are located on the place to be searched, there is no apparent basis in the language of the Amendment for also imposing the requirements for a valid arrest—probable cause to believe that the third party is implicated in the crime. The critical element in a reasonable search is not that the owner of the property is suspected of crime but that there is reasonable cause to believe that the specific "things" to be searched for and seized are located on the property to which entry is sought.

The District Court held, and respondents assert here, that whatever may be true of third-party searches generally, where the third party is a newspaper, there are additional factors derived from the First Amendment that justify a nearly per se rule forbidding the search warrant and permitting only the subpoena. The general submission is that searches of newspaper offices for evidence of crime reasonably believed to be on the premises will seriously threaten the ability of the press to gather, analyze, and disseminate news. This is said to be true for several reasons: First, searches will be physically disruptive to such an extent that timely publication will be impeded. Second, confidential sources of information will dry up, and the press will also lose opportunities to cover various events because of fears of the participants that press files will be readily available to the authorities. Third, reporters will be deterred from recording and preserving their recollections for future use if such information is subject to seizure. Fourth, the processing of news and its dissemination will be chilled by the prospects that searches will disclose internal editorial deliberations. Fifth, the press will resort to self-censorship to conceal its possession of information of potential interest to the police.

It is true that the struggle from which the Fourth Amendment emerged is largely a history of conflict between the Crown and the press, and that in issuing warrants and determining the reasonableness of a search, state and federal magistrates should be aware that unrestricted power of search and seizure could also be an instrument for stifling liberty of expression. Where the materials sought to be seized may be protected by the First Amendment, the requirements of the Fourth Amendment must be applied with scrupulous exactitude. Where presumptively protected materials are sought to be seized, the warrant requirement should be administered to leave as little as possible to the discretion or whim of the officer in the field.

Similarly, where seizure is sought of allegedly obscene materials, the judgment of the arresting officer alone is insufficient to justify issuance of a search warrant or a seizure without a warrant incident to arrest. Neither the Fourth Amendment nor the cases requiring consideration of First Amendment values in issuing search warrants, however, call for imposing the regime ordered by the District Court. Aware of the long struggle between Crown and press and desiring to curb unjustified official intrusions, the Framers took the enormously important step of subjecting searches to the test of reasonableness and to the general rule requiring search warrants issued by neutral magistrates. They nevertheless did not forbid warrants where the press was involved, did not require special showings that subpoenas would be impractical, and did not insist that the owner of the place to be searched, if connected with the press, must be shown to be implicated in the offense being investigated. Further, the prior cases do no more than insist that the courts apply the warrant requirements with particular exactitude when First Amendment interests would be endangered by the search. As we see it, no more than this is required where the warrant requested is for the seizure of criminal evidence reasonably believed to be on the premises occupied by a newspaper. Properly administered, the preconditions for a warrant—probable cause, specificity with respect to the place to be searched and the things to be seized, and overall reasonableness—should afford sufficient protection against the harms that are assertedly threatened by warrants for searching newspaper offices.

There is no reason to believe, for example, that magistrates cannot guard against searches of the type, scope, and intrusiveness that would actually interfere with the timely publication of a newspaper. Nor, if the requirements of specificity and reasonableness are properly applied, policed, and observed, will there be any occasion or opportunity for officers to rummage at large in newspaper files or to intrude into or to deter normal editorial and publication decisions. The warrant issued in this case authorized nothing of this sort. Nor are we convinced that confidential sources will disappear and that the press will suppress news because of fears of warranted searches. Whatever incremental effect there may be in this regard if search warrants, as well as subpoenas, are permissible in proper circumstances, it does not make a constitutional difference in our judgment.

The fact is that respondents and amici have pointed to only a very few instances in the entire United States since 1971 involving the issuance of warrants for searching newspaper premises. This reality hardly suggests abuse; and if abuse occurs, there will be time enough to deal with it. Furthermore, the press is not only an important, critical, and valuable asset to society, but it is not easily intimidated—nor should it be.

Respondents also insist that the press should be afforded opportunity to litigate the State's entitlement to the material it seeks before it is turned over or seized and that whereas the search warrant procedure is defective in this respect, resort to the subpoena would solve the problem. But presumptively protected materials are not necessarily immune from seizure under warrant for use at a criminal trial. A neutral magistrate carrying out his responsibilities under the Fourth Amendment has ample tools at his disposal to confine warrants to search within reasonable limits. We note finally that if the evidence sought by warrant is sufficiently connected with the crime to satisfy the probable-cause requirement, it will very likely be sufficiently relevant to justify a subpoena and to withstand a motion to quash.

We accordingly reject the reasons given by the District Court and adopted by the Court of Appeals for holding the search for photographs at the *Stanford Daily* to have been unreasonable within the meaning of the Fourth Amendment and in violation of the First Amendment. Nor has anything else presented here persuaded us that the Amendments forbade this search. It follows that the judgment of the Court of Appeals is reversed. So ordered.

POINTS FOR DISCUSSION

1. In *Branzburg v. Hayes*, the Supreme Court told reporters that they were not exempt from citizens' obligation to testify when called before a grand jury, but that they might not have to reveal the identity of their confidential sources. Is a newsroom search, as compared with a subpoena to reveal documents, more likely to result in the revealing of confidential sources? Why or why not?
2. Justice Stewart, in his dissenting opinion in the *Zurcher* case, wrote the following: "Perhaps as a matter of abstract policy a newspaper office should receive no more protection from unannounced police searches than, say, the office of a doctor or the office of a bank. But we are here to uphold a Constitution. And our Constitution does not explicitly protect the practice of medicine or the business of banking from all abridgment by government. It does explicitly protect the freedom of the press." Do you agree with him that the First Amendment's explicit mention of "the press" argues for a separate constitutional standard for newsroom searches? Why or why not?

■ *Cohen v. Cowles Media Company*
501 U.S. 663 (1991)
Justice White:

The question before us is whether the First Amendment prohibits a plaintiff from recovering damages, under state promissory estoppel law, for a newspaper's breach of a promise of confidentiality given to the plaintiff in exchange for information. We hold that it does not.

During the closing days of the 1982 Minnesota gubernatorial race, Dan Cohen, an active Republican associated with Wheelock Whitney's Independent-Republican gubernatorial campaign, approached reporters from the *St. Paul Pioneer Press Dispatch* (Pioneer Press) and the *Minneapolis Star and Tribune* (Star Tribune) and offered to provide documents relating to a candidate in the upcoming election. Cohen made clear to the reporters that he would provide the information only if he was given a promise of confidentiality. Reporters from both papers promised to keep Cohen's identity anonymous and Cohen turned over copies of two public court records concerning Marlene Johnson, the Democratic-Farmer-Labor candidate for Lieutenant Governor. The first record indicated that Johnson had been charged in 1969 with three counts of unlawful assembly, and the second that she had been convicted in 1970 of petit theft. Both newspapers interviewed Johnson for her explanation and one reporter tracked down the person who had found the records for Cohen. As it turned out, the unlawful assembly charges arose out of Johnson's participation in a protest of an alleged failure to hire minority workers on municipal construction projects, and the charges were eventually dismissed. The petit theft conviction was for leaving a store without paying for $6 worth of sewing materials. The incident apparently occurred at a time during which Johnson was emotionally distraught, and the conviction was later vacated.

After consultation and debate, the editorial staffs of the two newspapers independently decided to publish Cohen's name as part of their stories concerning Johnson. In their stories, both papers identified Cohen as the source of the court records, indicated his connection to the Whitney campaign, and included denials by Whitney campaign officials of any role in the matter. The same day the stories appeared, Cohen was fired by his employer.

Cohen sued respondents, the publishers of the Pioneer Press and Star Tribune, in Minnesota state court, alleging fraudulent misrepresentation and breach of contract. The trial court rejected respondents' argument that the First Amendment barred Cohen's lawsuit. A jury returned a verdict in Cohen's favor, awarding him $200,000 in compensatory damages and $500,000 in punitive damages. The Minnesota Court of Appeals, in a split decision, reversed the award of punitive damages after concluding that Cohen had failed to establish a fraud claim, the only claim which would support such an award. However, the court upheld the finding of liability for breach of contract and the $200,000 compensatory damages award. A divided Minnesota Supreme Court reversed the compensatory damages award.

The initial question we face is whether a private cause of action for promissory estoppel involves "state action" within the meaning of the Fourteenth

Amendment such that the protections of the First Amendment are triggered. For if it does not, then the First Amendment has no bearing on this case.

Our cases teach that the application of state rules of law in state courts in a manner alleged to restrict First Amendment freedoms constitutes "state action" under the Fourteenth Amendment. In this case, the Minnesota Supreme Court held that if Cohen could recover at all it would be on the theory of promissory estoppel, a state-law doctrine which, in the absence of a contract, creates obligations never explicitly assumed by the parties. These legal obligations would be enforced through the official power of the Minnesota courts. Under our cases, that is enough to constitute "state action" for purposes of the Fourteenth Amendment.

Generally applicable laws do not offend the First Amendment simply because their enforcement against the press has incidental effects on its ability to gather and report the news. Truthful information sought to be published must have been lawfully acquired. The press may not with impunity break and enter an office or dwelling to gather news. Neither does the First Amendment relieve a newspaper reporter of the obligation shared by all citizens to respond to a grand jury subpoena and answer questions relevant to a criminal investigation, even though the reporter might be required to reveal a confidential source. The press, like others interested in publishing, may not publish copyrighted material without obeying the copyright laws. Similarly, the media must obey the National Labor Relations Act and the Fair Labor Standards Act, may not restrain trade in violation of the antitrust laws, and must pay non-discriminatory taxes. Accordingly, enforcement of such general laws against the press is not subject to stricter scrutiny than would be applied to enforcement against other persons or organizations. There can be little doubt that the Minnesota doctrine of promissory estoppel is a law of general applicability. It does not target or single out the press. Rather, insofar as we are advised, the doctrine is generally applicable to the daily transactions of all the citizens of Minnesota. The First Amendment does not forbid its application to the press. Minnesota law simply requires those making promises to keep them. The parties themselves, as in this case, determine the scope of their legal obligations, and any restrictions that may be placed on the publication of truthful information are self-imposed. Also, it is not at all clear that respondents obtained Cohen's name "lawfully" in this case, at least for purposes of publishing it. Respondents obtained Cohen's name only by making a promise that they did not honor.

Nor is Cohen attempting to use a promissory estoppel cause of action to avoid the strict requirements for establishing a libel or defamation claim. As the Minnesota Supreme Court observed here, "Cohen could not sue for defamation because the information disclosed [his name] was true." Cohen is not seeking damages for injury to his reputation or his state of mind. He sought damages in excess of $50,000 for breach of a promise that caused him to lose his job and lowered his earning capacity.

Respondents and amici argue that permitting Cohen to maintain a cause of action for promissory estoppel will inhibit truthful reporting because news organizations will have legal incentives not to disclose a confidential source's identity even when that person's identity is itself newsworthy. But if this is the case, it is no more than the incidental, and constitutionally insignificant, consequence of applying to the press a generally applicable law that requires those who make certain kinds of promises to keep them.

Although we conclude that the First Amendment does not confer on the press a constitutional right to disregard promises that would otherwise be enforced under state law, we reject Cohen's request that in reversing the Minnesota Supreme Court's judgment we reinstate the jury verdict awarding him $200,000 in compensatory damages. The Minnesota Supreme Court's incorrect conclusion that the First Amendment barred Cohen's claim may well have truncated its consideration of whether a promissory estoppel claim had otherwise been established under Minnesota law and whether Cohen's jury verdict could be upheld on a promissory estoppel basis. Or perhaps the State Constitution may be construed to shield the press from a promissory estoppel cause of action such as this one. These are matters for the Minnesota Supreme Court to address and resolve in the first instance on remand. Accordingly, the judgment of the Minnesota Supreme Court is reversed, and the case is remanded for further proceedings not inconsistent with this opinion.

So ordered.

POINTS FOR DISCUSSION

1. If Cohen wanted the damaging information about Johnson to be printed without implicating himself or the Whitney campaign, why did he not just mail it anonymously to reporters? As it turns out, some evidence at trial suggested a reason. Cohen knew that the reporters' next step would be to make a visit themselves to the county clerk, where they would not only be able to examine the Johnson court records but would also see the list of persons who had recently had access to the records—including one person with known connections to the Whitney campaign. Does knowing this part of the story affect your belief about the wisdom of the Supreme Court's decision?

2. The doctrine of promissory estoppel does not seem to be limited to promises of confidentiality. What might happen if a source felt she was "promised" that an article flowing from an interview with her would paint her in a favorable light? If she later concludes that the reporter's portrayal of her was less than flattering, should she have a right to sue?

▪ *Chevron Corporation v. Berlinger*
629 F.3d 297 (2nd Cir. 2011)
Judge Leval:

This is an appeal from an order of the United States District Court for the Southern District of New York compelling disclosure for use in proceedings in foreign tribunals. The appeal involves the application of the qualified evidentiary privilege for information gathered during a journalistic investigation, sometimes described as the "press privilege" or "journalist's privilege."

The appeal is brought by Joseph Berlinger, who created a documentary film, entitled *Crude*, about a litigation being conducted in the courts of Ecuador at Lago Agrio (the "Lago Agrio litigation") over allegations of environmental damage in Ecuador from petroleum exploration and extraction operations conducted by an affiliate of petitioner Chevron Corp.[1]

The district court directed Berlinger to produce to the petitioners the videotape footage constituting the outtakes of the film. Berlinger contends the district court abused its discretion in ordering production of the outtake footage. He argues that his investigative journalism recorded in the raw footage is protected from such compelled disclosure by the press privilege. He therefore asks that we overturn the district court's order.

We reject Berlinger's contention. Given all the circumstances of the making of the film, particularly the fact that Berlinger's making of the film was solicited by the plaintiffs in the Lago Agrio litigation *for the purpose of telling their story*, and that changes to the film were made at their instance, Berlinger failed to carry his burden of showing that he collected information for the purpose of *independent* reporting and commentary. Accordingly, we cannot say it was error for the district court to conclude that petitioners had successfully overcome Berlinger's claim of privilege.

[This case] arises in the context of three decades of oil exploration and ex-

---

1. A relevant scene from *Crude* is available on my website, www.paulsiegelcommlaw.com; on the left side of the site (*Communication Law in America*), click on "Video Clips," then "Chapter 9," then on "Crude."

traction in Ecuador by Texaco, Inc., which became a wholly-owned subsidiary of Chevron in 2001. In 1964, Texaco Petroleum Company ("TexPet"), a subsidiary of Texaco, began oil exploration and drilling in the Oriente region of eastern Ecuador. In the following year, TexPet started operating a petroleum concession for a consortium owned in equal shares by TexPet and Gulf Oil Corporation (the "Consortium"). The government of Ecuador ("GOE") thereafter obtained Gulf Oil's interest through its state-owned oil company, Petroecuador, and became the majority stakeholder in the Consortium in 1976. TexPet operated a trans-Ecuadorian oil pipeline and the Consortium's drilling activities until 1990, when Petroecuador assumed those functions. Two years later, TexPet relinquished all of its interests in the Consortium, leaving it owned entirely by Petroecuador.

In 1993, a group of residents of the Oriente region of Ecuador brought a class action suit against Texaco arising from TexPet's operations in the Consortium. The complaint alleged that "between 1964 and 1992 Texaco's oil operation activities polluted the rain forests and rivers in Ecuador." The plaintiffs sought billions of dollars in damages on a variety of theories, including negligence, strict liability, and equity to "redress contamination of the water supplies and environment."

While the *Aguinda* litigation was pending, TexPet entered into a 1995 settlement agreement with the GOE and Petroecuador (the "Settlement") whereby TexPet agreed to perform specified environmental remedial work in exchange for a release of claims by the GOE. Three years later, the GOE entered into an agreement with TexPet (the "Final Release") according to which the GOE deemed the Settlement to have been "fully performed and concluded."

In the meantime, Texaco worked in earnest to transfer the *Aguinda* action from the U.S. District Court for the Southern District of New York to the courts of Ecuador. Texaco touted the ability of the Ecuadorian courts to "provide a fair and alternative forum" for the plaintiffs' claims. It argued also that the case did not belong in the U.S. court because the evidence and witnesses were predominantly in Ecuador. [Accordingly], after nine years of litigation, the U.S. district court dismissed the case. The Second Circuit affirmed the dismissal the following year.

In 2003, following the dismissal of the *Aguinda* action, a group of Ecuadorians including a substantial number of the *Aguinda* Plaintiffs brought an action against ChevronTexaco in Lago Agrio, Ecuador (the "Lago Agrio Litigation"). Plaintiffs asserted claims for, among other things, violations of an Ecuadorian environmental law enacted in 1999. The defendants contended that the law in effect impermissibly allowed plaintiffs to assert claims that belonged to the GOE but were released pursuant to the Settlement and Final

Release. The GOE announced that it would receive ninety percent of any recovery.

The Lago Agrio court ordered a "global" assessment of damages to be conducted by a team of expert witnesses led by Richard Stalin Cabrera Vega, who was required to "perform his work in an impartial matter" and to "maintain strict independence with regard to the parties." Dr. Carlos Beristain, who was appointed to Cabrera's team of expert witnesses, contributed to Cabrera's damages assessment for cancer deaths by meeting in "focus groups" with inhabitants of the region allegedly polluted by Chevron. Chevron maintains that Dr. Beristain failed to maintain "strict independence" with respect to counsel for the Lago Agrio plaintiffs.

The same year that the Lago Agrio Litigation was filed, the GOE filed a criminal complaint against two of Chevron's lawyers, petitioners Pallares and Veiga, and former GOE and Petroecuador officials, alleging that they had falsified public documents in connection with the Settlement and Final Release and had violated Ecuador's environmental laws. In 2004, the Ecuadorian Prosecutor General began an investigation of the criminal charges.

In 2005, Steven Donziger, one of the lead counsel for the plaintiffs in the Lago Agrio Litigation, solicited award-winning producer and filmmaker Joseph Berlinger to create a documentary depicting the Lago Agrio Litigation from the perspective of his clients. Berlinger recounted that: Donziger "was looking for a filmmaker *to tell his clients' story.*" For the next three years, Berlinger shadowed the plaintiffs' lawyers and filmed the events and people surrounding the trial, compiling six hundred hours of raw footage.

Chevron commenced an arbitration [in 2009] pursuant to the Bilateral Investment Treaty between the United States and Ecuador ("BIT") and United Nations Commission on International Trade Law ("UNCITRAL") rules (the "Arbitration"). Chevron there asserts that the GOE "abused the criminal justice system" in connection with the Lago Agrio Litigation and the criminal prosecutions and violated the BIT and the American Convention on Civil Rights. It seeks, among other things, dismissal of the Lago Agrio Litigation and a declaration that it "has no liability or responsibility for environmental impact arising out of the former Consortium that was jointly owned by TexPet and Ecuador."

In 2009, Berlinger released his documentary, entitled *Crude*, which, according to its own press package, "captures the evidentiary phase of the Lago Agrio trial, including field inspections and the appointment of independent expert Richard Cabrera to assess the region." The film depicts also the environmental damage allegedly caused by TexPet and interviews with Ecuadorians dying of diseases perhaps caused by oil spills.

Crude contains footage of a number of meetings that took place in the Dureno community of the indigenous Cofan people. A version of *Crude* "streamed" over Netflix depicts one such meeting, at which Dr. Beristain, an expert who contributed to Cabrera's neutral damages assessment, is shown working directly with both the Cofan people and plaintiffs' counsel. Berlinger, however, altered the scene at the direction of plaintiffs' counsel to conceal all images of Dr. Beristain before *Crude* was released on DVD. The interaction between plaintiffs' counsel and Dr. Beristain therefore does not appear in the final version of *Crude* sold on DVD in the United States.

In another scene of *Crude*, Donziger, one of plaintiffs' lead counsel, persuades an Ecuadorian judge, apparently in the presence of Chevron's lawyers and news media, to block the judicial inspection of a laboratory allegedly being used by the Lago Agrio plaintiffs to test for environmental contamination. Donziger describes his use of "pressure tactics" to influence the judge and concedes that "this is something you would never do in the United States, but Ecuador, you know, this is how the game is played, it's dirty."

In another scene, a representative of the plaintiffs informs Donziger that he had left the office of President Correa "after coordinating everything." Donziger declares, "Congratulations. We've achieved something very important in this case. Now we are friends with the President." The film then offers a glimpse of a meeting between President Correa and plaintiffs' counsel that takes place on a helicopter. Later on, President Correa embraces Donziger and says, "Wonderful, keep it up!"

Donziger explains also that President Correa had called for criminal prosecutions to proceed against those who engineered the Settlement and Final Release. "Correa just said that anyone in the Ecuador government who approved the so-called remediation is now going to be subject to litigation in Ecuador. Those guys are shittin' in their pants right now."

Chevron, Pérez, and Reis filed these petitions on April 9, 2010, asking the district court to direct Berlinger to disclose all footage shot or acquired in the making of *Crude* for use by Chevron in the Lago Agrio litigation and the treaty arbitration, and for use by Pérez and Reis in the prosecutions brought against them in Ecuador. In support of their applications, they contended that, because Berlinger had free access to plaintiffs' counsel and shot footage when plaintiffs' counsel were in court chambers and dealing with the supposedly neutral court expert, the footage excluded from the film would show improper influence by Plaintiffs' counsel on the court and the court's expert. The Lago Agrio plaintiffs moved to intervene in opposition and were permitted to do so. Upon consideration of the submissions of the parties, the district court granted the petitions, ordering disclosure of the outtakes.

As set out above, the district court found that Stephen Donziger, the legal adviser to the Lago Agrio plaintiffs, solicited Berlinger *to produce Crude "to tell his clients' story."* The court additionally found that Berlinger removed a scene from the final version of *Crude* at the request of the Lago Agrio plaintiffs. (Berlinger acknowledges editing the scene at the suggestion of the Lago Agrio plaintiffs, but he maintains he "retained complete editorial control" over the film and rejected other changes the Lago Agrio plaintiffs proposed.)

Turning to the merits of the applications, the court first determined that the statutory prerequisites for ordering discovery in aid of a foreign proceeding had been satisfied, and that the discretionary factors governing the availability of such discovery weighed in favor of granting the applications. The court then found that Chevron had demonstrated that the information in the footage was of likely relevance to significant issues in the Lago Agrio litigation, the treaty arbitration, and the criminal prosecutions of Pérez and Reis, and that the information was not reasonably obtainable from other sources.

Any interaction between plaintiffs' counsel and a supposedly neutral expert in the Lago Agrio Litigation, the court found, would be relevant to whether the expert is independent and his damages assessment reliable. Plaintiffs' counsel's interactions with the Ecuadorian judiciary and government officials would be relevant to Chevron's claims.

The court rejected Berlinger's argument that the more demanding standard for disclosure of confidential information collected during a journalistic investigation applied, because Berlinger did not carry his burden of showing that his sources reasonably expected him to maintain information in confidence. It also rejected Berlinger's argument that Chevron's request for *all* the *Crude* footage was overbroad, because Berlinger had not provided any proposal for distinguishing between relevant and assertedly non-relevant material.

The court's most pertinent conclusions for purposes of this appeal were to the effect that Berlinger failed to establish that in making the film he functioned with journalistic independence. Although the court did not *explicitly* state a finding that Berlinger lacked independence, it stressed that (1) "Donziger in fact solicited Berlinger to create a documentary of the litigation from the perspective of his clients," and (2) "Berlinger concededly removed at least one scene from the final version of *Crude* at their direction." The clear import of these findings is that Berlinger failed to establish that he did his research and made his film with independence from a subject of the film. On the basis of these findings and conclusions, the court directed the production of all footage related to *Crude* or the Lago Agrio litigation.

Berlinger appealed and moved for a stay of the district court's order. On June 8, 2010, a motions panel of this court stayed enforcement of the order until otherwise ordered by the panel assigned to hear the merits of the appeal. Following oral argument, we directed Berlinger to "promptly turn over to the petitioners copies of all footage that does not appear in publicly released versions of *Crude* showing: (a) counsel for the plaintiffs in the Lago Agrio litigation; (b) private or court-appointed experts in that proceeding; or (c) current or former officials of the Government of Ecuador." We directed that "Material produced under this order shall be used by the petitioners solely for litigation, arbitration, or submission to official bodies, either local or international." Our order noted that a further opinion would follow.

Berlinger contends the district court abused its discretion in rejecting his claim of press privilege and consequently ordering him to produce his outtakes. We disagree. This circuit has long recognized a qualified evidentiary privilege for information gathered in a journalistic investigation. The privilege for such information is intended to protect the public's interest in being informed by a vigorous, aggressive *and independent* press. It is at its highest when the information sought to be protected was acquired by the journalist through a promise of confidentiality. But the privilege is not limited to circumstances where the sources of information have been promised confidentiality. We have observed, even where there was no issue of betrayal of a promised confidence, that wholesale exposure of press files to litigant scrutiny would burden the press with heavy costs of subpoena compliance, and could otherwise impair its ability to perform its duties—particularly if potential sources were deterred from speaking to the press, or insisted on remaining anonymous, because of the likelihood that they would be sucked into litigation.

We have noted, furthermore, that unrestricted litigant access to press files would create socially wasteful incentives for press entities to clean out files containing potentially valuable information lest they incur substantial costs of subpoena compliance, and would risk the symbolic harm of making journalists appear to be an investigative arm of the judicial system, the government, or private parties. A person need not be a credentialed reporter working for an established press entity to establish entitlement to the privilege. Nonetheless, in collecting the information in question, the person must have acted in the role of the *independent* press.

The issue of the independence of the journalistic process is crucial to the present case. For determining the existence, or in any event the strength, of the press privilege, all forms of intention to publish or disseminate information are not on equal footing. While freedom of speech and of the press belongs to virtually anyone who intends to publish anything (with a few narrow exceptions), all those who intend to publish do not share an equal entitlement to the press privilege from compelled disclosure. Those who gather and publish information because they have been commissioned to publish in order to serve the objectives of others who have a stake in the subject of the reporting are not acting as an independent press. Those who do not retain independence as to what they will publish but are subservient to the objectives of others who have a stake in what will be published have either a weaker privilege or none at all.

This distinction is perhaps best understood through an illustrative example. Consider two persons, Smith and Jones, who separately undertake to investigate and write a book or article about a public figure in national politics. Smith undertakes to discover whatever she can through her investigations and to write a book that reflects whatever her investigations may show. Jones has been hired or commissioned by the public figure to write a book extolling his virtues and rebutting his critics. Smith unquestionably presents a stronger claim of entitlement to the press privilege (which is not to say the privilege might not be overcome, depending on the circumstances). Jones, who was commissioned to write a book promoting a particular point of view regardless of what her investigations may reveal, either possesses no privilege at all or, if she possesses the privilege, holds one that is weaker and more easily overcome.

The privilege is designed to support the press in its valuable public service of seeking out and revealing truthful information. An undertaking to publish matter in order to promote the interests of another, regardless of justification, does not serve the same public interest, regardless of whether the resultant work may prove to be one of high quality. It is not the policy of the law to exempt such undertakings from the obligation to produce information relevant to a dispute before a court of law.

Applying these principles here, we believe that the district court's findings adequately justified its denial of the press privilege. Our ruling in no way passes judgment on the value of Berlinger's film. We rule merely that the district court's factual findings were not clearly erroneous, and that those findings justified a conclusion that, given all the circumstances, Chevron overcame his claim of entitlement to withhold the outtakes under the press privilege.

Our ruling likewise does not imply that a journalist who has been solicited to investigate an issue and presents the story supporting the point of view of the entity that solicited her cannot establish the privilege. Without doubt, such a journalist can establish entitlement to the privilege by establishing the independence of her journalistic process, for example, through evidence of editorial and financial independence. But the burden is on the person who claims the privilege to show entitlement, and in this instance, Berlinger failed to persuade the district court that he undertook the task with independence.

A person (or entity) that undertakes to publish commentary but fails to establish that its research and reporting were done with independence from the subject of the reporting either has no press privilege at all, or in any event, possesses a privilege that is weaker and more easily overcome. We need not decide in this case whether the consequence of the failure of the claimant of the privilege to establish independence means it has a weaker privilege or no privilege at all. It is sufficient to rule that given Berlinger's failure to establish his independence from the Lago Agrio plaintiffs, the district court did not abuse its discretion in ordering the production notwithstanding Berlinger's claim that some of the footage was either irrelevant to the proceedings or could have been obtained from other sources.

Berlinger [also argues] that the district court erred in rejecting his claim that the persons who appear in *Crude* expected the unedited *Crude* footage to remain confidential. He contends that because his sources expected him to retain the unedited source footage in confidence, the district court ought to have applied the more demanding standard which applies to disclosure of confidential information. We cannot say, however, that the district court committed clear error in rejecting Berlinger's contention. Although Berlinger testified conclusorily that participants in his film "trusted that I would not turn over the raw footage to Chevron to be used against them," he did not submit corroborative evidence that the persons filmed demanded that the footage of them be held in confidence. To the contrary, the standard release form Berlinger submitted to persons whom he filmed specified that "the filmmakers may use my Contribution in connection with the creation of a nonfiction production which may be released in any media now known or hereafter invented." On the basis of this record, the district court was entitled to find that Berlinger did not sustain his burden of demonstrating information was conveyed to him in confidence.

Berlinger further argues that even if the journalist's privilege was overcome as to some of the *Crude* footage, the district court's disclosure order was overbroad. He argues that, even if *some* scenes in *Crude* contain relevant material, it does not follow that *all* of the footage is relevant. Berlinger asserts that the district court should have analyzed the film scene-by-scene, directing production of the source footage for only those scenes whose relevance, based on the publicly released version of the film, was apparent.

We reject this argument for two reasons. First, as we have explained, a district court enjoys greater discretion to order production of privileged material when the person asserting the press privilege fails to carry his burden of showing that he acted with journalistic independence. Second, Berlinger did not provide the district court with any proposal for distinguishing between relevant and assertedly non-relevant material. While in general it is desirable for a district court to tailor a production order to material likely to be relevant, the district court lacked any reliable means of doing so. The court is not obligated to undertake this burden without help from the party requesting the limitation.

We conclude that the district court's denial of the press privilege was adequately supported by its findings and conclusions, and, therefore, within the court's allowable discretion.

We hereby vacate the stay order which we entered on June 8, 2010, and affirm in full the district court's ruling of May 10, 2010. The material produced under the district court's order shall be used by the petitioners solely for litigation, arbitration, or submission to official bodies, either local or international. The case is remanded to the district court for all purposes.

POINTS FOR DISCUSSION

1. If most documentary filmmakers have a point of view about their topic, does this decision make it extremely difficult for them to ever claim a reporter's privilege?
2. Does the court make too much of the fact that the plaintiffs' attorney hoped that *Crude* would tell his clients' story (presumably from their point of view)? Is not the filmmaker's own objectivity or lack of it the more proper inquiry?

10

Regulation of Advertising

For most of this country's history, it was assumed that advertising is beyond the scope of the First Amendment. Not until 1976 did the U.S. Supreme Court bring purely commercial messages within the First Amendment umbrella. The first case in this chapter, *Virginia State Board of Pharmacy v. Virginia Citizens Consumer Council,* was the vehicle the Court used to effect this change.

The *Virginia Pharmacy* case, however, only said that advertising should enjoy some First Amendment protection; it did not say how much. The latter issue was addressed by the Court four years later in *Central Hudson Gas & Electric v. Public Service Commission of New York* (our second case).

Rubin v. Coors Brewing Company, from 1995, is an example of the Court applying the *Central Hudson* test to a specific factual situation, here involving a federal regulation prohibiting beer distributors from listing on their product labels the percentage of alcohol in each bottle.

Finally, *Citizens United v. FEC* is the landmark 2010 case in which the Supreme Court dramatically alters the rules by which money is made available for political advertising around the time of elections.

▪ *Virginia State Board of Pharmacy v. Virginia Citizens Consumer Council*
425 U.S. 748 (1976)
Justice Blackmun:

The plaintiff-appellees in this case attack, as violative of the First and Fourteenth Amendments, that portion of § 54-524.35 of Va. Code Ann. (1974), which provides that a pharmacist licensed in Virginia is guilty of unprofessional conduct if he "publishes, advertises or promotes, directly or indirectly, in any manner whatsoever, any amount, price, fee, premium, discount, rebate or credit terms for any drugs which may be dispensed only by prescription."

The plaintiffs are an individual Virginia resident who suffers from diseases that require her to take prescription drugs on a daily basis, and two nonprofit organizations. Their claim is that the First Amendment entitles the user of prescription drugs to receive information that pharmacists wish to communicate to them through advertising and other promotional means, concerning the prices of such drugs.

Certainly that information may be of value. Drug prices in Virginia, for both prescription and nonprescription items, strikingly vary from outlet to outlet even within the same locality. The phenomenon of widely varying drug prices is apparently national in scope.

The question first arises whether, even assuming that First Amendment protection attaches to the flow of drug price information, it is a protection enjoyed by the appellees as recipients of the information, and not solely, if at all, by the advertisers themselves who seek to disseminate that information. Freedom of speech presupposes a willing speaker. But where a speaker exists, as is the case here, the protection afforded is to the communication, to its source and to its recipients both.

The appellants contend that the advertisement of prescription drug prices is outside the protection of the First Amendment because it is "commercial speech." There can be no question that in past decisions the Court has given some indication that commercial speech is unprotected. Last Term, in *Bigelow v. Virginia*, 421 U.S. 809 (1975), the notion of unprotected "commercial speech" all but passed from the scene. We reversed a conviction for violation of a Virginia statute that made the circulation of any publication to encourage or promote the processing of an abortion in Virginia a misdemeanor. The defendant had published in his newspaper the availability of abortions in New York. The advertisement in question, in addition to announcing that abortions were legal in New York, offered the services of a referral agency in that State. We rejected the contention that the publication was unprotected because it was commercial. Some fragment of hope for the continuing validity of a "commercial speech" exception arguably might have persisted because of the subject matter of the advertisement in *Bigelow*. We noted that in announcing the availability of legal abortions in New York, the advertisement "did more than simply propose a commercial transaction. It contained factual material of clear 'public interest.'"

Here, in contrast, the question whether there is a First Amendment exception for "commercial speech" is squarely before us. Our pharmacist does not wish to editorialize on any subject, cultural, philosophical, or political. He does not wish to report any particularly newsworthy fact, or to make generalized observations even about commercial matters. The "idea" he wishes to communicate is simply this: "I will sell you the X prescription drug at the Y price." Our question, then, is whether this communication is wholly outside the protection of the First Amendment. Our answer is that it is not.

Those whom the suppression of prescription drug price information hits the hardest are the poor, the sick, and particularly the aged. A disproportionate amount of their income tends to be spent on prescription drugs; yet they are the least able to learn, by shopping from pharmacist to pharmacist, where their scarce dollars are best spent. When drug prices vary as strikingly as they do, information as to who is charging what becomes more than a convenience. It could mean the alleviation of physical pain or the enjoyment of basic necessities.

Society also may have a strong interest in the free flow of commercial information. Advertising, however tasteless and excessive it sometimes may seem, is nonetheless dissemination of information as to who is producing and selling what product, for what reason, and at what price. So long as we preserve a predominantly free enterprise economy, the allocation of our resources in large measure will be made through numerous private economic decisions. It is a matter of public interest that those decisions, in the aggregate, be intelligent and well informed. To this end, the free flow of commercial information is indispensable. And if it is indispensable to the proper allocation of resources in a free enterprise system, it is also indispensable to the formation of intelligent opinions as to how that system ought to be regulated or altered. Therefore, even if the First Amendment were thought to be primarily an instrument to enlighten public decision making in a democracy, we could not say that the free flow of information does not serve that goal.

Justifications for the advertising ban have to do principally with maintaining a high degree of professionalism on the part of licensed pharmacists. It is claimed that the aggressive price competition that will result from unlimited advertising will make it impossible for the pharmacist to supply professional services in the compounding, handling, and dispensing of prescription drugs. Such services are time consuming and expensive; if competitors who economize by eliminating them are permitted to advertise their resulting lower prices, the more painstaking and conscientious pharmacist will be forced either to follow suit or to go out of business.

The strength of these proffered justifications is greatly undermined by the fact that high professional standards, to a substantial extent, are guaranteed by the close regulation to which pharmacists in Virginia are subject. Surely, any pharmacist guilty of professional dereliction that actually endangers his customer will promptly lose his license.

On close inspection it is seen that the State's protectiveness of its citizens rests in large measure on the advantages of their being kept in ignorance. The advertising ban does not directly affect professional standards one way or the other. It affects them only through the reactions it is assumed people will have to the free flow of drug price information. There is no claim that the advertising ban in any way prevents the cutting of corners by the pharmacist who is so inclined. That pharmacist is likely to cut corners in any event. The only effect the advertising ban has on him is to insulate him from price competition and to open the way for him to make a substantial, and perhaps even excessive, profit in addition to providing an inferior service. The more painstaking pharmacist is also protected but, again, it is a protection based in large part on public ignorance.

It appears to be feared that if the pharmacist who wishes to provide low-cost, and assertedly low-quality, services is permitted to advertise, he will be taken up on his offer by too many unwitting customers. They will choose the low-cost, low-quality service and drive the "professional" pharmacist out of business. They will respond only to costly and excessive advertising, and end up paying the price. They will go from one pharmacist to another, following the discount, and destroy the pharmacist-customer relationship. They will lose respect for the profession because it advertises. All this is not in their best interests, and all this can be avoided if they are not permitted to know who is charging what.

There is, of course, an alternative to this highly paternalistic approach. That alternative is to assume that this information is not in itself harmful, that people will perceive their own best interests if only they are well enough informed, and that the best means to that end is to open the channels of communication rather than to close them. If they are truly open, nothing prevents the "professional" pharmacist from marketing his own assertedly superior product, and contrasting it with that of the low-cost, high-volume prescription drug retailer. But the choice among these alternative approaches is not ours to make or the Virginia General Assembly's. It is precisely this kind of choice, between the dangers of suppressing information, and the dangers of its misuse if it is freely available, that the First Amendment makes for us. Virginia is free to require whatever professional standards it wishes of its pharmacists; it may subsidize them or protect them from competition in other ways. But it may not do so by keeping the public in ignorance of the entirely lawful terms that competing pharmacists are offering. In this sense, the justifications Virginia has offered for suppressing the flow of prescription drug price information, far from persuading us that the flow is not protected by the First Amendment, have reinforced our view that it is. We so hold.

POINTS FOR DISCUSSION

1. Justice Blackmun's opinion makes clear that this ruling is the first time the Court will hold that purely commercial advertising is entitled to First Amendment protection. Yet he also argues that advertising is an important means of fostering "enlighten[ed] public decision making in a democracy." Does he thus equate commercial speech with political speech, and in fact suggest that smart shopping is, somehow, patriotic?
2. Most Americans have stronger opinions about which fast-food chain (if any) they prefer than which political candidate. Indeed, most Americans cannot even recognize their own representatives in Congress. Should these realities count as reasons for viewing commercial speech as at least as valuable as political speech?

Central Hudson Gas & Electric v. Public Service Commission of New York
447 U.S. 557 (1980)
Justice Powell:

This case presents the question whether a regulation of the Public Service Commission of the State of New York violates the First and Fourteenth Amendments because it completely bans promotional advertising by an electrical utility.

In December 1973, the [Public Service] Commission ordered electric utilities in New York State to cease all advertising that "promotes the use of electricity." The order was based on the Commission's finding that "the interconnected utility system in New York State does not have sufficient fuel stocks or sources of supply to continue furnishing all customer demands for the 1973-1974 winter." Three years later, when the fuel shortage had eased, the Commission requested comments from the public on its proposal to continue the ban on promotional advertising. Central Hudson Gas & Electric Corp., the appellant in this case, opposed the ban on First Amendment grounds. After reviewing the public comments, the Commission extended the prohibition in a Policy Statement issued on February 25, 1977.

The Policy Statement divided advertising expenses into two broad categories: promotional—advertising intended to stimulate the purchase of utility services—and institutional and informational, a broad category inclusive of all advertising not clearly intended to promote sales. The Commission declared all promotional advertising contrary to the national policy of conserving energy. It acknowledged that the ban is not a perfect vehicle for conserving energy. For example, the Commission's order prohibits promotional advertising to develop consumption during periods when demand for electricity is low. By limiting growth in "off-peak" consumption, the ban limits the "beneficial side effects" of such growth in terms of more efficient use of existing powerplants. And since oil dealers are not under the Commission's jurisdiction and thus remain free to advertise, it was recognized that the ban can achieve only "piecemeal conservationism." Still, the Commission adopted the restriction because it was deemed likely to result in some dampening of unnecessary growth in energy consumption.

The Commission's order explicitly permitted "informational" advertising designed to encourage "shifts of consumption" from peak demand times to periods of low electricity demand. Informational advertising would not seek to increase aggregate consumption, but would invite a leveling of demand throughout any given 24-hour period.

Appellant challenged the order in state court, arguing that the Commission had restrained commercial speech in violation of the First and Fourteenth Amendments. The Commission's order was upheld by the trial court and at the intermediate appellate level. The New York Court of Appeals affirmed. We noted probable jurisdiction, and now reverse.

The Commission's order restricts only commercial speech, that is, expression related solely to the economic interests of the speaker and its audience. In applying the First Amendment to this area, we have rejected the highly paternalistic view that government has complete power to suppress or regulate commercial speech. Even when advertising communicates only an incomplete version of the relevant facts, the First Amendment presumes that some accurate information is better than no information at all. Nevertheless, our decisions have recognized the commonsense distinction between speech proposing a commercial transaction, which occurs in an area traditionally subject to government regulation, and other varieties of speech. The Constitution therefore accords a lesser protection to commercial speech than to other constitutionally guaranteed expression. The protection available for particular commercial expression turns on the nature both of the expression and of the governmental interests served by its regulation.

The First Amendment's concern for commercial speech is based on the informational function of advertising. Consequently, there can be no constitutional objection to the suppression of commercial messages that do not accurately inform the public about lawful activity. The government may ban forms of communication more likely to deceive the public than to inform it, or commercial speech related to illegal activity.

If the communication is neither misleading nor related to unlawful activity, the government's power is more circumscribed. The State must assert a substantial interest to be achieved by restrictions on commercial speech. Moreover, the regulatory technique must be in proportion to that interest. The limitation on expression must be designed carefully to achieve the State's goal. Compliance with this requirement may be measured by two criteria. First, the restriction must directly advance the state interest involved; the regulation may not be sustained if it provides only ineffective or remote support for the government's purpose. Second, if the governmental interest could be served as well by a more limited restriction on commercial speech, the excessive restrictions cannot survive.

In commercial speech cases, then, a four-part analysis has developed. At the outset, we must determine whether the expression is protected by the First Amendment. For commercial speech to come within that provision, it at least must concern lawful activity and not be misleading. Next, we ask whether the asserted governmental interest is substantial. If both inquiries yield positive answers, we must determine whether the regulation directly advances the governmental interest asserted, and whether it is not more extensive than is necessary to serve that interest.

We now apply this four-step analysis for commercial speech to the Commission's arguments in support of its ban on promotional advertising. The Commission does not claim that the expression at issue either is inaccurate or relates to unlawful activity.

The Commission offers two state interests as justifications for the ban on promotional advertising. The first concerns energy conservation. Any increase in demand for electricity—during peak or off-peak periods—means greater consumption of energy. The Commission argues that the State's interest in conserving energy is sufficient to support suppression of advertising designed to increase consumption of electricity. In view of our country's dependence on energy resources beyond our control, no one can doubt the importance of energy conservation. Plainly, therefore, the state interest asserted is substantial.

The Commission also argues that promotional advertising will aggravate inequities caused by the failure to base the utilities' rates on marginal cost. The utilities argued to the Commission that if they could promote the use of electricity in periods of low demand, they would improve their utilization of generating capacity. The Commission responded that promotion of off-peak consumption also would increase consumption during peak periods. If peak demand were to rise, the absence of marginal cost rates would mean that the rates charged for the additional power would not reflect the true costs of expanding production. Instead, the extra costs would be borne by all consumers through higher overall rates. Without promotional advertising, the Commission stated, this inequitable turn of events would be less likely to occur. The choice among rate structures involves difficult and important questions of economic supply and distributional fairness. The State's concern that rates be fair and efficient represents a clear and substantial governmental interest.

Next, we focus on the relationship between the State's interests and the advertising ban. Under this criterion, the Commission's laudable concern over the equity and efficiency of appellant's rates does not provide a constitutionally adequate reason for restricting protected speech. The link between the advertising prohibition and appellant's rate structure is, at most, tenuous. The impact of promotional advertising on the equity of appellant's rates is highly speculative. Advertising to increase off-peak usage would have to increase peak usage, while other factors that directly affect the fairness and efficiency of appellant's rates remained constant. Such conditional and remote eventualities simply cannot justify silencing appellant's promotional advertising.

In contrast, the State's interest in energy conservation is directly advanced by the Commission order at issue here. There is an immediate connection between advertising and demand for electricity. Central Hudson would not contest the advertising ban unless it believed that promotion would increase its sales. Thus, we find a direct link between the state interest in conservation and the Commission's order.

We come finally to the critical inquiry in this case: whether the Commission's complete suppression of speech ordinarily protected by the First Amendment is no more extensive than necessary to further the State's interest in energy conservation. The Commission's order reaches all promotional advertising, regardless of the impact of the touted service on overall energy use. But the energy conservation rationale, as important as it is, cannot justify suppressing information about electric devices or services that would cause no net increase in total energy use. In addition, no showing has been made that a more limited restriction on the content of promotional advertising would not serve adequately the State's interests.

Appellant insists that but for the ban, it would advertise products and services that use energy efficiently. These include the "heat pump," which both parties acknowledge to be a major improvement in electric heating, and the use of electric heat as a "backup" to solar and other heat sources. Although the Commission has questioned the efficiency of electric heating before this

Court, neither the Commission's Policy Statement nor its order denying rehearing made findings on this issue. In the absence of authoritative findings to the contrary, we must credit as within the realm of possibility the claim that electric heat can be an efficient alternative in some circumstances.

The Commission's order prevents appellant from promoting electric services that would reduce energy use by diverting demand from less efficient sources, or that would consume roughly the same amount of energy as do alternative sources. In neither situation would the utility's advertising endanger conservation or mislead the public. To the extent that the Commission's order suppresses speech that in no way impairs the State's interest in energy conservation, the Commission's order violates the First and Fourteenth Amendments and must be invalidated.

The Commission also has not demonstrated that its interest in conservation cannot be protected adequately by more limited regulation of appellant's commercial expression. To further its policy of conservation, the Commission could attempt to restrict the format and content of Central Hudson's advertising. It might, for example, require that the advertisements include information about the relative efficiency and expense of the offered service, both under current conditions and for the foreseeable future. In the absence of a showing that more limited speech regulation would be ineffective, we cannot approve the complete suppression of Central Hudson's advertising.

Our decision today in no way disparages the national interest in energy conservation. We accept without reservation the argument that conservation, as well as the development of alternative energy sources, is an imperative national goal. Administrative bodies empowered to regulate electric utilities have the authority—and indeed the duty—to take appropriate action to further this goal. When, however, such action involves the suppression of speech, the First and Fourteenth Amendments require that the restriction be no more extensive than is necessary to serve the state interest. In this case, the record before us fails to show that the total ban on promotional advertising meets this requirement.

Accordingly, the judgment of the New York Court of Appeals is reversed.

POINTS FOR DISCUSSION

1. Commercial speech is defined by the Court here as "expression related solely to the economic interests of the speaker and its audience." Would not a labor leader's call for a strike fit that definition? Or a political candidate's promises of tax reforms? How, then, can we distinguish commercial speech from political speech?

2. Justice Powell accepts as common sense the assumption that advertising for a product or service will tend to increase demand for it. Thus, if the state wishes to decrease consumption of that product or service, the *Central Hudson* test would seem to penalize *effective* advertising. Is this a proper function of the First Amendment, or should the public be protected only from false, misleading advertising?

Rubin v. Coors Brewing Company
514 U.S. 476 (1995)
Justice Thomas:

Respondent brews beer. In 1987, respondent applied to the Bureau of Alcohol, Tobacco and Firearms (BATF), an agency of the Department of the Treasury, for approval of proposed labels and advertisements that disclosed the alcohol content of its beer. BATF rejected the application on the ground that the Federal Alcohol Administration Act [FAAA] prohibited disclosure of the alcohol content of beer on labels or in advertising. Respondent then filed suit in the District Court for the District of Colorado. The Government took the position that the ban was necessary to suppress the threat of "strength wars" among brewers, who, without the regulation, would seek to compete in the marketplace based on the potency of their beer.

The District Court upheld the ban on the disclosure of alcohol content in advertising but invalidated the ban as it applied to labels. Although the Government asked the Tenth Circuit to review the invalidation of the labeling ban, respondent did not appeal the court's decision sustaining the advertising ban. The Court of Appeals affirmed the District Court. We conclude that the ban infringes respondent's freedom of speech, and we therefore affirm.

Soon after the ratification of the Twenty-first Amendment, which repealed the Eighteenth Amendment and ended the Nation's experiment with Prohibition, Congress enacted the FAAA. The statute establishes national rules governing the distribution, production, and importation of alcohol and established a Federal Alcohol Administration to implement these rules. Section 5(e)(2) of the Act prohibits any producer, importer, wholesaler, or bottler of alcoholic beverages from selling, shipping, or delivering in interstate or foreign commerce any malt beverages, distilled spirits, or wines in bottles "unless such products are labeled [to] provide the consumer with adequate information as to the alcoholic content thereof (except that statements of, or statements likely to be considered as statements of, alcoholic content of malt beverages are prohibited unless required by State law and except that, in case of wines, statements of alcoholic content shall be required only for wines containing more than 14 per cent of alcohol by volume)."

The Act defines "malt beverage[s]" in such a way as to include all beers and ales. Implementing regulations promulgated by BATF prohibit the disclosure of alcohol content on beer labels. In addition to prohibiting numerical indications of alcohol content, the labeling regulations proscribe descriptive terms that suggest high content, such as "strong," "full strength," "extra strength," "high test," "high proof," "pre-war strength," and "full oldtime alcoholic strength." The prohibitions do not preclude labels from identifying a beer as "low alcohol," "reduced alcohol," "non-alcoholic," or "alcohol-free." By statute and by regulation, the labeling ban must give way if state law requires disclosure of alcohol content.

Both parties agree that the information on beer labels constitutes commercial speech. We now apply *Central Hudson* test to § 205(e)(2). Respondent seeks to disclose only truthful, verifiable, and nonmisleading factual information about alcohol content on its beer labels. Thus, our analysis focuses on the substantiality of the interest behind § 205(e)(2) and on whether the labeling ban bears an acceptable fit with the Government's goal.

The Government identifies two interests it considers sufficiently "substantial" to justify the labeling ban. First, the Government contends that it advances Congress' goal of curbing "strength wars" by beer brewers who might seek to compete for customers on the basis of alcohol content. Respondent counters that Congress actually intended the FAAA to achieve the far different purpose of preventing brewers from making inaccurate claims concerning alcohol content. According to respondent, when Congress passed the FAAA in 1935, brewers did not have the technology to produce beer with alcohol levels within predictable tolerances—a skill that modern beer producers now possess. Further, respondent argues that the true policy guiding federal alcohol regulation is not aimed at suppressing strength wars. If such were the goal, the Government would not pursue the opposite policy with respect to wines and distilled spirits. Although § 205(e)(2) requires BATF to promulgate regulations barring the disclosure of alcohol content on beer labels, it also orders BATF to require the disclosure of alcohol content on the labels of wines and spirits.

Rather than suppressing the free flow of factual information in the wine and spirits markets, the Government seeks to control competition on the basis of strength by monitoring distillers' promotions and marketing. Respondent quite correctly notes that the general thrust of federal alcohol policy appears to favor greater disclosure of information, rather than less. Respondent offers a plausible reading of the purpose behind § 205(e)(2), but the prevention of misleading statements of alcohol content need not be the exclusive government interest served. The Government here has a significant interest in protecting the health, safety, and welfare of its citizens by preventing brewers from competing on the basis of alcohol strength, which could lead to greater alcoholism and its attendant social costs.

The Government attempts to bolster its position by arguing that the labeling ban not only curbs strength wars, but also facilitates state efforts to regulate alcohol under the Twenty-first Amendment. [The FAAA] prohibits disclosure of alcohol content only in States that do not affirmatively require brewers to provide that information. In the Government's view, this saves States that might wish to ban such labels the trouble of enacting their own legislation, and it discourages beer drinkers from crossing state lines to buy beer they believe is stronger.

We conclude that the Government's interest in preserving state authority is not sufficiently substantial to meet the requirements of *Central Hudson*. Even if the Federal Government possessed the broad authority to facilitate state powers, in this case the Government has offered nothing that suggests that States are in need of federal assistance. States clearly possess ample authority to ban the disclosure of alcohol content—subject, of course, to the same First Amendment restrictions that apply to the Federal Government.

The remaining *Central Hudson* factors require that a valid restriction on commercial speech directly advance the governmental interest and be no more extensive than necessary to serve that interest. The Government attempts to meet its burden by pointing to current developments in the consumer market. It claims that beer producers are already competing and advertising on the basis of alcohol strength in the "malt liquor" segment of the beer market. The Government attempts to show that this competition threatens to spread to the rest of the market by directing our attention to respondent's motives in bringing this litigation. Respondent allegedly suffers from consumer misperceptions that its beers contain less alcohol than other brands. According to the Government, once respondent gains relief from § 205(e)(2), it will use its labels to overcome this handicap.

Under the Government's theory, § 205(e)(2) suppresses the threat of such competition by preventing consumers from choosing beers on the basis of alcohol content. It is assuredly a matter of common sense that a restriction on the advertising of a product characteristic will decrease the extent to which consumers select a product on the basis of that trait. In addition to common sense, the Government urges us to turn to history as a guide. According to the Government, at the time Congress enacted the FAAA, the use of labels displaying alcohol content had helped produce a strength war. Section 205(e)(2) allegedly relieved competitive pressures to market beer on the basis of alcohol content, resulting over the long term in beers with lower alcohol levels.

We conclude that § 205(e)(2) cannot directly and materially advance its asserted interest because of the overall irrationality of the Government's regulatory scheme. While the laws governing labeling prohibit the disclosure of alcohol content unless required by state law, federal regulations apply a contrary policy to beer advertising. These restrictions prohibit statements of alcohol content in advertising, but, unlike § 205(e)(2), they apply only in States that affirmatively prohibit such advertisements. As only 18 States at best prohibit disclosure of content in advertisements, brewers remain free to disclose alcohol content in advertisements, but not on labels, in much of the country. The failure to prohibit the disclosure of alcohol content in advertising, which would seem to constitute a more influential weapon in any strength war than labels, makes no rational sense if the Government's true aim is to suppress strength wars.

Other provisions of the FAAA and its regulations similarly undermine § 205(e)(2)'s efforts to prevent strength wars. While § 205(e)(2) bans the disclosure of alcohol content on beer labels, it allows the exact opposite in the case of wines and spirits. Thus, distilled spirits may contain statements of alcohol content, and such disclosures are required for wines with more than 14 percent alcohol. If combating strength wars were the goal, we would assume that Congress would regulate disclosure of alcohol content for the strongest beverages as well as for the weakest ones. Further, the Government permits brewers to signal high alcohol content through use of the term "malt liquor." Although the Secretary has proscribed the use of various colorful terms suggesting high alcohol levels, manufacturers still can distinguish a class of stronger malt beverages by identifying them as malt liquors. One would think that if the Government sought to suppress strength wars by prohibiting numerical disclosures of alcohol content, it also would preclude brewers from indicating higher alcohol beverages by using descriptive terms.

While we are mindful that respondent only appealed the constitutionality of § 205(e)(2), these exemptions and inconsistencies bring into question the purpose of the labeling ban. To be sure, the Government's interest in combating strength wars remains a valid goal. But the irrationality of this unique and puzzling regulatory framework ensures that the labeling ban will fail to achieve that end. There is little chance that § 205(e)(2) can directly and materially advance its aim, while other provisions of the same Act directly undermine and counteract its effects.

Nor do we think that respondent's litigating positions can be used against it as proof that the Government's regulation is necessary. That respondent wishes to disseminate factual information concerning alcohol content does not demonstrate that it intends to compete on the basis of alcohol content. Brewers may have many different reasons—only one of which might be a desire to wage a strength war—why they wish to disclose the potency of their beverages.

Respondent suggests several alternatives [to the labeling ban], such as directly limiting the alcohol content of beers, prohibiting marketing efforts emphasizing high alcohol strength (which is apparently the policy in some other western nations), or limiting the labeling ban only to malt liquors, which is the segment of the market that allegedly is threatened with a strength war. We agree that the availability of these options, all of which could advance the Government's asserted interest in a manner less intrusive to respondent's First Amendment rights, indicates that § 205(e)(2) is more extensive than necessary.

In sum, although the Government may have a substantial interest in suppressing strength wars in the beer market, the FAAA's countervailing provisions prevent § 205(e)(2) from furthering that purpose in a direct and material fashion. The FAAA's defects are further highlighted by the availability of alternatives that would prove less intrusive to the First Amendment's protections for commercial speech. Because we find that § 205(e)(2) fails the *Central Hudson* test, we affirm the decision of the court below.

POINTS FOR DISCUSSION

1. Justice Thomas's opinion tells us that, even if common sense suggests that a governmental regulation furthers a legitimate state's interest, it can be thrown out if the larger context of other, competing regulations calls into question the government's logic. What might be some implications of this stance? For example, can a beach town's laws against commercial highway billboards be thrown out because, if the town were *really* serious about protecting the aesthetics of its environment, it would have also banned the use of "fly-by" advertisements by airplanes with streamers?
2. Suppose that a nonprofit consumer magazine were to publish on its cover that "Coors beer has 4.73 per cent alcohol by volume." This statement would likely not be considered "commercial speech." Why, then, does the identical message become commercial when Coors itself disseminates it? Does the identity (and commercial motivation?) of the speaker make the difference? If so, why is it that we consider neither a book review, nor a publisher's insertion of excerpts from that review on a book's dust jacket, commercial speech?

▪ *Citizens United v. Federal Election Commission*

130 S. Ct. 876 (2010)
Justice Kennedy:

Federal law prohibits corporations and unions from using their general treasury funds to make independent expenditures for speech defined as an "electioneering communication" or for speech expressly advocating the election or defeat of a candidate. Limits on electioneering communications were upheld in *McConnell v. Federal Election Comm'n*, 540 U.S. 93 (2003). The holding of *McConnell* rested to a large extent on an earlier case, *Austin v. Michigan Chamber of Commerce*, 494 U.S. 652 (1990). *Austin* had held that political speech may be banned based on the speaker's corporate identity.

In this case we are asked to reconsider *Austin* and, in effect, *McConnell*. We hold that *stare decisis* does not compel the continued acceptance of *Austin*. The Government may regulate corporate political speech through disclaimer and disclosure requirements, but it may not suppress that speech altogether. We turn to the case now before us.

Citizens United is a nonprofit corporation, [with] an annual budget of about $12 million. Most of its funds are from donations by individuals; but, in addition, it accepts a small portion of its funds from for-profit corporations.

In January 2008, Citizens United released a film entitled *Hillary: The Movie*. We refer to the film as *Hillary*. It is a 90-minute documentary about then-Senator Hillary Clinton, who was a candidate in the Democratic Party's 2008 Presidential primary elections.[1]

Hillary mentions Senator Clinton by name and depicts interviews with political commentators and other persons, most of them quite critical of Senator Clinton. *Hillary* was released in theaters and on DVD, but Citizens United wanted to increase distribution by making it available through video-on-demand. Video-on-demand allows digital cable subscribers to select programming from various menus, including movies, television shows, sports, news, and music. The viewer can watch the program at any time and can elect to rewind or pause the program.

In December 2007, a cable company offered, for a payment of $1.2 million, to make *Hillary* available on a video-on-demand channel called "Elections

---

1. Scenes from the film are on my website. Go to www.paulsiegelcommlaw.com and then, on the left side of the site (*Communication Law in America*), click on "Video Clips," "Chapter 10," and finally on "Hillary: The Movie."

'08." Some video-on-demand services require viewers to pay a small fee to view a selected program, but here the proposal was to make *Hillary* available to viewers free of charge. To implement the proposal, Citizens United was prepared to pay for the video-on-demand; and to promote the film, it produced two 10-second ads and one 30-second ad for *Hillary*. Each ad includes a short (and, in our view, pejorative) statement about Senator Clinton, followed by the name of the movie and the movie's Website address. Citizens United desired to promote the video-on-demand offering by running advertisements on broadcast and cable television.

Before the Bipartisan Campaign Reform Act of 2002 (BCRA), [§ 441b of the U.S. Code] prohibited—and still does prohibit—corporations and unions from using general treasury funds to make direct contributions to candidates or independent expenditures that expressly advocate the election or defeat of a candidate, through any form of media, in connection with certain qualified federal elections. BCRA prohibited any "electioneering communication" as well. An electioneering communication is defined as "any broadcast, cable, or satellite communication" that "refers to a clearly identified candidate for Federal office" and is made within 30 days of a primary or 60 days of a general election. The Federal Election Commission's (FEC) regulations further define an electioneering communication as a communication that is "publicly distributed." In the case of a candidate for nomination for President *publicly distributed* means that the communication can be received by 50,000 or more persons in a State where a primary election is being held within 30 days.

Corporations and unions are barred from using their general treasury funds for express advocacy or electioneering communications. They may establish, however, a "separate segregated fund" (known as a political action committee, or PAC) for these purposes. The moneys received by the segregated fund are limited to donations from stockholders and employees of the corporation or, in the case of unions, members of the union.

Citizens United wanted to make *Hillary* available through video-on-demand within 30 days of the 2008 primary elections. It feared, however, that both the film and the ads would be covered by the ban on corporate-funded independent expenditures, thus subjecting the corporation to civil and criminal penalties. Citizens United sought declaratory and injunctive relief against the FEC. It argued that [the law] is unconstitutional as applied to *Hillary*; and (2) BCRA's disclaimer and disclosure requirements, are unconstitutional as applied to *Hillary* and to the three ads for the movie.

Before considering whether *Austin* should be overruled, we first address whether [the case] may be resolved on other, narrower grounds. Citizens United contends that the law does not cover *Hillary*, as a matter of statutory interpretation, because the film does not qualify as an "electioneering communication." Under the definition of electioneering communication, the video-on-demand showing of *Hillary* on cable television would have been a "cable ... communication" that "referred to a clearly identified candidate for Federal office" and that was made within 30 days of a primary election. Citizens United, however, argues that *Hillary* was not "publicly distributed," because a single video-on-demand transmission is sent only to a requesting cable converter box and each separate transmission, in most instances, will be seen by just one household—not 50,000 or more persons.

This argument ignores the regulation's instruction on how to determine whether a cable transmission "can be received by 50,000 or more persons." The regulation provides that the number of people who can receive a cable transmission is determined by the number of cable subscribers in the relevant area. Here, Citizens United wanted to use a cable video-on-demand system that had 34.5 million subscribers nationwide. Thus, *Hillary* could have been received by 50,000 persons or more.

Citizens United next argues that § 441b may not be applied to *Hillary* [because it does not constitute] "express advocacy" for or against a specific candidate. [But] the movie, in essence, is a feature-length negative advertisement that urges viewers to vote against Senator Clinton for President. In light of historical footage, interviews with persons critical of her, and voiceover narration, the film would be understood by most viewers as an extended criticism of Senator Clinton's character and her fitness for the office of the Presidency. The narrative may contain more suggestions and arguments than facts, but there is little doubt that the thesis of the film is that she is unfit for the Presidency. The movie concentrates on alleged wrongdoing during the Clinton administration, Senator Clinton's qualifications and fitness for office, and policies the commentators predict she would pursue if elected President. It calls Senator Clinton "Machiavellian," and asks whether she is "the most qualified to hit the ground running if elected President." The narrator reminds viewers that "Americans have never been keen on dynasties" and that "a vote for Hillary is a vote to continue 20 years of a Bush or a Clinton in the White House."

Citizens United argues that *Hillary* is just "a documentary film that examines certain historical events." We disagree. The movie's consistent emphasis is on the relevance of these events to Senator Clinton's candidacy for President. The narrator begins by asking "could Senator Clinton become the first female President in the history of the United States?" And the narrator reiterates the movie's message in his closing line: "Finally, before America decides on our next president, voters should need no reminders of what's at stake—

the well being and prosperity of our nation." There is no reasonable interpretation of *Hillary* other than as an appeal to vote against Senator Clinton. The film qualifies as the functional equivalent of express advocacy.

Citizens United further contends that § 441b [cannot be applied to] movies shown through video-on-demand, arguing that this delivery system has a lower risk of distorting the political process than do television ads. On what we might call conventional television, advertising spots reach viewers who have chosen a channel or a program for reasons unrelated to the advertising. With video-on-demand, by contrast, the viewer selects a program after taking a series of affirmative steps: subscribing to cable; navigating through various menus; and selecting the program.

While some means of communication may be less effective than others at influencing the public in different contexts, any effort by the Judiciary to decide which means of communications are to be preferred for the particular type of message and speaker would raise questions as to the courts' own lawful authority. Substantial questions would arise if courts were to begin saying what means of speech should be preferred or disfavored. And in all events, those differentiations might soon prove to be irrelevant or outdated by technologies that are in rapid flux.

Courts, too, are bound by the First Amendment. We must decline to draw, and then redraw, constitutional lines based on the particular media or technology used to disseminate political speech from a particular speaker. It must be noted, moreover, that this undertaking would require substantial litigation over an extended time, all to interpret a law that beyond doubt discloses serious First Amendment flaws. The interpretive process itself would create an inevitable, pervasive, and serious risk of chilling protected speech pending the drawing of fine distinctions that, in the end, would themselves be questionable.

Citizens United also asks us to carve out an exception to the expenditure ban for nonprofit corporate political speech funded overwhelmingly by individuals. This line of analysis, however, would be unavailing.

[We have previously struck down the law's] restrictions on corporate expenditures as applied to nonprofit corporations that were formed for the sole purpose of promoting political ideas, did not engage in business activities, and did not accept contributions from for-profit corporations or labor unions. Citizens United does not qualify for the exemption, however, since some funds used to make the movie were donations from for-profit corporations.

We decline to adopt an interpretation that requires intricate case-by-case determinations to verify whether political speech is banned, especially if we are convinced that, in the end, this corporation has a constitutional right to speak on this subject.

The Court cannot resolve this case on a narrower ground without chilling political speech, speech that is central to the meaning and purpose of the First Amendment. It is not judicial restraint to accept an unsound, narrow argument just so the Court can avoid another argument with broader implications. Here, the lack of a valid basis for an alternative ruling requires full consideration of the continuing effect of the speech suppression upheld in *Austin*.

The law before us is an outright ban, backed by criminal sanctions. Section 441b makes it a felony for all corporations—including nonprofit advocacy corporations—either to expressly advocate the election or defeat of candidates or to broadcast electioneering communications within 30 days of a primary election and 60 days of a general election. Thus, the following acts would all be felonies under § 441b: The Sierra Club runs an ad, within the crucial phase of 60 days before the general election, that exhorts the public to disapprove of a Congressman who favors logging in national forests; the National Rifle Association publishes a book urging the public to vote for the challenger because the incumbent U.S. Senator supports a handgun ban; and the American Civil Liberties Union creates a Web site telling the public to vote for a Presidential candidate in light of that candidate's defense of free speech. These prohibitions are classic examples of censorship.

Section 441b is a ban on corporate speech notwithstanding the fact that a PAC created by a corporation can still speak. A PAC is a separate association from the corporation. So the PAC exemption from § 441b's expenditure ban does not allow corporations to speak. Even if a PAC could somehow allow a corporation to speak—and it does not—the option to form PACs does not alleviate the First Amendment problems with § 441b. PACs are burdensome alternatives; they are expensive to administer and subject to extensive regulations. For example, every PAC must appoint a treasurer, forward donations to the treasurer promptly, keep detailed records of the identities of the persons making donations, preserve receipts for three years, and file an organization statement and report changes to this information within 10 days.

And that is just the beginning. PACs must file detailed monthly reports with the FEC, which are due at different times depending on the type of election that is about to occur. PACs have to comply with these regulations just to speak. This might explain why fewer than 2,000 of the millions of corporations in this country have PACs. PACs, furthermore, must exist before they can speak. Given the onerous restrictions, a corporation may not be able to establish a PAC in time to make its views known regarding candidates and issues in a current campaign.

Section 441b's prohibition on corporate independent expenditures is thus a ban on speech. Were the Court to uphold these restrictions, the Government could repress speech by silencing certain voices at any of the various points in the speech process. If § 441b applied to individuals, no one would believe that it is merely a time, place, or manner restriction on speech. Its purpose and effect are to silence entities whose voices the Government deems to be suspect.

Laws that burden political speech are subject to strict scrutiny, which requires the Government to prove that the restriction furthers a compelling interest and is narrowly tailored to achieve that interest. Premised on mistrust of governmental power, the First Amendment stands against attempts to disfavor certain subjects or viewpoints. Prohibited, too, are restrictions distinguishing among different speakers, allowing speech by some but not others. As instruments to censor, these categories are interrelated: Speech restrictions based on the identity of the speaker are all too often simply a means to control content.

Quite apart from the purpose or effect of regulating content, moreover, the Government may commit a constitutional wrong when by law it identifies certain preferred speakers. By taking the right to speak from some and giving it to others, the Government deprives the disadvantaged person or class of the right to use speech to strive to establish worth, standing, and respect for the speaker's voice. The Government may not by these means deprive the public of the right and privilege to determine for itself what speech and speakers are worthy of consideration. At least before *Austin*, the Court had not allowed the exclusion of a class of speakers from the general public dialogue.

The Court has recognized that First Amendment protection extends to corporations. This protection has been extended by explicit holdings to the context of political speech. Political speech does not lose First Amendment protection simply because its source is a corporation.

At least since the latter part of the 19th century, the laws of some States and of the United States imposed a ban on corporate direct contributions to candidates. Yet not until 1947 did Congress first prohibit independent expenditures by corporations and labor unions in § 304 of the Labor Management Relations Act 1947. In passing this Act Congress overrode the veto of President Truman, who warned that the expenditure ban was a "dangerous intrusion on free speech." For almost three decades thereafter, the Court did not reach the question whether restrictions on corporate and union expenditures are constitutional.

In *Buckley v. Valeo*, 424 U.S. 1 (1976) the Court addressed various challenges to the Federal Election Campaign Act of 1971 (FECA) as amended in 1974. These amendments created an expenditure ban that applied to individuals as well as corporations and labor unions.

Buckley upheld FECA's limits on direct contributions to candidates. The *Buckley* Court recognized a "sufficiently important" governmental interest in "the prevention of corruption and the appearance of corruption." The *Buckley* Court explained that the potential for *quid pro quo* corruption distinguished direct contributions to candidates from independent expenditures. The Court emphasized that "the independent expenditure ceiling fails to serve any substantial governmental interest in stemming the reality or appearance of corruption in the electoral process because the absence of prearrangement and coordination alleviates the danger that expenditures will be given as a *quid pro quo* for improper commitments from the candidate." *Buckley* invalidated restrictions on independent expenditures. (*Buckley* did not consider the separate ban on corporate and union independent expenditures.)

Notwithstanding this precedent, Congress recodified [the FECA's] corporate and union expenditure ban at 2 U.S.C. § 441b four months after *Buckley* was decided. Section 441b is the independent expenditure restriction challenged here.

Thus the law stood until *Austin*, [which] upheld a direct restriction on the independent expenditure of funds for political speech for the first time in this Court's history. There, the Michigan Chamber of Commerce sought to use general treasury funds to run a newspaper ad supporting a specific candidate. Michigan law, however, prohibited corporate independent expenditures that supported or opposed any candidate for state office. A violation of the law was punishable as a felony. The Court sustained the speech prohibition. The *Austin* Court identified a new governmental interest in limiting political speech: an antidistortion interest. *Austin* found a compelling governmental interest in preventing "the corrosive and distorting effects of immense aggregations of wealth that are accumulated with the help of the corporate form and that have little or no correlation to the public's support for the corporation's political ideas." No case before *Austin* had held that Congress could prohibit independent expenditures for political speech based on the speaker's corporate identity.

In its defense of the corporate-speech restrictions in § 441b, the Government notes the antidistortion rationale on which *Austin* and its progeny rest in part, yet it all but abandons reliance upon it. It argues instead that two other compelling interests support *Austin*'s holding that corporate expenditure restrictions are constitutional: an anticorruption interest and a shareholder-protection interest.

As for *Austin*'s antidistortion rationale, the Government does little to defend it. And with good reason, for the rationale cannot support § 441b. If the First Amendment has any force, it prohibits Congress from fining or jailing citizens, or associations of citizens, for simply engaging in political speech. If the antidistortion rationale were to be accepted, however, it would permit Government to ban political speech simply because the speaker is an association that has taken on the corporate form.

The Government contends that *Austin* permits it to ban corporate expenditures for almost all forms of communication stemming from a corporation. If *Austin* were correct, the Government could prohibit a corporation from expressing political views in media beyond those presented here, such as by printing books. *Austin* sought to defend the antidistortion rationale as a means to prevent corporations from obtaining "an unfair advantage in the political marketplace" by using "resources amassed in the economic marketplace." [But we reject] the premise that the Government has an interest in equalizing the relative ability of individuals and groups to influence the outcome of elections. The First Amendment's protections do not depend on the speaker's financial ability to engage in public discussion. [We have previously] invalidated the BCRA provision that increased the cap on contributions to one candidate if the opponent made certain expenditures from personal funds. The rule that political speech cannot be limited based on a speaker's wealth is a necessary consequence of the premise that the First Amendment generally prohibits the suppression of political speech based on the speaker's identity.

It is irrelevant for purposes of the First Amendment that corporate funds may have little or no correlation to the public's support for the corporation's political ideas. All speakers, including individuals and the media, use money amassed from the economic marketplace to fund their speech. The First Amendment protects the resulting speech, even if it was enabled by economic transactions with persons or entities who disagree with the speaker's ideas.

By suppressing the speech of manifold corporations, both for-profit and nonprofit, the Government prevents their voices and viewpoints from reaching the public and advising voters on which persons or entities are hostile to their interests. Factions will necessarily form in our Republic, but the remedy of destroying the liberty of some factions is worse than the disease. Factions should be checked by permitting them all to speak and by entrusting the people to judge what is true and what is false. When Government seeks to use its full power, including the criminal law, to command where a person may get his or her information or what distrusted source he or she may not hear, it uses censorship to control thought. This is unlawful. The First Amendment confirms the freedom to think for ourselves.

What we have said also shows the invalidity of other arguments made by the Government. For the most part relinquishing the antidistortion rationale, the Government falls back on the argument that corporate political speech can be banned in order to prevent corruption or its appearance. In *Buckley*, the Court found this interest "sufficiently important" to allow limits on contributions but did not extend that reasoning to expenditure limits. When *Buckley* examined an expenditure ban, it found that the governmental interest in preventing corruption and the appearance of corruption was inadequate to justify the ban on independent expenditures. The absence of prearrangement and coordination of an expenditure with the candidate or his agent not only undermines the value of the expenditure to the candidate, but also alleviates the danger that expenditures will be given as a *quid pro quo* for improper commitments from the candidate.

Limits on independent expenditures, such as § 441b, have a chilling effect extending well beyond the Government's interest in preventing *quid pro quo* corruption. The anticorruption interest is not sufficient to displace the speech here in question. Indeed, 26 States do not restrict independent expenditures by for-profit corporations. The Government does not claim that these expenditures have corrupted the political process in those States.

The appearance of influence or access, furthermore, will not cause the electorate to lose faith in our democracy. By definition, an independent expenditure is political speech presented to the electorate that is not coordinated with a candidate. The fact that a corporation, or any other speaker, is willing to spend money to try to persuade voters presupposes that the people have the ultimate influence over elected officials. This is inconsistent with any suggestion that the electorate will refuse to take part in democratic governance because of additional political speech made by a corporation or any other speaker.

When Congress finds that a problem exists, we must give that finding due deference; but Congress may not choose an unconstitutional remedy. If elected officials succumb to improper influences from independent expenditures; if they surrender their best judgment; and if they put expediency before principle, then surely there is cause for concern. We must give weight to attempts by Congress to seek to dispel either the appearance or the reality of these influences. The remedies enacted by law, however, must comply with the First Amendment; and, it is our law and our tradition that more speech, not less, is the governing rule. An outright ban on corporate political speech during the critical preelection period is not a permissible remedy.

The Government contends further that corporate independent expenditures can be limited because of its interest in protecting dissenting shareholders from being compelled to fund corporate political speech. This asserted interest would allow the Government to ban the political speech even of media corporations. Assume, for example, that a shareholder of a corporation that owns a newspaper disagrees with the political views the newspaper expresses. Under the Government's view, that potential disagreement could give the Government the authority to restrict the media corporation's political speech. The First Amendment does not allow that power.

Moreover, the statute is both underinclusive and overinclusive. As to the first, if Congress had been seeking to protect dissenting shareholders, it would not have banned corporate speech in only certain media within 30 or 60 days before an election. A dissenting shareholder's interests would be implicated by speech in any media at any time. As to the second, the statute is overinclusive because it covers all corporations, including nonprofit corporations and for-profit corporations with only single shareholders. As to other corporations, the remedy is not to restrict speech but to consider and explore other regulatory mechanisms. The regulatory mechanism here, based on speech, contravenes the First Amendment.

Our precedent is to be respected unless the most convincing of reasons demonstrates that adherence to it puts us on a course that is sure error. Beyond workability, the relevant factors in deciding whether to adhere to the principle of *stare decisis* include the antiquity of the precedent, the reliance interests at stake, and of course whether the decision was well reasoned, [and] whether experience has pointed up the precedent's shortcomings. These considerations counsel in favor of rejecting *Austin*. This Court has not hesitated to overrule decisions offensive to the First Amendment. For the reasons above, it must be concluded that *Austin* was not well reasoned. *Austin* is undermined by experience since its announcement. Political speech is so ingrained in our culture that speakers find ways to circumvent campaign finance laws. Our Nation's speech dynamic is changing, and informative voices should not have to circumvent onerous restrictions to exercise their First Amendment rights. Speakers have become adept at presenting citizens with sound bites, talking points, and scripted messages that dominate the 24-hour news cycle. Corporations, like individuals, do not have monolithic views. On certain topics corporations may possess valuable expertise, leaving them the best equipped to point out errors or fallacies in speech of all sorts, including the speech of candidates and elected officials.

Rapid changes in technology—and the creative dynamic inherent in the concept of free expression—counsel against upholding a law that restricts political speech in certain media or by certain speakers. Today, 30-second television ads may be the most effective way to convey a political message. Soon, however, it may be that Internet sources, such as blogs and social networking Web sites, will provide citizens with significant information about political candidates and issues. Yet, § 441b would seem to ban a blog post expressly advocating the election or defeat of a candidate if that blog were created with corporate funds. The First Amendment does not permit Congress to make these categorical distinctions based on the corporate identity of the speaker and the content of the political speech.

Austin is overruled, so it provides no basis for allowing the Government to limit corporate independent expenditures. Section 441b's restrictions on corporate independent expenditures are therefore invalid and cannot be applied to *Hillary*. Given our conclusion we are further required to overrule the part of *McConnell* that upheld BCRA's extension of § 441b's restrictions on corporate independent expenditures. The *McConnell* Court relied on the antidistortion interest recognized in *Austin* to uphold a greater restriction on speech than the restriction upheld in *Austin*, and we have found this interest unconvincing and insufficient. This part of *McConnell* is now overruled.

Citizens United next challenges BCRA's disclaimer and disclosure provisions as applied to *Hillary* and the three advertisements for the movie. Under BCRA § 311, televised electioneering communications funded by anyone other than a candidate must include a disclaimer that "_____ is responsible for the content of this advertising." The required statement must be made in a "clearly spoken manner," and displayed on the screen in a "clearly readable manner" for at least four seconds. It must state that the communication "is not authorized by any candidate or candidate's committee"; it must also display the name and address (or Web site address) of the person or group that funded the advertisement. Under BCRA § 201, any person who spends more than $10,000 on electioneering communications within a calendar year must file a disclosure statement with the FEC. That statement must identify the person making the expenditure, the amount of the expenditure, the election to which the communication was directed, and the names of certain contributors.

Disclaimer and disclosure requirements may burden the ability to speak, but they impose no ceiling on campaign-related activities and do not prevent anyone from speaking. For the reasons stated below, we find the statute valid as applied to the ads for the movie and to the movie itself.

Citizens United sought to broadcast one 30-second and two 10-second ads to promote *Hillary*. Under FEC regulations, a communication that proposes a commercial transaction was not subject to 2 U.S.C. § 441b's restrictions on corporate or union funding of electioneering communications. The regulations, however, do not exempt those communications from the disclaimer and disclosure requirements.

Citizens United argues that the disclaimer requirements in § 311 are unconstitutional as applied to its ads. It contends that the governmental interest in providing information to the electorate does not justify requiring disclaimers for any commercial advertisements, including the ones at issue here. We disagree. The ads fall within BCRA's definition of an "electioneering communication": They referred to then-Senator Clinton by name shortly before a primary and contained pejorative references to her candidacy. The disclaimers required by § 311 provide the electorate with information and insure that the voters are fully informed about the person or group who is speaking. At the very least, the disclaimers avoid confusion by making clear that the ads are not funded by a candidate or political party.

Citizens United argues that § 311 is underinclusive because it requires disclaimers for broadcast advertisements but not for print or Internet advertising. It asserts that § 311 decreases both the quantity and effectiveness of the group's speech by forcing it to devote four seconds of each advertisement to the spoken disclaimer. We rejected these arguments in *McConnell*, and we now adhere to that decision as it pertains to the disclosure provisions.

As a final point, Citizens United claims that, in any event, the disclosure requirements in § 201 must be confined to speech that is the functional equivalent of express advocacy. We reject this contention. The Court has explained that disclosure is a less restrictive alternative to more comprehensive regulations of speech. The Court has upheld registration and disclosure requirements on lobbyists, even though Congress has no power to ban lobbying itself.

Citizens United also disputes that an informational interest justifies the application of § 201 to its ads, which only attempt to persuade viewers to see the film. Even if it disclosed the funding sources for the ads, Citizens United says, the information would not help viewers make informed choices in the political marketplace. This is similar to the argument rejected above with respect to disclaimers. Even if the ads only pertain to a commercial transaction, the public has an interest in knowing who is speaking about a candidate shortly before an election. Because the informational interest alone is sufficient to justify application of § 201 to these ads, it is not necessary to consider the Government's other asserted interests.

Last, Citizens United argues that disclosure requirements can chill donations to an organization by exposing donors to retaliation. [We] recognize that § 201 would be unconstitutional as applied to an organization if there were a reasonable probability that the group's members would face threats, harassment, or reprisals if their names were disclosed. Citizens United, however, has offered no evidence that its members may face [such] threats or reprisals. To the contrary, Citizens United has been disclosing its donors for years and has identified no instance of harassment or retaliation.

For the same reasons we uphold the application of BCRA §§ 201 and 311 to the ads, we affirm their application to *Hillary*. We find no constitutional impediment to the application of BCRA's disclaimer and disclosure requirements to a movie broadcast via video-on-demand. And there has been no showing that, as applied in this case, these requirements would impose a chill on speech or expression.

When word concerning the plot of the movie *Mr. Smith Goes to Washington* reached the circles of Government, some officials sought, by persuasion, to discourage its distribution. Under *Austin*, though, officials could have done more than discourage its distribution—they could have banned the film. After all, it, like *Hillary*, was speech funded by a corporation that was critical of Members of Congress. *Mr. Smith Goes to Washington* may be fiction and caricature; but fiction and caricature can be a powerful force.

Modern day movies, television comedies, or skits on Youtube.com might portray public officials or public policies in unflattering ways. Yet if a covered transmission during the blackout period creates the background for candidate endorsement or opposition, a felony occurs solely because a corporation, other than an exempt media corporation, has made the "purchase, payment, distribution, loan, advance, deposit, or gift of money or anything of value" in order to engage in political speech. Speech would be suppressed in the realm where its necessity is most evident: in the public dialogue preceding a real election. Governments are often hostile to speech, but under our law and our tradition it seems stranger than fiction for our Government to make this political speech a crime. Yet this is the statute's purpose and design.

The judgment of the District Court is reversed with respect to the constitutionality of 2 U.S.C. § 441b's restrictions on corporate independent expenditures. The judgment is affirmed with respect to BCRA's disclaimer and disclosure requirements. The case is remanded for further proceedings consistent with this opinion.

POINTS FOR DISCUSSION

1. After looking at the excerpts from *Hillary: The Movie*, on my website, ask yourself—is it more than simply a movie-length "political ad," and if so, could not the Court have produced a far narrower ruling refusing to apply the relevant laws to this film, but upholding the overall provisions of the BCRA?
2. Throughout the Court's opinion we see reference to a long-accepted notion in First Amendment law to the effect that more and more varied speech,

rather than government censorship, is the proper remedy to "bad" speech. Is it ever possible to reconcile this principle with the fear that there might not be enough time to formulate and disseminate "more speech" (such as, for example, within seven days of an election, instead of the thirty-day rule at issue here)?

11

Sexually Oriented Speech

This chapter looks at a category of speech—graphic sexual content—that the U.S. Supreme Court says is protected only marginally, if at all, by the First Amendment. *Miller v. California* is the landmark 1973 ruling providing the definition of obscenity still used by the Court. Two key components of that definition are that otherwise prohibitable works may be protected if they boast "serious literary, artistic, political, or scientific value" (often called the SLAPS test), and that the scope of prohibited works can vary from community to community.

Although the Court has said that truly obscene works are exceptions to the general principle that the government may not proscribe speech on the basis of its content, *Stanley v. Georgia* creates an exception to that exception. Unlike Miller, who was a commercial purveyor of pornography, Stanley was convicted of reading obscene materials in the privacy of his own home. This difference was of constitutional import, the Court determined.

And if *Stanley* counts as an exception to an exception, the rest of our cases in this chapter deal with various features of third-order exception. First we have *Osborne v. Ohio*, a 1990 decision in which the Court rules that states may criminalize the mere possession of *child* pornography (material that need not be obscene, but that does depict juveniles in lewd ways).

So, one may not own child pornography. But what exactly *is* child pornography? Must its production involve the participation of child actors, or can it be "virtual," or based on computer graphics alone? That is the question posed by *Ashcroft v. Free Speech Coalition*.

Finally we look at *U.S. v. Williams*, in which the Court holds that one can be sanctioned for even a false offer to provide child pornography.

▪ *Miller v. California*
413 U.S. 15 (1973)
Chief Justice Burger:

Appellant conducted a mass mailing campaign to advertise the sale of illustrated books, euphemistically called "adult" material. After a jury trial, he was convicted of violating California Penal Code § 311.2 (a), a misdemeanor, by knowingly distributing obscene matter. Appellant's conviction was specifically based on his conduct in causing five unsolicited advertising brochures to be sent through the mail in an envelope addressed to a restaurant in Newport Beach, California. The envelope was opened by the manager of the restaurant and his mother. They had not requested the brochures; they complained to the police. The brochures primarily consist of pictures and drawings very explicitly depicting men and women in groups of two or more engaging in a variety of sexual activities, with genitals often prominently displayed.

This Court has recognized that the States have a legitimate interest in prohibiting dissemination or exhibition of obscene material when the mode of dissemination carries with it a significant danger of offending the sensibilities of unwilling recipients or of exposure to juveniles. It is in this context that we are called on to define the standards which must be used to identify obscene material that a State may regulate without infringing on the First Amendment as applicable to the States through the Fourteenth Amendment.

We acknowledge the inherent dangers of undertaking to regulate any form of expression. State statutes designed to regulate obscene materials must be carefully limited. As a result, we now confine the permissible scope of such regulation to works which depict or describe sexual conduct. That conduct must be specifically defined by the applicable state law, as written or authoritatively construed. The basic guidelines for the trier of fact must be: (a) whether the average person, applying contemporary community standards would find that the work, taken as a whole, appeals to the prurient interest; (b) whether the work depicts or describes, in a patently offensive way, sexual conduct specifically defined by the applicable state law; and (c) whether the work, taken as a whole, lacks serious literary, artistic, political, or scientific value.

We emphasize that it is not our function to propose regulatory schemes for the States. That must await their concrete legislative efforts. It is possible, however, to give a few plain examples. State statutes [might legitimately cover] patently offensive representations or descriptions of ultimate sexual acts, normal or perverted, actual or simulated; and/or patently offensive representations or descriptions of masturbation, excretory functions, and lewd exhibition of the genitals.

Sex and nudity may not be exploited without limit by films or pictures exhibited or sold in places of public accommodation any more than live sex and nudity can be exhibited or sold without limit in such public places. At a minimum, prurient, patently offensive depiction or description of sexual conduct must have serious literary, artistic, political, or scientific value to merit First Amendment protection. For example, medical books for the education of physicians and related personnel necessarily use graphic illustrations and descriptions of human anatomy. In resolving the inevitably sensitive questions of fact and law, we must continue to rely on the jury system, accompanied by the safeguards that judges, rules of evidence, presumption of innocence, and other protective features provide, as we do with rape, murder, and a host of other offenses against society and its individual members.

Under the holdings announced today, no one will be subject to prosecution for the sale or exposure of obscene materials unless these materials depict or describe patently offensive "hard core" sexual conduct specifically defined by the regulating state law, as written or construed. We are satisfied that these specific prerequisites will provide fair notice to a dealer in such materials that his public and commercial activities may bring prosecution. If the inability to define regulated materials with ultimate, god-like precision altogether removes the power of the States or the Congress to regulate, then "hard core" pornography may be exposed without limit to the juvenile, the passerby, and the consenting adult alike.

Under a National Constitution, fundamental First Amendment limitations on the powers of the States do not vary from community to community, but this does not mean that there are, or should or can be, fixed, uniform national standards of precisely what appeals to the prurient interest or is patently offensive. These are essentially questions of fact, and our Nation is simply too big and too diverse for this Court to reasonably expect that such standards could be articulated for all 50 States in a single formulation, even assuming the prerequisite consensus exists. When triers of fact are asked to decide whether "the average person, applying contemporary community standards" would consider certain materials "prurient," it would be unrealistic to require that the answer be based on some abstract formulation. The adversary system, with lay jurors as the usual ultimate fact finders in criminal prosecutions, has historically permitted triers of fact to draw on the standards of their community, guided always by limiting instructions on the law. To require a State to structure obscenity proceedings around evidence of a national "community standard" would be an exercise in futility. It is neither realistic nor constitutionally sound to read the First Amendment as requiring that the people of Maine or

Mississippi accept public depiction of conduct found tolerable in Las Vegas, or New York City.

The primary concern with requiring a jury to apply the standard of "the average person, applying contemporary community standards" is to be certain that, so far as material is not aimed at a deviant group, it will be judged by its impact on an average person, rather than a particularly susceptible or sensitive person—or indeed a totally insensitive one. We hold that the requirement that the jury evaluate the materials with reference to "contemporary standards of the State of California" [as was done in this case] serves this protective purpose and is constitutionally adequate.

In our view, to equate the free and robust exchange of ideas and political debate with commercial exploitation of obscene material demeans the grand conception of the First Amendment and its high purposes in the historic struggle for freedom. The First Amendment protects works which, taken as a whole, have serious literary, artistic, political, or scientific value, regardless of whether the government or a majority of the people approve of the ideas these works represent. There is no evidence, empirical or historical, that the stern 19th century American censorship of public distribution and display of material relating to sex in any way limited or affected expression of serious literary, artistic, political, or scientific ideas. On the contrary, it is beyond any question that the era following Thomas Jefferson to Theodore Roosevelt was an extraordinarily vigorous period, not just in economics and politics, but in belles lettres and in the outlying fields of social and political philosophies. We do not see the harsh hand of censorship of ideas—good or bad, sound or unsound—and "repression" of political liberty lurking in every state regulation of commercial exploitation of human interest in sex. One can concede that the "sexual revolution" of recent years may have had useful byproducts in striking layers of prudery from a subject long irrationally kept from needed ventilation. But it does not follow that no regulation of patently offensive "hard core" materials is needed or permissible; civilized people do not allow unregulated access to heroin because it is a derivative of medicinal morphine.

The judgment of the Appellate Department of the Superior Court, Orange County, California, is vacated and the case remanded to that court for further proceedings not inconsistent with the First Amendment standards established by this opinion. Vacated and remanded.

[*Editor's note*: "Vacating" the lower court judgment in this way is not at all the same thing as "overturning" the judgment would have been. Indeed, because the definition of obscenity offered by Chief Justice Burger gives states more freedom to prosecute than the one used at Miller's trial, Burger is really inviting the California courts to uphold the initial conviction.]

POINTS FOR DISCUSSION

1. The majority says, without fanfare, that sexual messages may be prohibited "when the mode of dissemination carries with it a significant danger of offending the sensibilities of unwilling recipients or of exposure to juveniles." But why single out *sexual* messages for this treatment? Might a Jew be equally offended by the local church marquee's claim that "Jesus is the *only* way?" Isn't the pro-life demonstrator's shouting that "abortion is murder" designed, at least in part, to offend the sensibilities of abortion clinics' approaching clients?
2. Suppose that you are a juror in an obscenity case, and also that you are not especially offended by the materials you are called on to judge. Yet you are not supposed to apply your own feelings. Rather, you are asked to call to mind the "average person" in your community. How would you figure out what such a person's reaction would be to this material? Would the average person find the work appeals to the "prurient interest," or was "patently offensive"? How would you guess?

Stanley v. Georgia
394 U.S. 557 (1969)
Justice Marshall:

An investigation of appellant's alleged bookmaking activities led to the issuance of a search warrant for appellant's home. Federal and state agents found very little evidence of bookmaking activity, but while looking through a desk drawer in an upstairs bedroom, one of the federal agents, accompanied by a state officer, found three reels of eight-millimeter film. Using a projector and screen found in an upstairs living room, they viewed the films. The state officer concluded that they were obscene and seized them. Appellant was charged with possession of obscene matter and placed under arrest. He was tried before a jury and convicted. The Supreme Court of Georgia affirmed.

Appellant argues that the Georgia obscenity statute, insofar as it punishes mere private possession of obscene matter, violates the First Amendment, as made applicable to the States by the Fourteenth Amendment. For reasons set forth below, we agree that the mere private possession of obscene matter cannot constitutionally be made a crime. Georgia contends that since obscenity is not within the area of constitutionally protected speech or press, the States are free, subject to the limits of other provisions of the Constitution, to deal with it any way deemed necessary, just as they may deal with possession of other things thought to be detrimental to the welfare of their citizens. If the State can protect the body of a citizen, may it not, argues Georgia, protect his mind?

It is true that [our previous decisions] declare, seemingly without qualification, that obscenity is not protected by the First Amendment. However, [no] decision of this Court dealt with the precise problem involved in the present case—private possession of obscene materials. [The earlier cases] dealt with the power of the State and Federal Governments to prohibit or regulate certain public actions taken or intended to be taken with respect to obscene matter, [such as] sale or distribution of obscene materials or possession with intent to sell or distribute, [or] sale of obscene material to children.

It is now well established that the Constitution protects the right to receive information and ideas. This right to receive information and ideas, regardless of their social worth, is fundamental to our free society. Moreover, in the context of this case—a prosecution for mere possession of printed or filmed matter in the privacy of a person's own home—that right takes on an added dimension. For also fundamental is the right to be free, except in very limited circumstances, from unwanted governmental intrusions into one's privacy.

These are the rights that appellant is asserting in the case before us. He is asserting the right to read or observe what he pleases—the right to satisfy his intellectual and emotional needs in the privacy of his own home. He is asserting the right to be free from state inquiry into the contents of his library. Georgia contends that appellant does not have these rights, that there are certain types of materials that the individual may not read or even possess. Georgia justifies this assertion by arguing that the films in the present case are obscene. But we think that mere categorization of these films as "obscene" is insufficient justification for such a drastic invasion of personal liberties guaranteed by the First and Fourteenth Amendments. Whatever may be the justifications for other statutes regulating obscenity, we do not think they reach into the privacy of one's own home. If the First Amendment means anything, it means that a State has no business telling a man, sitting alone in his own house, what books he may read or what films he may watch. Our whole constitutional heritage rebels at the thought of giving government the power to control men's minds. And yet, in the face of these traditional notions of individual liberty, Georgia asserts the right to protect the individual's mind from the effects of obscenity. We are not certain that this argument amounts to anything more than the assertion that the State has the right to control the moral content of a person's thoughts. To some, this may be a noble purpose, but it is wholly inconsistent with the philosophy of the First Amendment.

Nor is it relevant that obscene materials in general, or the particular films before the Court, are arguably devoid of any ideological content. The line between the transmission of ideas and mere entertainment is much too elusive for this Court to draw, if indeed such a line can be drawn at all. Whatever the power of the state to control public dissemination of ideas inimical to the public morality, it cannot constitutionally premise legislation on the desirability of controlling a person's private thoughts.

Perhaps recognizing this, Georgia asserts that exposure to obscene materials may lead to deviant sexual behavior or crimes of sexual violence. There appears to be little empirical basis for that assertion. But more important, if the State is only concerned about printed or filmed materials inducing antisocial conduct, we believe that in the context of private consumption of ideas and information we should adhere to the view that among free men, the deterrents ordinarily to be applied to prevent crime are education and punishment for violations of the law. Given the present state of knowledge, the State may no more prohibit mere possession of obscene matter on the ground that it may lead to antisocial conduct than it may prohibit possession of chemistry books on the ground that they may lead to the manufacture of homemade spirits.

There is always the danger that obscene material might fall into the hands of children, or that it might intrude upon the sensibilities or privacy of the general public. No such dangers are present in this case.

Finally, we are faced with the argument that prohibition of possession of obscene materials is a necessary incident to statutory schemes prohibiting distribution. That argument is based on alleged difficulties of proving an intent to distribute or in producing evidence of actual distribution. We are not convinced that such difficulties exist, but even if they did we do not think that they would justify infringement of the individual's right to read or observe what he pleases. Because that right is so fundamental to our scheme of individual liberty, its restriction may not be justified by the need to ease the administration of otherwise valid criminal laws.

We hold that the First and Fourteenth Amendments prohibit making mere private possession of obscene material a crime. The States retain broad power to regulate obscenity; that power simply does not extend to mere possession by the individual in the privacy of his own home. Accordingly, the judgment of the court below is reversed and the case is remanded for proceedings not inconsistent with this opinion.

POINTS FOR DISCUSSION

1. In other decisions, the Court upheld laws making it illegal to send obscene works through the mails, or through such interstate public transport as air-

planes or trains, or to import them from another country. Such rulings led Justice Douglas to comment that he could not understand "how the right to possession enunciated in *Stanley* has any meaning when States are allowed to outlaw the commercial transactions which give rise to such possession." How would you answer Justice Douglas?

2. The Court says here that "the line between the transmission of ideas and mere entertainment" is an elusive one, suggesting that works are more likely to be protected by the First Amendment to the extent that they contain "ideas." Yet isn't that which upsets many people most about some kinds of pornography precisely the "ideas" they convey? Many pornographic films, after all, depict women enjoying being penetrated by force in every available orifice. Do not such depictions convey "ideas" about women, and about relationships between the sexes generally?

▪ *Osborne v. Ohio*

495 U.S. 103 (1990)
Justice White:

In order to combat child pornography, Ohio enacted Rev. Code Ann. § 2907.323(A)(3) (Supp. 1989), which provides in pertinent part:

(A) No person shall do any of the following:

(3) Possess or view any material or performance that shows a minor who is not the person's child or ward in a state of nudity, unless one of the following applies:

(a) The material or performance is sold, disseminated, displayed, possessed, controlled, brought or caused to be brought into this state, or presented for a bona fide artistic, medical, scientific, educational, religious, governmental, judicial, or other proper purpose, by or to a physician, psychologist, sociologist, scientist, teacher, person pursuing bona fide studies or research, librarian, clergyman, prosecutor, judge, or other person having a proper interest in the material or performance.
(b) The person knows that the parents, guardian, or custodian has consented in writing to the photographing or use of the minor in a state of nudity and to the manner in which the material or performance is used or transferred.

Petitioner, Clyde Osborne, was convicted of violating this statute and sentenced to six months in prison, after the Columbus, Ohio, police, pursuant to a valid search, found four photographs in Osborne's home. Each photograph depicts a nude male adolescent posed in a sexually explicit position. The Ohio Supreme Court affirmed Osborne's conviction. The court first rejected Osborne's contention that the First Amendment prohibits the States from proscribing the private possession of child pornography. Next, the Court found that § 2907.323(A)(3) is not unconstitutionally overbroad. In so doing, the Court, read § 2907.323(A)(3) as only applying to depictions of nudity involving a lewd exhibition or graphic focus on a minor's genitals. The Court also found that scienter [i.e., that the defendant was aware of the sexually graphic nature of the photos] is an essential element of a § 2907.323(A)(3) offense. Osborne objected that the trial judge had not insisted that the government prove lewd exhibition and scienter as elements of his crime. The Ohio Supreme Court rejected these contentions because Osborne had failed to object to the jury instructions given at his trial and the court did not believe that the failures of proof amounted to plain error.

The threshold question in this case is whether Ohio may constitutionally proscribe the possession and viewing of child pornography or whether, as Osborne argues, our decision in *Stanley v. Georgia*, 394 U.S. 557 (1969), compels the contrary result. In *Stanley*, we struck down a Georgia law outlawing the private possession of obscene material. We recognized that the statute impinged upon Stanley's right to receive information in the privacy of his home, and we found Georgia's justifications for its law inadequate.

Stanley should not be read too broadly. [It] was a narrow holding and, since the decision in that case, the value of permitting child pornography has been characterized [by this Court] as "exceedingly modest, if not *de minimis*." But assuming, for the sake of argument, that Osborne has a First Amendment interest in viewing and possessing child pornography, we nonetheless find this case distinct from *Stanley* because the interests underlying child pornography prohibitions far exceed the interests justifying the Georgia law at issue in *Stanley*. In *Stanley*, Georgia primarily sought to proscribe the private possession of obscenity because it was concerned that obscenity would poison the minds of its viewers. We responded that "whatever the power of the state to control public dissemination of ideas inimical to the public morality, it cannot constitutionally premise legislation on the desirability of controlling a person's private thoughts." The difference here is obvious: The State does not rely on a paternalistic interest in regulating Osborne's mind. Rather, Ohio has enacted § 2907.323(A)(3) in order to protect the victims of child pornography; it hopes to destroy a market for the exploitative use of children.

The use of children as subjects of pornographic materials is harmful to the physiological, emotional, and mental health of the child. It is also surely reasonable for the State to conclude that it will decrease the production of child pornography if it penalizes those who possess and view the product, thereby decreasing demand. The advertising and selling of child pornography provide an economic motive for and are thus an integral part of the production of such materials, an activity illegal throughout the Nation. It rarely has been suggested that the constitutional freedom for speech and press extends its immunity to speech or writing used as an integral part of conduct in violation of a valid criminal statute.

Osborne contends that the State should use other measures, besides penalizing possession, to dry up the child pornography market. Osborne points out that in *Stanley* we rejected Georgia's argument that its prohibition on obscenity possession was a necessary incident to its proscription on obscenity distribution. This holding, however, must be viewed in light of the weak interests asserted by the State in that case. *Stanley* itself emphasized that we did not "mean to express any opinion on statutes making criminal possession of other types of printed, filmed, or recorded materials," [that] "in such cases, compelling reasons may exist for overriding the right of the individual to possess those materials."

Given the importance of the State's interest in protecting the victims of child pornography, we cannot fault Ohio for attempting to stamp out this vice at all levels in the distribution chain. Much of the child pornography market [is] underground; as a result, it is difficult, if not impossible, to solve the child pornography problem by only attacking production and distribution.

Other interests also support the Ohio law. First, the materials produced by child pornographers permanently record the victim's abuse. The pornography's continued existence causes the child victims continuing harm by haunting the children in years to come. The State's ban on possession and viewing encourages the possessors of these materials to destroy them. Second, encouraging the destruction of these materials is also desirable because evidence suggests that pedophiles use child pornography to seduce other children into sexual activity. Given the gravity of the State's interests in this context, we find that Ohio may constitutionally proscribe the possession and viewing of child pornography.

Osborne next argues that even if the State may constitutionally ban the possession of child pornography, his conviction is invalid because § 2907.323(A)(3) is unconstitutionally overbroad in that it criminalizes an intolerable range of constitutionally protected conduct. The Ohio statute, on its face, purports to prohibit the possession of "nude" photographs of minors. We have stated that depictions of nudity, without more, constitute protected expression. Relying on this observation, Osborne argues that the statute as written is substantially overbroad. We are skeptical of this claim because, in light of the statute's exemptions and "proper purposes" provisions, the statute may not be substantially overbroad. However that may be, Osborne's overbreadth challenge, in any event, fails because the statute, as construed by the Ohio Supreme Court on Osborne's direct appeal, plainly survives overbreadth scrutiny. Under the Ohio Supreme Court reading, the statute prohibits "the possession or viewing of material or performance of a minor who is in a state of nudity, where such nudity constitutes a lewd exhibition or involves a graphic focus on the genitals, and where the person depicted is neither the child nor the ward of the person charged." By limiting the statute's operation in this manner, the Ohio Supreme Court avoided penalizing persons for viewing or possessing innocuous photographs of naked children. We have upheld similar language against overbreadth challenges in the past.

The Ohio Supreme Court also concluded that the State had to establish scienter in order to prove a violation of § 2907.323(A)(3). Osborne contends that it was impermissible for the Ohio Supreme Court to apply its construction of § 2907.323(A)(3) to him—i.e., to rely on the narrowed construction of the statute when evaluating his overbreadth claim. Our cases, however, have long held that a statute as construed may be applied to conduct occurring prior to the construction, provided such application affords fair warning to the defendant. Osborne had notice that his conduct was proscribed. It is obvious from the face of § 2907.323(A)(3) that the goal of the statute is to eradicate child pornography. The provision criminalizes the viewing and possessing of material depicting children in a state of nudity for other than "proper purposes." The provision appears in the "Sex Offenses" chapter of the Ohio Code. That Osborne's photographs of adolescent boys in sexually explicit situations constitute child pornography hardly needs elaboration. Therefore, although § 2907.323(A)(3) as written may have been imprecise at its fringes, someone in Osborne's position would not be surprised to learn that his possession of the four photographs at issue in this case constituted a crime.

Osborne contends that a court may not construe the statute to avoid overbreadth problems and then apply the statute, as construed, to past conduct. The implication of this argument is that if a statute is overbroad as written, then the statute is void and incurable. As a result, when reviewing a conviction under a potentially overbroad statute, a court must either affirm or strike down the statute on its face, but the court may not, as the Ohio Supreme court did in this case, narrow the statute, affirm on the basis of the narrowing construction, and leave the statute in full force. We disagree.

If we accepted this proposition, it would require a radical reworking of our law. Courts routinely construe statutes so as to avoid the statutes' potentially overbroad reach, apply the statute in that case, and leave the statute in place.

Osborne contends that when courts construe statutes so as to eliminate overbreadth, convictions of those found guilty of unprotected conduct covered by the statute must be reversed and any further convictions for prior reprehensible conduct are barred. Furthermore, because he contends that overbroad laws implicating First Amendment interests are nullities and incapable of valid application from the outset, this would mean that judicial construction could not save the statute even as applied to subsequent conduct unprotected by the First Amendment. The overbreadth doctrine, as we have recognized, is indeed strong medicine, and requiring that statutes be facially invalidated whenever overbreadth is perceived would very likely invite reconsideration or redefinition of the doctrine in a way that would not serve First Amendment interests.

[*Editor's note*: Although Osborne's First Amendment claims were rejected, the Supreme Court overturned his conviction, finding that the jury had not been properly instructed as to all the elements of the Ohio obscenity statute.]

POINTS FOR DISCUSSION

1. The Ohio statute provided an exception for images gathered for "a bona fide . . . educational . . . or other proper purpose, by or to a . . . person pursuing bona fide studies or research." One of the state's major interests in prohibiting child pornography, however, is to protect the child victims' privacy; the material's "continued existence causes the child victims continuing harm by haunting the children in years to come." From the child victim's perspective, what difference does it make if the images of their abuse are in the hands of a researcher—a reporter?—or a bus driver? Does the exception ignore the state's interest?
2. Do the statute's exemptions also suffer from a degree of vagueness? Would a sex manual, for example, qualify as an "educational" purpose?

Ashcroft v. Free Speech Coalition
535 U.S. 234 (2002)
Justice Kennedy:

We consider in this case whether the Child Pornography Prevention Act of 1996 (CPPA), abridges the freedom of speech. The CPPA extends the federal prohibition against child pornography to sexually explicit images that appear to depict minors but were produced without using any real children. The statute prohibits, in specific circumstances, possessing or distributing these images, which may be created by using adults who look like minors or by using computer imaging. The new technology, according to Congress, makes it possible to create realistic images of children who do not exist.

By prohibiting child pornography that does not depict an actual child, the statute goes beyond [the scope of our precedents], which distinguished child pornography from other sexually explicit speech because of the State's interest in protecting the children exploited by the production process. As a general rule, pornography can be banned only if obscene, but pornography showing minors can be proscribed whether or not the images are obscene.

While we have not had occasion to consider the question, we may assume that the apparent age of persons engaged in sexual conduct is relevant to whether a depiction offends community standards. Pictures of young children engaged in certain acts might be obscene where similar depictions of adults, or perhaps even older adolescents, would not. The CPPA, however, is not directed at speech that is obscene; Congress has proscribed those materials through a separate statute. The CPPA seeks to reach beyond obscenity; for instance, the statute would reach visual depictions, such as movies, even if they have redeeming social value.

The principal question to be resolved, then, is whether the CPPA is constitutional where it proscribes a significant universe of speech that is neither obscene nor [fits the accepted definition of] child pornography.

Before 1996, Congress defined child pornography as images made using actual minors. The CPPA retains that prohibition and adds three other prohibited categories of speech, of which the first and the third are at issue in this case. [The one section] prohibits "any visual depiction, including any photograph, film, video, picture, or computer or computer-generated image or picture" that "is, or appears to be, of a minor engaging in sexually explicit conduct." The prohibition on "any visual depiction" does not depend at all on how the image is produced. The section captures a range of depictions, sometimes called "virtual child pornography," which include computer-generated images, as well as images produced by more traditional means. For instance, the literal terms of the statute embrace a Renaissance painting depicting a scene from classical mythology, a "picture" that "appears to be, of a minor engaging in sexually explicit conduct." The statute also prohibits Hollywood movies, filmed without any child actors, if a jury believes an actor "appears to be" a minor engaging in "actual or simulated sexual intercourse."

These images do not involve, let alone harm, any children in the production process; but Congress decided the materials threaten children in other, less direct, ways. Pedophiles might use the materials to encourage children to participate in sexual activity. "A child who is reluctant to engage in sexual activity with an adult, or to pose for sexually explicit photographs, can sometimes be convinced by viewing depictions of other children "having fun" participating in such activity. Furthermore, pedophiles might "whet their own sexual appetites" with the pornographic images, "thereby increasing the creation and distribution of child pornography and the sexual abuse and exploitation of actual children." Under these rationales, harm flows from the content of the images, not from the means of their production. In addition, Congress identified another problem created by computer-generated images: Their existence can make it harder to prosecute pornographers who do use real minors. As imaging technology improves, Congress found, it becomes more difficult to prove that a particular picture was produced using actual children. To ensure that defendants possessing child pornography using real minors cannot evade prosecution, Congress extended the ban to virtual child pornography.

[The second section at issue here] defines child pornography to include any sexually explicit image that was "advertised, promoted, presented, described, or distributed in such a manner that conveys the impression" it depicts "a minor engaging in sexually explicit conduct." One Committee Report identified the provision as directed at sexually explicit images pandered as child pornography. The statute is not so limited in its reach, however, as it punishes even those possessors who took no part in pandering. Once a work has been described as child pornography, the taint remains on the speech in the hands of subsequent possessors, making possession unlawful even though the content otherwise would not be objectionable.

Fearing that the CPPA threatened the activities of its members, respondent Free Speech Coalition and others challenged the statute. The District Court granted summary judgment to the Government. The Court of Appeals for the Ninth Circuit reversed. While the Ninth Circuit found the CPPA invalid on its face, four other Courts of Appeals have sustained it. We granted certiorari.

A law imposing criminal penalties on protected speech is a stark example of speech suppression. The CPPA's penalties are indeed severe. A first offender may be imprisoned for 15 years. A repeat offender faces a prison sentence of not less than 5 years and not more than 30 years in prison. This case provides a textbook example of why we permit facial challenges to statutes that burden expression. With these severe penalties in force, few legitimate movie producers or book publishers, or few other speakers in any capacity, would risk distributing images in or near the uncertain reach of this law. The Constitution gives significant protection from overbroad laws that chill speech within the

First Amendment's vast and privileged sphere. Under this principle, the CPPA is unconstitutional on its face if it prohibits a substantial amount of protected expression.

The sexual abuse of a child is a most serious crime and an act repugnant to the moral instincts of a decent people. In its legislative findings, Congress recognized that there are subcultures of persons who harbor illicit desires for children and commit criminal acts to gratify the impulses. Congress also found that surrounding the serious offenders are those who flirt with these impulses and trade pictures and written accounts of sexual activity with young children.

Congress may pass valid laws to protect children from abuse, and it has. The prospect of crime, however, by itself does not justify laws suppressing protected speech.

The CPPA is much more than a supplement to the existing federal prohibition on obscenity. Under [traditional obscenity law], the Government must prove that the work, taken as a whole, appeals to the prurient interest, is patently offensive in light of community standards, and lacks serious literary, artistic, political, or scientific value. The CPPA, however, extends to images that appear to depict a minor engaging in sexually explicit activity without regard to these requirements. The materials need not appeal to the prurient interest. Any depiction of sexually explicit activity, no matter how it is presented, is proscribed. The CPPA applies to a picture in a psychology manual, as well as a movie depicting the horrors of sexual abuse. It is not necessary, moreover, that the image be patently offensive. Pictures of what appear to be 17-year-olds engaging in sexually explicit activity do not in every case contravene community standards.

The CPPA prohibits speech despite its serious literary, artistic, political, or scientific value. The statute proscribes the visual depiction of an idea—that of teenagers engaging in sexual activity—that is a fact of modern society and has been a theme in art and literature throughout the ages. Under the CPPA, images are prohibited so long as the persons appear to be under 18 years of age. This is higher than the legal age for marriage in many States, as well as the age at which persons may consent to sexual relations. It is, of course, undeniable that some youths engage in sexual activity before the legal age, either on their own inclination or because they are victims of sexual abuse.

Both themes—teenage sexual activity and the sexual abuse of children—have inspired countless literary works. William Shakespeare created [in *Romeo and Juliet*] the most famous pair of teenage lovers, one of whom is just 13 years of age. In the drama, Shakespeare portrays the relationship as something splendid and innocent, but not juvenile. The work has inspired no less than 40 motion pictures, some of which suggest that the teenagers consummated their relationship. Shakespeare may not have written sexually explicit scenes for the Elizabethan audience, but were modern directors to adopt a less conventional approach, that fact alone would not compel the conclusion that the work was obscene.

Contemporary movies pursue similar themes. [The 2001] Academy Awards featured the movie, *Traffic*, which was nominated for Best Picture. The film portrays a teenager, identified as a 16-year-old, who becomes addicted to drugs. The viewer sees the degradation of her addiction, which in the end leads her to a filthy room to trade sex for drugs. The year before, *American Beauty* won the Academy Award for Best Picture. In the course of the movie, a teenage girl engages in sexual relations with her teenage boyfriend, and another yields herself to the gratification of a middle-aged man.[1] The film also contains a scene where, although the movie audience understands the act is not taking place, one character believes he is watching a teenage boy performing a sexual act on an older man.

Whether or not the films we mention violate the CPPA, they explore themes within the wide sweep of the statute's prohibitions. If these films, or hundreds of others of lesser note that explore those subjects, contain a single graphic depiction of sexual activity within the statutory definition, the possessor of the film would be subject to severe punishment without inquiry into the work's redeeming value. This is inconsistent with an essential First Amendment rule: The artistic merit of a work does not depend on the presence of a single explicit scene.

The Government seeks to address this deficiency by arguing that speech prohibited by the CPPA is virtually indistinguishable from child pornography, which may be banned without regard to whether it depicts works of value. Where the images are themselves the product of child sexual abuse, the State has an interest in stamping it out without regard to any judgment about its content. The production of the work, not its content, was the target of the statute. The fact that a work contained serious literary, artistic, or other value did not excuse the harm it caused to its child participants.

[We have] upheld a prohibition on the distribution and sale of child pornography, as well as its production, because these acts were "intrinsically related" to the sexual abuse of children in two ways. First, as a permanent record of a child's abuse, the continued circulation itself would harm the child who had participated. Like a defamatory statement, each new publication of the

---

1. The latter scene referenced here is on my website. Go to www.paulsiegelcomm law.com, then, on the left side of the screen (*Communication Law in America*), click on "Video Clips," then "Chapter 11," and finally on "American Beauty."

speech would cause new injury to the child's reputation and emotional well-being. Second, because the traffic in child pornography was an economic motive for its production, the State had an interest in closing the distribution network. The most expeditious if not the only practical method of law enforcement may be to dry up the market for this material by imposing severe criminal penalties on persons selling, advertising, or otherwise promoting the product. Under either rationale, the speech had what the Court in effect held was a proximate link to the crime from which it came.

[We have also held] that these same interests justified a ban on the possession of pornography produced by using children. Given the importance of the State's interest in protecting the victims of child pornography, the state was justified in attempting to stamp out this vice at all levels in the distribution chain. [We have] also noted the State's interest in preventing child pornography from being used as an aid in the solicitation of minors. The Court, however, anchored its holding in the concern for the participants, those whom it called the "victims of child pornography." It did not suggest that, absent this concern, other governmental interests would suffice.

In contrast to the [earlier cases], the CPPA prohibits speech that records no crime and creates no victims by its production. Virtual child pornography is not "intrinsically related" to the sexual abuse of children. While the Government asserts that the images can lead to actual instances of child abuse, the causal link is contingent and indirect. The harm does not necessarily follow from the speech, but depends upon some unquantified potential for subsequent criminal acts.

The Government says these indirect harms are sufficient because child pornography rarely can be valuable speech. This argument, however, suffers from two flaws. First, [our earlier child pornography cases] were based upon how it was made, not on what it communicated. [We even] reaffirmed that where the speech is neither obscene nor the product of sexual abuse, it does not fall outside the protection of the First Amendment.

The second flaw in the Government's position is that [we have never held] that child pornography is by definition without value. On the contrary, the Court recognized some works in this category might have significant value, but relied on virtual images—the very images prohibited by the CPPA—as an alternative and permissible means of expression: "If it were necessary for literary or artistic value, a person over the statutory age who perhaps looked younger could be utilized. Simulation outside of the prohibition of the statute could provide another alternative."

The Government seeks to justify [CPPA's] prohibitions in other ways. It argues that the CPPA is necessary because pedophiles may use virtual child pornography to seduce children. There are many things innocent in themselves, however, such as cartoons, video games, and candy, that might be used for immoral purposes, yet we would not expect those to be prohibited because they can be misused. The Government, of course, may punish adults who provide unsuitable materials to children, and it may enforce criminal penalties for unlawful solicitation. The precedents establish, however, that speech within the rights of adults to hear may not be silenced completely in an attempt to shield children from it. The State [may] not reduce the adult population to reading only what is fit for children.

Here, the Government wants to keep speech from children not to protect them from its content but to protect them from those who would commit other crimes. The principle, however, remains the same: The Government cannot ban speech fit for adults simply because it may fall into the hands of children. The evil in question depends upon the actor's unlawful conduct, conduct defined as criminal quite apart from any link to the speech in question. This establishes that the speech ban is not narrowly drawn. The objective is to prohibit illegal conduct, but this restriction goes well beyond that interest by restricting the speech available to law-abiding adults.

The Government submits further that virtual child pornography whets the appetites of pedophiles and encourages them to engage in illegal conduct. This rationale cannot sustain the provision in question. The mere tendency of speech to encourage unlawful acts is not a sufficient reason for banning it. The government cannot constitutionally premise legislation on the desirability of controlling a person's private thoughts. The government may not prohibit speech because it increases the chance an unlawful act will be committed at some indefinite future time.

The Government next argues that its objective of eliminating the market for pornography produced using real children necessitates a prohibition on virtual images as well. Virtual images, the Government contends, are indistinguishable from real ones; they are part of the same market and are often exchanged. In this way, it is said, virtual images promote the trafficking in works produced through the exploitation of real children. The hypothesis is somewhat implausible. If virtual images were identical to illegal child pornography, the illegal images would be driven from the market by the indistinguishable substitutes. Few pornographers would risk prosecution by abusing real children if fictional, computerized images would suffice.

Finally, the Government says that the possibility of producing images by using computer imaging makes it very difficult for it to prosecute those who produce pornography by using real children. Experts, we are told, may have difficulty in saying whether the pictures were made by using real children or by using computer imaging. The necessary solution, the argument runs, is to prohibit both kinds of images. The argument, in essence, is that protected speech may be banned as a means to ban unprotected speech. This analysis turns the First Amendment upside down. The Government may not suppress lawful speech as the means to suppress unlawful speech. Protected speech does not become unprotected merely because it resembles the latter.

To avoid the force of this objection, the Government would have us read the CPPA not as a measure suppressing speech but as a law shifting the burden to the accused to prove the speech is lawful. In this connection, the Government relies on an affirmative defense under the statute, which allows a defendant to avoid conviction for nonpossession offenses by showing that the materials were produced using only adults and were not otherwise distributed in a manner conveying the impression that they depicted real children.

The Government raises serious constitutional difficulties by seeking to impose on the defendant the burden of proving his speech is not unlawful. An affirmative defense applies only after prosecution has begun, and the speaker must himself prove, on pain of a felony conviction, that his conduct falls within the affirmative defense. In cases under the CPPA, the evidentiary burden is not trivial. Where the defendant is not the producer of the work, he may have no way of establishing the identity, or even the existence, of the actors. If the evidentiary issue is a serious problem for the Government, as it asserts, it will be at least as difficult for the innocent possessor.

We need not decide, however, whether the Government could impose this burden on a speaker. Even if an affirmative defense can save a statute from First Amendment challenge, here the defense is incomplete and insufficient, even on its own terms. It allows persons to be convicted in some instances where they can prove children were not exploited in the production. A defendant charged with possessing, as opposed to distributing, proscribed works may not defend on the ground that the film depicts only adult actors. So while the affirmative defense may protect a movie producer from prosecution for the act of distribution, that same producer, and all other persons in the subsequent distribution chain, could be liable for possessing the prohibited work. Furthermore, the affirmative defense provides no protection to persons who produce speech by using computer imaging, or through other means that do not involve the use of adult actors who appear to be minors. In these cases, the defendant can demonstrate no children were harmed in producing the images, yet the affirmative defense would not bar the prosecution. For this reason, the affirmative defense cannot save the statute, for it leaves unprotected a substantial amount of speech not tied to the Government's interest in distinguishing images produced using real children from virtual ones.

Respondents [also] challenge [the CPPA provision that] bans depictions of sexually explicit conduct that are "advertised, promoted, presented, described, or distributed in such a manner that conveys the impression that the material is or contains a visual depiction of a minor engaging in sexually explicit conduct." The parties treat the section as nearly identical to the provision prohibiting materials that appear to be child pornography. In the Government's view, the difference between the two is that "the 'conveys the impression' provision requires the jury to assess the material at issue in light of the manner in which it is promoted." The Government's assumption, however, is that the determination would still depend principally upon the content of the prohibited work.

We disagree with this view. The CPPA prohibits sexually explicit materials that "convey the impression" they depict minors. While that phrase may sound like the "appears to be" prohibition, it requires little judgment about the content of the image. Under [CPPA's anti-pandering section], the work must be sexually explicit, but otherwise the content is irrelevant. Even if a film contains no sexually explicit scenes involving minors, it could be treated as child pornography if the title and trailers convey the impression that the scenes would be found in the movie. The determination turns on how the speech is presented, not on what is depicted. While the legislative findings address at length the problems posed by materials that look like child pornography, they are silent on the evils posed by images simply pandered that way.

The Government does not offer a serious defense of this provision, and the other arguments it makes in support of the CPPA do not bear on [this section]. The materials, for instance, are not likely to be confused for child pornography in a criminal trial. The Court has recognized that pandering may be relevant, as an evidentiary matter, to the question whether particular materials are obscene. Where a defendant engages in the "commercial exploitation of erotica solely for the sake of their prurient appeal," the context he or she creates may itself be relevant to the evaluation of the materials. [But] materials falling within the [anti-pandering] proscription are tainted and unlawful in the hands of all who receive it, though they bear no responsibility for how it was marketed, sold, or described. The statute, furthermore, does not require that the context be part of an effort at "commercial exploitation." As a consequence, the CPPA does more than prohibit pandering. It prohibits possession of material described, or pandered, as child pornography by someone earlier in the distribution chain. The provision prohibits a sexually explicit film containing no youthful actors, just because it is placed in a box suggesting a prohibited movie. Possession is a crime even when the possessor knows the movie was mislabeled. The First Amendment requires a more precise restriction.

For the reasons we have set forth, the [challenged CPPA] prohibitions are overbroad and unconstitutional. Having reached this conclusion, we need not address respondents' further contention that the provisions are unconstitutional because of vague statutory language. The judgment of the Court of Appeals is affirmed.

It is so ordered.

POINTS FOR DISCUSSION

1. Do you think that technology has so far reached the point where "virtual" images are frequently confused with "real" ones? Perhaps you saw the film, *Polar Express*. Were you ever confused about whether you were looking at the real Tom Hanks or the virtual Tom Hanks?
2. Continuing with the same theme, if and when technology improves to the point where images—including ones that appear to be children engaged in sexual acts—are truly indistinguishable from "the real thing," should Congress and the Court revisit this issue?

▪ *U.S. v. Williams*

553 U.S. 285 (2008)
Justice Scalia:

Section 2252A(a)(3)(B) of Title 18, United States Code, criminalizes, in certain specified circumstances, the pandering or solicitation of child pornography. This case presents the question whether that statute is overbroad under the First Amendment or impermissibly vague under the Due Process Clause of the Fifth Amendment.

We have long held that obscene speech—sexually explicit material that violates fundamental notions of decency—is not protected by the First Amendment. But to protect explicit material that has social value, we have limited the scope of the obscenity exception, and have overturned convictions for the distribution of sexually graphic but nonobscene material. Over the last 25 years, we have confronted a related and overlapping category of proscribable speech: child pornography. This consists of sexually explicit visual portrayals that feature children. We have held that a statute which proscribes the distribution of all child pornography, even material that does not qualify as obscenity, does not on its face violate the First Amendment. Moreover, we have held that the government may criminalize the possession of child pornography, even though it may not criminalize the mere possession of obscene material involving adults.

The broad authority to proscribe child pornography is not, however, unlimited. Four Terms ago, we held facially overbroad two provisions of the federal Child Pornography Protection Act of 1996 (CPPA). The first of these banned the possession and distribution of "any visual depiction" that "is, or appears to be, of a minor engaging in sexually explicit conduct," even if it contained only youthful-looking adult actors or virtual images of children generated by a computer. This was invalid, we explained, because the child-protection rationale for speech restriction does not apply to materials produced without children. The second provision at issue [then] criminalized the possession and distribution of material that had been pandered as child pornography, regardless of whether it actually was that. A person could thus face prosecution for possessing unobjectionable material that someone else had pandered. We held that this prohibition, which did "more than prohibit pandering," was also facially overbroad.

After our decision, Congress went back to the drawing board and produced legislation with the unlikely title of the Prosecutorial Remedies and Other Tools to end the Exploitation of Children Today Act of 2003. We shall refer to it as the Act. Section 503 of the Act amended 18 U.S.C. § 2252A to add a new pandering and solicitation provision, relevant portions of which now read as follows:

> Any person who, knowingly, advertises, promotes, presents, distributes, or solicits through the mails, or in interstate or foreign commerce by any means, including by computer, any material or purported material in a manner that reflects the belief, or that is intended to cause another to believe, or contains—(1) an obscene visual depiction of a minor engaging in sexually explicit conduct; or (2) a visual depiction of an actual minor engaging in sexually explicit conduct, shall be punished as provided in subsection (b).

Section 2256(2)(A) defines "sexually explicit conduct" as "actual or simulated sexual intercourse, including genital-genital, oral-genital, anal-genital, or oral-anal, whether between persons of the same or opposite sex; bestiality; masturbation; sadistic or masochistic abuse; or lascivious exhibition of the genitals or pubic area of any person." Violation of § 2252A(a)(3)(B) incurs a minimum sentence of 5 years imprisonment and a maximum of 20 years.

The Act's express findings indicate that Congress was concerned that limiting the child-pornography prohibition to material that could be *proved* to feature actual children would enable many child pornographers to evade conviction. The emergence of new technology and the repeated retransmission of picture files over the Internet could make it nearly impossible to prove that a particular image was produced using real children—even though "there is no substantial evidence that any of the child pornography images being trafficked today were made other than by the abuse of real children," virtual imaging being prohibitively expensive.

On April 26, 2004, respondent Michael Williams, using a sexually explicit screen name, signed in to a public Internet chat room. A Secret Service agent had also signed in to the chat room under the moniker "Lisa n Miami." The agent noticed that Williams had posted a message that read: "Dad of toddler has 'good' pics of her an [sic] me for swap of your toddler pics, or live cam." The agent struck up a conversation with Williams, leading to an electronic exchange of nonpornographic pictures of children. (The agent's picture was in fact a doctored photograph of an adult.) Soon thereafter, Williams messaged that he had photographs of men molesting his 4-year-old daughter. Suspicious that "Lisa n Miami" was a law-enforcement agent, before proceeding further Williams demanded that the agent produce additional pictures. When he did not, Williams posted the following public message in the chat room: "HERE ROOM; I CAN PUT UPLINK CUZ IM FOR REAL—SHE CANT." Appended to this declaration was a hyperlink that, when clicked, led to seven pictures of actual children, aged approximately 5 to 15, engaging in sexually explicit conduct and displaying their genitals. The Secret Service then obtained a search warrant for Williams's home, where agents seized two hard drives containing at least 22 images of real children engaged in sexually explicit conduct, some of it sadomasochistic.

Williams was charged with one count of pandering child pornography under § 2252A(a)(3)(B) and one count of possessing child pornography under § 2252A(a)(5)(B). He pleaded guilty to both counts but reserved the right to challenge the constitutionality of the pandering conviction. The District Court rejected his challenge, and imposed concurrent 60-month prison terms on the two counts and a statutory assessment of $100 for each count. The United States Court of Appeals for the Eleventh Circuit reversed the pandering conviction, holding that the statute was both overbroad and impermissibly vague.

According to our First Amendment overbreadth doctrine, a statute is facially invalid if it prohibits a substantial amount of protected speech. The doctrine seeks to strike a balance between competing social costs. On the one hand, the threat of enforcement of an overbroad law deters people from engaging in constitutionally protected speech, inhibiting the free exchange of ideas. On the other hand, invalidating a law that in some of its applications is perfectly constitutional—particularly a law directed at conduct so antisocial that it has been made criminal—has obvious harmful effects. In order to maintain an appropriate balance, we have vigorously enforced the requirement that a statute's overbreadth be *substantial*, not only in an absolute sense, but also relative to the statute's plainly legitimate sweep. Invalidation for overbreadth is "strong medicine" that is not to be "casually employed."

The first step in overbreadth analysis is to construe the challenged statute; it is impossible to determine whether a statute reaches too far without first knowing what the statute covers. Generally speaking, § 2252A(a)(3)(B) prohibits offers to provide and requests to obtain child pornography. The statute does not require the actual existence of child pornography. Rather than targeting the underlying material, this statute bans the collateral speech that introduces such material into the child-pornography distribution network. Thus, an Internet user who solicits child pornography from an undercover agent violates the statute, even if the officer possesses no child pornography. Likewise, a person who advertises virtual child pornography as depicting actual children also falls within the reach of the statute.

The statute's definition of the material or purported material that may not be pandered or solicited precisely tracks the material held constitutionally proscribable in [our precedents]: obscene material depicting (actual or virtual) children engaged in sexually explicit conduct, and any other material depicting actual children engaged in sexually explicit conduct. A number of features of the statute are important to our analysis.

First, the statute includes a *scienter* requirement. The first word of § 2252A(a)(3)—"knowingly"—applies to both of the immediately following subdivisions, both the previously existing § 2252A(a)(3)(A) and the new § 2252A(a)(3)(B) at issue here. We think that the best reading of the term in context is that it applies to every element of the two provisions. This is not a case where grammar or structure enables the challenged provision or some of its parts to be read apart from the "knowingly" requirement. Here "knowingly" introduces the challenged provision itself, making clear that it applies to that provision in its entirety; and there is no grammatical barrier to reading it that way.

Second, the statute's string of operative verbs—"advertises, promotes, presents, distributes, or solicits"—is reasonably read to have a transactional connotation. That is to say, the statute penalizes speech that accompanies or seeks to induce a transfer of child pornography—via reproduction or physical delivery—from one person to another. For three of the verbs, this is obvious: Advertising, distributing, and soliciting are steps taken in the course of an actual or proposed transfer of a product, typically but not exclusively in a commercial market. When taken in isolation, the two remaining verbs—"promotes" and "presents"—are susceptible of multiple and wide-ranging meanings. In context, however, those meanings are narrowed by the commonsense canon of *noscitur a sociis*, which counsels that a word is given more precise content by the neighboring words with which it is associated. "Promotes," in a list that includes "solicits," "distributes," and "advertises," is most sensibly read to mean the act of recommending purported child pornography to another person for his acquisition. Similarly, "presents," in the context of the other verbs with which it is associated, means showing or offering the child pornography to another person with a view to his acquisition. The envisioned acquisition, of course, could be an electronic one, for example, reproduction of the image on the recipient's computer screen.

To be clear, our conclusion that all the words in this list relate to transactions is not to say that they relate to *commercial* transactions. One could certainly "distribute" child pornography without expecting payment in return. Indeed, in much Internet file sharing of child pornography each participant makes his files available for free to other participants—as Williams did in this case. To run afoul of the statute, the speech need only accompany or seek to induce the transfer of child pornography from one person to another.

Third, the phrase "in a manner that reflects the belief" includes both subjective and objective components. "A manner that reflects the belief" is quite different from "a manner that would give one cause to believe." The first formulation suggests that the defendant must actually have held the subjective "belief" that the material or purported material was child pornography. Thus, a misdescription that leads the listener to believe the defendant is offering child pornography, when the defendant in fact does not believe the material is child pornography, does not violate this prong of the statute. (It may, however, violate the "manner . . . that is intended to cause another to believe" prong if the misdescription is intentional.) There is also an objective component to the phrase "manner that reflects the belief." The statement or action must objectively manifest a belief that the material is child pornography; a mere belief, without an accompanying statement or action that would lead a reasonable person to understand that the defendant holds that belief, is insufficient.

Fourth, the other key phrase, "in a manner . . . that is intended to cause another to believe," contains only a subjective element: The defendant must "intend" that the listener believe the material to be child pornography, and must select a manner of "advertising, promoting, presenting, distributing, or soliciting" the material that *he* thinks will engender that belief, whether or not a reasonable person would think the same. (Of course in the ordinary case the proof of the defendant's intent will be the fact that, as an objective matter, the manner of "advertising, promoting, presenting, distributing, or soliciting" plainly sought to convey that the material was child pornography.)

Fifth, the definition of "sexually explicit conduct" (the visual depiction of which, engaged in by an actual minor, is covered by the Act's pandering and soliciting prohibition even when it is not obscene) is very similar to the definition of "sexual conduct" in the New York statute we [previously] upheld against an overbreadth challenge. Congress used essentially the same constitutionally approved definition in the present Act. If anything, the fact that the defined term here is "sexually *explicit* conduct," rather than merely "sexual conduct," renders the definition more immune from facial constitutional attack. "Sexually *explicit* conduct" connotes actual depiction of the sex act rather than merely the suggestion that it is occurring. And "simulated" sexual intercourse is not sexual intercourse that is merely suggested, but rather sexual intercourse that is explicitly portrayed, even though (through camera tricks or otherwise) it may not actually have occurred. The portrayal must cause a reasonable viewer to believe that the actors actually engaged in that conduct on camera. Critically, [the Act's] requirement of a "visual depiction of an actual minor" makes clear that, although the sexual intercourse may be simulated, it must involve actual children (unless it is obscene). This change eliminates any possibility that virtual child pornography or sex between youthful-looking adult actors might be covered by the term "simulated sexual intercourse."

We now turn to whether the statute, as we have construed it, criminalizes a substantial amount of protected expressive activity. Offers to engage in illegal transactions are categorically excluded from First Amendment protection. One would think that this principle resolves the present case, since the statute criminalizes only offers to provide or requests to obtain contraband—child obscenity and child pornography involving actual children, both of which are proscribed, and the proscription of which is constitutional. Many long established criminal proscriptions—such as laws against conspiracy, incitement, and solicitation—criminalize speech (commercial or not) that is intended to induce or commence illegal activities. Offers to provide or requests to obtain unlawful material, whether as part of a commercial exchange or not, are similarly undeserving of First Amendment protection. It would be an odd constitutional principle that permitted the government to prohibit offers to sell illegal drugs, but not offers to give them away for free.

To be sure, there remains an important distinction between a proposal to engage in illegal activity and the abstract advocacy of illegality. The Act before us does not prohibit advocacy of child pornography, but only offers to provide or requests to obtain it. There is no doubt that this prohibition falls well within constitutional bounds. In sum, we hold that offers to provide or requests to obtain child pornography are categorically excluded from the First Amendment.

The Eleventh Circuit believed it a constitutional difficulty that no child pornography need exist to trigger the statute. In its view, the fact that the statute could punish a "braggart, exaggerator, or outright liar" rendered it unconstitutional. That seems to us a strange constitutional calculus. Although we have held that the government can ban *both* fraudulent offers *and* offers to provide illegal products, the Eleventh Circuit would forbid the government from punishing *fraudulent offers to provide illegal products*. We see no logic in that position; if anything, such statements are doubly excluded from the First Amendment.

The Eleventh Circuit held that the "non-commercial, non-inciteful promotion of illegal child pornography" is protected, and § 2252A(a)(3)(B) therefore overreaches by criminalizing the promotion of child pornography. As we have discussed earlier, however, the term "promotes" does not refer to abstract advocacy, such as the statement "I believe that child pornography should be legal" or even "I encourage you to obtain child pornography." It refers to the recommendation of a particular piece of purported child pornography with the intent of initiating a transfer.

The Eleventh Circuit found "particularly objectionable" the fact that the "reflects the belief" prong of the statute could ensnare a person who mistakenly believes that material is child pornography. This objection has two conceptually distinct parts. First, the Eleventh Circuit thought that it would be unconstitutional to punish someone for mistakenly distributing virtual child pornography as real child pornography. We disagree. Offers to deal in illegal products or otherwise engage in illegal activity do not acquire First Amendment protection when the offeror is mistaken about the factual predicate of his offer. The pandering and solicitation made unlawful by the Act are sorts of inchoate crimes—acts looking toward the commission of another crime, the delivery of child pornography. Impossibility of completing the crime because the facts were not as the defendant believed is not a defense.

The Eleventh Circuit also thought that the statute could apply to someone who subjectively believes that an innocuous picture of a child is "lascivious." That is not so. The defendant must believe that the picture contains certain material, and that material in fact (and not merely in his estimation) must meet the statutory definition. Where the material at issue is a harmless picture of a child in a bathtub and the defendant, knowing that material, erroneously believes that it constitutes a "lascivious exhibition of the genitals," the statute has no application.

Williams and *amici* raise other objections, which demonstrate nothing so forcefully as the tendency of our overbreadth doctrine to summon forth an endless stream of fanciful hypotheticals. Williams argues, for example, that a person who offers non-pornographic photographs of young girls to a pedophile could be punished under the statute if the pedophile secretly expects that the pictures will contain child pornography. That hypothetical does not implicate the statute, because the offeror does not hold the belief or intend the recipient to believe that the material is child pornography.

Amici contend that some advertisements for mainstream Hollywood movies that depict underage characters having sex violate the statute. We think it implausible that a reputable distributor of Hollywood movies, such as Amazon.com, believes that one of these films contains *actual* children engaging in *actual or simulated* sex on camera; and even more implausible that Amazon.com would *intend* to make its customers believe such a thing. The average person understands that sex scenes in mainstream movies use nonchild actors, depict sexual activity in a way that would not rise to the explicit level necessary under the statute, or, in most cases, both.

There was raised at oral argument the question whether turning child pornography over to the police might not count as "presenting" the material. An interpretation of "presents" that would include turning material over to the authorities would of course be self-defeating in a statute that looks to the prosecution of people who deal in child pornography. And it would effectively nullify § 2252A(d), which provides an affirmative defense to the possession ban if a defendant promptly delivers child pornography to a law-enforcement agency. (The possession offense would simply be replaced by a pandering offense for delivering the material to law-enforcement officers.) In any event, the verb "present"—along with "distribute" and "advertise," as well as "give," "lend," "deliver," and "transfer"—was used in the definition of "promote" in [the New York law we upheld in 1982]. Despite that inclusion, we had no difficulty concluding that the New York statute survived facial challenge. And in the period since, despite similar statutory definitions in other state statutes, we are aware of no prosecution for giving child pornography to the police. We can hardly say, therefore, that there is a "realistic danger" that § 2252A(a)(3)(B) will deter such activity.

It was also suggested at oral argument that the statute might cover documentary footage of atrocities being committed in foreign countries, such as soldiers raping young children. Perhaps so, if the material rises to the high level of explicitness that we have held is required. That sort of documentary footage could of course be the subject of an as-applied challenge. The courts presumably would weigh the educational interest in the dissemination of information about the atrocities against the government's interest in preventing the distribution of materials that constitute "a permanent record" of the children's degradation whose dissemination increases "the harm to the child." Assuming that the constitutional balance would have to be struck in favor of the documentary, the existence of that exception would not establish that the statute is *substantially* overbroad. The mere fact that one can conceive of some impermissible applications of a statute is not sufficient to render it susceptible to an overbreadth challenge. In the vast majority of its applications, this statute raises no constitutional problems whatever.

Finally, the dissent accuses us of silently overruling our prior decisions. According to the dissent, Congress has made an end run around the First Amendment's protection of virtual child pornography by prohibiting proposals to transact in such images rather than prohibiting the images themselves. But an offer to provide or request to receive virtual child pornography is not prohibited by the statute. A crime is committed only when the speaker believes or intends the listener to believe that the subject of the proposed transaction depicts *real* children. It is simply not true that this means "a protected category of expression will inevitably be suppressed." Simulated child pornography will be as available as ever, so long as it is offered and sought *as such*, and not as real child pornography. The dissent would require an exception from the statute's prohibition when, unbeknownst to one or both of the parties to the proposal, the completed transaction would not have been unlawful because it is (we have said) protected by the First Amendment. We fail to see what First Amendment interest would be served by drawing a distinction between two defendants who attempt to acquire contraband, one of whom happens to be mistaken about the contraband nature of what he would acquire. Is Congress prohibited from punishing those who attempt to acquire what they believe to be national-security documents, but which are actually fakes? To ask is to answer. There is no First Amendment exception from the general principle of criminal law that a person attempting to commit a crime need not be exonerated because he has a mistaken view of the facts.

As an alternative ground for facial invalidation, the Eleventh Circuit held that § 2252A(a)(3)(B) is void for vagueness. Vagueness doctrine is an outgrowth not of the First Amendment, but of the Due Process Clause of the Fifth Amendment. A conviction fails to comport with due process if the statute under which it is obtained fails to provide a person of ordinary intelligence fair notice of what is prohibited, or is so standardless that it authorizes or encourages seriously discriminatory enforcement. Although ordinarily a plaintiff who engages in some conduct that is clearly proscribed cannot complain of the vagueness of the law as applied to the conduct of others, we have relaxed that requirement in the First Amendment context, permitting plaintiffs to argue that a statute is overbroad because it is unclear whether it regulates a substantial amount of protected speech. But perfect clarity and precise guidance have never been required even of regulations that restrict expressive activity.

The Eleventh Circuit believed that the phrases "in a manner that reflects the belief" and "in a manner that is intended to cause another to believe" are vague and standardless. The court gave two examples. First, an e-mail claiming to contain photograph attachments and including a message that says "little Janie in the bath—hubba, hubba!" According to the Eleventh Circuit, given that the statute does not require the actual existence of illegal material, the Government would have "virtually unbounded discretion" to deem such a statement in violation of the "reflects the belief" prong. The court's second example was an e-mail entitled "Good pics of kids in bed" with a photograph attachment of toddlers in pajamas asleep in their beds. The court described three hypothetical senders: a proud grandparent, a "chronic forwarder of cute photos with racy tongue-in-cheek subject lines," and a child molester who seeks to trade the photographs for more graphic material. According to the Eleventh Circuit, because the "manner" in which the photographs are sent is the same in each case, and because the identity of the sender and the content of the photographs are irrelevant under the statute, all three senders could arguably be prosecuted for pandering.

We think that neither of these hypotheticals, without further facts, would enable a reasonable juror to find, beyond a reasonable doubt, that the speaker believed and spoke in a manner that reflected the belief, or spoke in a manner intended to cause another to believe, that the pictures displayed actual children engaged in "sexually explicit conduct" as defined in the Act. The prosecutions would be thrown out at the threshold.

But the Eleventh Circuit's error is more fundamental than merely its selection of unproblematic hypotheticals. Its basic mistake lies in the belief that the mere fact that close cases can be envisioned renders a statute vague. That is not so. Close cases can be imagined under virtually any statute. The problem that poses is addressed, not by the doctrine of vagueness, but by the requirement of proof beyond a reasonable doubt.

What renders a statute vague is not the possibility that it will sometimes be difficult to determine whether the incriminating fact it establishes has been proved; but rather the indeterminacy of precisely what that fact is. Thus, we have struck down statutes that tied criminal culpability to whether the defendant's conduct was "annoying" or "indecent"—wholly subjective judgments without statutory definitions, narrowing context, or settled legal meanings.

There is no such indeterminacy here. The statute requires that the defendant hold, and make a statement that reflects, the belief that the material is child pornography; or that he communicate in a manner intended to cause another so to believe. Those are clear questions of fact. Whether someone held a belief or had an intent is a true-or-false determination, not a subjective judgment such as whether conduct is "annoying" or "indecent." Similarly true or false is the determination whether a particular formulation reflects a belief that material or purported material is child pornography. To be sure, it may be difficult in some cases to determine whether these clear requirements have been met. But courts and juries every day pass upon knowledge, belief and intent—the state of men's minds—having before them no more than evidence of their words and conduct, from which, in ordinary human experience, mental condition may be inferred. Thus, the Eleventh Circuit's contention that § 2252A(a)(3)(B) gives law-enforcement officials "virtually unfettered discretion" has no merit. No more here than in the case of laws against fraud, conspiracy, or solicitation.

Child pornography harms and debases the most defenseless of our citizens. Both the State and Federal Governments have sought to suppress it for many years, only to find it proliferating through the new medium of the Internet. This Court held unconstitutional Congress's previous attempt to meet this new threat, and Congress responded with a carefully crafted attempt to eliminate the First Amendment problems we identified. As far as the provision at issue in this case is concerned, that effort was successful. The judgment of the Eleventh Circuit is reversed.

POINTS FOR DISCUSSION

1. The Eleventh Circuit's hypotheticals, especially the one contrasting the "proud grandparent" with the child molester, are rather clever, are they not? Does the Court dismiss them a bit too hastily?
2. In previous cases the Court has struck down laws that would criminalize possession of distribution of images that merely looked like child pornography (whether computer generated or where the actors are really not minors). Does it seem at all odd for the Court here to uphold a law that it admits could be used to prosecute persons who simply express an intent to distribute images that turn out themselves to be, for the same reasons, protected by the First Amendment?

12

Broadcast and Cable TV Regulation

In this chapter we look at cases involving laws and regulations that would be clearly unconstitutional if applied to the print media. The system of communication law in the United States, however, has long embraced the notion that the electromagnetic spectrum, the "airwaves," belong to the public. Thus, those who are granted a license to broadcast TV or radio programming using those airwaves must do so in the public interest. The Federal Communications Commission (FCC) was created in 1934 to promulgate and enforce broadcast regulations.

We begin with *FCC v. Pacifica Foundation*, which dealt with a New York radio station that was sanctioned by the Commission for playing a comedy routine by George Carlin called "Filthy Words." We follow this with *Fox Television Stations, Inc. v. FCC* from 2010, in which a federal appellate court tells the FCC that its more recent crackdown on broadcast indecency runs afoul of the First Amendment because the Commission's regulations were too vague.

Next we examine *Turner Broadcasting System v. FCC*, a case that deals with the complicated relationship between over-the-air broadcasters and local cable TV franchisees. Regulations affecting the latter industry, the Court tells us, will be subjected by the Court to a level of scrutiny somewhere between the strictness it uses when adjudicating laws affecting print media, and the more lax standard used with respect to broadcast regulations.

Finally we look at *MPAA v. FCC*, in which the D.C. Circuit Court of Appeals contrasts for us key pieces of federal law governing two technologies designed to enhance accessibility of TV signals: closed captioning and descriptive video services.

▪ *FCC v. Pacifica Foundation*
438 U.S. 726 (1978)

Justice Stevens:

This case requires that we decide whether the Federal Communications Commission has any power to regulate a radio broadcast that is indecent but not obscene. A satiric humorist named George Carlin recorded a 12-minute monologue entitled "Filthy Words" before a live audience in a California theater. He began by referring to his thoughts about "the words you couldn't say on the public, ah, airwaves, um, the ones you definitely wouldn't say, ever." He proceeded to list those words and repeat them over and over again in a variety of colloquialisms.

At about 2 o'clock in the afternoon on Tuesday, October 30, 1973, a New York radio station, owned by respondent Pacifica Foundation, broadcast the Filthy Words monologue. A few weeks later a man, who stated that he had heard the broadcast while driving with his young son, wrote a letter complaining to the Commission. He stated that, although he could perhaps understand the "record's being sold for private use, I certainly cannot understand the broadcast of same over the air that, supposedly, you control." The complaint was forwarded to the station for comment. In its response, Pacifica explained that the monologue had been played during a program about contemporary society's attitude toward language and that, immediately before its broadcast, listeners had been advised that it included "sensitive language which might be regarded as offensive to some." Pacifica characterized George Carlin as "a significant social satirist" who examines "the language of ordinary people." Pacifica stated that it was not aware of any other complaints about the broadcast.

On February 21, 1975, the Commission issued a declaratory order granting the complaint and holding that Pacifica "could have been the subject of administrative sanctions." The Commission did not impose formal sanctions, but it did state that the order would be "associated with the station's license file, and in the event that subsequent complaints are received, the Commission will then decide whether it should utilize any of the available sanctions it has been granted by Congress."

In its memorandum opinion the Commission stated that it intended to clarify the standards which will be utilized in considering the growing number of complaints about indecent speech on the airwaves. Advancing several reasons for treating broadcast speech differently from other forms of expression, the Commission found a power to regulate indecent broadcasting in two statutes: 18 U.S.C. § 1464, which forbids the use of "any obscene, indecent, or profane language by means of radio communications," and 47 U.S.C. § 303(g), which requires the Commission to "encourage the larger and more effective use of radio in the public interest."

The Commission characterized the language used in the Carlin monologue as "patently offensive," though not necessarily obscene: "The concept of indecent is intimately connected with the exposure of children to language that describes, in terms patently offensive as measured by contemporary community standards for the broadcast medium, sexual or excretory activities and organs, at times of the day when there is a reasonable risk that children may be in the audience." Thus, the Commission suggested, if an offensive broadcast had literary, artistic, political, or scientific value, and were preceded by warnings, it might not be indecent in the late evening, but would be so during the day, when children are in the audience.

Applying these considerations to the language used in the monologue as broadcast by respondent, the Commission concluded that certain words depicted sexual and excretory activities in a patently offensive manner, noted that they "were broadcast at a time when children were undoubtedly in the audience (i.e., in the early afternoon)." In summary, the Commission stated: "We therefore hold that the language as broadcast was indecent."

After the order issued, the Commission was asked to clarify its opinion by ruling that the broadcast of indecent words as part of a live newscast would not be prohibited. The Commission issued another opinion in which it pointed out that it "never intended to place an absolute prohibition on the broadcast of this type of language, but rather sought to channel it to times of day when children most likely would not be exposed to it."

The relevant statutory questions are whether the Commission's action is forbidden "censorship" within the meaning of 47 U.S.C. § 326 and whether speech that concededly is not obscene may be restricted as "indecent" under the authority of 18 U.S.C. § 1464. The questions are not unrelated, for the two statutory provisions have a common origin. Nevertheless, we analyze them separately.

Section 29 of the Radio Act of 1927 provided: "Nothing in this Act shall be understood or construed to give the licensing authority the power of censorship over the radio communications or signals transmitted by any radio station." The prohibition against censorship unequivocally denies the Commission any power to edit proposed broadcasts in advance and to excise material considered inappropriate for the airwaves. The prohibition, however, has never been construed to deny the Commission the power to review the content of completed broadcasts in the performance of its regulatory duties.

Entirely apart from the fact that the subsequent review of program content is not the sort of censorship at which the statute was directed, its history makes it perfectly clear that it was not intended to limit the Commission's power to regulate the broadcast of obscene, indecent, or profane language. A single section of the 1927 Act is the source of both the anticensorship provision and the Commission's authority to impose sanctions for the broadcast of indecent or obscene language. Quite plainly, Congress intended to give meaning to both provisions. Respect for that intent requires that the censorship language be read as inapplicable to the prohibition on broadcasting obscene, indecent, or profane language. We conclude, therefore, that § 326 does not limit the Commission's authority to impose sanctions on licensees who engage in obscene, indecent, or profane broadcasting.

The only other statutory question presented by this case is whether the afternoon broadcast of the "Filthy Words" monologue was indecent within the meaning of § 1464. The Commission identified several words that referred to excretory or sexual activities or organs, stated that the repetitive, deliberate use of those words in an afternoon broadcast when children are in the audience was patently offensive, and held that the broadcast was indecent. Pacifica takes issue with the Commission's definition of indecency, but does not dispute the Commission's preliminary determination that each of the components of its definition was present. Specifically, Pacifica does not quarrel with the conclusion that this afternoon broadcast was patently offensive. Pacifica's claim that the broadcast was not indecent within the meaning of the statute rests entirely on the absence of prurient appeal. The plain language of the statute does not support Pacifica's argument. The words "obscene, indecent, or profane" are written in the disjunctive, implying that each has a separate meaning. Prurient appeal is an element of the obscene, but the normal definition of "indecent" merely refers to nonconformance with accepted standards of morality.

[*Editor's note*: The next three paragraphs come from a section of Justice Stevens's opinion joined by only two other justices; it is thus not majority doctrine.]

Pacifica argues that, inasmuch as the recording is not obscene, the Constitution forbids any abridgment of the right to broadcast it on the radio. When the issue is narrowed to the facts of this case, the question is whether the First Amendment denies government any power to restrict the public broadcast of indecent language in any circumstances. For if the government has any such power, this was an appropriate occasion for its exercise.

The words of the Carlin monologue are unquestionably "speech" within the meaning of the First Amendment. It is equally clear that the Commission's objections to the broadcast were based in part on its content. The question in this case is whether a broadcast of patently offensive words dealing with sex and excretion may be regulated because of its content. Obscene materials have been denied the protection of the First Amendment because their content is so offensive to contemporary moral standards. But the fact that society may find speech offensive is not a sufficient reason for suppressing it. Indeed, if it is the speaker's opinion that gives offense, that consequence is a reason for according it constitutional protection. For it is a central tenet of the First Amendment that the government must remain neutral in the marketplace of ideas. If there were any reason to believe that the Commission's characterization of the Carlin monologue as offensive could be traced to its political content—or even to the fact that it satirized contemporary attitudes about four-letter words—First Amendment protection might be required. But that is simply not this case. These words offend for the same reasons that obscenity offends. Such utterances are no essential part of any exposition of ideas, and are of such slight social value as a step to truth that any benefit that may be derived from them is clearly outweighed by the social interest in order and morality.

Although these words ordinarily lack literary, political, or scientific value, they are not entirely outside the protection of the First Amendment. Some uses of even the most offensive words are unquestionably protected. Indeed, we may assume, [for argument's sake], that this monologue would be protected in other contexts. Nonetheless, the constitutional protection accorded to a communication containing such patently offensive sexual and excretory language need not be the same in every context. It is a characteristic of speech such as this that both its capacity to offend and its social value vary with the circumstances. Words that are commonplace in one setting are shocking in another.

We have long recognized that each medium of expression presents special First Amendment problems. And of all forms of communication, it is broadcasting that has received the most limited First Amendment protection. Thus, although other speakers cannot be licensed except under laws that carefully define and narrow official discretion, a broadcaster may be deprived of his license and his forum if the Commission decides that such an action would serve the public interest, convenience, and necessity. Similarly, although the First Amendment protects newspaper publishers from being required to print the replies of those whom they criticize, it affords no such protection to broadcasters; on the contrary, they must give free time to the victims of their criticism.

The reasons for these distinctions are complex, but two have relevance to the present case. First, the broadcast media have established a uniquely pervasive presence in the lives of all Americans. Patently offensive, indecent material presented over the airwaves confronts the citizen, not only in public, but also in the privacy of the home, where the individual's right to be left alone plainly outweighs the First Amendment rights of an intruder. Because the broadcast audience is constantly tuning in and out, prior warnings cannot completely protect the listener or viewer from unexpected program content. To say that one may avoid further offense by turning off the radio when he hears indecent language is like saying that the remedy for an assault is to run away after the first blow. One may hang up on an indecent phone call, but that option does not give the caller a constitutional immunity or avoid a harm that has already taken place.

Second, broadcasting is uniquely accessible to children, even those too young to read. Pacifica's broadcast could have enlarged a child's vocabulary in an instant. Other forms of offensive expression may be withheld from the young without restricting the expression at its source. Bookstores and motion picture theaters, for example, may be prohibited from making indecent material available to children. [Similarly], the government's interest in the well-being of its youth and in supporting parents' claim to authority in their own household [can justify] the regulation of otherwise protected expression.

It is appropriate, in conclusion, to emphasize the narrowness of our holding. This case does not involve a two-way radio conversation between a cab driver and a dispatcher, or a telecast of an Elizabethan comedy. We have not decided that an occasional expletive in either setting would justify any sanction or, indeed, that this broadcast would justify a criminal prosecution. The Commission's decision rested entirely on a nuisance rationale under which context is all-important. The concept requires consideration of a host of variables. The time of day was emphasized by the Commission. The content of the program in which the language is used will also affect the composition of the audience, and differences between radio, television, and perhaps closed-circuit transmissions, may also be relevant. As Mr. Justice Sutherland wrote, a "nuisance may be merely a right thing in the wrong place—like a pig in the parlor instead of the barnyard." We simply hold that when the Commission finds that a pig has entered the parlor, the exercise of its regulatory power does not depend on proof that the pig is obscene.

POINTS FOR DISCUSSION

1. In his dissenting opinion, Justice Brennan charges the Court with usurping parental authority in the name of protecting children. "Some parents may actually find Mr. Carlin's unabashed attitude towards the seven 'dirty

words' healthy, and deem it desirable to expose their children to the manner in which Mr. Carlin defuses the taboo surrounding the words." How would you answer Brennan?
2. Currently, the FCC permits the broadcast of admittedly indecent (but not obscene) programming between 10 p.m. and 6 a.m. Do you think that is a reasonable compromise? Why or why not? Do you think any of the more popular "shock jock" programs on radio are indecent?

▪ Fox Television Stations, Inc. v. FCC
613 F.3d 317 (2nd Cir. 2010)
Judge Pooler:

Section 1464 of Title 18 of United States Code provides that "whoever utters any obscene, indecent, or profane language by means of radio communication shall be fined under this title or imprisoned not more than two years, or both." In 1960, Congress authorized the FCC to impose civil forfeitures for violations of Section 1464. It was not until 1975, however, that the FCC first exercised its authority to regulate speech it deemed indecent but not obscene. The speech at issue was comedian George Carlin's "Filthy Words" monologue, a 12-minute string of expletives broadcast on the radio at 2:00 in the afternoon. The Commission defined "indecent" speech as "language that describes, in terms patently offensive as measured by contemporary community standards for the broadcast medium, sexual or excretory activities and organs, at times of the day when there is a reasonable risk that children may be in the audience." The Supreme Court [held, in *FCC v. Pacifica Foundation*] that the FCC could, at least in the situation before it, restrict indecent speech in the broadcast context that did not meet the legal definition of obscenity. Resting on a nuisance rationale, the Court first noted that "of all forms of communication, it is broadcasting that has received the most limited First Amendment protection" because of its "uniquely pervasive presence in the lives of all Americans." Moreover, the nature of broadcast television—as opposed to printed materials—made it "uniquely accessible to children, even those too young to read."

In the years after *Pacifica* the FCC did indeed pursue a restrained enforcement policy, taking the position that its enforcement powers were limited to the seven specific words in the Carlin monologue. Then, in 1987, the FCC abandoned its focus on specific words, [reasoning] that under the prior standard, patently offensive material was permissible as long as it avoided certain words. This, the Commission concluded, "made neither legal nor policy sense." The Commission instead decided to adopt a contextual approach to indecent speech.

Despite its move to a more flexible standard, the FCC continued to exercise restraint. In particular, it consistently held that a single, non-literal use of an expletive was not actionably indecent. In 2001, in an attempt to "provide guidance to the broadcast industry regarding its enforcement policies with respect to broadcast indecency," the FCC issued a policy statement in which it set forth its indecency standard in more detail ["Industry Guidance"]. The FCC explained that an indecency finding involved the following two determinations: (1) whether the material "describes or depicts sexual or excretory organs or activities"; and (2) whether the broadcast is "patently offensive as measured by contemporary community standards for the broadcast medium." The FCC further explained that it considered the following three factors in determining whether a broadcast is patently offensive: (1) "the explicitness or graphic nature of the description or depiction"; (2) "whether the material dwells on or repeats at length" the description or depiction; and (3) "whether the material appears to pander or is used to titillate, or whether the materials appears to have been presented for its shock value." The Industry Guidance reiterated that under the second prong of the patently offensive test, "fleeting and isolated" expletives were not actionably indecent.

In 2004, however, the FCC's policy on indecency changed. During the 2003 Golden Globe Awards, U2 band member Bono exclaimed, upon receiving an award, "this is really, really, fucking brilliant. Really, really, great." In response to complaints filed after the incident, the FCC declared, for the first time, that a single, nonliteral use of an expletive (a so-called "fleeting expletive") could be actionably indecent. Finding that "the 'F-Word' is one of the most vulgar, graphic, and explicit descriptions of sexual activity in the English language," and therefore "inherently has a sexual connotation," the FCC concluded that the fleeting and isolated use of the word was irrelevant and overruled all prior decisions in which fleeting use of an expletive was held per se not indecent. The FCC's increased enforcement efforts—as well as Congress's decision to increase the maximum fines—were in large part caused by the broadcast of the 2004 Super Bowl, during which Justin Timberlake exposed Janet Jackson's breast for a fraction of a second during their halftime show.

At the same time that the FCC expanded its enforcement efforts to include even fleeting expletives, the FCC also began issuing record fines for indecency violations. While the Commission had previously interpreted the maximum fines in the statute as applying on a per-program basis, it began treating each licensee's broadcast of the same program as a separate violation, thereby multiplying the maximum fine the FCC could order for each instance of indecent speech. In addition, Congress amended Section 503(b)(2)(C)(ii) to increase the maximum fine permitted by a factor of 10—from $32,500 to $325,000—meaning that the fine for a single expletive uttered during a broadcast could easily run into the tens of millions of dollars.

NBC, along with numerous other parties, filed petitions for reconsideration of the Golden Globes Order before the FCC, raising statutory and constitutional challenges to the new policy. While the petitions for reconsideration were pending, the FCC applied the Golden Globes Order policy [a 2006 document, "Omnibus Order"]. In the Omnibus Order (which dealt with many more programs than are at issue in the present case), the Commission found four programs—the 2002 Billboard Music Awards, the 2003 Billboard Music Awards, various episodes of ABC's *NYPD Blue*, and CBS's *The Early Show*—indecent and profane under the Golden Globes standard.

All four programs involved what could be characterized as fleeting expletives. For instance, during the 2002 Billboard Music Awards, Cher, in an unscripted moment from her acceptance speech, stated: "People have been telling me I'm on the way out every year, right? So fuck 'em." Similarly, during the 2003 Billboard Music Awards, Nicole Ritchie—on stage to present an award with Paris Hilton—made the following unscripted remark: "Have you ever tried to get cow shit out of a Prada purse? It's not so fucking simple."[1] Episodes of *NYPD Blue* were found indecent based on several instances of the word "bullshit," while the CBS's *The Early Show* was found indecent on the basis of a guest's use of the word "bullshitter" to describe a fellow contestant on the reality TV show, *Survivor: Vanuatu*.

In finding these programs indecent and profane, the FCC reaffirmed its decision in the Golden Globes Order that any use of the word "fuck" was presumptively indecent and profane, further concluding that any use of the word "shit" was also presumptively indecent and profane. It also held that the four broadcasts in question were "patently offensive" because the material was explicit, shocking, and gratuitous, notwithstanding the fact that the expletives were fleeting and isolated.

Fox, CBS, and ABC, as well as several network affiliates, filed petitions for review of the Omnibus Order. The FCC moved for a voluntary remand, which we granted, so that it could have the opportunity to address petitioners' argu-

---

1. The Cher, Nicole Richie, and Bono incidents are on my website, as is the famous "wardrobe malfunction" involving Janet Jackson. Go to www.paulsiegelcommlaw.com, and on the left side of the site (*Communication Law in America*), click on "Video Clips," and then on "Chapter 12." There you will find "Cher and Nicole Richie," "U2's Bono and Edge: 'Fucking Brilliant!'" and "Wardrobe Malfunction."

ments and could ensure that all licensees had a full opportunity to be heard before the FCC issued a final decision. After soliciting public comments, the FCC issued a second order on November 6, 2006. In the Remand Order, the FCC reaffirmed its finding that the 2002 and 2003 Billboard Music Awards were indecent and profane. However, the FCC reversed its finding with respect to *The Early Show* and dismissed the complaint against *NYPD Blue* on procedural grounds.

In the Remand Order, the FCC rejected the petitioners' argument that nonliteral uses of expletives were not indecent, reasoning that "an expletive's power to offend derives from its sexual or excretory meaning." However, the Commission did not take the position that any occurrence of an expletive is indecent or profane under its rules, allowing that expletives that were "integral" to an artistic work or occurring during a "bona fide news interview" might not run afoul of the indecency standard. As such, it reversed its previous decision concerning the CBS's *The Early Show* because the utterance of the word "bullshitter" took place during a bona fide news interview. The Commission made clear, however, that "there is no outright news exemption from our indecency rules."

Petitioners and intervenors, which collectively represented all the major broadcast networks as well as local affiliates affected by the FCC's indecency policy, returned to this Court for review of the Remand Order, making a variety of administrative, statutory, and constitutional arguments. In a 2-1 decision (with Judge Leval in dissent), we held that the FCC's indecency policy was arbitrary and capricious under the Administrative Procedures Act [APA]. We reached this decision because we believed that the FCC had failed to adequately explain why it had changed its nearly-30-year policy on fleeting expletives. Moreover, we noted that the FCC's justification for the policy—that children could be harmed by hearing even one fleeting expletive (the so-called "first blow" theory)—bore "no rational connection to the Commission's actual policy," because the FCC had not instituted a blanket ban on expletives.

Because we struck down the indecency policy on APA grounds, we declined to reach the constitutional issues in the case. In a 5-4 decision, the Supreme Court reversed our APA ruling, holding that the FCC's "fleeting expletive" policy was not arbitrary and capricious because "the Commission could reasonably conclude that the pervasiveness of foul language, and the coarsening of public entertainment in other media such as cable, justify more stringent regulation of broadcast programs so as to give conscientious parents a relatively safe haven for their children." The Court remanded for us to consider [the constitutional issues]. Thus, we now turn to the question that we deferred in our previous decision—whether the FCC's indecency policy violates the First Amendment.

It is well-established that indecent speech is fully protected by the First Amendment. In most contexts, the Supreme Court has considered restrictions on indecent speech to be content-based restrictions subject to strict scrutiny. Broadcast radio and television, however, have always occupied a unique position when it comes to First Amendment protection. The categorization of broadcasting as different from all other forms of communication pre-dates *Pacifica*. However, it was in *Pacifica* that the Supreme Court gave its fullest explanation for why restrictions on broadcast speech were subject to a lower level of scrutiny, relying on the twin pillars of pervasiveness and accessibility to children. While *Pacifica* did not specify what level of scrutiny applies to restrictions on broadcast speech, subsequent cases have applied something akin to intermediate scrutiny.

The Networks argue that the world has changed since *Pacifica* and the reasons underlying the decision are no longer valid. Indeed, we face a media landscape that would have been almost unrecognizable in 1978. Cable television was still in its infancy. The Internet was a project run out of the Department of Defense with several hundred users. Not only did YouTube, Facebook, and Twitter not exist, but their founders were either still in diapers or not yet conceived.

The past thirty years has seen an explosion of media sources, and broadcast television has become only one voice in the chorus. Cable television is almost as pervasive as broadcast—almost 87 percent of households subscribe to a cable or satellite service—and most viewers can alternate between broadcast and non-broadcast channels with a click of their remote control. The Internet, too, has become omnipresent, offering access to everything from viral videos to feature films and, yes, even broadcast television programs.

Moreover, technological changes have given parents the ability to decide which programs they will permit their children to watch. Every television, 13 inches or larger, sold in the United States since January 2000 contains a V-chip, which allows parents to block programs based on a standardized rating system. Moreover, since June 11, 2009, when the United States made the transition to digital television, anyone using a digital converter box also has access to a V-chip. In short, there now exists a way to block programs that contain indecent speech in a way that was not possible in 1978.

Nevertheless, we are bound by Supreme Court precedent, regardless of whether it reflects today's realities. The Supreme Court may decide in due course to overrule *Pacifica* and subject speech restrictions in the broadcast context to strict scrutiny. This Court, however, is not at liberty to depart from binding Supreme Court precedent unless and until the Court reinterprets that precedent.

There is considerable disagreement among the parties, however, as to what framework *Pacifica* established. The FCC interprets *Pacifica* as permitting it to exercise broad regulatory authority to sanction indecent speech. In its view, the Carlin monologue was only the most extreme example of a large category of indecent speech that the FCC can constitutionally prohibit. The Networks, on the other hand, view *Pacifica* as establishing the limit of the FCC's authority. In other words, they believe that only when indecent speech rises to the level of "verbal shock treatment," exemplified by the Carlin monologue, can the FCC impose a civil forfeiture. Because *Pacifica* was an intentionally narrow opinion, it does not provide us with a clear answer to this question. Fortunately, we do not need to wade into the brambles in an attempt to answer it ourselves. For we conclude that, regardless of where the outer limit of the FCC's authority lies, the FCC's indecency policy is unconstitutional because it is impermissibly vague. It is to this issue that we now turn.

It is a basic principle that a law or regulation is void for vagueness if its prohibitions are not clearly defined. A law or regulation is impermissibly vague if it does not give the person of ordinary intelligence a reasonable opportunity to know what is prohibited. The First Amendment places a special burden on the government to ensure that restrictions on speech are not impermissibly vague.

The vagueness doctrine serves several important objectives in the First Amendment context. First, the doctrine is based on the principle of fair notice. Notice is particularly important with respect to content-based speech restrictions because of their obvious chilling effect on free speech. Vague regulations inevitably lead citizens to steer far wider of the unlawful zone than if the boundaries of the forbidden areas were clearly marked.

The Networks argue that the FCC's indecency test is unconstitutionally vague because it provides no clear guidelines as to what is covered and thus forces broadcasters to "steer far wider of the unlawful zone," rather than risk massive fines. In support of their position, the Networks rely on the Supreme Court's decision in *Reno v. ACLU*, (1997). Section 223(a) of the Communications Decency Act ("CDA") prohibited transmitting "indecent" material to minors over the Internet while section 223(d) prohibited material that "in context, depicts or describes, in terms patently offensive as measured by contemporary community standards, sexual or excretory activities or organs." In addition to finding that the statute was not narrowly tailored, the Court found the statute unconstitutionally vague because "the many ambiguities concerning the scope of its coverage rendered it problematic for purposes of the First

Amendment." The Networks argue that since *Reno* found this indecency regulation unconstitutionally vague, the FCC's identically-worded indecency test for broadcasting must fall as well.

FCC argues the opposite—that *Reno* forecloses a vagueness challenge to the FCC's policy. In *Reno*, the government argued that the CDA was "plainly constitutional" under the *Pacifica* decision. The Supreme Court rejected this argument, distinguishing *Pacifica* on the grounds that (1) the FCC is an expert agency that had been regulating the radio for decades; (2) the CDA was a categorical ban on speech while the FCC's indecency regulation designated "when—rather than whether—it would be permissible to air such a program"; (3) the order at issue in *Pacifica* was not punitive; and (4) the broadcast medium had traditionally received the most limited First Amendment protection. According to the FCC, because the Court refused to find *Pacifica* controlling of the constitutional challenges to the CDA, we must find *Reno* equally inapplicable here.

As an initial matter, we reject the FCC's argument that *Reno* forecloses the Networks' vagueness challenge. When the Supreme Court distinguished *Pacifica* in *Reno*, it did so with respect to the level of First Amendment scrutiny that should be applied to the Internet, not to its analysis of whether the statute was unconstitutionally vague. Broadcasters are entitled to the same degree of clarity as other speakers, even if restrictions on their speech are subject to a lower level of scrutiny. It is the language of the rule, not the medium in which it is applied, that determines whether a law or regulation is impermissibly vague.

We also reject the Networks' argument that *Reno* requires us to find the FCC's policy vague. To be sure, the CDA's definition of indecency was almost identical to the Commission's, and language that is unconstitutionally vague in one context cannot suddenly become the model of clarity in another. However, unlike in *Reno*, the FCC has further elaborated on the definition of indecency in the broadcast context. For example, the FCC has outlined three factors that it purportedly uses to determine whether a broadcast is patently offensive, and has declared "fuck" and "shit" presumptively indecent. This additional guidance may not be sufficient to survive a vagueness challenge, but it certainly distinguishes the FCC policy from the one struck down in *Reno*.

Finally, we reject the FCC's argument that the Networks' vagueness challenge is foreclosed by *Pacifica* itself. *Pacifica*, which did not reach the question of whether the FCC's policy was unconstitutionally vague, was an intentionally narrow opinion predicated on the FCC's "restrained" enforcement policy. The FCC's policy has now changed and we would be hard pressed to characterize it as "restrained." Thus, the questions left unresolved by *Pacifica* are now squarely before us.

Having concluded that neither *Pacifica* nor *Reno* resolves the question, we must now decide whether the FCC's indecency policy provides a discernible standard by which broadcasters can accurately predict what speech is prohibited. The FCC set forth its indecency policy in its 2001 Industry Guidance, in which the FCC explained that an indecency finding involved the following two determinations: (1) whether the material "describes or depicts sexual or excretory organs or activities"; and (2) whether the broadcast is "patently offensive as measured by contemporary community standards for the broadcast medium." Under the policy, whether a broadcast is patently offensive depends on the following three factors: (1) "the explicitness or graphic nature of the description or depiction"; (2) "whether the material dwells on or repeats at length" the description or depiction; and (3) "whether the material appears to pander or is used to titillate, or whether the materials appears to have been presented for its shock value." Since 2001, the FCC has interpreted its indecency policy in a number of decisions, including Golden Globes Order and the orders on review here.

The FCC argues that the indecency policy in its Industry Guidance, together with its subsequent decisions, give the broadcasters sufficient notice as to what will be considered indecent. The Networks argue that the policy is impermissibly vague and that the FCC's decisions interpreting the policy only add to the confusion of what will be considered indecent.

We agree with the Networks that the indecency policy is impermissibly vague. The first problem arises in the FCC's determination as to which words or expressions are patently offensive. For instance, while the FCC concluded that "bullshit" in an *NYPD Blue* episode was patently offensive, it concluded that "dick" and "dickhead" were not. Other expletives such as "pissed off," up yours," "kiss my ass," and "wiping his ass" were also not found to be patently offensive. The Commission argues that its three-factor "patently offensive" test gives broadcasters fair notice of what it will find indecent. However, in each of these cases, the Commission's reasoning consisted of repetition of one or more of the factors without any discussion of how it applied them. Thus, the word "bullshit" is indecent because it is "vulgar, graphic and explicit" while the word "dickhead" was not indecent because it was "not sufficiently vulgar, explicit, or graphic." This hardly gives broadcasters notice of how the Commission will apply the factors in the future.

The English language is rife with creative ways of depicting sexual or excretory organs or activities, and even if the FCC were able to provide a complete list of all such expressions, new offensive and indecent words are invented every day. For many years after *Pacifica*, the FCC decided to focus its enforcement efforts solely on the seven "dirty" words in the Carlin monologue. This strategy had its limitations—it meant that some indecent speech that did not employ these seven words slipped through the cracks. However, it had the advantage of providing broadcasters with a clear list of words that were prohibited. Not surprisingly, in the nine years between *Pacifica* and the FCC's abandonment of this policy, not a single enforcement action was brought. This could be because we lived in a simpler time before such foul language was common. Or, it could be that the FCC's policy was sufficiently clear that broadcasters knew what was prohibited.

The FCC argues that a flexible standard is necessary precisely because the list was not effective—broadcasters simply found offensive ways of depicting sexual or excretory organs or activities without using any of the seven words. In other words, because the FCC cannot anticipate how broadcasters will attempt to circumvent the prohibition on indecent speech, the FCC needs the maximum amount of flexibility to be able to decide what is indecent. The observation that people will always find a way to subvert censorship laws may expose a certain futility in the FCC's crusade against indecent speech, but it does not provide a justification for implementing a vague, indiscernible standard. If the FCC cannot anticipate what will be considered indecent under its policy, then it can hardly expect broadcasters to do so. And while the FCC characterizes all broadcasters as consciously trying to push the envelope on what is permitted, much like a petulant teenager angling for a later curfew, the Networks have expressed a good faith desire to comply with the FCC's indecency regime. They simply want to know with some degree of certainty what the policy is so that they can comply with it. The First Amendment requires nothing less.

The same vagueness problems plague the FCC's presumptive prohibition on the words "fuck" and "shit" and the exceptions thereto. Under the FCC's current policy, all variants of these two words are indecent unless one of two exceptions apply. The first is the "bona fide news" exception, which the FCC has failed to explain except to say that it is not absolute. The second is the artistic necessity exception, in which fleeting expletives are permissible if they are "demonstrably essential to the nature of an artistic or educational work or essential to informing viewers on a matter of public importance."

Although the Commission has declared that all variants of "fuck" and "shit" are presumptively indecent and profane, repeated use of those words in *Saving Private Ryan*, for example, was neither indecent nor profane. And while multiple occurrences of expletives in *Saving Private Ryan* was not gratuitous, a single occurrence of "fucking" in the Golden Globe Awards was "shocking and gratuitous." Parental ratings and advisories were important in finding *Saving Private Ryan* not patently offensive under contemporary community standards, but irrelevant in evaluating a rape scene in another fictional movie. The use of numerous expletives was "integral" to a fictional movie about war, but occasional expletives spoken by real musicians were indecent and profane because the educational purpose of the documentary "could have been fulfilled and all viewpoints expressed without the repeated broadcast of expletives." The "S-Word" on *The Early Show* was not indecent because it was in the context of a "bona fide news interview," but "there is no outright news exemption from our indecency rules."

There is little rhyme or reason to these decisions and broadcasters are left to guess whether an expletive will be deemed "integral" to a program or whether the FCC will consider a particular broadcast a "bona fide news interview."

The FCC created these exceptions because it recognized that an outright ban on certain words would raise grave First Amendment concerns. The FCC's current indecency policy undoubtedly gives the FCC more flexibility, but this flexibility comes at a price. The "artistic necessity" and "bona fide news" exceptions allow the FCC to decide, in each case, whether the First Amendment is implicated. The policy may maximize the amount of speech that the FCC can prohibit, but it results in a standard that even the FCC cannot articulate or apply consistently.

With the FCC's indiscernible standards comes the risk that such standards will be enforced in a discriminatory manner. We have no reason to suspect that the FCC is using its indecency policy as a means of suppressing particular points of view. But even the risk of such subjective, content-based decision-making raises grave concerns under the First Amendment. Take, for example, the disparate treatment of *Saving Private Ryan* and the documentary, *The Blues*. The FCC decided that the words "fuck" and "shit" were integral to the "realism and immediacy of the film experience for viewers" in *Saving Private Ryan*, but not in *The Blues*. We query how fleeting expletives could be more essential to the "realism" of a fictional movie than to the "realism" of interviews with real people about real life events, and it is hard not to speculate that the FCC was simply more comfortable with the themes in *Saving Private Ryan*, a mainstream movie with a familiar cultural milieu, than it was with *The Blues*, which largely profiled an outsider genre of musical experience. But even if there were a perfectly benign way of explaining these particular outcomes, nothing would prevent the FCC from applying its indecency policy in a discriminatory manner in the future.

The FCC argues that its context-based approach is consistent with, indeed even required by, *Pacifica*. Of course, context is always relevant, and we do not mean to suggest otherwise in this opinion. But the FCC still must have discernible standards by which individual contexts are judged. The FCC assures us that it will "bend over backwards" to protect editorial judgment, at least in the news context, but such assurances are not sufficient given the record before us. Instead, the FCC should bend over backwards to create a standard that gives broadcasters the notice that is required by the First Amendment.

Under the current policy, broadcasters must choose between not airing or censoring controversial programs and risking massive fines or possibly even loss of their licenses, and it is not surprising which option they choose. Indeed, there is ample evidence in the record that the FCC's indecency policy has chilled protected speech. For instance, several CBS affiliates declined to air the Peabody Award–winning *9/11* documentary, which contains real audio footage—including occasional expletives—of firefighters in the World Trade Center on September 11th. Although the documentary had previously aired twice without complaint, following the Golden Globes Order affiliates could no longer be sure whether the expletives contained in the documentary could be found indecent. In yet another example, a radio station cancelled a planned reading of Tom Wolfe's novel *I Am Charlotte Simmons*, based on a single complaint it received about the "adult" language in the book, because the station feared FCC action. When the program was reinstated two weeks later, the station decided that it could only safely air the program during the "safe harbor" period [after 10 p.m.].

The FCC's application of its policy to live broadcasts creates an even more profound chilling effect. In the case of the 2003 Billboard Music Awards broadcasts, Fox had an audio delay system in place to bleep fleeting expletives. It also pre-cleared the scripts of the presenters. Ritchie, however, departed from her script and used three expletives in rapid sequence. While the person employed to monitor and bleep expletives was bleeping the first, the following two slipped through. Even elaborate precautions will not protect a broadcaster against such occurrences. The FCC argues that Fox should simply implement a more effective screening system, but, short of giving up live broadcasting altogether, no system will ever be one hundred percent effective.

This chilling effect extends to news and public affairs programming as well. Broadcasters may well decide not to invite controversial guests on to their programs for fear that an unexpected fleeting expletive will result in fines. The FCC points to its "bona fide news" exception to show that such fears would be unfounded. But the FCC has made clear that it considers the decision to apply this exception a matter within its discretion. Otherwise, why not simply make an outright news exception? During the previous proceedings before this

Court, amicus curiae gave the example of a local station in Vermont that refused to air a political debate because one of the local politicians involved had previously used expletives on air. The record contains other examples of local stations that have forgone live programming in order to avoid fines. For instance, Phoenix TV stations dropped live coverage of a memorial service for Pat Tillman, the former football star killed in Afghanistan, because of language used by Tillman's family members to express their grief. A station in Moosic, Pennsylvania submitted an affidavit stating that in the wake of the FCC's new policy, it had decided to no longer provide live, direct-to-air coverage of news events "unless they affect matters of public safety or convenience." If the FCC's policy is allowed to remain in place, there will undoubtedly be countless other situations where broadcasters will exercise their editorial judgment and decline to pursue contentious people or subjects, or will eschew live programming altogether, in order to avoid the FCC's fines. This chill reaches speech at the heart of the First Amendment.

The chill of protected speech has even extended to programs that contain no expletives, but which contain reference to or discussion of sex, sexual organs, or excretion. For instance, Fox decided not to re-broadcast an episode of *That 70s Show* that dealt with masturbation, even though it neither depicted the act nor discussed it in specific terms. The episode subsequently won an award from the Kaiser Family Foundation for its honest and accurate depiction of a sexual health issue. Similarly, an episode of *House* was re-written after concerns that one of the character's struggles with psychiatric issues related to his sexuality would be considered indecent by the FCC.

As these examples illustrate, the absence of reliable guidance in the FCC's standards chills a vast amount of protected speech dealing with some of the most important and universal themes in art and literature. Sex and the magnetic power of sexual attraction are surely among the most predominant themes in the study of humanity since the Trojan War. The digestive system and excretion are also important areas of human attention. By prohibiting all "patently offensive" references to sex, sexual organs, and excretion without giving adequate guidance as to what "patently offensive" means, the FCC effectively chills speech, because broadcasters have no way of knowing what the FCC will find offensive. To place any discussion of these vast topics at the broadcaster's peril has the effect of promoting wide self-censorship of valuable material which should be completely protected under the First Amendment.

For the foregoing reasons, we strike down the FCC's indecency policy. We do not suggest that the FCC could not create a constitutional policy. We hold only that the FCC's current policy fails constitutional scrutiny.

POINTS FOR DISCUSSION

1. How much do you think the FCC hurt its own credibility by arguing that every instance of "fuck" and "shit" call to mind sexual and excretory matters? Indeed, a major theme of George Carlin's "Filthy Words" monologue at issue in *Pacifica* was that we cuss a lot, and in ways that have nothing to do with the literal meaning of the cuss words—for example, "Shit! Burnt the broccoli!"
2. On the other hand, do not the networks go a bit too far when they claim they feared that even non-indecent discussions of "taboo" topics could get them into trouble with the FCC? *House*, for example, certainly deals with mature themes, but it does not typically have characters "dropping the F-bomb."

▪ *Turner Broadcasting System v. FCC*
520 U.S. 180 (1997)
Justice Kennedy:

Sections 4 and 5 of the Cable Television Consumer Protection and Competition Act of 1992 require cable television systems to dedicate some of their channels to local broadcast television stations. Earlier in this case, we held the so-called "must-carry" provisions to be content-neutral restrictions on speech, subject to intermediate First Amendment scrutiny. A plurality of the Court considered the record as then developed insufficient. The case now presents the two questions left open during the first appeal: First, whether the record as it now stands supports Congress' predictive judgment that the must-carry provisions further important governmental interests; and second, whether the provisions do not burden substantially more speech than necessary to further those interests. We answer both questions in the affirmative, and conclude the must-carry provisions are consistent with the First Amendment.

Soon after Congress enacted the Cable Television Consumer Protection and Competition Act of 1992, appellants brought suit against the United States and the Federal Communications Commission, challenging the constitutionality of the must-carry provisions under the First Amendment.

A content-neutral regulation will be sustained under the First Amendment if it advances important governmental interests unrelated to the suppression of free speech and does not burden substantially more speech than necessary to further those interests. Must-carry was designed to serve three interrelated interests: (1) preserving the benefits of free, over-the-air local broadcast television, (2) promoting the widespread dissemination of information from a multiplicity of sources, and (3) promoting fair competition in the market for television programming. Each of those is an important governmental interest. Forty percent of American households continue to rely on over-the-air signals for television programming. Despite the growing importance of cable television and alternative technologies, broadcasting is demonstrably a principal source of information and entertainment for a great part of the Nation's population.

We have identified a corresponding governmental purpose of the highest order in ensuring public access to a multiplicity of information sources. And it is undisputed the Government has an interest in eliminating restraints on fair competition, even when the individuals or entities subject to particular regulations are engaged in expressive activity protected by the First Amendment.

The Government downplays the importance of showing a risk to the broadcast industry as a whole and suggests the loss of even a few broadcast stations is a matter of critical importance. Taking the opposite approach, appellants argue Congress' interest in preserving broadcasting is not implicated unless it is shown the industry as a whole would fail without must-carry, and suggest Congress' legitimate interest extends only as far as preserving a minimum amount of television broadcast service.

These alternative formulations are inconsistent with Congress' stated interests in enacting must-carry. The congressional findings do not reflect concern that, absent must-carry, "a few voices" would be lost from the television marketplace. In explicit factual findings, Congress expressed clear concern that the "marked shift in market share from broadcast television to cable television services," resulting from increasing market penetration by cable services, as well as the expanding horizontal concentration and vertical integration of cable operators, combined to give cable systems the incentive and ability to delete, reposition, or decline carriage to local broadcasters in an attempt to favor affiliated cable programmers. Congress predicted that "absent the reimposition of [must-carry], additional local broadcast signals will be deleted, repositioned, or not carried," with the end result that "the economic viability of free local broadcast television and its ability to originate quality local programming will be seriously jeopardized." At the same time, Congress was under no illusion that there would be a complete disappearance of broadcast television nationwide in the absence of must-carry. Congress recognized broadcast programming (and network programming in particular) "remains the most popular programming on cable systems." Indeed, reflecting the popularity and strength of some broadcasters, Congress included in the Cable Act a provision permitting broadcasters to charge cable systems for carriage of the broadcasters' signals. Congress was concerned not that broadcast television would disappear in its entirety without must-carry, but that without it, "significant numbers of broadcast stations will be refused carriage on cable systems," and those "broadcast stations denied carriage will either deteriorate to a substantial degree or fail altogether."

Nor do the congressional findings support appellants' suggestion that legitimate legislative goals would be satisfied by the preservation of a rump broadcasting industry providing a minimum of broadcast service to Americans without cable. It has long been a basic tenet of national communications policy that the widest possible dissemination of information from diverse and antagonistic sources is essential to the welfare of the public. Consistent with this objective, the Cable Act's findings reflect a concern that congressional action was necessary to prevent a reduction in the number of media voices available to consumers. Congress found must-carry necessary to serve the goals of the original Communications Act of 1934 of "providing a fair, efficient, and equitable distribution of broadcast services." Although Congress set no definite number of broadcast stations sufficient for these purposes, the Cable Act's requirement that all cable operators with more than 12 channels set aside one-third of their channel capacity for local broadcasters, refutes the notion that Congress contemplated preserving only a bare minimum of stations. To the extent the appellants question the substantiality of the Government's interest in preserving something more than a minimum number of stations in each community, their position is meritless.

Broadcast television is an important source of information to many Americans. Though it is but one of many means for communication, by tradition and use for decades now it has been an essential part of the national discourse on subjects across the whole broad spectrum of speech, thought, and expression. Congress has an independent interest in preserving a multiplicity of broadcasters to ensure that all households have access to information and entertainment on an equal footing with those who subscribe to cable.

[We now] consider whether the must-carry provisions were designed to address a real harm, and whether those provisions will alleviate it in a material way. We turn first to the harm or risk which prompted Congress to act. The Government's assertion that the economic health of local broadcasting is in genuine jeopardy and in need of the protections afforded by must-carry rests on two component propositions: First, significant numbers of broadcast stations will be refused carriage on cable systems absent must-carry. Second, the broadcast stations denied carriage will either deteriorate to a substantial degree or fail altogether. In reviewing the constitutionality of a statute, courts must accord substantial deference to the predictive judgments of Congress. This principle has special significance in cases, like this one, involving congressional judgments concerning regulatory schemes of inherent complexity and assessments about the likely interaction of industries undergoing rapid economic and technological change.

We have no difficulty in finding a substantial basis to support Congress' conclusion that a real threat justified enactment of the must-carry provisions. There was specific support for its conclusion that cable operators had considerable and growing market power over local video programming markets. Cable served at least 60 percent of American households in 1992, and evidence indicated cable market penetration was projected to grow beyond 70 percent. As Congress noted, cable operators possess a local monopoly over cable households. Only one percent of communities are served by more than one cable system. Cable operators thus exercise control over most (if not all) of the television programming that is channeled into the subscriber's home and can thus silence the voice of competing speakers with a mere flick of the switch.

Evidence indicated the structure of the cable industry would give cable operators increasing ability and incentive to drop local broadcast stations from their systems, or reposition them to a less-viewed channel. Horizontal concentration was increasing as a small number of multiple system operators (MSOs) acquired large numbers of cable systems nationwide. The trend was accelerating, giving the MSOs increasing market power. In 1985, the 10 largest MSOs controlled cable systems serving slightly less than 42 percent of all cable subscribers; by 1989, the figure was nearly 54 percent. Vertical integration in the industry also was increasing. As Congress was aware, many MSOs owned or had affiliation agreements with cable programmers. Evidence indicated that before 1984 cable operators had equity interests in 38 percent of cable programming networks. In the late 1980s, 64 percent of new cable programmers were held in vertical ownership. Congress concluded that vertical integration gives cable operators the incentive and ability to favor their affiliated programming services. Extensive testimony indicated that cable operators would have an incentive to drop local broadcasters and to favor affiliated programmers. After hearing years of testimony, and reviewing volumes of documentary evidence and studies offered by both sides, Congress concluded that the cable industry posed a threat to broadcast television.

In addition, evidence before Congress indicated that cable systems would have incentives to drop local broadcasters in favor of other programmers less likely to compete with them for audience and advertisers. Independent local broadcasters tend to be the closest substitutes for cable programs, because their programming tends to be similar, and because both primarily target the same type of advertiser: those interested in cheaper (and more frequent) ad spots than are typically available on network affiliates. The ability of broadcast stations to compete for advertising is greatly increased by cable carriage, which increases viewership substantially. With expanded viewership, broadcast presents a more competitive medium for television advertising. Empirical studies indicate that cable-carried broadcasters so enhance competition for advertising that even modest increases in the numbers of broadcast stations carried on cable are correlated with significant decreases in advertising revenue to cable systems. Empirical evidence also indicates that demand for premium cable services (such as pay-per-view) is reduced when a cable system carries more independent broadcasters.

Cable systems also have more systemic reasons for seeking to disadvantage broadcast stations: Simply stated, cable has little interest in assisting, through carriage, a competing medium of communication. The incentive to subscribe to cable is lower in markets with many over-the-air viewing options. Evidence adduced on remand indicated cable systems have little incentive to carry, and a significant incentive to drop, broadcast stations that will only be strengthened by access to the 60% of the television market that cable typically controls. Congress could therefore reasonably conclude that cable systems would drop broadcasters in favor of programmers—even unaffiliated ones—less likely to compete with them for audience and advertisers.

It was more than a theoretical possibility in 1992 that cable operators would take actions adverse to local broadcasters; indeed, significant numbers of broadcasters had already been dropped. The record before Congress contained extensive anecdotal evidence about scores of adverse carriage decisions against broadcast stations. [One study] indicated that in 1988, 280 out of 912 responding broadcast stations had been dropped or denied carriage in 1,533 instances. Even assuming that every station dropped or denied coverage responded to the survey, it would indicate that nearly a quarter (21 percent) of the approximately 1,356 broadcast stations then in existence had been denied carriage. The same study reported 869 of 4,303 reporting cable systems had denied carriage to 704 broadcast stations in 1,820 instances, and 279 of those stations had qualified for carriage under the prior must-carry rules. A contemporaneous study of public television stations indicated that in the vast majority of cases, dropped stations were not restored to the cable service.

Substantial evidence demonstrated that absent must-carry the already serious problem of noncarriage would grow worse. The record included anecdotal evidence showing the cable industry was acting with restraint in dropping broadcast stations in an effort to discourage reregulation. There was also substantial evidence that advertising revenue would be of increasing importance to cable operators as subscribership growth began to flatten, providing a steady, increasing incentive to deny carriage to local broadcasters in an effort to capture their advertising revenue.

The harm Congress feared was that stations dropped or denied carriage would be at a serious risk of financial difficulty, and would deteriorate to a substantial degree or fail altogether. Congress had before it substantial evidence to support its conclusion.

Considerable evidence, consisting of statements compiled from dozens of broadcasters who testified before Congress and the FCC, confirmed that broadcast stations had fallen into bankruptcy, curtailed their broadcast operations, and suffered serious reductions in operating revenues as a result of adverse carriage decisions by cable systems. Congress thus had ample basis to conclude that attaining cable carriage would be of increasing importance to ensuring a station's viability. We hold Congress could conclude from the substantial body of evidence before it that absent legislative action, the free local off-air broadcast system is endangered.

To be sure, the record also contains evidence to support a contrary conclusion. Appellants (and the dissent in the District Court) make much of the fact that the number of broadcast stations and their advertising revenue continued to grow during the period without must-carry, albeit at a diminished rate. Evidence indicated that only 31 broadcast stations actually went dark during the period without must-carry (one of which failed after a tornado destroyed its transmitter), and during the same period some 263 new stations signed on the air. New evidence appellants produced indicates the average cable system voluntarily carried local broadcast stations accounting for about 97 percent of television ratings in noncable households. Appellants, as well as the dissent in the District Court, contend that in light of such evidence, it is clear the must-carry law is not necessary to assure the economic viability of the broadcast system as a whole. This assertion misapprehends the relevant inquiry. The question is not whether Congress, as an objective matter, was correct to determine must-carry is necessary to prevent a substantial number of broadcast stations from losing cable carriage and suffering significant financial hardship. Rather, the question is whether the legislative conclusion was reasonable and supported by substantial evidence in the record.

Content-neutral regulations do not pose the same inherent dangers to free expression that content-based regulations do, and thus are subject to a less rigorous analysis, which affords the Government latitude in designing a regulatory solution.

Under intermediate scrutiny, the Government may employ the means of its choosing so long as the regulation promotes a substantial governmental interest that would be achieved less effectively absent the regulation, and does not burden substantially more speech than is necessary to further that interest. The must-carry provisions have the potential to interfere with protected speech in two ways. First, the provisions restrain cable operators' editorial discretion in creating programming packages by reducing the number of channels over which they exercise unfettered control. Second, the rules render it more difficult for cable programmers to compete for carriage on the limited channels remaining. Appellants say the burden of must-carry is great, but the evidence indicates the actual effects are modest. Significant evidence indicates the vast majority of cable operators have not been affected in a significant manner by must-carry. Cable operators have been able to satisfy their must-carry obligations 87 percent of the time using previously unused channel capacity; 94.5 percent of the 11,628 cable systems nationwide have not had to drop any programming in order to fulfill their must-carry obligations; the remaining 5.5 percent have had to drop an average of only 1.22 services from their programming; and cable operators nationwide carry 99.8 percent of the programming they carried before enactment of must-carry. Appellees note that only 1.18 percent of the approximately 500,000 cable channels nationwide [are] channels added because of must-carry; weighted for subscribership, the figure is 2.4 percent. Appellees contend the burdens of must-carry will soon diminish as cable channel capacity increases, as is occurring nationwide.

We do not understand appellants to dispute in any fundamental way the accuracy of those figures, only their significance. They note national averages fail to account for greater crowding on certain (especially urban) cable systems, and contend that half of all cable systems, serving two-thirds of all cable subscribers, have no available capacity. Appellants argue that the rate of growth in cable programming outstrips cable operators' creation of new channel space, that the rate of cable growth is lower than claimed, and that must-carry infringes First Amendment rights now irrespective of future growth. Finally, they say that regardless of the percentage of channels occupied, must-carry still represents thousands of real and individual infringements of speech. While the parties' evidence is susceptible of varying interpretations, a few definite conclusions can be drawn about the burdens of must-carry. It is undisputed that broadcast stations gained carriage on 5,880 channels as a result of must-carry. While broadcast stations occupy another 30,006 cable channels nationwide, this carriage does not represent a significant First Amendment harm to either system operators or cable programmers because those stations were carried voluntarily before 1992, and even appellants represent that the vast majority of those channels would continue to be carried in the absence of any legal obligation to do so.

The 5,880 channels occupied by added broadcasters represent the actual burden of the regulatory scheme. Appellants concede most of those stations would be dropped in the absence of must-carry, so the figure approximates the benefits of must-carry as well. Because the burden imposed by must-carry is congruent to the benefits it affords, we conclude must-carry is narrowly tailored to preserve a multiplicity of broadcast stations for the 40 percent of American households without cable. Congress took steps to confine the breadth and burden of the regulatory scheme. For example, the more popular stations (which appellants concede would be carried anyway) will likely opt to be paid for cable carriage under the "retransmission consent" provision of the Cable Act; those stations will nonetheless be counted towards systems' must-carry obligations. Congress exempted systems of 12 or fewer channels, and limited the must-carry obligation of larger systems to one-third of capacity; allowed cable operators discretion in choosing which competing and qualified signals would be carried; and permitted operators to carry public stations on unused public, educational, and governmental channels in some circumstances. Appellants say the must-carry provisions are overbroad because they require carriage in some instances when the Government's interests are not implicated: the must-carry rules prohibit a cable system operator from dropping a broadcaster even if the operator has no anticompetitive motives, and even if the broadcaster that would have to be dropped would survive without cable access. We are not persuaded that either possibility is so prevalent that must-carry is substantially overbroad. Cable systems serving 70 percent of subscribers are vertically integrated with cable programmers, so anticompetitive motives may be implicated in a majority of systems' decisions not to carry broadcasters. Some broadcasters will opt for must-carry although they would not suffer serious financial harm in its absence. Broadcasters with stronger finances tend, however, to be popular ones that ordinarily seek payment from cable systems for transmission, so their reliance on must-carry should be minimal. It appears, for example, that no more than a few hundred of the 500,000 cable channels nationwide are occupied by network affiliates opting for must-carry, a number insufficient to render must-carry substantially broader than necessary to achieve the government's interest. Even on the doubtful assumption that a narrower but still practicable must-carry rule could be drafted to exclude all instances in which the Government's interests are not implicated, our cases establish that content-neutral regulations are not invalid simply because there is some imaginable alternative that might be less burdensome on speech.

Appellants urge [in lieu of must-carry rules] the use of input selector or "A/

B" switches, which, in combination with antennas, would permit viewers to switch between cable and broadcast input, allowing cable subscribers to watch broadcast programs not carried on cable. Congress examined the use of A/B switches as an alternative. The data showed that: many households lacked adequate antennas to receive broadcast signals; A/B switches suffered from technical flaws; viewers might be required to reset channel settings repeatedly in order to view both UHF and cable channels; and installation and use of the switch with other common video equipment (such as videocassette recorders) could be cumbersome or impossible.

Appellants [alternatively] suggest a system of subsidies for financially weak stations. Appellants have not proposed any particular subsidy scheme, so it is difficult to determine whether this option presents a feasible means of achieving the Government's interests, let alone one preferable to must-carry under the First Amendment. To begin with, a system of subsidies would serve a very different purpose than must-carry. Must-carry is intended not to guarantee the financial health of all broadcasters, but to ensure a base number of broadcasters survive to provide service to noncable households. Must-carry is simpler to administer and less likely to involve the Government in making content-based determinations about programming. The must-carry rules distinguish between categories of speakers based solely on the technology used to communicate.

Appellants also suggest a system of antitrust enforcement or an administrative complaint procedure to protect broadcasters from cable operators' anti-competitive conduct. Congress could conclude, however, that the considerable expense and delay inherent in antitrust litigation, and the great disparities in wealth and sophistication between the average independent broadcast station and average cable system operator, would make these remedies inadequate substitutes for guaranteed carriage.

Judgments about how competing economic interests are to be reconciled in the complex and fast-changing field of television are for Congress to make. Appellants' challenges to must-carry reflect little more than disagreement over the level of protection broadcast stations are to be afforded and how protection is to be attained. We cannot displace Congress' judgment respecting content-neutral regulations with our own, so long as its policy is grounded on reasonable factual findings supported by evidence that is substantial for a legislative determination. Those requirements were met in this case, and in these circumstances the First Amendment requires nothing more. The judgment of the District Court is affirmed. It is so ordered.

POINTS FOR DISCUSSION

1. Justice Kennedy's opinion is rather complex, requiring the reader to follow his evaluation of Congress's analysis of the economics of the cable industry. Can you, in your own words, explain the differences between "horizontal" and "vertical" concentration of ownership?
2. Congress and the Supreme Court seem to agree that the main reason for must-carry rules is to ensure the survival of free, over-the-air TV stations—so that one need not be able to afford to pay a monthly cable bill in order to have television service. If this is indeed the basis for the rules, why not restrict their application to broadcast stations that can demonstrate likely financial hardship if not carried by their local cable system?

▪ *Motion Picture Association of America v. FCC*

309 F.3d 796 (D.C. Cir. 2002)

Judge Edwards:

The Telecommunications Act of 1996, added new provisions covering video programming accessibility to the Communications Act of 1934. The new provisions, codified in § 713 of the Communications Act, specifically dealt with "closed captioning" and "video description" technologies that can be employed to enhance television video services for hearing and visually impaired individuals. Closed captioning displays the audio portion of television signals as words displayed on the screen and can be activated at a viewer's discretion. Video descriptions provide aural descriptions of a television program's key visual elements (such as the movement of a person in a scene) that are inserted during pauses in the program dialogue. Video descriptions change program content because they require the creation of new script to convey program details, whereas closed captions present a verbatim transcription of the program's spoken words.

Congress treated the two technologies quite differently when it passed the Telecommunications Act, which added § 713 to the Communications Act. Section 713(a) required the Commission to complete a closed captioning inquiry and to report its findings to Congress within 180 days of the Act's passage. Sections 713(b) and (c) required the Commission to prescribe closed captioning regulations and established compliance deadlines. In contrast, subsections 713(f) and (g)—the sole subsections dealing with video description—merely defined "video description" and required the FCC to prepare a report to Congress. Unlike the provisions covering closed captioning, § 713 did not authorize the Commission to adopt regulations implementing video descriptions.

After releasing a report on video description, the FCC announced that it was seeking commentary on proposed rules mandating video description. The FCC then adopted rules mandating television programming with video descriptions. The Motion Picture Association of America ("MPAA") and the National Federation of the Blind ("NFB") both petitioned this court for review of the agency's regulations mandating video descriptions.

Video description is defined in the statute to include "the insertion of audio narrated descriptions of a television program's key visual elements into natural pauses between the program's dialogue." Video descriptions are usually transmitted over a secondary audio programming channel, a subcarrier that allows video distributors to transmit additional soundtracks, such as foreign language programming.

After the enactment of § 713, the FCC issued the report that the Act mandated. The report stated that "the best course is . . . to continue to collect information and monitor the deployment of video description and the development of standards for new video technologies that are likely to affect the availability of video description." Then, in 1999, the FCC announced that it was seeking commentary on proposed rules that would mandate video description. The Commission sought commentary about whether the FCC possessed statutory authority to enact such rules. After reviewing the comments, the FCC voted 3-2 to adopt rules requiring certain video programmers to supplement certain programming with video descriptions.

The FCC concluded that it possessed the statutory authority to adopt these rules pursuant to § 1 of the Act, [which] gives the FCC authority to regulate "interstate and foreign commerce in communication by wire and radio so as to make available, so far as possible, to all the people of the United States, a rapid, efficient, Nation-wide, and world-wide wire and radio communication service." The FCC majority also rejected the argument that § 713 precluded the agency from mandating video description merely because the provision only authorized the FCC to conduct an inquiry. Finally, the FCC found that the record demonstrated "the importance of video description to persons with visual disabilities." The FCC primarily based this conclusion on the American Council for the Blind's submission, which contained more than 250 e-mails and letters of support for the rules.

The FCC's video description rules require commercial television broadcasters affiliated with the top four commercial networks (ABC, CBS, Fox, and NBC) to provide fifty hours of video description per quarter during either prime time or children's programming. The rules also require multichannel video programming distributors that serve 50,000 or more subscribers to provide fifty hours of video description per quarter during prime time or children's programming on each channel that carries one of the top five nonbroadcast networks. Various parties sought reconsideration of the FCC's Order, primarily on the ground that the rules exceeded the FCC's legal authority. The FCC denied reconsideration, although it did refine certain implementation issues related to the new rules. MPAA and NFB then filed petitions for review.

The principal question is whether Congress "delegated authority" to the FCC to promulgate visual description regulations. Absent such authority, we need not decide whether the regulations are otherwise "reasonable." An agency may not promulgate even reasonable regulations that claim a force of law without delegated authority from Congress.

MPAA argues that § 713 precludes the adoption of rules mandating video description and that § 1 does not otherwise authorize the FCC to adopt video description rules. We largely agree, although we rest principally on the latter point.

There is no doubt that § 713, by its terms, does not provide the FCC with the authority to enact video description rules, and the FCC does not suggest that it does. The harder question is whether the provision effectively bars the FCC from mandating video description. [The relevant sub-section] provides:

> Within 6 months after the date of enactment of the Telecommunications Act of 1996 [enacted Feb. 8, 1996], the Commission shall commence an inquiry to examine the use of video descriptions on video programming in order to ensure the accessibility of video programming to persons with visual impairments, and report to Congress on its findings. The Commission's report shall assess appropriate methods and schedules for phasing video descriptions into the marketplace, technical and quality standards for video descriptions, a definition of programming for which video descriptions would apply, and other technical and legal issues that the Commission deems appropriate.

We need not decide whether § 713 positively forecloses agency rules mandating video description. Rather, we find that § 713 does not authorize the FCC to adopt such rules. We also find that, when coupled with the absence of authority under § 1 (discussed below), § 713 clearly supports the conclusion that the FCC is barred from mandating video description. We now turn to the question whether § 1, or any other provision in the Act, authorizes the Commission to mandate video description.

The FCC [argues that its] authority to mandate video description is derived from the combination of § 1 of the Communications Act, [which states] that "the provisions of this Act shall apply to all interstate and foreign communication by wire or radio, and to all persons engaged within the United States in such communication," [and that] "the Commission may perform any and all acts, make such rules and regulations, and issue such orders, not inconsistent with this Act, as may be necessary in the execution of its functions." At oral argument, counsel for the FCC essentially conceded that if the agency cannot find its authority in § 1 then the video description regulations must be vacated by the court. We agree.

There is no doubt that the video description rules regulate programming content. Video description is not a regulation of television transmission that only incidentally and minimally affects program content; it is a direct and significant regulation of program content. The rules require programmers to create a second script, select actors, decide what to describe, decide how to describe it and choose what style or what pace. In contrast, closed captioning is a straight translation of dialogue into text. Ultimately, video descriptions require a writer to amend a script to fill in audio pauses that were not originally intended to be filled. Not only will producers and script writers be required to decide on what to describe, how to characterize it, and the style and pace of video descriptions, but script writers will have to describe subtleties in movements and mood that may not translate easily. And many movements in a scene admit of several interpretations, or their meaning is purposely left vague to enhance the program content. In short, it is clear that the implementation of video descriptions invariably would entail subjective and artistic judgments that concern and affect program content.

The FCC's arguments to the contrary are entirely unpersuasive. First, the Commission is wrong in its claim that video descriptions are the same as closed captioning. One is a simple transcript, a precise repetition of the spoken words. The other requires an interpretation of visual scenes. They are not the same. Second, the FCC's statement that video descriptions are "not related to content" is specious. FCC's counsel would not even endorse that position at oral argument. Requiring someone to change or add to a program script is related to the program's content. Finally, the FCC claims that the video description regulations are "content-neutral." We need not decide that issue, because it is irrelevant. The question that we face is whether § 1 provides the FCC with authority to promulgate regulations that significantly regulate programming content. The content-neutrality of the rules is irrelevant to the inquiry of the FCC's delegated authority.

During oral argument, counsel for the FCC acknowledged that it was not self-evident from the statute that the FCC is authorized to regulate *program content* pursuant to § 1. Counsel's hesitation was well placed, because § 1 merely authorizes the agency to ensure that all people of the United States, without discrimination, have access to wire and radio communication transmissions. Section 1 does not otherwise authorize the FCC to regulate program content, as the video description regulations clearly do. Both the terms of § 1 and the case law amplifying it focus on the FCC's power to promote the accessibility and universality of transmission, not to regulate program content. Neither the FCC's Order nor its brief to this court cite any authority to suggest otherwise.

The Communications Act was implemented for the purpose of consolidating federal authority over communications in a single agency to assure an adequate communication system for this country. Given the limited distribution of communications facilities in 1934, § 1's mandate to serve "all the people of the United States" is a reference to the geographic availability of service. Section 1 does not address the *content* of the programs with respect to which accessibility is to be ensured. In other words, the FCC's authority under § 1 is broad, but not without limits.

One of the reasons why § 1 has not been construed to allow the FCC to regulate programming content is because such regulations invariably raise First Amendment issues. Government regulation over the content of program broadcasting must be narrow; broadcast licensees must retain abundant discretion over programming choices.

The parties in this case have argued over whether the video description rules infringe free speech precepts. To avoid potential First Amendment issues, the very general provisions of § 1 have not been construed to go so far as to authorize the FCC to regulate program content. Rather, Congress has been scrupulously clear when it intends to delegate authority to the FCC to address areas significantly implicating program content.

The FCC's position seems to be that the adoption of rules mandating video description is permissible because Congress did not expressly foreclose the possibility. This is an entirely untenable position. Were courts to *presume* a delegation of power absent an express *withholding* of such power, agencies would enjoy virtually limitless hegemony, a result plainly out of keeping with [precedent] and quite likely with the Constitution as well.

Congress enacted the closed captioning and video description provisions of § 713 together. After originally entertaining the possibility of providing the FCC with authority to adopt video description rules, Congress declined to do so. This silence surely cannot be read as ambiguity resulting in delegated authority to the FCC to promulgate the disputed regulations.

The Commission's brief to this court advances the somewhat opaque argument that the video description rules are "obviously a 'valid communications policy goal' and in the public interest." The Commission thus claims that the regulations are justified under § 303(r), which permits the FCC to regulate in the public interest "as may be necessary to carry out the provisions of the Act." But this statutory provision simply cannot carry the weight of the Commission's argument. The FCC cannot act in the "public interest" if the agency does not otherwise have the authority to promulgate the regulations at issue. An action in the public interest is not necessarily taken to "carry out the provisions of the Act," nor is it necessarily authorized by the Act. The FCC must act pursuant to *delegated authority* before any "public interest" inquiry is made under § 303(r).

In short, the FCC can point to no statutory provision that gives the agency authority to mandate visual description rules. The rules may be highly salutary. But that is not the issue before this court and we offer no judgment on the question. What is determinative here is the FCC acted without delegated authority from Congress. Section 1 does not furnish the authority sought, because the regulations significantly implicate program content and the FCC can cite no authority in which a court has upheld agency action under § 1 where program content was at the core of the regulations at issue. And it does not matter that the disputed rules here are arguably "content-neutral." The point is that the rules are about program content and therefore can find no authorization in § 1.

Finally, if there were any serious question about the proper result in this case, all doubt is resolved by reference to § 713. In § 713(f), Congress authorized and ordered the Commission to *produce a report*—nothing more, nothing less. The statute does not, as with closed captioning, instruct (or even permit) the FCC to promulgate regulations mandating video description. Once the Commission completed the task of preparing the report on video description, its delegated authority on the subject ended.

We hereby grant the petition for review filed by MPAA, and reverse and vacate the Commission's Order insofar as it requires broadcasters to implement video description.

POINTS FOR DISCUSSION

1. Judge Edwards admits that, as far back as 1934, Congress empowered the FCC to create regulations that would ensure that broadcast messages are "accessible." He claims that accessibility back then referred only to geographic limitations on receiving signals; cannot the same language be interpreted to refer to sensory limitations in select audiences, such as the blind?

2. Much more than he had to in order to decide this case, Judge Edwards pointed out what differences he saw between video descriptions and closed captioning. You likely have experienced closed captioning. Are there not times when it is much more than "a verbatim transcription of the program's spoken words." Captioners must decide when a speaker's accent is an important part of the message, or how to characterize the voice of an off-stage speaker, or even of non-vocal sound effects. If Edwards is wrong in his exaggerated distinction between the two technologies, does that error affect the legal analysis?

13

The Internet

In this final chapter, we take a look at the emerging area of communication law as applied to cyberspace. The cases here were carefully selected so as to provide examples of how different judges have perceived the Internet. Is it just one more new medium of communication, such as cable TV? Or, does it represent a revolutionary change in the communication landscape? Readers are encouraged to focus especially on those portions of these decisions where judges struggle to make sense of this new medium by analogizing it to other, more familiar means of communication.

We begin with *Reno v. ACLU*, the Supreme Court's first foray into Internet law, striking down key elements of the Communications Decency Act, itself a portion of the Telecommunications Act of 1996. Next we examine *MGM v. Grokster*, the first time the Supreme Court weighed in on the issue of peer-to-peer sharing software.

We move on to *Fair Housing Council of San Fernando Valley v. Roommates .com*, in which a court considers whether "Section 230" protections for websites against liability for their clients' transgressions apply to the defendant's business model.

Our final case, *Bradburn v. North Central Regional Library*, is a challenge to the constitutionality of a public library system choosing to filter Internet content for all its patrons, adults and children alike.

▪ *Reno v. ACLU*

521 U.S. 844 (1997)
Justice Stevens:

At issue is the constitutionality of two statutory provisions enacted to protect minors from "indecent" and "patently offensive" communications on the Internet. Notwithstanding the legitimacy and importance of the congressional goal of protecting children from harmful materials, we agree with the three-judge District Court that the statute abridges the freedom of speech protected by the First Amendment.

The Internet is an international network of interconnected computers, a unique and wholly new medium of worldwide human communication. About 40 million people used the Internet [by 1996], a number that is expected to mushroom to 200 million by 1999.

Anyone with access to the Internet may take advantage of a wide variety of communication and information retrieval methods. These methods are constantly evolving and difficult to categorize precisely. But, as presently constituted, those most relevant to this case are e-mail, listservs ("mail exploders"), newsgroups, chat rooms, and the World Wide Web. All of these methods can be used to transmit text; most can transmit sound, pictures, and moving video images.

Navigating the Web is relatively straightforward. A user may either type the address of a known page or enter one or more keywords into a commercial search engine in an effort to locate sites on a subject of interest. A particular Web page may contain the information sought by the "surfer," or, through its links, it may be an avenue to other documents located anywhere on the Internet. Users generally explore a given Web page, or move to another, by clicking a computer mouse on one of the page's icons or links. Access to most Web pages is freely available, but some allow access only to those who have purchased the right from a commercial provider. The Web is thus comparable, from the readers' viewpoint, to both a vast library including millions of readily available and indexed publications and a sprawling mall offering goods and services.

From the publishers' point of view, it constitutes a vast platform from which to address and hear from a world-wide audience of millions of readers, viewers, researchers, and buyers. Any person or organization with a computer connected to the Internet can "publish" information. Publishers include government agencies, educational institutions, commercial entities, advocacy groups, and individuals. Publishers may either make their material available to the entire pool of Internet users, or confine access to a selected group, such as those willing to pay for the privilege.

Sexually explicit material on the Internet includes text, pictures, and chat and extends from the modestly titillating to the hardest-core. These files are created, named, and posted in the same manner as material that is not sexually explicit, and may be accessed either deliberately or unintentionally during the course of an imprecise search. Once a provider posts its content on the Internet, it cannot prevent that content from entering any community.

Though such material is widely available, users seldom encounter such content accidentally. A document's title or a description of the document will usually appear before the document itself, and in many cases the user will receive detailed information about a site's content before he or she need take the step to access the document. Almost all sexually explicit images are preceded by warnings as to the content. For that reason, the odds are slim that a user would enter a sexually explicit site by accident. Unlike communications received by radio or television, the receipt of information on the Internet requires a series of affirmative steps more deliberate and directed than merely turning a dial. A child requires some sophistication and some ability to read to retrieve material and thereby to use the Internet unattended.

Systems have been developed to help parents control the material that may be available on a home computer with Internet access. A system may either limit a computer's access to an approved list of sources that have been identified as containing no adult material, it may block designated inappropriate sites, or it may attempt to block messages containing identifiable objectionable features. Although parental control software currently can screen for certain suggestive words or for known sexually explicit sites, it cannot now screen for sexually explicit images. Nevertheless, the evidence indicates that a reasonably effective method by which parents can prevent their children from accessing sexually explicit and other material which parents may believe is inappropriate for their children will soon be available.

The problem of age verification differs for different uses of the Internet. The District Court categorically determined that there is no effective way to determine the identity or the age of a user who is accessing material through e-mail, [listservs], newsgroups, or chat rooms. The Government offered no evidence that there was a reliable way to screen recipients and participants in such fora for age. Moreover, even if it were technologically feasible to block minors' access to newsgroups and chat rooms containing discussions of art, politics, or other subjects that potentially elicit "indecent" or "patently offensive" contributions, it would not be possible to block their access to that material and still allow them access to the remaining content, even if the overwhelming majority of that content was not indecent.

Technology exists by which an operator of a Web site may condition access on the verification of requested information such as a credit card number or an adult password. Credit card verification is only feasible, however, either in connection with a commercial transaction in which the card is used, or by payment to a verification agency. Using credit card possession as a surrogate for proof of age would impose costs on non-commercial Web sites that would require many of them to shut down.

Commercial pornographic sites that charge their users for access have assigned them passwords as a method of age verification. The record does not contain any evidence concerning the reliability of these technologies. Even if passwords are effective for commercial purveyors of indecent material, the District Court found that an adult password requirement would impose significant burdens on noncommercial sites, both because they would discourage users from accessing their sites and because the cost of creating and maintaining such screening systems would be beyond their reach.

The Telecommunications Act of 1996 was an unusually important legislative enactment. Title V—known as the "Communications Decency Act of 1996" (CDA)—[includes] the two statutory provisions challenged in this case. The first prohibits the knowing transmission of obscene or indecent messages to any recipient under 18 years of age. The second provision prohibits the knowing sending or displaying of "patently offensive messages" in a manner that is available to a person under 18 years of age.

The breadth of these prohibitions is qualified by two affirmative defenses. One covers those who take "good faith, reasonable, effective, and appropriate actions" to restrict access by minors to the prohibited communications. The other covers those who restrict access to covered material by requiring certain designated forms of age proof, such as a verified credit card or an adult identification number or code.

Immediately after the President signed the statute, 20 plaintiffs challenged the constitutionality of [the CDA]. A three-judge District Court was convened, [which] entered a preliminary injunction against enforcement of both of the challenged provisions.

The judgment of the District Court enjoins the Government from enforcing the prohibitions in CDA insofar as they relate to indecent communications, but expressly preserves the Government's right to investigate and prosecute the obscenity or child pornography activities. The Government argues that the District Court erred in holding that the CDA violated both the First Amendment because it is overbroad and the Fifth Amendment because it is vague. While we discuss the vagueness of the CDA because of its relevance to the First Amendment overbreadth inquiry, we conclude that the judgment should be affirmed without reaching the Fifth Amendment issue.

In arguing for reversal, the Government contends that the CDA is plainly constitutional under three of our prior decisions: *Ginsberg v. New York*, 390 U.S. 629 (1968); *FCC v. Pacifica Foundation*, 438 U.S. 726 (1978); and *Renton v. Playtime Theatres, Inc.*, 475 U.S. 41 (1986). A close look at these cases, however, raises—rather than relieves—doubts concerning the constitutionality of the CDA.

In *Ginsberg*, we upheld the constitutionality of a New York statute that prohibited selling to minors under 17 years of age material that was considered obscene as to them even if not obscene as to adults. In four important respects, the statute upheld in *Ginsberg* was narrower than the CDA. First, we noted in *Ginsberg* that the prohibition against sales to minors does not bar parents who so desire from purchasing the magazines for their children. Under the CDA, by contrast, neither the parents' consent—nor even their participation—in the communication would avoid the application of the statute. Second, the New York statute applied only to commercial transactions, whereas the CDA contains no such limitation. Third, the New York statute cabined its definition of material that is harmful to minors with the requirement that it be "utterly without redeeming social importance for minors." The CDA fails to provide us with any definition of the term "indecent" and, importantly, omits any requirement that "patently offensive" material lack serious literary, artistic, political, or scientific value. Fourth, the New York statute defined a minor as a person under the age of 17, whereas the CDA, in applying to all those under 18 years, includes an additional year of those nearest majority.

In *Pacifica*, we upheld a declaratory order of the Federal Communications Commission, holding that the broadcast of a recording of a 12-minute monologue entitled "Filthy Words" that had previously been delivered to a live audience could have been the subject of administrative sanctions. The Commission had found that the repetitive use of certain words referring to excretory or sexual activities or organs in an afternoon broadcast when children are in the audience was patently offensive and concluded that the monologue was indecent "as broadcast." The Court concluded that the ease with which children may obtain access to broadcasts justified special treatment of indecent broadcasting.

There are significant differences between the order upheld in *Pacifica* and the CDA. First, the order in *Pacifica*, issued by an agency that had been regulating radio stations for decades, targeted a specific broadcast that represented a rather dramatic departure from traditional program content in order to designate when—rather than whether—it would be permissible to air such a program in that particular medium. The CDA's broad categorical prohibitions are not limited to particular times and are not dependent on any evaluation by an agency familiar with the unique characteristics of the Internet. Second, unlike the CDA, the Commission's declaratory order was not punitive; we expressly refused to decide whether the indecent broadcast would justify a criminal prosecution. Finally, the Commission's order applied to a medium which as a matter of history had received the most limited First Amendment protection, in large part because warnings could not adequately protect the listener from unexpected program content. The Internet, however, has no comparable history. Moreover, the District Court found that the risk of encountering indecent material by accident is remote because a series of affirmative steps is required to access specific material.

In *Renton*, we upheld a zoning ordinance that kept adult movie theatres out of residential neighborhoods. The ordinance was aimed not at the content of the films shown in the theaters, but rather at the "secondary effects"—such as crime and deteriorating property values—that these theaters fostered. According to the Government, the CDA is constitutional because it constitutes a sort of "cyberzoning" on the Internet. But the CDA applies broadly to the entire universe of cyberspace. And the purpose of the CDA is to protect children from the primary effects of "indecent" and "patently offensive" speech, rather than any "secondary" effect of such speech. Thus, the CDA is a content-based blanket restriction on speech, and, as such, cannot be properly analyzed as a form of time, place, and manner regulation. Listeners' reaction to speech is not a content-neutral basis for regulation.

These precedents, then, surely do not require us to uphold the CDA and are fully consistent with the application of the most stringent review of its provisions. [They] provide no basis for qualifying the level of First Amendment scrutiny that should be applied to this medium.

Regardless of whether the CDA is so vague that it violates the Fifth Amendment, the many ambiguities concerning the scope of its coverage render it problematic for purposes of the First Amendment. Could a speaker confidently assume that a serious discussion about birth control practices, homosexuality, the First Amendment issues raised by [George Carlin's "Filthy Words"], or the consequences of prison rape would not violate the CDA? This uncertainty undermines the likelihood that the CDA has been carefully tailored to the congressional goal of protecting minors from potentially harmful materials.

The vagueness of the CDA is a matter of special concern for two reasons. First, the CDA is a content-based regulation of speech. The vagueness of such a regulation raises special First Amendment concerns because of its obvious chilling effect on free speech. Second, the CDA is a criminal statute. In addition to the opprobrium and stigma of a criminal conviction, the CDA threatens violators with penalties including up to two years in prison for each act of violation. The severity of criminal sanctions may well cause speakers to remain silent rather than communicate even arguably unlawful words, ideas, and images. As a practical matter, this increased deterrent effect, coupled with the risk of discriminatory enforcement of vague regulations, poses great First Amendment concerns.

We are persuaded that the CDA lacks the precision that the First Amendment requires when a statute regulates the content of speech. In order to deny minors access to potentially harmful speech, the CDA effectively suppresses a large amount of speech that adults have a constitutional right to receive and to address to one another. That burden on adult speech is unacceptable if less restrictive alternatives would be at least as effective in achieving the legitimate purpose that the statute was enacted to serve. The District Court found that despite its limitations, currently available user-based software suggests that a reasonably effective method by which parents can prevent their children from accessing sexually explicit and other material which parents may believe is inappropriate for their children will soon be widely available.

The breadth of the CDA's coverage is wholly unprecedented, not limited to commercial speech or commercial entities. Its open-ended prohibitions embrace all nonprofit entities and individuals posting indecent messages or displaying them on their own computers in the presence of minors. The general, undefined terms "indecent" and "patently offensive" cover large amounts of nonpornographic material with serious educational or other value. Moreover, the "community standards" criterion as applied to the Internet means that any communication available to a nation-wide audience will be judged by the standards of the community most likely to be offended by the message. The regulated subject matter may extend to discussions about prison rape or safe sexual practices, artistic images that include nude subjects, and arguably the card catalogue of the Carnegie Library. Under the CDA, a parent allowing her 17-year-old to use the family computer to obtain information on the Internet that she, in her parental judgment, deems appropriate could face a lengthy prison term. Similarly, a parent who sent his 17-year-old college freshman information on birth control via e-mail could be incarcerated even though neither he, his child, nor anyone in their home community, found the material indecent or patently offensive, if the college town's community thought otherwise.

The breadth of this content-based restriction of speech imposes an especially heavy burden on the Government to explain why a less restrictive provision would not be as effective as the CDA. It has not done so. The arguments in this Court have referred to possible alternatives such as requiring that indecent material be "tagged" in a way that facilitates parental control of material coming into their homes, making exceptions for messages with artistic or educational value, providing some tolerance for parental choice, and regulating some portions of the Internet—such as commercial web sites—differently than others, such as chat rooms. Particularly in the light of the absence of any detailed findings by the Congress, or even hearings addressing the special problems of the CDA, we are persuaded that the CDA is not narrowly tailored if that requirement has any meaning at all.

Relying on the "good faith, reasonable, effective, and appropriate actions" provision, the Government suggests that "tagging" provides a defense that saves the constitutionality of the Act. The suggestion assumes that transmitters may encode their indecent communications in a way that would indicate their contents, thus permitting recipients to block their reception with appropriate software. It is the requirement that the good faith action must be "effective" that makes this defense illusory. The Government recognizes that its proposed screening software does not currently exist. Even if it did, there is no way to know whether a potential recipient will actually block the encoded material.

We agree with the District Court's conclusion that the CDA places an unacceptably heavy burden on protected speech, and that the defenses do not constitute the sort of narrow tailoring that will save an otherwise patently invalid unconstitutional provision.

The Government asserts that—in addition to its interest in protecting children—its "equally significant" interest in fostering the growth of the Internet provides an independent basis for upholding the constitutionality of the CDA. The Government apparently assumes that the unregulated availability of "indecent" and "patently offensive" material on the Internet is driving countless citizens away from the medium because of the risk of exposing themselves or their children to harmful material. We find this argument singularly unpersuasive. The dramatic expansion of this new marketplace of ideas contradicts the factual basis of this contention. The record demonstrates that the growth of the Internet has been and continues to be phenomenal. As a matter of constitutional tradition, in the absence of evidence to the contrary, we presume that governmental regulation of the content of speech is more likely to interfere with the free exchange of ideas than to encourage it. The interest in encouraging freedom of expression in a democratic society outweighs any theoretical but unproven benefit of censorship.

For the foregoing reasons, the judgment of the district court is affirmed. It is so ordered.

POINTS FOR DISCUSSION

1. Much of Justice Stevens's ultimate decision seems to rest on his belief, based on the lower court's findings, that "the odds are slim that [an In-

ternet] user would enter a sexually explicit site by accident." How does this fit with your own experience in surfing the Web?
2. Justice Stevens's invoking of the hypothetical parent of a seventeen-year-old college student might make you wonder why the same concern did not persuade the Court in the earlier *Pacifica* decision (see chapter 11) that the rights of parents who *want* their mature kids to be able to listen to George Carlin's routines on the radio should be respected. Are you satisfied with the way Stevens distinguishes *Pacifica* from the *Reno* case? Why or why not?

▪ *MGM Studios v. Grokster*
545 U.S. 913 (2005)
Justice Souter:

Grokster, Ltd., and StreamCast Networks, Inc. distribute free software products that allow computer users to share electronic files through peer-to-peer networks, so called because users' computers communicate directly with each other, not through central servers. The advantage of peer-to-peer networks over information networks of other types shows up in their substantial and growing popularity. Because they need no central computer server to mediate the exchange of information or files among users, the high-bandwidth communications capacity for a server may be dispensed with, and the need for costly server storage space is eliminated. Since copies of a file (particularly a popular one) are available on many users' computers, file requests and retrievals may be faster than on other types of networks, and since file exchanges do not travel through a server, communications can take place between any computers that remain connected to the network without risk that a glitch in the server will disable the network in its entirety. Given these benefits in security, cost, and efficiency, peer-to-peer networks are employed to store and distribute electronic files by universities, government agencies, corporations, and libraries, among others.

Other users of peer-to-peer networks include individual recipients of Grokster's and StreamCast's software, and although the networks that they enjoy through using the software can be used to share any type of digital file, they have prominently employed those networks in sharing copyrighted music and video files without authorization. A group of copyright holders (MGM for short, but including motion picture studios, recording companies, songwriters, and music publishers) sued Grokster and StreamCast for their users' copyright infringements, alleging that they knowingly and intentionally distributed their software to enable users to reproduce and distribute the copyrighted works in violation of the Copyright Act.

Discovery during the litigation revealed the way the software worked, the business aims of each defendant company, and the predilections of the users. Grokster's eponymous software employs what is known as FastTrack technology, a protocol developed by others and licensed to Grokster. StreamCast distributes a very similar product except that its software, called Morpheus, relies on what is known as Gnutella technology. A user who downloads and installs either software possesses the protocol to send requests for files directly to the computers of others using software compatible with FastTrack or Gnutella. On the FastTrack network opened by the Grokster software, the user's request goes to a computer given an indexing capacity by the software and designated a supernode, or to some other computer with comparable power and capacity to collect temporary indexes of the files available on the computers of users connected to it. The supernode (or indexing computer) searches its own index and may communicate the search request to other supernodes. If the file is found, the supernode discloses its location to the computer requesting it, and the requesting user can download the file directly from the computer located. The copied file is placed in a designated sharing folder on the requesting user's computer, where it is available for other users to download in turn, along with any other file in that folder.

In the Gnutella network made available by Morpheus, the process is mostly the same, except that in some versions of the Gnutella protocol there are no supernodes. In these versions, peer computers using the protocol communicate directly with each other. When a user enters a search request into the Morpheus software, it sends the request to computers connected with it, which in turn pass the request along to other connected peers. The search results are communicated to the requesting computer, and the user can download desired files directly from peers' computers. As this description indicates, Grokster and StreamCast use no servers to intercept the content of the search requests or to mediate the file transfers conducted by users of the software, there being no central point through which the substance of the communications passes in either direction.

Although Grokster and StreamCast do not therefore know when particular files are copied, a few searches using their software would show what is available on the networks the software reaches. MGM commissioned a statistician to conduct a systematic search, and his study showed that nearly 90% of the files available for download on the FastTrack system were copyrighted works. Grokster and StreamCast dispute this figure, raising methodological problems and arguing that free copying even of copyrighted works may be authorized by the rightholders. They also argue that potential noninfringing uses of their software are significant in kind, even if infrequent in practice. Some musical performers, for example, have gained new audiences by distributing their copyrighted works for free across peer-to-peer networks, and some distributors of unprotected content have used peer-to-peer networks to disseminate files, Shakespeare being an example. Indeed, StreamCast has given Morpheus users the opportunity to download the briefs in this very case, though their popularity has not been quantified.

As for quantification, the parties' anecdotal and statistical evidence entered thus far to show the content available on the FastTrack and Gnutella networks does not say much about which files are actually downloaded by users, and no one can say how often the software is used to obtain copies of unprotected material. But MGM's evidence gives reason to think that the vast majority of users' downloads are acts of infringement, and because well over 100 million copies of the software in question are known to have been downloaded, and billions of files are shared across the FastTrack and Gnutella networks each month, the probable scope of copyright infringement is staggering.

Grokster and StreamCast concede the infringement in most downloads, and it is uncontested that they are aware that users employ their software primarily to download copyrighted files, even if the decentralized FastTrack and Gnutella networks fail to reveal which files are being copied, and when. From time to time, moreover, the companies have learned about their users' infringement directly, as from users who have sent e-mail to each company with questions about playing copyrighted movies they had downloaded, to whom the companies have responded with guidance. And MGM notified the companies of 8 million copyrighted files that could be obtained using their software.

Grokster and StreamCast are not, however, merely passive recipients of information about infringing use. The record is replete with evidence that from the moment Grokster and StreamCast began to distribute their free software, each one clearly voiced the objective that recipients use it to download copyrighted works, and each took active steps to encourage infringement.

After the notorious file-sharing service, Napster, was sued by copyright holders for facilitation of copyright infringement, StreamCast gave away a software program of a kind known as OpenNap, designed as compatible with the Napster program and open to Napster users for downloading files from other Napster and OpenNap users' computers. Evidence indicates that it was always StreamCast's intent to use its OpenNap network to be able to capture email addresses of its initial target market so that it could promote its StreamCast Morpheus interface to them. Indeed, the OpenNap program was engineered to leverage Napster's 50 million user base.

StreamCast monitored both the number of users downloading its OpenNap program and the number of music files they downloaded. It also used the resulting OpenNap network to distribute copies of the Morpheus software and to encourage users to adopt it. Internal company documents indicate that StreamCast hoped to attract large numbers of former Napster users if that company was shut down by court order or otherwise, and that StreamCast planned to be the next Napster. A kit developed by StreamCast to be delivered to advertisers, for example, contained press articles about StreamCast's potential to capture former Napster users, and it introduced itself to some potential advertisers as a company "which is similar to what Napster was."

Thus, StreamCast developed promotional materials to market its service as the best Napster alternative. One proposed advertisement read: "Napster Inc. has announced that it will soon begin charging you a fee. That's if the courts don't order it shut down first. What will you do to get around it?" StreamCast even planned to flaunt the illegal uses of its software; when it launched the OpenNap network, the chief technology officer of the company averred that "[t]he goal is to get in trouble with the law and get sued. It's the best way to get in the new[s]."

The evidence that Grokster sought to capture the market of former Napster users is sparser but revealing, for Grokster launched its own OpenNap system called Swaptor and inserted digital codes into its Web site so that computer users using Web search engines to look for "Napster" or "[f]ree filesharing" would be directed to the Grokster Web site, where they could download the Grokster software. And Grokster's name is an apparent derivative of Napster.

StreamCast's executives monitored the number of songs by certain commercial artists available on their networks, and an internal communication indicates they aimed to have a larger number of copyrighted songs available on their networks than other file-sharing networks. The point, of course, would be to attract users of a mind to infringe, just as it would be with their promotional materials developed showing copyrighted songs as examples of the kinds of files available through Morpheus. Morpheus in fact allowed users to search specifically for "Top 40" songs, which were inevitably copyrighted. Similarly, Grokster sent users a newsletter promoting its ability to provide particular, popular copyrighted materials.

In addition to this evidence of express promotion, marketing, and intent to promote further, the business models employed by Grokster and StreamCast confirm that their principal object was use of their software to download copyrighted works. Grokster and StreamCast receive no revenue from users, who obtain the software itself for nothing. Instead, both companies generate income by selling advertising space, and they stream the advertising to Grokster and Morpheus users while they are employing the programs. As the number of users of each program increases, advertising opportunities become worth more. While there is doubtless some demand for free Shakespeare, the evidence shows that substantive volume is a function of free access to copyrighted work. Users seeking Top 40 songs, for example, or the latest release by Modest Mouse, are certain to be far more numerous than those seeking a free *Decameron*, and Grokster and StreamCast translated that demand into dollars.

Finally, there is no evidence that either company made an effort to filter copyrighted material from users' downloads or otherwise impede the sharing of copyrighted files. Although Grokster appears to have sent e-mails warning users about infringing content when it received threatening notice from the copyright holders, it never blocked anyone from continuing to use its software to share copyrighted files. StreamCast not only rejected another company's offer of help to monitor infringement, but blocked the Internet Protocol addresses of entities it believed were trying to engage in such monitoring on its networks.

The District Court held that those who used the Grokster and Morpheus software to download copyrighted media files directly infringed MGM's copyrights, a conclusion not contested on appeal, but the court nonetheless granted summary judgment in favor of Grokster and StreamCast as to any liability arising from distribution of their software. The Court of Appeals affirmed.

MGM and many of the *amici* fault the Court of Appeals's holding for upsetting a sound balance between the respective values of supporting creative pursuits through copyright protection and promoting innovation in new communication technologies by limiting the incidence of liability for copyright infringement. The more artistic protection is favored, the more technological innovation may be discouraged; the administration of copyright law is an exercise in managing the trade-off. The tension between the two values is the subject of this case, with its claim that digital distribution of copyrighted material threatens copyright holders as never before, because every copy is identical to the original, copying is easy, and many people (especially the young) use file-sharing software to download copyrighted works. This very breadth of the software's use may well draw the public directly into the debate over copyright policy, and the indications are that the ease of copying songs or movies using software like Grokster's and Napster's is fostering disdain for copyright protection. As the case has been presented to us, these fears are said to be offset by the different concern that imposing liability, not only on infringers but on distributors of software based on its potential for unlawful use, could limit further development of beneficial technologies.

Despite the currency of these principles of secondary liability, this Court has dealt with secondary copyright infringement in only one recent case, and because MGM has tailored its principal claim to our opinion there, a look at our earlier holding is in order. In *Sony Corp. v. Universal City Studios* (1984), this Court addressed a claim that secondary liability for infringement can arise from the very distribution of a commercial product. There, the product, novel at the time, was what we know today as the videocassette recorder or VCR. Copyright holders sued Sony as the manufacturer, claiming it was contributorily liable for infringement that occurred when VCR owners taped copyrighted programs because it supplied the means used to infringe, and it had constructive knowledge that infringement would occur. At the trial on the merits, the evidence showed that the principal use of the VCR was for time-shifting, or taping a program for later viewing at a more convenient time, which the Court found to be a fair, not an infringing, use. There was no evidence that Sony had expressed an object of bringing about taping in violation of copyright or had taken active steps to increase its profits from unlawful taping. Although Sony's advertisements urged consumers to buy the VCR to "record favorite shows" or "build a library" of recorded programs, neither of these uses was necessarily infringing.

On those facts, with no evidence of stated or indicated intent to promote infringing uses, the only conceivable basis for imposing liability was on a theory of contributory infringement arising from its sale of VCRs to consumers with knowledge that some would use them to infringe. But because the VCR was "capable of commercially significant noninfringing uses," we held the manufacturer could not be faulted solely on the basis of its distribution.

This analysis reflected patent law's traditional staple article of commerce doctrine, now codified, that distribution of a component of a patented device will not violate the patent if it is suitable for use in other ways. The doctrine was devised to identify instances in which it may be presumed from distribution of an article in commerce that the distributor intended the article to be used to infringe another's patent, and so may justly be held liable for that infringement.

In sum, where an article is "good for nothing else" but infringement, there is no legitimate public interest in its unlicensed availability, and there is no injustice in presuming or imputing an intent to infringe. Conversely, the doctrine absolves the equivocal conduct of selling an item with substantial lawful as well as unlawful uses, and limits liability to instances of more acute fault than the mere understanding that some of one's products will be misused. It leaves breathing room for innovation and a vigorous commerce.

The parties and many of the *amici* in this case think the key to resolving it is the *Sony* rule and, in particular, what it means for a product to be "capable of commercially significant noninfringing uses. MGM advances the argument that granting summary judgment to Grokster and StreamCast as to their current activities gave too much weight to the value of innovative technology, and too little to the copyrights infringed by users of their software, given that 90% of works available on one of the networks was shown to be copyrighted. Assuming the remaining 10% to be its noninfringing use, MGM says this should not qualify as "substantial," and the Court should quantify *Sony* to the extent of holding that a product used "principally" for infringement does not qualify. As mentioned before, Grokster and StreamCast reply by citing evidence that their software can be used to reproduce public domain works, and they point to copyright holders who actually encourage copying. Even if infringement is the principal practice with their software today, they argue, the noninfringing uses are significant and will grow.

We agree with MGM that the Court of Appeals misapplied *Sony*, which it read as limiting secondary liability quite beyond the circumstances to which the case applied. *Sony* barred secondary liability based on presuming or imputing intent to cause infringement solely from the design or distribution of a product capable of substantial lawful use, which the distributor knows is in fact used for infringement. The Ninth Circuit has read *Sony*'s limitation to mean that whenever a product is capable of substantial lawful use, the producer can never be held contributorily liable for third parties' infringing use of it; it read the rule as being this broad, even when an actual purpose to cause infringing use is shown by evidence independent of design and distribution of the product, unless the distributors had specific knowledge of infringement at a time at which they contributed to the infringement, and failed to act upon that information. Because the Circuit found the StreamCast and Grokster software capable of substantial lawful use, it concluded on the basis of its reading of *Sony* that neither company could be held liable, since there was no showing that their software, being without any central server, afforded them knowledge of specific unlawful uses. This view of *Sony*, however, was error, converting the case from one about liability resting on imputed intent to one about liability on any theory.

Sony's rule limits imputing culpable intent as a matter of law from the characteristics or uses of a distributed product. But nothing in *Sony* requires courts to ignore evidence of intent if there is such evidence, and the case was never meant to foreclose rules of fault-based liability derived from the common law. Where evidence goes beyond a product's characteristics or the knowledge that it may be put to infringing uses, and shows statements or actions directed to promoting infringement, *Sony*'s staple-article rule will not preclude liability.

The classic case of direct evidence of unlawful purpose occurs when one induces commission of infringement by another, or entices or persuades another to infringe, as by advertising. Thus at common law a copyright or patent defendant who not only expected but invoked infringing use by advertisement was liable for infringement on principles recognized in every part of the law. The rule on inducement of infringement as developed in the early cases is no different today.

For the same reasons that *Sony* took the staple-article doctrine of patent law as a model for its copyright safe-harbor rule, the inducement rule, too, is a sensible one for copyright. We adopt it here, holding that one who distributes a device with the object of promoting its use to infringe copyright, as shown by clear expression or other affirmative steps taken to foster infringement, is liable for the resulting acts of infringement by third parties. Mere knowledge of infringing potential or of actual infringing uses would not be enough here to subject a distributor to liability. Nor would ordinary acts incident to product distribution, such as offering customers technical support or product updates, support liability in themselves. The inducement rule, instead, premises liability on purposeful, culpable expression and conduct, and thus does nothing to compromise legitimate commerce or discourage innovation having a lawful promise.

The only apparent question about treating MGM's evidence as sufficient to withstand summary judgment under the theory of inducement goes to the need on MGM's part to adduce evidence that StreamCast and Grokster communicated an inducing message to their software users. The classic instance of inducement is by advertisement or solicitation that broadcasts a message designed to stimulate others to commit violations. MGM claims that such a message is shown here. It is undisputed that StreamCast beamed onto the computer screens of users of Napster-compatible programs ads urging the adoption of its OpenNap program, which was designed, as its name implied, to invite the custom of patrons of Napster, then under attack in the courts for facilitating massive infringement. Those who accepted StreamCast's OpenNap program were offered software to perform the same services, which a factfinder could conclude would readily have been understood in the Napster market as the ability to download copyrighted music files. Grokster distributed an electronic newsletter containing links to articles promoting its software's ability to access popular copyrighted music. And anyone whose Napster or free file-sharing searches turned up a link to Grokster would have understood Grokster to be offering the same file-sharing ability as Napster, and to the same people who probably used Napster for infringing downloads; that would also have been the understanding of anyone offered Grokster's suggestively named Swaptor software, its version of OpenNap. And both companies communicated a clear message by responding affirmatively to requests for help in locating and playing copyrighted materials.

In StreamCast's case the evidence just described was supplemented by other unequivocal indications of unlawful purpose in the internal communications and advertising designs aimed at Napster users ("When the lights went off at Napster . . . where did the users go?"). Whether the messages were communicated is not to the point on this record. The function of the message in the theory of inducement is to prove by a defendant's own statements that his unlawful purpose disqualifies him from claiming protection (and incidentally to point to actual violators likely to be found among those who hear or read the message). Proving that a message was sent out, then, is the preeminent but not exclusive way of showing that active steps were taken with the purpose of bringing about infringing acts, and of showing that infringing acts took place by using the device distributed. Here, the summary judgment record is replete with other evidence that Grokster and StreamCast, unlike the manufacturer and distributor in *Sony*, acted with a purpose to cause copyright violations by use of software suitable for illegal use.

Three features of this evidence of intent are particularly notable. First, each company showed itself to be aiming to satisfy a known source of demand for copyright infringement, the market comprising former Napster users. StreamCast's internal documents made constant reference to Napster, it initially distributed its Morpheus software through an OpenNap program compatible with Napster, it advertised its OpenNap program to Napster users, and its Morpheus software functions as Napster did except that it could be used to distribute more kinds of files, including copyrighted movies and software programs. Grokster's name is apparently derived from Napster, it too initially offered an OpenNap program, its software's function is likewise comparable to Napster's, and it attempted to divert queries for Napster onto its own Web site. Grokster and StreamCast's efforts to supply services to former Napster users, deprived of a mechanism to copy and distribute what were overwhelmingly infringing files, indicate a principal, if not exclusive, intent on the part of each to bring about infringement.

Second, this evidence of unlawful objective is given added significance by MGM's showing that neither company attempted to develop filtering tools or other mechanisms to diminish the infringing activity using their software. While the Ninth Circuit treated the defendants' failure to develop such tools as irrelevant because they lacked an independent duty to monitor their users' activity, we think this evidence underscores Grokster's and StreamCast's intentional facilitation of their users' infringement.

Third, there is a further complement to the direct evidence of unlawful objective. It is useful to recall that StreamCast and Grokster make money by selling advertising space, by directing ads to the screens of computers employing their software. As the record shows, the more the software is used, the more ads are sent out and the greater the advertising revenue becomes. Since the extent of the software's use determines the gain to the distributors, the commercial sense of their enterprise turns on high-volume use, which the record shows is infringing. This evidence alone would not justify an inference of unlawful intent, but viewed in the context of the entire record its import is clear.

In addition to intent to bring about infringement and distribution of a device suitable for infringing use, the inducement theory of course requires evidence of actual infringement by recipients of the device, the software in this case. As the account of the facts indicates, there is evidence of infringement on a gigantic scale, and there is no serious issue of the adequacy of MGM's showing on this point in order to survive the companies' summary judgment requests. Although an exact calculation of infringing use, as a basis for a claim of damages, is subject to dispute, there is no question that the summary judgment evidence is at least adequate to entitle MGM to go forward with claims for damages and equitable relief.

In sum, this case is significantly different from *Sony* and reliance on that case to rule in favor of StreamCast and Grokster was error. *Sony* dealt with a claim of liability based solely on distributing a product with alternative lawful and unlawful uses, with knowledge that some users would follow the unlawful course. The case struck a balance between the interests of protection and innovation by holding that the product's capability of substantial lawful employment should bar the imputation of fault and consequent secondary liability for the unlawful acts of others.

MGM's evidence in this case most obviously addresses a different basis of liability for distributing a product open to alternative uses. Here, evidence of the distributors' words and deeds going beyond distribution as such shows a purpose to cause and profit from third-party acts of copyright infringement. If liability for inducing infringement is ultimately found, it will not be on the basis of presuming or imputing fault, but from inferring a patently illegal objective from statements and actions showing what that objective was.

There is substantial evidence in MGM's favor on all elements of inducement, and summary judgment in favor of Grokster and StreamCast was error. On remand, reconsideration of MGM's motion for summary judgment will be in order. The judgment of the Court of Appeals is vacated, and the case is remanded for further proceedings consistent with this opinion. It is so ordered.

POINTS FOR DISCUSSION

1. Many commentators have suggested that Justice Souter exaggerates the factual differences between *Grokster* and the earlier *Sony* case. He admits that ads for the Sony Betamax touted the machine's ability to let you "Watch What You Want, When You Want." This would seem to encourage users to build home libraries of videotapes, a large portion of which would presumably be copyright-protected materials. Is this really so different from the defendants in this more recent case demonstrating an awareness that clients might use the software to share music that is also protected by copyright?
2. Critics of the movie industry often point out that the real lesson from the earlier *Sony* case is the futility of the plaintiffs' strategy. The VCR (and, more recently, DVR/Tivo) create whole new markets for the industry, and only a fool or a Luddite or both would try to slow these technologies. Do you believe that the movie industry will learn to cooperate with (or even co-opt) the peer sharing aspect of the Internet?

▪ *Fair Housing Council of San Fernando Valley v. Roommates.com*
421 F.3d 1157 (9th Cir. 2008)
Judge Kosinski:

We plumb the depths of the immunity provided by section 230 of the Communications Decency Act of 1996 ("CDA"). Defendant Roommate.com, LLC ("Roommate") operates a website designed to match people renting out spare rooms with people looking for a place to live. At the time of the district court's disposition, Roommate's website featured approximately 150,000 active listings and received around a million page views a day. Roommate seeks to profit by collecting revenue from advertisers and subscribers.

Before subscribers can search listings or post housing opportunities on Roommate's website, they must create profiles, a process that requires them to answer a series of questions. In addition to requesting basic information—such as name, location and email address—Roommate requires each subscriber to disclose his sex, sexual orientation and whether he would bring children to a household. Each subscriber must also describe his preferences in roommates with respect to the same three criteria: sex, sexual orientation and whether they will bring children to the household. The site also encourages subscribers to provide "Additional Comments" describing themselves and their desired roommate in an open-ended essay. After a new subscriber completes the application, Roommate assembles his answers into a "profile page." The profile page displays the subscriber's pseudonym, his description and his preferences, as divulged through answers to Roommate's questions.

Subscribers can choose between two levels of service: Those using the site's free service level can create their own personal profile page, search the profiles of others and send personal email messages. They can also receive periodic emails from Roommate, informing them of available housing opportunities matching their preferences. Subscribers who pay a monthly fee also gain the ability to read emails from other users, and to view other subscribers' "Additional Comments."

The Fair Housing Councils of the San Fernando Valley and San Diego ("Councils") sued Roommate in federal court, alleging that Roommate's business violates the federal Fair Housing Act ("FHA") and California housing discrimination laws. Councils claim that Roommate is effectively a housing broker doing online what it may not lawfully do off-line. The district court held that Roommate is immune under section 230 of the CDA.

Section 230 of the CDA immunizes providers of interactive computer services against liability arising from content created by third parties: "No provider of an interactive computer service shall be treated as the publisher or speaker of any information provided by another information content provider." This grant of immunity applies only if the interactive computer service provider is not also an "information content provider," which is defined as someone who is "responsible, in whole or in part, for the creation or development of" the offending content.

A website operator can be both a service provider and a content provider: If it passively displays content that is created entirely by third parties, then it is only a service provider with respect to that content. But as to content that it creates itself, or is "responsible, in whole or in part" for creating or developing, the website is also a content provider. Thus, a website may be immune from liability for some of the content it displays to the public but be subject to liability for other content.

In passing section 230, Congress sought to [allow] interactive computer services to perform some editing on user-generated content without thereby becoming liable for all defamatory or otherwise unlawful messages that they didn't edit or delete. In other words, Congress sought to immunize the *removal* of user-generated content, not the *creation* of content. With this backdrop in mind, we examine three specific functions performed by Roommate that are alleged to violate the Fair Housing Act and California law.

Councils first argue that the questions Roommate poses to prospective subscribers during the registration process violate the Fair Housing Act and the analogous California law. Councils allege that requiring subscribers to disclose their sex, family status and sexual orientation "indicates" an intent to discriminate against them, and thus runs afoul of both the FHA and state law.

Roommate created the questions and choice of answers, and designed its website registration process around them. Therefore, Roommate is undoubtedly the "information content provider" as to the questions and can claim no immunity for posting them on its website, or for forcing subscribers to answer them as a condition of using its services.

We must determine whether Roommate has immunity under the CDA because Councils have at least a plausible claim that Roommate violated state and federal law by merely posing the questions. We need not decide whether any of Roommate's questions actually violate the Fair Housing Act or California law, or whether they are protected by the First Amendment or other constitutional guarantees; we leave those issues for the district court on remand. Rather, we examine the scope of plaintiffs' substantive claims only insofar as necessary to determine whether section 230 immunity applies. However, we note that asking questions certainly *can* violate the Fair Housing Act and analogous laws in the physical world. For example, a real estate broker may not inquire as to the race of a prospective buyer, and an employer may not inquire as to the religion of a prospective employee. If such questions are unlawful when posed face-to-face or by telephone, they don't magically become lawful when asked electronically online. The Communications Decency Act was not meant to create a lawless no-man's-land on the Internet.

Councils also claim that requiring subscribers to answer the questions as a condition of using Roommate's services unlawfully "causes subscribers to make a statement with respect to the sale or rental of a dwelling that indicates a preference, limitation, or discrimination," in violation of FHA. The CDA does not grant immunity for inducing third parties to express illegal preferences. Roommate's own acts—posting the questionnaire and requiring answers to it—are entirely its doing and thus section 230 of the CDA does not apply to them. Roommate is entitled to no immunity.

Councils also charge that Roommate's development and display of subscribers' discriminatory preferences is unlawful. Roommate publishes a "profile page" for each subscriber on its website. The page describes the client's personal information—such as his sex, sexual orientation and whether he has children—as well as the attributes of the housing situation he seeks. The content of these pages is drawn directly from the registration process: For example, Roommate requires subscribers to specify, using a drop-down menu provided by Roommate, whether they are "Male" or "Female" and then displays that information on the profile page. Roommate also requires subscribers who are listing available housing to disclose whether there are currently "Straight male(s)," "Gay male(s)," "Straight female(s)" or "Lesbian(s)" living in the dwelling. Subscribers who are seeking housing must make a selection from a drop-down menu, again provided by Roommate, to indicate whether they are willing to live with "Straight or gay" males, only with "Straight" males, only with "Gay" males or with "No males." Similarly, Roommate requires subscribers listing housing to disclose whether there are "Children present" or "Children not present" and requires housing seekers to say "I will live with children" or "I will not live with children." Roommate then displays these answers, along with other information, on the subscriber's profile page. This information is obviously included to help subscribers decide which housing opportunities to pursue and which to bypass. In addition, Roommate itself uses this information to channel subscribers away from listings where the individual offering housing has expressed preferences that aren't compatible with the subscriber's answers.

Here, the part of the profile that is alleged to offend the Fair Housing Act and state housing discrimination laws—the information about sex, family status and sexual orientation—is provided by subscribers in response to Roommate's questions, which they cannot refuse to answer if they want to use defendant's services. By requiring subscribers to provide the information as a condition of accessing its service, and by providing a limited set of pre-populated answers, Roommate becomes much more than a passive transmitter of information provided by others; it becomes the developer, at least in part, of that information. And section 230 provides immunity only if the interactive computer service does not "create or develop" the information "in whole or in part." Roommate argues that it is not responsible for the information on the profile page because it is each subscriber's action that leads to publication of his particular profile—in other words, the user pushes the last button or takes the last act before publication. We are not convinced that this is even true, but don't see why it matters anyway. The projectionist in the theater may push the last button before a film is displayed on the screen, but surely this doesn't make him the sole producer of the movie. By any reasonable use of the English language, Roommate is "responsible" at least "in part" for each subscriber's profile page, because every such page is a collaborative effort between Roommate and the subscriber.

Similarly, Roommate is not entitled to CDA immunity for the operation of its search system, which filters listings, or of its email notification system, which directs emails to subscribers according to discriminatory criteria. Roommate designed its search system so it would steer users based on the preferences and personal characteristics that Roommate itself forces subscribers to disclose. If Roommate has no immunity for asking the discriminatory questions, as we concluded above, it can certainly have no immunity for using the answers to the unlawful questions to limit who has access to housing.

For example, a subscriber who self-identifies as a "Gay male" will not receive email notifications of new housing opportunities supplied by owners who limit the universe of acceptable tenants to "Straight male(s)," "Straight female(s)" and "Lesbian(s)." Similarly, subscribers with children will not be notified of new listings where the owner specifies "no children." Councils charge that limiting the information a subscriber can access based on that subscriber's protected status violates the Fair Housing Act and state housing discrimination laws. It is, Councils allege, no different from a real estate broker saying to a client: "Sorry, sir, but I can't show you any listings on this block because you are [gay/female/black/a parent]." If such screening is prohibited when practiced in person or by telephone, we see no reason why Congress would have wanted to make it lawful to profit from it online.

Roommate's search function is similarly designed to steer users based on discriminatory criteria. Roommate's search engine thus differs materially from generic search engines such as Google, Yahoo! and MSN Live Search, in that Roommate designed its system to use allegedly unlawful criteria so as to limit the results of each search, and to force users to participate in its discriminatory process. In other words, Councils allege that Roommate's search is designed to make it more difficult or impossible for individuals with certain protected characteristics to find housing—something the law prohibits. By contrast, ordinary search engines do not use unlawful criteria to limit the scope of searches conducted on them, nor are they designed to achieve illegal ends—as Roommate's search function is alleged to do here. Therefore, such search engines play no part in the "development" of any unlawful searches.

It's true that the broadest sense of the term "develop" could include the functions of an ordinary search engine—indeed, just about any function performed by a website. But to read the term so broadly would defeat the purposes of section 230 by swallowing up every bit of the immunity that the section otherwise provides. At the same time, reading the exception for co-developers as applying only to content that originates entirely with the website ignores the words "development . . . in part" in the statutory passage "creation *or development* in whole *or in part.*" We believe that both the immunity for passive conduits and the exception for co-developers must be given their proper scope and, to that end, we interpret the term "development" as referring not merely to augmenting the content generally, but to materially contributing to its alleged unlawfulness. In other words, a website helps to develop unlawful content, and thus falls within the exception to section 230, if it contributes materially to the alleged illegality of the conduct.

In an abundance of caution, we offer a few examples to elucidate what does and does not amount to "development" under section 230 of the Communications Decency Act: If an individual uses an ordinary search engine to query for a "white roommate," the search engine has not contributed to any alleged unlawfulness in the individual's conduct; providing *neutral* tools to carry out what may be unlawful or illicit searches does not amount to "development" for purposes of the immunity exception. A dating website that requires users to enter their sex, race, religion and marital status through drop-down menus, and that provides means for users to search along the same lines, retains its CDA immunity insofar as it does not contribute to any alleged illegality; this immunity is retained even if the website is sued for libel based on these characteristics because the website would not have contributed materially to any alleged defamation. Similarly, a housing website that allows users to specify whether they will or will not receive emails by means of *user-defined* criteria might help some users exclude email from other users of a particular race or sex. However, that website would be immune, so long as it does not require the use of discriminatory criteria. A website operator who edits user-created content—such as by correcting spelling, removing obscenity or trimming for length—retains his immunity for any illegality in the user-created content, provided that the edits are unrelated to the illegality. However, a website operator who edits in a manner that contributes to the alleged illegality—such as by removing the word "not" from a user's message reading "[Name] did *not* steal the artwork" in order to transform an innocent message into a libelous one—is directly involved in the alleged illegality and thus not immune.

Here, Roommate's connection to the discriminatory filtering process is direct and palpable: Roommate designed its search and email systems to limit the listings available to subscribers based on sex, sexual orientation and presence of children. Roommate selected the criteria used to hide listings, and Councils allege that the act of hiding certain listings is itself unlawful under the Fair Housing Act, which prohibits brokers from steering clients in accordance with discriminatory preferences. We need not decide the merits of Councils' claim to hold that Roommate is sufficiently involved with the design and operation of the search and email systems—which are engineered to limit access to housing on the basis of the protected characteristics elicited by the registration process—so as to forfeit any immunity to which it was otherwise entitled under section 230.

Councils finally argue that Roommate should be held liable for the discriminatory statements displayed in the "Additional Comments" section of profile pages. At the end of the registration process, on a separate page from the other registration steps, Roommate prompts subscribers to "take a moment to personalize your profile by writing a paragraph or two describing yourself and what you are looking for in a roommate." The subscriber is presented with a blank text box, in which he can type as much or as little about himself as he wishes. Such essays are visible only to paying subscribers.

Subscribers provide a variety of provocative, and often very revealing, answers. The contents range from subscribers who "prefer white Male roommates" or require that "the person applying for the room MUST be a BLACK GAY MALE" to those who are "NOT looking for black Muslims." Some common themes are a desire to live without "drugs, kids or animals" or "smokers, kids or druggies," while a few subscribers express more particular preferences, such as preferring to live in a home free of "psychos or anyone on mental medication." Some subscribers are just looking for someone who will get along with their significant other or with their most significant Other ["our Lord Jesus Christ"].

Roommate publishes these comments as written. It does not provide any specific guidance as to what the essay should contain, nor does it urge subscribers to input discriminatory preferences. Roommate is not responsible, in whole or in part, for the development of this content, which comes entirely from subscribers and is passively displayed by Roommate. Without reviewing every essay, Roommate would have no way to distinguish unlawful discriminatory preferences from perfectly legitimate statements. Nor can there be any doubt that this information was tendered to Roommate for publication online. This is precisely the kind of situation for which section 230 was designed to provide immunity.

Councils argue that—given the context of the discriminatory questions presented earlier in the registration process—the "Additional Comments" prompt impliedly suggests that subscribers should make statements expressing a desire to discriminate on the basis of protected classifications; in other words, Councils allege that, by encouraging *some* discriminatory preferences, Roommate encourages other discriminatory preferences when it gives subscribers a chance to describe themselves. But the encouragement that bleeds over from one part of the registration process to another is extremely weak, if it exists at all. Such weak encouragement cannot strip a website of its section 230 immunity, lest that immunity be rendered meaningless as a practical matter.

We must keep firmly in mind that this is an immunity statute we are expounding, a provision enacted to protect websites against the evil of liability for failure to remove offensive content. Websites are complicated enterprises, and there will always be close cases where a clever lawyer could argue that *something* the website operator did encouraged the illegality. Such close cases, we believe, must be resolved in favor of immunity, lest we cut the heart out of section 230 by forcing websites to face death by ten thousand duck-bites, fighting off claims that they promoted or encouraged—or at least tacitly assented to—the illegality of third parties. Where it is very clear that the website directly participates in developing the alleged illegality—as it is clear here with respect to Roommate's questions, answers and the resulting profile pages—immunity will be lost. But in cases of enhancement by implication or development by inference—such as with respect to the "Additional Comments" here—section 230 must be interpreted to protect websites not merely from ultimate liability, but from having to fight costly and protracted legal battles.

In light of our determination that the CDA does not provide immunity to Roommate for all of the content of its website and email newsletters, we remand for the district court to determine in the first instance whether the alleged actions for which Roommate is not immune violate the Fair Housing Act. We do not address Roommate's claim that its activities are protected by the First Amendment. The district court based its decision entirely on the CDA and we refrain from deciding an issue that the district court has not had the opportunity to evaluate.

POINTS FOR DISCUSSION

1. It appears that Roommate.com's clients are forced to offer demographic information about themselves but are not forced to indicate any discriminatory intentions. (They can say "yes, that would be OK with me" in response to all categories of hypothetical roommate characteristics.) Has Roommate.com thus encouraged illegal discrimination?
2. Kosinsky correctly points out, in passing, that the law may preclude us from making hiring decisions and commercial housing decisions based on certain characteristics, but not dating decisions. Isn't a roommate relationship more akin to a dating relationship than to, say, a truly commercial rental relationship involving an apartment in a huge housing complex?

▪ *Bradburn v. North Central Regional Library District*

231 P.3d 166 (Wash. 2010)
Chief Justice Madsen:

The question in this case has been certified to us from the United States District Court for the Eastern District of Washington: Whether a public library, consistent with Article I, § 5 of the Washington Constitution, may filter Internet access for all patrons without disabling Web sites containing constitutionally-protected speech upon the request of an adult library patron. We conclude that a library can, subject to the limitations set forth in this opinion, filter Internet access for all patrons, including adults, without violating article I, section 5 of the Washington State Constitution.

North Central Regional Library (NCRL) is an intercounty rural library district with 28 branch libraries, established in 1960 by citizens of Chelan, Douglas, Ferry, Grant, and Okanogan Counties. Its mission is to promote reading and lifelong learning. It is also committed to support of public education, with 26 school districts operating within its area. In 14 of these districts, the branch libraries act as de facto school libraries. NCRL maintains a collection of more than 675,000 books and other materials that are available to its patrons at the branch libraries, by order through its web site, or by mail order. Only one branch has a wall or partition separating the children's section of the library from the rest of it. Twenty of the branches are staffed by one librarian.

NCRL provides public Internet access in all of its branches, access subject to two policies, the Collection Development Policy and the Internet Public Use Policy. NCRL's director and director of public services interpret and apply these policies. The Collection Development Policy states:

> The North Central Regional Library District's Board of Trustees recognizes that the library was created to serve all of the people within the District's service area, regardless of race, age, creed, or political persuasions, individuals and groups with widely disparate and diverse interests, cultural backgrounds, and needs. Library materials shall be selected and retained in the library on the basis of their value for the interest, information, and enlightenment of all the people of the community in conformance with the District's mission. Some of the factors which will be considered in adding to or removing materials from the library collection shall include: present collection composition, collection development objectives, interest, demand, timeliness, audience, significance of subject, diversity of viewpoint, effective expression, and limitation of budget and facilities. No library materials shall be excluded because of the views of the author. Not all materials will be suitable for all members of the community. Reading, listening to, and viewing library materials are individual, private matters. While individuals are free to select or to reject materials for themselves, they cannot restrict the freedom of others to read, view, or inquire. The Board of Trustees recognizes that parents have the primary responsibility to guide and direct the reading and viewing of their own minor children.
>
> The Board of Trustees recognizes the right of individuals to question materials in the District collection. A library customer questioning material in the collection is encouraged to talk with designated members of the staff concerning

such material. To formally state his or her opinion and receive a written response, a customer may submit the form provided for that purpose.

NCRL's Internet Public Use Policy states:

> The Internet is currently an unregulated medium. While the Internet offers access to materials that are enriching to users of all ages, the Internet also enables access to some materials that may be offensive, disturbing, or illegal. There is no guarantee that information obtained through the Internet is accurate or that individuals are who they represent themselves to be. The library district recognizes that it cannot fully control the amount of material accessible through the Internet but will take reasonable steps to apply to the Internet the selection criteria stated in the Collection Development Guidelines and Procedures.
>
> All Internet access on NCRL library computers is filtered. The library district does not host customer e-mail accounts or provide access to chat rooms. The library district cannot guarantee privacy for individuals using library public access computers to search the Internet and computer screens may be visible to people of all ages, backgrounds, and sensibilities. Customers are requested to exercise appropriate discretion in viewing materials or submitting sensitive personal information. Minors, in particular, are discouraged from sharing personal information online.

In October 2006, following its earlier use of other software, NCRL implemented the "FortiGuard Web Filtering Service," a widely used filtering service. FortiGuard sorts web sites into 76 categories based upon predominant content. The database catalogues over 43 million web sites and over 2 billion individual web pages. It is continually updated. Anyone can ask for FortiGuard to review its classification of a particular site or page by using an electronic form available on the Fortinet site.

NCRL's FortiGuard filter is configured to block the following of the 76 categories that can be blocked using the FortiGuard system: Hacking; Phishing; Spyware; Malware; Adult Materials (Mature content websites that feature or promote sexuality, strip clubs, sex shops, etc. excluding sex education, without the intent to sexually arouse); Nudity and Risqué (Mature content sites that depict the human body in full or partial nudity without the intent to sexually arouse); Pornography; Gambling; Web Chat; and Instant Messaging.

NCRL also blocks the "Image Search," "Video Search," and "Spam" classifications, certain specific image search web sites, and the "personals" section of craigslist.org. NCRL also initially blocked but subsequently unblocked access to youtube.com, myspace.com, and craigslist.org (except for the "personals" section).

In addition, to qualify for certain federal funding, i.e., discounted Internet access and grants available to state libraries, NCRL is required to certify its compliance with the Children's Internet Protection Act (CIPA), [which] requires libraries to employ measures that prohibit access by minors to depictions that are obscene, child pornography, or otherwise harmful to minors.

NCRL also has a policy that its Internet filter not be disabled at the request of an adult patron. This means that if material is appropriately blocked under the Internet Use Policy, it is not unblocked upon request. However, if the material is erroneously blocked, it can be unblocked upon request.

Plaintiffs Sarah Bradburn, Pearl Cherrington, and Charles Heinlen are patrons of NCRL who use or have used computers that NCRL has made available to access the Internet. Each claims that access to certain web sites was blocked by NCRL's Internet filter. Plaintiff Second Amendment Foundation (SAF) is a Washington nonprofit corporation dedicated to issues associated with the constitutional right to keep and bear firearms, with about 1,000 members in the counties served by NCRL. SAF has a web site and sponsors on-line publications, including *Women and Guns*. SAF was advised by a member or members that access to its publication www.womenandguns was blocked on NCRL's computers. Prior to this lawsuit, NCRL had not received any report that this site was blocked and does not contend that it should be blocked. It is not presently blocked. SAF is concerned about possible future blocking.

Plaintiffs brought suit against NCRL, challenging the filtering policy's constitutionality and, in particular, NCRL's decision that it would not disable the filter at the request of an adult (except in the case of a site being blocked when it did not in fact fall within a prohibited category such as spyware, gambling, or pornography).

Article I, section 5 of the Washington State Constitution provides that "every person may freely speak, write and publish on all subjects, being responsible for the abuse of that right." [Here], our analytical approach aligns with the approach taken under the First Amendment.

The first question here is whether, as the plaintiffs claim, NCRL's filtering policy acts as a prior restraint in violation of article I, section 5. NCRL maintains that its policy is neither a prior restraint nor its functional equivalent. Rather, it is an operational rule that applies in the same way as any other collection decision by NCRL managers.

We first note that the plaintiffs' complaint is that they are prevented from accessing the speech of others in violation of article I, section 5. The First Amendment protects the right to receive information and ideas. We believe that a comparable right exists under article I, section 5.

There are very few appellate cases involving Internet filters and free speech issues, and no cases decided under article I, section 5. However, the United States Supreme Court termed it a mistake to extend prior restraint to the context of public libraries' collection decisions. A library's decision to use filtering software is a collection decision, not a restraint on private speech. NCRL's filtering policy does not constitute a prior restraint within the meaning of article I, section 5.

A public library provides Internet access for the same reasons it offers other library resources: to facilitate research, learning, and recreational pursuits by furnishing materials of requisite and appropriate quality. To fulfill their traditional missions, public libraries must have broad discretion to decide what material to provide to their patrons. This discretion is not unlimited; it may not be exercised in a narrowly partisan or political manner.

NCRL's filtering policy does not prevent any speech and in particular it does not ban or attempt to ban online speech before it occurs. Rather, it is a standard for making determinations about what will be included in the collection available to NCRL's patrons.

The plaintiffs maintain, however, that NCRL's policy is overbroad and in fact is so overbroad that it rises to the level of a prior restraint in violation of article I, section 5.

A public library has no obligation to make available any and all constitutionally protected material, and the goal of libraries has never been to provide "universal coverage." The librarian's responsibility is to separate out the gold from the garbage, not to preserve everything. The principle that a library has no obligation to provide universal coverage of all constitutionally protected speech applies to Internet access just as it does to the printed word in books, periodicals, and other material physically collected and made available to patrons. Just as NCRL is entitled to exercise its acknowledged discretion in amassing a collection of printed materials physically placed on the shelves in order to carry out its mission, it is entitled to exercise discretion when it comes to Internet access involving its facilities and equipment.

The discretion that public libraries enjoy in selecting materials for their collections is not merely a function of what a library can afford in terms of costs and space. Even if one were to assume a public library with unlimited funds and space, that library would be under no obligation to make all constitutionally protected printed materials available. For example, regardless of its resources a library need not place pornographic materials on its shelves, although such materials are constitutionally protected. It need not place children's comic books on its shelves, although these, too, are constitutionally protected.

In short, a library simply does not have to include all constitutionally protected materials in its collection and it follows that no overbreadth problem necessarily results under article I, section 5 as a result of a public library's Internet filtering policy under which access to certain categories of constitutionally protected materials is denied.

Next, turning to the plaintiffs' overbreadth claim based on filtering errors, NCRL concedes that its filter on some occasions incorrectly includes inoffensive web sites in the prohibited categories, a circumstance known as "overblocking." This means that the filter blocks web sites that do not actually fall within the categories that the filter is intended to block. The parties make vastly different statements about the degree of overblocking. Regardless of the disparities, *even if* any constitutional issue is implicated by overblocking, it is dispelled if the material that is erroneously blocked is easily unblocked upon the request of an adult.

Here, if a library patron wants to access a web site or page that has been blocked by FortiGuard, he or she may send an e-mail to NCRL administrators asking for a manual override of the block. The site or page is reviewed to ascertain whether allowing access would accord with NCRL's mission, its policy, and CIPA requirements. If not, the request is denied. If the request is approved, access will be allowed on all of NCRL's public access computers. Because adults can request and obtain unblocking of erroneously blocked sites, we conclude that on this record no overbreadth problem exists under article I, section 5 as a result of overblocking.

The plaintiffs next contend that an overbreadth problem results when entire web sites are blocked rather than just the specific pages that contain material within the prohibited categories. This claim is similar to the overblocking claim, i.e., a claim that material is blocked that should not be blocked because it does not fall within a prohibited category. It differs in that at least a part of what is on the blocked site falls within one of the categories that the filter is designed to block.

Again, the crux of the issue is NCRL's discretion regarding what will be added to its collection. Given that a public library simply has no obligation to include all types of constitutionally protected printed material in its collection, and is not, for example, required to include a book with three pages of pornography and three hundred pages that are not pornographic, it does not have to include access to an Internet site that contains some matter falling within a prohibited category even if other matter on the site does not. We do not believe an overbreadth problem occurs under article I, section 5 when the filter blocks sites containing matter falling within one of the prohibited categories, even if other material on the site does not.

The plaintiffs contend that the filtering policy is an overbroad restriction on adult speech because, they assert, no person can access on-line material that NCRL decides is inappropriate for a child. [But] just as a public library has discretion to make content-based decisions about which magazines and books to include in its collection, it has discretion to make decisions about Internet content. A public library can decide that it will not include pornography and other adult materials in its collection in accord with its mission and policies and, as explained, no unconstitutionality necessarily results. It can make the same choices about Internet access.

A public library does not come readily to mind as having been a source of pornography and other adult material before the advent of the Internet (and the current dispute), and should not be forced to become one just because it makes Internet access available to its patrons. We conclude that no overbreadth in violation of article I, section 5 occurs as a result of NCRL's choice to block Internet access to pornography, adult materials, and nudity/risqué materials.

The plaintiffs also argue that NCRL's filtering policy constitutes an unconstitutional content-based restriction under article I, section 5. According to the plaintiffs, any content-based restriction is presumptively invalid and ordinarily upheld only if it is meets the strict scrutiny standard of review. Contrary to the plaintiffs' apparent position, not all content-based standards are presumptively invalid or reviewed under a strict scrutiny standard. A public library necessarily considers content when making collection decisions and must do so to fulfill its mission. Given the traditional and historical role of a public library, and the discretion necessarily entailed to make content-based judgments about what to include in its collection, we conclude that article I, section 5 is not violated by a public library's Internet filtering policy if it is reasonable when measured in light of the library's mission and policies, and is viewpoint neutral.

It appears to us that NCRL's filtering policy is reasonable and accords with its mission and these policies and is viewpoint neutral. It appears that no article I, section 5 content-based violation exists in this case. NCRL's essential mission is to promote reading and lifelong learning. As NCRL maintains, it is reasonable to impose restrictions on Internet access in order to maintain an environment that is conducive to study and contemplative thought.

NCRL points out that more than half of its branches serve as the de facto school library for local school districts. While the Internet provides opportunities for educational enrichment, exposure to unfiltered Internet access on demand by adults in these branches is not suited to education of children.

Children are not the only patrons who might be adversely affected by unlimited Internet access in the public libraries. Even adults may find such exposure ill-suited to their use and enjoyment of a public library as a place for reading and contemplative thought. As NCRL says, limited restrictions on Internet access may help to minimize circumstances that staff and other patrons, including adults, may find threatening, hostile, or disruptive.

The filtering policy is neutral in application, applying to all patrons alike. It is viewpoint neutral because it makes no distinctions based on the perspective of the speaker.

We conclude that on the factual record presented to us in the district court's order on certification, the filtering policy suffers from none of the constitutional infirmities under article I, section 5 claimed by the plaintiffs. In response to the question certified by the United States District Court for the Eastern District of Washington, we answer that in accord with our analysis in this opinion a public library may, consistent with article I, section 5 of the Washington State Constitution, filter Internet access for all patrons without disabling the filter to allow access to web sites containing constitutionally protected speech upon the request of an adult library patron.

POINTS FOR DISCUSSION

1. When adult patrons of the library complain about blocked access to a specific site, the library's response depends on whether the site is of a category that the library intends to block. Should this be the relevant criterion, or rather whether the site is constitutionally protected or not?
2. Would it have been wise, or too cumbersome, to have one policy for "true" public libraries, and another for those that also have to function as a de facto school library?

About the Author

Paul Siegel is professor of communication at the University of Hartford. For sixteen years Siegel taught at Gallaudet University, the world's only comprehensive university designed especially for deaf and hard of hearing students. He has also taught communication law courses at American University, the Catholic University of America, George Mason University, Illinois State University, Keene State College (New Hampshire), Quinnipiac University, Tulane University, the University of Connecticut, the University of Missouri–Kansas City, and the University of North Carolina.

Siegel has published dozens of essays in journals of communication, sociology, and anthropology, as well as in law reviews and as book chapters. Topics have ranged from product placement in movies and the development of the Supreme Court's commercial speech doctrine to the gays-in-the-military debate and the interaction of privacy and communication law. Siegel also edited a collection of readings on the Clarence Thomas Supreme Court confirmation hearings.

A graduate of Northwestern University's doctoral program in communication studies, Siegel also earned degrees from the University of Wisconsin and the University of New Mexico.

Beyond work in the academy, Siegel was the founding executive director of the Kansas and Western Missouri office of the American Civil Liberties Union and has been on the ACLU's affiliate boards in Illinois, Washington, D.C., and Connecticut. He is also a past president of the Text and Academic Authors Association.